D0708310

WHITE BEECH

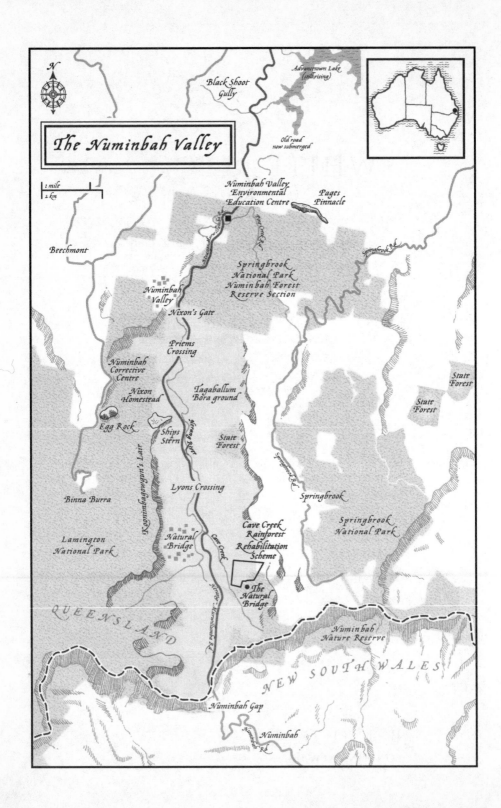

WHITE BEECH

The Rainforest Years

GERMAINE GREER

BLOOMSBURY

LONDON · NEW DELHI · NEW YORK · SYDNEY

First published in Great Britain 2014

Copyright © 2013 by Germaine Greer
Map by Liane Payne

Bloomsbury Publishing Plc
50 Bedford Square
London
WC1B 3DP

www.bloomsbury.com

Bloomsbury Publishing is a trademark of Bloomsbury PLC

Bloomsbury Publishing, London, New Delhi, New York and Sydney

A CIP catalogue record for this book is available from the British Library

ISBN 978 1 4088 4671 1

10 9 8 7 6 5 4 3

Typeset by Hewer Text UK Ltd, Edinburgh
Printed and bound in Great Britain by CPI Group (UK) Ltd, Croydon CR0 4YY

To the CCRRS workforce, past, present and to come,
this work is respectfully dedicated.

CONTENTS

LIST OF ABBREVIATIONS

ADB	*Australian Dictionary of Biography*
APNI	Australian Plant Name Index (on line)
BC	*Brisbane Courier*
BMAD	Bell Miner Associated Dieback
CCRRS	Cave Creek Rainforest Rehabilitation Scheme
CP	*Cairns Post*
CSIRO	Commonwealth Scientific and Industrial Research Organisation
DNB	*Dictionary of National Biography* (UK)
IATSIS	Institute of Aboriginal and Torres Strait Islander Studies
IPNI	International Plant Name Index (on line)
ISN	*Illustrated Sydney News*
LW	*Logan Witness*
MLA	Member of the Legislative Assembly (lower house of state parliament)
MLC	Member of the Legislative Council (upper house of state parliament)
MM	*Maitland Mercury and Hunter River General Advertiser*
NA	National Archives (UK)
NLA	National Library of Australia
Q	*The Queenslander*
QSA	Queensland State Archives
QPWS	Queensland Parks and Wildlife Service
SMH	*Sydney Morning Herald*
spp.	species (plural)

ssp.   subspecies
USDA   United States Department of Agriculture
var.   variety
WA   *Warwick Argus*
WIRES   NSW Wildlife Rescue and Information Service Inc.

PROLOGUE

This is the story of an extraordinary stroke of luck. You could call it 'life-changing', if only every woman's life were not an inexorable series of changes to which she has to adapt as well as she can. What happened at Cave Creek in December 2001 is that life grabbed me by the scruff of the neck. I went there as a lamb to the slaughter, without the faintest inkling that my life was about to be taken over by a forest. Some of my friends tell me now that they saw it coming. Had I not quit London in 1984 and removed to rural Essex? Was not the first thing I did there to plant a wood? Was I not prouder of my English wood (which is all the wrong trees and in quite the wrong place) than anything else I had ever done? They may not have been surprised when I bought land at Cave Creek, but I was.

Great strokes of luck are usually disastrous. People who win millions on the lottery tell us that their lives have been ruined: their friends have turned into spongers; their families are dissatisfied; tradesmen, lawyers, bankers and accountants have swindled them and too much of the money was frittered away before they could secure their future. I was sixty-two when the forest became my responsibility, with no idea of how long I might be able to go on earning a living by my pen and my tongue. Our culture is not sympathetic to old women, and I was definitely an old woman, with a creaky knee and shockingly arthritic feet. Everyone else my age was buying a unit on the Sunshine Coast. What did I think I was doing buying sixty hectares of steep rocky country most of it impenetrable scrub?

As will become evident, I didn't think. I followed a series of signs
and portents that led beyond thought, to find myself in a realm that
was unimaginably vast and ancient. My horizons flew away, my notion
of time expanded and deepened, and my self disappeared. I hadn't
been the centre of my world since menopause shook me free of vanity
and self-consciousness; once I became the servant of the forest I was
just one more organism in its biomass, the sister of its mosses and fungi,
its mites and worms. I would be its interface with the world of humans,
arguing its case for as long as I could, doing my best to protect it from
exploitation and desecration. For ten years I could call it 'my' forest,
because I had bought the freehold, but that was only for convenience.
To be sure the signs I put all along the unfenced boundary said that any
person found removing anything whatsoever from the property would
be prosecuted, but that was not because I would consider myself to
have been robbed, but because the forest would have been plundered.
I never thought of the forest as mine.

I would walk down the creek, gazing up at the Bangalow Palms and
Rose Apples that soared into the sky, and say to myself over and over
again, 'Who could own this?' The Azure Kingfisher perched on a
trembling frond to scan the creek for fish had more right to it than I.
The Long-finned Eel nosing under the rocks, the White-browed
Scrubwren washing itself in a rock pool, the Bladder Cicada living its
one glorious day of airborne life, all were co-owners with me. It was
only a matter of time before the forest would be given back to itself, and
a fund accumulated for its management. So I gave the place a name that
referred to the project rather than the property, Cave Creek Rainforest
Rehabilitation Scheme, CCRRS for short. Perhaps one day I shall earn
the place's true, historic, Aboriginal name, but for now CCRRS it is.

How did I know on that bright December day in 2001 that the
forest at Cave Creek could be rehabilitated? I thought I knew the
answer to that question until I tried to answer it. On my first visit I
couldn't even guess at the rainforest on the upper slopes. What I could
see was acres of exotic pasture grass with cattle dribbling into it and as
many acres of soft weed. Maybe it was the entrance to the national
park, with its Macadamias carrying strings of unripe nuts, Black Beans
dangling their giant pea pods and watervines hanging in huge swags
over the road, that told me louder than words what I should have

found in the perched valley beneath. I didn't know then how much of that exuberant vegetation was exotic weed species. I do now. Now I know that the Queensland Parks and Wildlife Service is short of everything it needs to carry out its job of conservation, and that what funds it does have are exhausted by the cost of maintaining the infrastructure that is meant to protect the tourists from themselves. Governments having failed, the restoration of the most biodiverse rainforest outside the wet tropics will have to be done by dedicated individuals.

That day I saw a pasture bounded not by forest but by impenetrable curtains of tangled Lantana canes. I had no idea how to remove them, but I knew they could be removed. The other thing I knew was that it was my responsibility to remove them. Why? Because I could. I had money, enough to get started at least. Once I got started I wouldn't have money for anything else, but that didn't scare me. I didn't need anything nearly as much as I needed to heal some part of the fabulous country where I was born. Everywhere I had ever travelled across its vast expanse I had seen devastation, denuded hills, eroded slopes, weeds from all over the world, feral animals, open-cut mines as big as cities, salt rivers, salt earth, abandoned townships, whole beaches made of beer cans. Give me just a chance to clean something up, sort something out, make it right, I thought, and I will take it. I wasn't doing it out of altruism; I didn't think I was saving the world. I was in search of heart's ease and this was my chance to find it. I didn't know it until a bird showed me, as you shall see if you read on. I needed a sign and the bird was it.

The bird was an ambassador from the realm of biodiversity, which is every Earthling's birthright. Biodiversity is our real heritage as the ostentation of extinct aristocracies is not. We have inherited a planet that is richer and more various than could ever have been imagined. Every day brings discoveries of new riches, coral reefs in the darkest depths of arctic seas, crustaceans living in boiling sulphuric water, thousands of species in thousands of genera, some older than history and some brand-new. Biodiversity is the name we give to the extravagant elaboration of this our planet, to the continuing creativity of evolution. Every one of the millions of life forms on Earth is an Earthling like us, closer to us than any yet to be discovered life form in a distant solar system. The tiny snail negotiating the edge of that lettuce leaf is my cousin; it and I share most of our genes. Its survival and the survival of its kind depend on me. I could pick the little creature off the leaf and crush it under my boot, or I could leave it for a hungry thrush, or I could bless it unaware, as Coleridge's Ancient Mariner blessed the snakes of the Sargasso Sea:

> Within the shadow of the ship
> I watched their rich attire:
> Blue, glossy green and velvet black,
> They coiled and swam; and every track
> Was a flash of golden fire.
>
> O happy living things! no tongue
> Their beauty might declare:
> A spring of love gushed from my heart,
> And I blessed them unaware:
> Sure my kind saint took pity on me,
> And I blessed them unaware.
>
> That self-same moment I could pray;
> And from my neck so free
> The Albatross fell off, and sank
> Like lead into the sea.

We all carry our own version of the dead Albatross hung around the Mariner's neck. Our Albatross is the guilt that should weigh on us for making war on other Earthlings, invading and disrupting their habitat, slaughtering them in their millions and condemning millions of others to death and extinction. The Ancient Mariner didn't know why he shot the Albatross, any more than the early settlers in Queensland could explain why they shot and killed vast numbers of koalas. The Mariner's sudden surge of love for the snakes (snakes!) was like the sudden awareness of kinship that overtakes some of us as we enter the contemplative phase of life, when we find ourselves watching flies and midges instead of swatting them. The Ancient Mariner didn't know, as Coleridge didn't, that the opalescent sea snakes that were thronging about him were eels that had travelled halfway round the world to breed in the Sargasso Sea. The truth is even more wonderful than Coleridge's fiction.

The Mariner learnt that 'he prayeth well, who loveth well Both man and bird and beast'; true it is that entering fully into the multifarious life that is the Earthling's environment, while giving up delusions of controlling it, is a transcendental experience. To give up fighting against nature, struggling to tame it and make it bring forth profit, is to enter a new kind of existence which has nothing to do with serenity or relaxation. It is rather a state of heightened awareness and deep excitement. As I limp back down the mountain with my pockets full of fruit, on my way to prepare the seed for planting, I know that as many will grow as should grow. I am like Ganymede in the talons of the eagle, caught up and carried along by the prodigious energy of the forest. If the forest has its way, paucity will be replaced by plenty; once the vanished trees return, an invasion will follow. Mosses, lichens, ferns, orchids, mites, weevils, beetles, moths, butterflies, phasmids, frogs, snakes, lizards, gliders, possums, wallabies, echidnas, all will reappear in their own sweet time.

The forest is the bottom line. Without it the thousands of species that have evolved with it will fade from the earth. Technology has no solutions to the problem of biodepletion. There is little point in accumulating gene banks and none whatever in breeding threatened species in captivity. The only way of keeping the extraordinary richness and exuberance of this small planet is to rebuild habitat. If you put nets into the Wenlock River to trap Green Sawfish, and then truck them hundreds of kilometres to Cairns, where they will be loaded into an aircraft and flown to an aquarium in Missouri, you will be doing nothing to aid their survival, though you may be earning yourself as much as fifty thousand US dollars. The sawfish may survive in the aquarium, but they will survive as White Beeches do when they're planted as street trees. They will have been forced to exchange a life of astounding plenitude for mere existence. If their habitat has disappeared, they can never return to it; if their habitat was restored, they would never need to go to the other side of the world, there to dwell in a tank.

The good news is that as soon as a depleted ecosystem begins to rebuild, the creatures that have evolved with it will flock to it. As soon as the Sloaneas we reared at CCRRS were shoulder-high, we found in the domatia on the undersides of their leaves mites that were practically identical with those found in the domatia of their fossil ancestors (O'Dowd *et al.*). It really doesn't matter what ecosystem any might be, the creatures that belong within it are unique. They may be the same species as elsewhere, but their inter-action with diverse habitats and different co-residents creates diverse behaviours. Monitor lizards lay their eggs in termite nests. There are few termite species in subtropical rainforest; the few there are make their nests high in the trees. The gravid lizard must climb the tree, break into the termite nest, get inside and lay her eggs, which might explain why in our local version of the Lace Monitor (*Varanus varius*) the female is less than a third the size of the male. The eggs laid, she leaves the nest, and the termites reseal it, so the eggs will be incubated in constant warmth and humidity. Legend has it that when the eggs are ready to hatch, the mother lizard will visit the nest once again and tear it open to free her hatchlings. Nobody seems to have actually witnessed this event but we keep watching.

As any threatened ecosystem begins to recover it may wobble. When the weevils that evolved many millennia ago with our Bolwarras found the ones we had planted at Cave Creek, they overwhelmed them (Williams and Adam). The creamy-white porcelain flowers were nothing but writhing brown knots of insect bodies, until the weevils' predator caught up and lunched largely and long. Balance in the rainforest is largely a matter of stalemate, for no single species can opt out of the eternal struggle and no single species can be allowed to win it. Any species that dominates is doomed. Survival depends on finding your niche and keeping it.

I had no idea in December 2001 that what was about to fall into my hands was a hotspot of biodiversity. Gondwana was nothing but a name, no realer to me than Middle Earth. The first botanist to take a look at what I had was excited; those who followed were more excited. I knew that my patch was surrounded on two sides by national park, which was a plus, and I knew the national park was at the northern extremity of a World Heritage Site that was then called the Central Eastern Rainforest Reserve Area. That area, consisting of a broken string of small rainforest remnants, is now called Gondwana Rainforests of Australia. The forest fragments are of major conservation importance because of their high rate of endemism; what that means is that surviving in them are many species that can survive nowhere else. The rate of endemism grows higher in the northernmost fragments; it is highest in the Springbrook National Park, and that system includes Cave Creek. This is the astonishing stroke of luck.

I didn't go shopping for exceptional biodiversity. I would have taken whatever came my way. When our first planting stopped holding its breath and shot up to make a forest, I was amazed. As I walked under its low canopy I felt a special kind of comfort in the knowledge that here at least the devastation of Australia's astonishing biodiversity could be reversed. When I saw that caterpillars were already feeding on the leaves of the new little trees, I rejoiced that the system could still rebuild itself, that insects and plants that had evolved together many millennia ago could find each other again. For years I had wandered Australia with an aching heart. Here was balm indeed, worth every cent of the millions of dollars I have since turned into trees. The stock market may stagger, but the trees grow on.

This book could have been named for any of the myriad species that have their being in that small chunk of rainforest. I could have called it 'Platypus' or 'Gastric-brooding Frog', or 'Pencil Orchid' or 'Blue Crayfish' or even 'Green Mountains' but 'White Beech' is the name by which the book announced itself to me. I didn't know that I wanted to write a book about the rainforest, until I woke up in the middle of the night with those two words written in white neon under my eyelids. I began to write the story before I knew the half of it. I still don't know the half of it; I didn't know till a few weeks ago that the fruit of the Cave Creek quandongs is blue not because of a pigment but because of nanoscale photonic crystals like the ones that give us the blue feathers of the peacock and the blue scales on butterflies (Lee). Every day brings a new encounter with the wonderful. There are as well encounters of a different kind.

I had all but finished this book, when a last terrible twist was given to the tale of the forest. I thought I knew all the outrages and insults that had been inflicted on it. The land had been stripped naked, the forest knocked down, burnt, the ground flattened and dug up time and again. It never occurred to me that the area might have been poisoned, and that with the deadliest compound that man has ever made.

I was innocently stowing my recyclables in the big yellow wheelie bin at the Resource Recovery Centre, when one of the locals came over for a natter.

'I notice those people over the road from the national park are trying to grow organic vegetables,' he said. 'Bloody ridiculous.'

(I didn't tell him that they had lost so much money trying to distribute their organic vegetables that they had already given up.)

'All those signs along the fence saying no spraying. Bloody ridiculous. That whole place used to be sprayed from one end to the other with 2,4,5-T. Regularly. For years.'

His words hit me like a fist in the solar plexus. I knew 2,4,5-T only too well; 2,4,5-T was one of the two compounds that made up the defoliant known as Agent Orange. For years I carried a can of Agent Orange in my luggage, ready at the first opportunity to spray it on the White House rhododendrons. Agent Orange was the herbicide used by the Americans in their vain struggle to crush the Vietnamese National Liberation Front by 'intentional destruction of both the natural and human ecologies of the region', the most colossal onslaught ever inflicted on any natural system anywhere. By drenching the Vietnamese rainforest with herbicide the Americans hoped to strip the vegetation that provided cover for the Viet Cong and, by destroying the people's crops, to starve them out of the countryside. In Operation Ranch Hand something like 20 million gallons of herbicide was sprayed on Vietnamese forest and cropland. By the time the operation came to an end in January 1971 a fifth of the forest cover in Vietnam, as well as some on the borders of Laos and Cambodia, had been destroyed. The American military stopped using 2,4,5-T, not out of remorse at the devastation they had wrought, but because of the growing body of evidence that it was contaminated with 2,3,7,8-TCDD, a dioxin. Dioxins are so toxic that they are measured in parts per trillion; at a tenth of a part per trillion they are still mutagenic, carcinogenic and teratogenic. They are also indestructible; even distillation will not remove them from water. They resist biological breakdown, are concentrated in fatty tissue, and are not easily excreted. By far the most dangerous of them is 2,3,7,8-TCDD which persists, accumulates and aggregates in the environment, becoming even more toxic when exposed to heat or light.

From the beginning of Operation Ranch Hand, scientists all over the world had been protesting at its savagery and recklessness. As one of the London-based Australians against the Vietnam War I had seen images of Vietnamese infants born appallingly deformed, apparently because of dioxins in the water table. In December 1971 I took a plane from Saigon to Vientiane. For a half-hour, as we flew north from Saigon, I saw nothing below but bare pitted mud latticed with tree skeletons, the accumulated result of nine years of ecocidal warfare. In 2006 the Vietnamese government informed the international community that dioxin poisoning had claimed 4 million victims and begged for help. Vietnam is a poor country, with few resources to put into a proper assessment of the damage done to its people or to deal with the burden of illness that will blight their future, as the teratogenic effects of dioxin exposure manifest themselves in a third and fourth generation of Vietnamese babies. In forty years the forest has not regenerated; in place of the rainforest dipterocarps there is a coarse scrub of bamboos and Pogon Grass, which is identical with the Blady Grass of southern Queensland. The lowland tropical forest of the Mekong delta is cousin to the forest at Cave Creek, with Gondwanan elements like podocarps and casuarinas; that meant less than nothing to me in 1971 but it matters a lot to me now.

The Americans drenched Vietnam with Agent Orange as an act of war. Could Australians have willingly poisoned their own country in peacetime? Surely my neighbour was mistaken.

'Right up to the foot of the scarps. Year on year,' he went on, 'for years, 2,4,5-T. And now those people are growing purple carrots and blue potatoes on it and trying to pretend that they're organic. All bullshit. You couldn't farm organically anywhere round here.'

Surely he meant 2,4-D, Agent Orange's other ingredient, I thought, as I turned the car around. I was wrong. I know now to my great sorrow that 2,4,5-T was widely used in south-east Queensland for thirty years or more.

Australia was one place where, as the Vietnam War wound down, the American military could profitably offload their unused chemicals. Much of the Agent Orange that entered Australia between 1969 and 1971 came via Singapore; some went to Western Australia, where vigorous campaigning has brought to light the extent of its malevolent action on the Aboriginal workers who were made to use it in the Kimberley. Ten times as much Agent Orange came into Queensland, via Farm Chemicals Pty Ltd at Eagle Farm near Brisbane, but of the kind of indignation that convulsed Western Australia there is no trace. By all accounts this old stock was unstable and heavily contaminated with dioxin (Hall and Selinger). Some of it was reportedly fire-damaged. It was dangerous, but it was cheap. It was to be used in forestry, to thin native hardwoods to the required eight-metre centres and to eliminate competing vegetation, and in agriculture, to control weed infestation in pasture, particularly Groundsel. It was also used by local authorities for brush control along roadsides and railway lines.

By 1970 the effects of exposure to 2,4,5-T on the health of military personnel were pretty well understood. The result would be a series of long-drawn-out and largely unsuccessful class action suits in Canada and the US. Nevertheless the widespread use of 2,4,5-T as a defoliant in state forestry programmes continued into the Seventies and Eighties in northern Ontario, in New Brunswick, in California and the Pacific north-west, and in Brazil. In forestry programmes in south-east Queensland use of 2,4,5-T continued until 1995. Local farmers continued to use it until Picloram, another systemic herbicide for broad-leaf evergreens which was also used in Vietnam, became readily available as Tordon and Grazon. North American forestry workers who were exposed to 2,4,5-T are now pursuing class action suits of their own against Dow Chemical and Monsanto, but the Queensland experience seems to have been utterly forgotten.

It was not as if Australian scientists were unaware of the risks. In 1981 researchers at Monash University published results of their admin-istration of tiny doses of 2,4,5-T to fertilised hen eggs, which produced pronounced and undeniable teratogenic effects. The 2,4,5-T they were using contained much lower levels of dioxin than the version that was being routinely sprayed on Australian blackberries (Sanderson and Rogers). The next year researchers at Sydney University published results of an epidemiological study that found that the proportion of babies born with neural tube defects in any year displays positive correlation with the amounts of 2,4,5-T used in the previous year (Field, Kerr and Mathers, 1982, also Field and Kerr, 1988). In 1985 there was a Royal Commission on the Use and Effects of Chemical

Agents on Australian Personnel in Vietnam. Yet there has never been any kind of investigation into what Australian civilians did to themselves and their birthplace by the peacetime use of 2,4,5-T.

Back at CCRRS, I trawled the net, hunting for information on how repeated dowsing with 2,4,5-T might have affected the forest. Though there was a vast amount of information about contamination with an array of dioxins resulting from faulty manufacturing processes, there was almost nothing about the long-term consequences of routine use of 2,4,5-T. About the only relevant data came from an air force base in north-western Florida where 2,4,5-T had been repeatedly used over a nine-year period, from 1961 to 1970. Twelve years later 2,3,7,8-TCDD was detected in soils, rodents, birds, lizards, fish and insects. One of the highest residues, 1,360 parts per trillion, was found in an amphibian, the Southern Toad (*Bufo terrestris*) (Eisler, 7). Two years after the escape of dioxin at Seveso, Italy, in 1976, high levels were detected in toads (Fanelli *et al.*). Yet nobody studying the decline in frog populations in south-east Queensland has ever suggested that spraying their environment with 2,4,5-T cannot have been good for them.

Surely, I thought, nobody would have been so wanton as to have sprayed the headwaters of the Nerang River with 2,4,5-T. The river is after all the main source of drinking water for the whole Gold Coast. As I poked about, hunting in vain for an account of the use of 2,4,5-T in forestry in south-east Queensland, I came across a mention of its use to control 'weed' vegetation in plantations of Pinus and Araucaria (Wells and Lewty, 215). One of the doomed enterprises at Cave Creek was a plantation of Hoop Pine (*Araucaria cunninghamii*), part of which still stands. Rainforest natives have sprung up under the planted pines and are giving them a run for their money; when the pines were a cash crop such competition would have been ruthlessly eliminated. Trees do die in the forest, but now whenever I see branches of an established tree withering and dying, I feel a clutch of fear, that somewhere underground there is a sump full of poison that is slowly leaking out. All the water that drains through the Cave Creek roots and rocks ends up in the Advancetown Lake; I wonder whether anyone is testing the water for dioxin residues. If anyone is, nobody's saying.

If you'd told me forty years ago that I was destined to come across 2,4,5-T again, and that then it would be my problem, I'd have been appalled. I am older and wiser now, and not even surprised. I'm only glad that I was offered an opportunity to make some small amends, and that I was in a position to take it. The same opportunity is out there for everyone. Supposing you live on an average suburban street. Under the tarmac there is geology, a soil type, a seed bank, and a memory of what used to be there, before the bush was ripped up, trashed and thrown away to be replaced by Norfolk Island Pines or Canary Island Date Palms and Buffalo Grass. You can stop mowing and weeding and mending what passes for lawn, and let your quarter-acre revert to Moonah Woodland and Coast Banksia or whatever. No need to put out the bird feeders, because Wattlebirds will come as soon as the Banksias flower and the Possums will move out of the roof space and back into the trees. If you can get your neighbours on side, you can combine your backyards, to make a safe place for kids to explore and for echidnas to mosey about in.

If I have written this book properly, it will convey the deep joy that rebuilding wild nature can bring. Not that the forest is peaceful, anything but. The only forest creatures that live long are the trees; they can live for aeons unless a cyclone comes to suck them out of the ground or a scarp collapses over them or the earth slides out from under them. Then all the other little trees that have waited in their shade will start racing for their bit of sky. The trees create the habitat for a vast horde of species most of which will be eaten by other species that will be eaten in their turn. The sweetest tree frog is a ruthless predator on hundreds of species including other frogs. The Spiny Rainforest Katydid that has just landed on my keyboard, dressed in his mad suit of particoloured fronds, is a voracious killer too. I sit quiet to watch him as he takes off. He is barely airborne before a Rufous Fantail flirts out of the Cheese Tree and snares him for her fledglings. Both bird and prey are wonderfully special. The katydid is dressed with such crazy excess that he looks more like a Green Man crossed with a Leafy Seadragon than a flycatcher's meal on wings. The Rufous Fantail turns hunting into an aerial circus, whirling her wings and tail so that she tumbles and spins, only feet from my face. Her fanned brick-red tail is edged with a white so bright that it seems to leave tracks in the sunlit air.

THE TREE

The hero of this story is a tree or, rather, a tree species. Though it is called White Beech, it is neither white nor a beech. The beech family, which includes beeches, oaks and chestnuts, is unrepresented in Australia, unless you count the genus *Nothofagus*, the Southern Beech. The three Australian species of Southern Beech are now thought to belong to a family of their own, the Nothofagaceae. Antarctic Beeches, some of which were alive when Christ was born, stand on the misty heights of the Lamington Plateau to the west of Cave Creek, and on the heights of Springbrook to the north-east, but there is none in our wet nook amid the headwaters of the Nerang River. The White Beech of this story is not related in any way to beeches of any kind.

The settlers who turned up in southern Queensland in the second half of the nineteenth century were confronted by a vast array of tree species that were not related even distantly to the trees they had grown up with. Many were bigger than any trees they had ever seen. They knew Red Cedar by reputation, because ever since the beginning of white settlement generations of loggers all along the coast of New South Wales had been hard at work felling it and shipping it away. Many books have been written about Red Cedar. No book has ever celebrated the even more charismatic species known to the few who have ever heard of it as White Beech. White Beech is endemic to a far smaller and less continuous range than Red Cedar, from the Illawarra south of Sydney to Proserpine on the Queensland central coast. Rarer, and easier to work than Red Cedar,

it was the first of the subtropical rainforest tree species to be logged
out. It is estimated that in the Illawarra, scattered over thirty disjunct
sites, fewer than a hundred White Beeches can now be found
(Bofeldt).

The local Aboriginal name for White Beech is 'binna burra', spelt
by whitefellas in the usual variety of ways (Gresty, 70). Another very
different Aboriginal name for the species is 'cullonen', though where
it is called that and by whom I could not say. Binna Burra, a well-
known tourist centre on the edge of the Lamington Plateau, was
named for the White Beech, and refers to itself as the place 'where the
beech tree grows'. The neighbouring town of Beechmont is thought
by many of the people who visit it and even some who write about
it, to have been named for the Antarctic Beech, when in fact it was
originally dubbed Beech Mountain because of the number of White
Beeches to be found there. There are very few growing there now.

On 1 February 2008 the Beechmont Landcare Group announced
that 'from now until April 2008, Beechmont Landcare members will
be collecting White Beech seeds. These will then be propagated and
grown at Council's Nursery at Beaudesert. When ready, expected to
be in late 2009, the plants will be distributed by Beechmont Landcare
to local residents at the Beechmont markets.' A district councillor
declared that she had 'no doubt that the community will put the
beech back into Beechmont'. But the rainforest was in no hurry. The
beeches did not fruit that year. The organisers were obliged to report
that: 'Rains have stimulated vegetative growth instead of flowers
from mature trees, interrupting plans for seed collection this year.
However it's hoped that seeds will be available for propagation next
summer.' The summer of 2008–9 proved to be even wetter.

Summer in subtropical rainforest is usually a rainy season and
bumper crops of White Beech fruit the exception rather than the rule.
Some rainforest species fruit only once every five years or so. Others
will flower profusely on only one or two branches. As Margaret
Lowman, who pioneered canopy science, reported in 1999:

After thirty-five years of annual surveys on 4 hectares of rain forests in
Australia, the seedling teams have found a large variability in the
patterns of seed rain, seedling germination and growth of tropical

trees. Mast seeding, annual seed production, and intermittent seed
rain triggered by environmental conditions such as seasonal rains or
high light were all successful patterns utilized by neighbouring species.
Some adult trees never flowered or fruited during the thirty-five years
of observations.

Among these last Lowman listed the Rose Marara, *Pseudoweinmannia
lachnocarpa*. 'We hypothesized that these species typically flowered
infrequently – perhaps every fifty years or more – or that subtle
climatic changes had led to their sterility. Only patient observations
will yield these secrets of the great forest floor lottery' (Lowman,
102). At Cave Creek in August, the last month of the Australian
winter, Rose Mararas can be seen in cloudy white bloom up and
down the forest slopes. The fruit ripens slowly and doesn't begin to
drift to earth till steamy February. It is not every year that the spent
blossom ripens to shed clouds of fine seeds clad in brown fluff, that
float down through the forest to settle on every moss-covered rock
and drift into every crevice. We collect the seed by the bucketful and
dump it in trays. Stout little seedlings appear in due course. It may be
that the trees that were the subject of the study in which Lowman
was involved were growing outside their range, and therefore lacked
the stimulus to flower, which might indeed be the consequence of
accelerated climate change. Lowman was working with the famed
Joseph H. Connell, distinguished professor of zoology at the
University of California, Santa Barbara. In 1963 Connell set up a
long-term observation in which transects were marked across two
Australian rainforest plots; along these every tree, sapling or seedling
had to be identified, counted, marked and mapped, to document
how succession actually worked. Over the years a procession of
distinguished American biologists has visited Australia to work on
the Connell project. If any of them had wandered further afield than
their two plots, or even consulted the odd Australian dendrologist,
other possibilities might have occurred to them.

The name White Beech could refer to any one of half-a-dozen
subtropical tree species (Munir). It is used for any of five Australian
tree species, *Gmelina leichhardtii*, *G. dalrympleana*, *G. fasciculiflora*, *G.
schlechteri* and one member of a totally different genus, *Elaeocarpus*

kirtonii. G. fasciculiflora is native to Cairns and the Atherton Tableland, and *G. dalrympleana* (sometimes called *G. macrophylla*), with leaves twenty-five centimetres long and reddish-pink fruits, grows in northern Australia and Papua New Guinea, where *G. schlechteri* is also to be found. Further north still, in New Guinea and the Solomon Islands, the name White Beech is given to yet another Gmelina, *G. moluccana*. Far away in the rainforest of Martinique *Symplocos martinicensis* is also called White Beech. Seven of the thirty-five species in the genus Gmelina are native to China, the rest to other parts of Asia, New Guinea and Australia.

The White Beech this book is named after is *Gmelina leichhardtii*. This is a stupendous tree, growing to forty metres in height, with a straight cylindrical trunk, only slightly flanged at the base, just asking to be cut down, slabbed up and shipped off, which is what had already happened to most White Beeches by the beginning of the twentieth century. To my anglophone sensibility the misleading imprecision of the name 'White Beech' conveys something of the mystery that veils my whole crackbrained enterprise, something of the riddle of the rainforest.

Forests are not just bunches of trees. Supposing you plant a few hundred trees on an acre of ground, for a few years they will grow on side by side like a plantation, until gradually the faster-growing trees will shade the others out. Some of the outstripped trees will die, others will accept life in the understorey, and still more will wait for a neighbouring tree to fall. Meanwhile the trees that are pushing towards the sky will sacrifice their lateral branches, as the canopy lifts further and further off the ground. Trees that top out over the others will spread their canopies, snaring more and more of the light. On the forest floor a galaxy of shade-loving organisms will begin to appear – mosses, fungi, groundcovers, ferns. With them will come hundreds of invertebrate species. Eventually the forest achieves equilibrium, but this is not static. The key to the forest's survival is competition. Trees growing in forest communities behave differently from trees of the same species growing in the open. Even as the forest trees vie with each other for light, they are protected from extreme weather, from wind and frost and parching sun; often they are bound together by vines. The more time you spend in a forest the more aware you become that it is an organism intent upon its own survival.

Chief members of the forest community are the trees that together create the shelter, the mild temperatures and the humidity upon which the other plant and animal life depends. In most of the subtropical rainforest of eastern Australia, sixty or so species of trees support a couple of hundred other plant species. In the Cave Creek forest, which is both riparian and montane, there are more than twice as many tree species as the norm. Some of the vines that knit the trees together can grow to such massive size that they drag their supporters to the ground. Looping along the slopes at Cave Creek you can find the great writhing trunks of woody vines that have outlived several generations of rainforest trees. Conversely many mature trees have barley-sugar trunks, showing where a now-vanished vine once constricted them. The trees being the underpinning, the armature of the forest, it stands to reason that anyone thinking of rebuilding a forest would choose to begin by planting them. This is not the only way however, and there are good reasons for clearing weeds and leaving the forest to regenerate spontaneously. I chose to take the planting option.

Many people who plant trees live to rue the day, as their chosen tree grows much bigger than they expected, cracking drains, ripping up pavements, filling guttering with shed leaves and twiggery. Suburban gardens are full of trees that have outgrown the available space, looming dangerously over houses, cars and passers-by. My mother took steps to eliminate any tree that she suspected of shading the house, regardless of whether it grew on her own ground or somebody else's. Any eucalypt that dared to shed a single sheet of bark onto our lawn was doomed. My mother's intolerance of trees may have been exacerbated by my father's habit of warbling Joyce Kilmer's famous but fatuous poem when he was in the shower. This, in the setting by Oscar Rasbach, had been a great hit for Paul Robeson in the year I was born.

> I think that I shall never see
> A poem lovely as a tree.
>
> A tree whose hungry mouth is prest
> Against the earth's sweet flowing breast;

A tree that looks at God all day
And lifts her leafy arms to pray;

A tree that may in summer wear
A nest of robins in her hair;

Upon whose bosom snow has lain;
Who intimately lives with rain.

Poems are made by fools like me,
But only God can make a tree.

The poem is arrant nonsense, with which my mother had as little patience as I. Trees don't have mouths or hair or bosoms, don't have to be sexualised in order to be praised and shouldn't be encumbered with gender. You have to wonder whether Kilmer had ever really looked at a tree. What you get to understand when you live with trees is that they are not to be trifled with. The lords of the forest are mysterious and frightening, utterly beyond caring about us and our petty concerns, as they live on through the centuries into millennia. The longest-lived and biggest creatures on Earth are not whales but trees. They are emblems of the interrelatedness of all Earthlings, typified in the notion of the Tree of Life. Evolution itself is tree-shaped, as are the dendrites, the tiny structures that carry electrostimulation to all the cells in our bodies.

When it comes to defining a tree or even a tree shape, language fails. The dictionary can do no better than to tell us that a tree is a perennial plant with a self-supporting woody stem that usually develops woody branches at some height off the ground. The essence of treehood would appear to be this very branchingness; figuratively at least a tree is any structure that can branch, as in 'family tree'. Trees are everywhere, whether in the Usenet hierarchy of the Internet or the binary search tree of computer science, or the von Neumann hierarchy of sets in mathematics. Botanically speaking, the tiny bonsai in its earthenware tray and the ninety-metre-high California Redwood are both trees. The tree fern however is not a tree but a fern, the banana is not a tree but a herb, and the palm is not a tree either, because it lacks some other attributes of treehood, having no cambial layers, and hence no continuous production of bark and wood.

There is more to a tree than meets the eye. Its woody trunk, or xylem, has an inner core called heartwood, within an outer layer called sapwood, which transports water from the root to all parts of the tree. As the tree ages the sapwood gradually becomes heartwood. The xylem is encased within a sleeve of cambium that transports its nutrients, which is in turn encased in the phloem, which carries the sugars made by the leaves during photosynthesis, and the whole is wrapped in a protective layer of bark. Most of the cells that make up wood are dead; they serve as the support for a complex system of vessels. When the leaves exhale moisture through their pores, the drying cells exert pressure on the leaf vein to make it suck up more water from the roots.

The forest tree is a powerhouse, converting light, gas and moisture to nutrients, not only for itself but for a whole population that lives on and by it. Some of these dependants are spectacular, like the epiphytic ferns and orchids, and the mistletoes; others are subtle, like the mites that live in the water-filled cavities in the bark, and the mycorrhizas that convey and convert nutrients from the tree for the ground-dwelling plants. The tree is not only important in itself, it is also important as a contributor to the canopy, which governs the microclimate that makes possible the massive biodiversity of the forest. It is now thought that one way Australia's tree frogs escape chytrid fungus disease is by taking to the canopy; if there is no canopy, there is no escape. We now know that canopies are universal; all kinds of organisms from seaweeds and corals and mosses to the loftiest trees tend to form canopies if they can. Canopy science is only fifteen years old and has still to formulate its basic questions, let alone answer them, but we are beginning to understand that canopies are an optimum form of vegetation (Nadkarni *et al.,* 3–20).

Most Australians have never heard of White Beech but, for thirty years or so when it was enthusiastically promoted as an export timber, White Beech was internationally famous. In the Paris Exhibition of 1855 it was exhibited as No. 193. In the Great Exhibition in London in 1862 it was exhibited as No. 30 among the Queensland woods and as Nos 68 and 171 among the New South Wales woods. When I was little I was very proud of a ruler my father gave me. It was inlaid with specimens of Australian timber in a kind of sampler that was developed in association with timber-trade promotions. Nowadays you will find one in every local museum, each with a sample of White Beech.

Because White Beech timber was 'durable, easily worked and non-shrinking', the early timber-getters sold their Red Cedar and kept the White Beech for themselves. The first dwellings, barns, stables, schools and churches in the Numinbah Valley were built of White Beech because, as an enthusiast wrote to *The Queenslander* (6 November 1875, 4S), its 'most useful wood . . . never shrinks in drying, and is unequalled for ships' decks and verandah floors, where it sits close, and like one homogeneous marble slab, under the foot'. The schoolhouse that opened at Nerang in 1876 was built by William Duncan from pit-sawn White Beech (Lentz, 33). Like all the other buildings made of White Beech in those early years, the schoolhouse seems to have disappeared.

In 1883 local man Carl Lentz visited Beechmont: he recalls in his typescript 'Memoirs and Some History', compiled at the end of his long life, that: 'There was a small clearing and a new pitsawn weatherboard house on it of beech timber, which is the easiest to cut out and the best to last. Besides, white ants won't touch it'(15). The Queensland Department of Primary Industry and Fisheries would disagree; its website baldly states that White Beech is not termite-resistant. Lentz's father probably knew better: 'When Dad was preparing to start dairy farming the sawn timber needed for the milking shed was all pitsawn . . . These logs were cut from some of those beech trees that gave the mountain its name'(71). People who had the choice continued to use White Beech for as long as they could find it. In the mid-1890s Duncan McKenzie, the first permanent settler on Beechmont, built his first farmhouse from pit-sawn tongue-and-groove joined beech boards.

Despite its high value much of the White Beech that was felled was left to rot, sometimes because there was no way of getting the bullock teams within reach of the fallen timber, but as often because the timber-getters couldn't afford the cost of transporting it. Only the biggest butt-logs were worth enough to cover the cost of cartage;

the rest was wasted. By 1911, 'Disturbing stories were coming out of the hills . . . There were tales of fallen white beech-trees, monarchs of the plateaux jungles, felled by past bullockies and timber-fellers, and forgotten.' (Groom, 88–9)

White Beeches cannot grow as fast as the pioneer species that shot up wherever the timber-getters tore down the ancient canopy. They couldn't have replaced themselves quickly even if they had been given a chance, and they weren't. The *Sydney Morning Herald* for 1 November 1912 reported that the supply of White Beech in southern Queensland was exhausted. Within ten years it had become the mythical hero of a forestry legend. In an article on 'The Timbers of Queensland' published on 28 November 1925 *The Queenslander* declared:

> Of all the softwood timber-trees known to bushmen and timber-getters, White Beech is generally regarded as the ideal. It is a splendid timber-tree and is recognised as such by the timber trade; but only those who have seen the sound logs and limbs in the scrubs, some of them over 50 years old, lying on wet ground, could form any exact idea of its remarkable durability. It often seems impossible for the timber to decay . . .

It must not be thought that the wanton destruction of the Queensland forests went unnoticed. In 1916 the English Chief Forest Officer visited Queensland and was scandalised to find that: 'There has been no survey of the forests . . . and though there has been for long a forest office in Brisbane, no forest map of Queensland, I believe, has been produced . . . Forest continued to be given away to anyone who would undertake to destroy it . . .' In reporting this on 9 December *The Queenslander* added its own comment: 'A sharp warning is given that three valuable Queensland timbers are nearly extinct – cedar, silky oak and white beech.' Cave Creek is one of the very few places where White Beech survived.

In the age of colonial expansion, trees in the new world were valued only as they could be exploited for the benefit of the old. What the adventurers saw as they scanned the rainforests was not whole majestic trees but a massive, soaring colonnade of potentially valuable tree-trunks, which they sampled, probably by slicing off wedges. When they saw the diffuse–porous pattern of the heartwood of the Gmelina species of Asia and Oceania, they called them beeches after the European tree that manifested a similar pattern. It took the botanists to investigate and argue about the tribe to which these tropical and subtropical 'beech' trees actually belonged. At first they were thought to be tree verbenas and placed in the Verbenaceae but, since about 1985 when doubts first began to be voiced about the appropriateness of this classification, White Beech and allied species have begun to be placed with the dead nettles in the Lamiaceae. The botanists have not yet reached conclusion; in most reference books you will find White Beech placed in the Verbenaceae still. It will probably take biotechnology to decide the issue once for all, proving by molecular analysis of the plants' DNA whether the Gmelinas are more closely related to the verbenas or to the dead nettles.

Australian botanists, no matter how deeply concerned they might be about the vulnerable status of so many of Australia's indigenous tree species, still find themselves under an obligation to assess them in terms of the usefulness or otherwise of their timber. The Department of Primary Industries and Fisheries of the Queensland government is anxious to inform the world that White Beech is the 'premier carving timber in Queensland', that it has been used for decking and planking of boats, for 'furniture, joinery, carvery, turnery, picture frames', 'draughtsperson's implements, templates, pattern making, cask bungs, brush stocks, Venetian blind slats and beehives'. 'Highly resistant to decay in ground contact or in persistently damp or ill-ventilated situations', in the early 1900s it was used for building frames, as well as flooring, lining, mouldings, joinery and cladding.

In the 1920s attempts were made to grow White Beech in plantations. A visitor to the state forestry nursery at Imbil on the Mary River reported to the *Brisbane Courier* on 28 June 1924:

> During the last two years attention has been paid to white beech, which takes from six to twelve months to germinate. Propagation in the nursery is easy, but being tremendously deep-rooted there is a difficult task to prevent injury when raising for transferring to the plantations . . . With the use of tube planting the difficulty of damaging the young plants has been overcome. In white beech plantation it is

necessary to enclose the areas with wire netting, as wallabies eat the leaves as fast as they grow. Growth is thus checked. For this reason, and the expense involved, growing of white beech has not been extensively undertaken.

Rainforest trees are seldom 'deep-rooted', let alone 'tremendously deep-rooted'. They live by clutching at rocks with fans of spreading buttresses. The mistake that was made at Imbil is to be found in the word 'plantation'; if the foresters had planted White Beeches as members of a forest community and not as a monoculture, the wallabies that graze all over the forest, sampling rainforest fungi, grasses, ferns and palms as well as trees, would not have eaten all their leaves.

Since the Imbil experiment few if any forestry projects have featured White Beech. Recently Super Forests Plantations called their new 74-hectare plantation which will 'produce quality saw-logs from a range of quality hardwoods' 'White Beech', but of the more than twenty thousand trees that have been planted there, not one is a White Beech. Just over the southern lip of the Mount Warning caldera, at Rocky Creek Dam, the local county council has used White Beech in plantations of 'cabinet species' on abandoned dairy farms within the catchment; out of a total of twelve species White Beech is coming ninth in the growing race, so the proliferating plans for 'farm forestry', in which landowners cease clearing and replant native forest for sustainable wood production, are unlikely to feature it. There is now no White Beech timber to be had anywhere. A recently updated statement on the Queensland Department of Primary Industries and Fisheries website tells us simply that 'Sawn timber of these [Gmelina] species is not readily available. Other species of *Gmelina* are imported from Papua New Guinea, Solomon Islands and Fiji.'

The old-growth White Beeches at Cave Creek survived either because they were crooked or because they grew in places that the timber-getters couldn't get into, or couldn't get the timber out of, whichever. Fewer than a dozen mature White Beeches in sixty hectares is not much, but it will be enough. We have literally thousands of Red Cedars in all phases of growth from the oldest to the youngest, but the tree that for me typifies the specialness of Cave Creek as a Gondwanan refugium is White Beech.

Here's the how-and-why.

I hadn't been responsible for the forest long, when I paused on my pre-breakfast walk to watch Golden Whistlers popping in and out of an immense pyramid of Lantana on the creek edge. As the whistlers skimmed about me, I turned my binoculars upward till there was nothing to see but sky. Such a vast pyramid of Lantana had to be sprawling over a seriously big tree, but what? Most of the leaves that I could pick out among the canes arching out of the top of the towering heap were still Lantana, pale-stemmed, matt, bright green, cordate. Others, a very few, were different, bigger, denser, with a stout network of leaf veins visible against the light. I poked around on the ground under the Lantana canes and found a thick yellowing leaf, still greenish on one side, buff-gold and slightly felted on the other. I tested it against the faraway shape I could see outlined against the light. It matched. I hunted about for more but found none. I put the single leaf in my trouser pocket and took it back to the house.

An hour later, when the white flare of the sun had spilled over the scarp and the air was full of sizzling radiance, I betook me to the shade of the verandah for a homemade caffe latte and a bit of botanising with the field guide we call the Red Book (Harden, McDonald and Williams). My sister Jane, who was on holidays and hence not expected to go marching off at the first light of dawn, was having a late breakfast. Jane is a proper botanist and my willing but demanding preceptor in matters botanical.

'So?' she asked, mopping up the last of her stewed tomatoes with her last bit of toast.

'It's a leaf,' I said.

'Was that all you could get?'

'The tree's enormous, a hundred feet high or so, but it's completely covered by Lantana.'

(If you look up White Beech on the net, you may come across an advertisement that assures you that it is 'a fast growing, deciduous, small to medium tree' that will grow no more than eight to ten metres in your garden. A White Beech recorded at Terania Creek, New South Wales, came in at 59 metres tall and 2.65 metres round.)

My sister was unimpressed by my lack of enterprise. I went on, 'I couldn't even see the branches, let alone climb them.'

'As if,' said Jane, who is six years younger and a good deal fitter than I. 'Describe what you've got then.'

'Simple. Well, I think it's simple. It doesn't look like a leaflet. Largish.' Even in its slightly withered state the leaf was eight centimetres long, with a stalk more than two centimetres long. 'Stout, er, kind of tough.'

'What's the word for kind of tough?'

'Coriaceous?'

'Go on. Shape?'

'Egg-shaped, I mean, ovate or obovate. With a slight point. Hairless, or glabrous, if you'd rather, on the upper side, softly felted on the under.'

'Felted?'

'Tomentose.'

'What about the base of the leaf?'

I was stumped. Jane took the leaf. 'See how it doesn't narrow into the petiole? That structure's probably diagnostic. It's certainly not common.'

I believed her, although to me it seemed like the quintessential leaf, leaf-coloured, leaf-shaped, leaf-ish. Jane was warming to her task.

'You've already got a stack of identifying characteristics, even in this one leaf. You should be able to key the whole tree out just from that. Palaeobotanists often have to work with less. What you don't know is leaf arrangement; you don't know if it's opposite or alternate, but you do know that it's not compound. This leaf is as simple as they come.'

'It looks verbenaceous,' I said.

'Don't speculate. Investigate,' said Jane sternly, and got up to clear away. While she washed the dishes, I struggled with the key.

'It begins with leaf arrangement,' I whinged. 'I can't key it out if I don't know that.'

'What about the edge of the leaf? Is it toothed or frilly or lobed?'

'No. It's, um, straight.'

'No, it's not. It's curved. We describe a leaf that has an uninterrupted margin as what?'

'Oh, entire.'

'What else have I taught you to look for?'

I knew that one. 'Oil dots.'

'So get the glass and look for them.'

I squinted through the loupe looking for translucent dots like a jeweller looking for flaws in a diamond. 'No oil dots, as far as I can see.'

'What about the venation? What can you tell me about that?'

That was interesting. The veins were not arranged symmetrically. 'The veins seem sort of haphazard, and, they're incised on the upper surface and really prominent on the underside.'

Jane took the leaf from me.

'Impressed. Not incised, impressed.'

I ploughed through the Red Book until I was only one page from the end. 'What about this?' I read out,

> Leaves 8 to 18 centimetres long, ovate or broad-ovate, bluntly pointed or acute, rather thick and tough, the main veins impressed above, strongly raised and prominent below ... leaf-under surfaces, softly and densely hairy with fawn hairs—

'Use your glass again.'

'It's just like thick blond fur! So this must be White Beech.'

'Not must exactly.' Jane was still looking at the leaf. 'More may. That petiole's interesting. It's quite stout, and channelled on the upper surface.'

The Red Book didn't say anything about the leafstalks. 'Can I work backwards now? Can I look up White Beech in Floyd?' Alex Floyd is the daddy of everyone who works on our rainforest. Although his *Rainforest Trees of Mainland South-eastern Australia* was published more than twenty-five years ago it remains by far our most useful reference book; for all those years the publishers, the New South Wales Forestry Commission, remained deaf to all pleas for a new issue. The CCRRS copy had seen such hard service that its boards had fallen off and were now held on by a sticky mess of yellowing sellotape. I had orders in with every specialist bookshop in the world for another copy but nothing was forthcoming. A university press advertised it; we sent off an order only to receive the entirely unnecessary information that the book was out of print. At some

point two heroes of the rainforest, Nan and Hugh Nicholson, decided
that they would take the matter in hand. They had the original publication electronically scanned, and carefully edited every entry. Then
they formed themselves into Terania Rainforest Publishing and
published the revised edition in 2008, which was long after the day I
sat on the verandah puzzling over my single White Beech leaf.

'Here we go,

Leaf stalks 15–37mm long, somewhat thick, densely hairy . . . lateral
veins eight to ten, straight and forking toward the margin, at 45° to
the midrib. (Floyd, 1989, 173)

'What family's it in?'
'The Verbenaceae.'
'So you guessed right. What made you say you thought it was
verbenaceous?'
'The leaf shape, for one. And its feltedness.' Jane was to have the
last laugh after all, because White Beech is not now in the Verbenaceae.

If my tree was a White Beech, it would bear flowers 'in large
panicles at the end of the branchlets', followed by blue fruit. It would
be those flowers that would remove the White Beech from the
company of the verbenaceous, because they are white velvet versions
of dead nettle flowers, with petals fused into a tubular bell with a
protuberant lower lip marked with 'two yellow flight-path bars' and
four stamens, 'a long and a short pair overarching the flight paths'.

I couldn't bear the thought of a tree so sumptuous smothered under
the heap of rampant Lantana. The CCRRS workforce was supposed to
be proceeding in an orderly fashion, clearing zones in sequence, but this
was a case for ETR, emergency tree rescue, our first but by no means
our last. Nothing is more rewarding than to spy an ancient rainforest
aristocrat struggling under a blanket of suffocating Lantana or Kangaroo
Vine, and gently to remove its load. It can't be done quickly; to rip out
canes or vines is to rip the tree. Instead we hack our way in under the
marauder, scraping and poisoning as we go until all its connections with
the ground are severed. The stock and roots are then painted with neat
glyphosate stained turquoise blue with a vegetable dye.

If we'd dragged the Lantana canes out of the old White Beech hundreds of epiphytes, orchids, ferns and mosses would have come out with them. Instead we waited for the canes to die, to become light and brittle and finally to break and fall. The first bearded branches to emerge from the twiggy mess of dead Lantana seemed half-rotten themselves. I watched them anxiously week by week until they began to push out furry new leaves of a thick pastel green unusual in the rainforest. Before the leaves had finished coming in, the great old tree sent up a silent shout of victory and gushed torrents of blossom, china-white cymes that turned violet-blue as they aged. The struggle to get a sight of them involved a good deal of rock-scrambling and tree-climbing and subsequent tick infestation, but the sight of the tree in its glory was well worth it. Amongst the blossoms in the canopy, Sulphur-crested Cockatoos eyed us quizzically, never pausing as they nipped off the big dead nettle flowers at the neck and threw them to the forest floor, while around them a billion insects plundered the pollen and the nectar, laying their eggs in the flower hearts as they went.

After the torrent of blossom came loads of fruit, flattened spherical drupes of the same china-white and violet-blue as the flowers. We waited till the fruit began to rain down, turning the forest floor fluorescent lavender-blue. As soon as the sun slid behind the edge of the Lamington Plateau, and only minutes ahead of the hordes of small nocturnal herbivores who would grab the fruit and hide it away for future consumption, we would gather up all we could find, mindful of Floyd's grim account of propagating White Beech.

> Germination is very slow, such as 37% after five months. Percussion and shell removal is either not feasible or beneficial. Flesh should be removed and seed soaked for 2 months, then dried in the sun for one day, followed by further soaking before sowing. (1989, 173)

Half the fruit I gave away to a professional grower. The rest I prepared myself. Nothing about soaking seed for two months made sense to me. As my eyes had become attuned to the green of the White Beeches in the canopy I knew that the species did not specially favour creek sides. Immersion of the seeds for two months sounded too much like drowning, but I guessed they did need an alternation of very wet and quite dry. Most growers of rainforest species soak the freshly gathered fruits overnight to drown the larvae that will otherwise hatch in almost every one and eat the seed kernel before it can germinate. The activities of the larvae clearly reduce the fertility outcome for the tree, but in the crowded rainforest environment long-lived trees like the White Beech are in no immediate need of hordes of descendants. Seedlings that germinate from the fruit might have to wait years, even generations, before a gap will open in the canopy and trigger their upward surge. Most of the extravagant crop of the White Beech was destined to be used by the other denizens of the forest, and they included me. My self-appointed task was temporarily to maximise the White Beech's reproductive potential so that it could reoccupy its old niche in the forest. Whether this is a realistic aim or a useful objective was by no means clear to me, but I felt in my bones that I had no choice. Someone, something else was calling the shots.

After the fruit had soaked for a full twenty-four hours, I took on the toil of peeling off the drupe, which was more woody than fleshy, to lay bare the squat round nut with its inset lid. Within minutes my hands were thickly coated in an odd-smelling brownish exudate, that so stuck my fingers together that I could hardly wield my knife. I struggled on for hour after hour as my fingers got pulpy from repeated immersion and stiffened under the relentless build-up of the exudate, which I had regularly to peel off my fingers with the knife blade. As I got progressively clumsier the knife found more opportunities to slip off the small wet nut and bury its short blade in my palm. I had no way of knowing, as the uncomfortable hours crept by, whether what I was doing was for the best, or even necessary. I let the seeds dry off, but not in the sun, tucked them into a special compost in an old broccoli box scavenged from the supermarket, wetted them through, and put over them a car-window pane that I had found lying under the old farmhouse. For six months the box remained forgotten on a shelf, among old woolsacks, broken furniture and rusting machine parts. It was one of my mad ideas. No one else was interested, and anyway, it would never work.

When I came back from England six months later, I made sure that my box was one of those placed in our makeshift propagation unit, where it would be watered automatically twice a day. A month went by. I didn't even ask about my box because I was so sure that the effort had been wasted. Now and then I'd check to see that the lads hadn't thrown it out or planted something else in the box. I was fussing over Garry's bull terrier bitch one morning when Garry stuck his head out of the door of the propagation unit and said, 'Sump'm here you should see.'

At first I didn't recognise the five plantlings that stood stiff and erect in the loose planting medium, five furry stems each bearing a single pair of leaves, not entire like the leaves of the adult parent, but with five teeth on each margin. (This phenomenon of dissimilarity between juveniles and adults is not uncommon among the primitive Australian flora.) Though the first five leaf pairs of the baby beeches were different in shape from those of the parent tree, they were the same unmistakeable kitchen-cabinet green. Every day more baby beech trees popped up until we had 150 of them standing proudly side-by-side in their old polystyrene box. I don't know how people feel when they win the lottery, but I'll bet they're no happier than I was then.

We could have grown more, but White Beech is not dominant in our forest. Rightly or wrongly (and there is disagreement on the point) we are concerned to keep our own races pure, at least until we know more about the exact identities of our species, subspecies and varieties, and the extent of their variability. In none of the books could I find any account of the asymmetric venation of our leaves, which can make them look quite lopsided. I know now that the leaves are opposite, but the leaf veins are mostly subalternate, and some actually fork where they leave the midrib. I don't know if the oddity of the leaves on the CCRRS trees puts them in a different variety or subspecies, but I do know that we won't mix them up with White Beeches from further away, not yet anyway. The issue is more important than it might seem. Speciation is an ongoing process; the Cave Creek Gmelinas with their lopsided leaves may be in the process of turning into a distinct subspecies or even a species, in which case we should let nature take its course rather than acciden-tally or deliberately causing our clones to revert to an earlier type.

Botany is an inexact science. What is more, frequent name changes make Australian plant taxonomy rather more challenging than it needs to be, especially as the ill-tempered factionalism that characterises all academic disciplines leads some botanists to leap on the new names as soon as they appear while others steadfastly refuse to use them. *Gmelina leichhardtii* has been that for a good while now; what is not clear is just who has accepted that the genus is in the Lamiaceae, or why. The taxonomic problems presented by the genus Gmelina and allied genera are currently being investigated by the Lamiaceae Team of the Royal Botanic Gardens at Kew. As long as they think White Beeches are lamiaceous that's good enough for me.

When Victorian government botanist Ferdinand Mueller came to identify the specimen of White Beech that had been collected by Ludwig Leichhardt at Myall Creek on 20 November 1843, he decided that it was in the related genus Vitex, and gave it thé species name *leichhardtii* (*Fragmenta*, 3:58). At Kew George Bentham had the advantage of being able to compare the specimen he was sent with other members of both genera, Vitex and Gmelina so, when the name was published in Volume 66 of his *Flora Australiensis*, it was silently corrected to *Gmelina leichhardtii*, the specific name being allowed to stand. Mueller greatly admired Leichhardt, which is about the only thing I am happy to have in common with him. Other observers have expressed less favourable opinions (Chisholm, *passim*). Because Leichhardt's way of being a naturalist (as distinct from his way of conducting expeditions) seems to me the right way, I shall impose upon your patience by telling you more than you probably want to know about him.

Ludwig Leichhardt was born in Trebatsch, Prussia in 1813, sixth of the eight children of the Royal Peat Inspector. He was accepted by the universities of both Berlin and Göttingen to study philology, but in November 1833 he met a young Englishman called John Nicholson who turned him on to natural science. When Nicholson's younger brother William came to Germany in 1835, he persuaded Leichhardt to change his field of academic study at the University of Berlin to natural science. As Leichhardt's family did not have the funds to support him, he had been living in direst poverty. William Nicholson offered not only to share his accommodation with Leichhardt, but also to pay his tuition fees and other expenses. When Nicholson returned to England he invited Leichhardt to join him there so that they could collaborate in studying natural science, in preparation for a career as explorers of Australia. The two travelled and studied together in France, Italy and Switzerland. They were together in Clermont-Ferrand when, on 24 September 1840, Nicholson announced that he no longer intended to follow a career as a naturalist in Australia but would return to England and practise as a physician. Nicholson paid for Leichhardt's passage to Australia, and his clothing and equipment, and gave him £200 in cash.

Leichhardt arrived in Port Jackson on Valentine's Day, 1842. For six months he looked for employment in Sydney; then he set off alone on an expedition from Newcastle along the Hunter and across the Liverpool Range to New England, collecting and annotating as he went. After resting a while at Lindesay Station he travelled to Wide Bay and it was on this part of his journey that he collected the first specimen of White Beech at Myall Creek. He was then invited by Thomas Archer to accompany him to his brothers' property at Durundur on the Stanley River and use it as the base for his explorations of the district. Leichhardt remained at Durundur for seven months, and then set off back to Sydney. On the way he stopped at Cecil Station on the Darling Downs where preliminary plans were laid for his next, far more ambitious enterprise.

An overland expedition from Sydney to Port Essington had been recommended by the Legislative Council in the hope that it would open a lucrative trade route between south-east Asia, India and the colony. The surveyor-general Sir Thomas Mitchell had agreed to lead the expedition but Governor Sir George Gipps refused to authorise 'an expedition of so hazardous and expensive a nature' without support from the British government. When Leichhardt offered to lead an expedition of volunteers, newspaper editors decided to assist him in raising a private subscription. The route chosen led from the Darling Downs to Port Essington on the shores of the Arafura Sea, a total of 4,800 kilometres. The ten men involved, with their 17 horses, 16 bullocks, 550 kilos of flour, 90 kilos of sugar, 40 kilos of tea and 10 kilos of gelatine, left Jimbour on 1 October 1844.

They travelled north along the Burdekin, the Lynd and the Mitchell rivers to the shore of the Gulf of Carpentaria, which they followed to the mouth of the Roper River before turning inland, skirting Arnhem Land to the east. Though Leichhardt had few bush skills, and was happier rambling and botanising than working out logistics, it took them less than fifteen months. They reached Port Essington on 17 December 1845. On the way two men had left the expedition and John Gilbert, himself an expert bushman and naturalist, had been killed by Aborigines. No one had suffered from the scurvy that had crippled Sturt's expedition inland from Adelaide, because of Leichhardt's awareness of the nutritional value of the native herbage he saw around him. The team returned by sea to Sydney where Leichhardt was greeted as a hero.

Leichhardt lost no time in raising money for a second expedition and this time the government came on board. The plan was to cross the continent from east to west. The team left in December 1846, but managed to cover only 800 kilometres before flooding, malaria and starvation forced them back. Leichhardt then set off on his own to explore the country around the Condamine River.

In his next attempt to cross the continent from east to west, Leichhardt was determined to travel light. He added to the team of seven Europeans two Aborigines, who would help them to live off the land they were travelling through. As they had no more than one spare horse for each man, it is hard to see how they could have completed a journey of more than four thousand kilometres. The small party left Cogoon Station, on the northern edge of the Darling Downs, on 3 April 1848 and was never heard of again. Since then nine expeditions have been organised in attempts to trace the party but none has been successful.

'Listen to this!' I said to my mate Ann, who was reading Rex Stout as she sunned her knees on the verandah. 'This is Leichhardt's first encounter with Gondwanan rainforest – it's in a letter to a fellow naturalist:

> And oh that you could have been with me in these brushes. Here grows the nettle tree about 80 and 90 feet high with its large leaves, and the noble red cedar (what is its scientific name?) the red Sterculia, the Sassafras, the Ricinus, the Rosewood, the cohiti wood. It will take some time before we find even their real names . . .

– that was certainly true –

In little gullies, where the waters went down the fern trees grew luxuriantly about 12–15 feet high long leaves of 8–9 feet long. Polypodium,
Asplenium, Acrostichum grew everywhere, mosses hung down in
festoons and a species of birds had knowingly made use of them to hide
its nest – Lichens of various colour covered the rotten and the living
trees. The lyre bird, the native turkey with its peculiar nest of leaves,
the fermentation of which hatches the eggs, a kind of rat, the Echidna
and many curious animals live here. (Aurousseau, ii, 632)

'Where was he? It sounds just like here,' said Ann.

'He was camping on Mount Royal.' (The Mount Royal National
Park is one of the southernmost of the Gondwana Rainforests of
Australia.) 'You have to love him. He's so full of optimism and confidence and generosity. He's fascinated by the country he's in, no
matter whether it's spectacular or fertile or dull and stony. He finds
something to intrigue him everywhere, and he describes it simply
and vividly. He gives attention to all kinds of animals, vertebrate and
invertebrate, and all kinds of plants from lichens to forest giants. He
knows his botany so well that he recognises plants he's never seen
before from descriptions he has read. He names natural features after
ordinary people, including the boy and the convict and the black-
fellow in his team. He's special.'

Ann was unimpressed. 'Surely the man was a leech. How could he
have shared Nicholson's small allowance and his narrow lodgings and
let him pay for everything, even his passage to Australia?'

'It wasn't as if he could work as well as study,' I said uncertainly,
because I too found Leichhardt's willingness to live off Nicholson
faintly contemptible.

Ann went on. 'The key to Leichhardt's whole messy career is that
he was desperate to avoid being drafted into the Prussian army. He's
supposed to do a year's military service after he completes high
school, doesn't do it, goes to university instead. Hops from one
course to another, doesn't graduate, but he still lets people call him
"Dr" Leichhardt. Then he wants to join Nicholson in England and
tries really hard to convince the Prussian government that he's unfit
for service, fails, but gets a deferment and is allowed to go to England.
The Prussian government won't let him travel to France so he goes

on forged identity papers. Then instead of going home to do his service, he sneaks off to Australia at Nicholson's expense. The man was a lightweight. A chancer.'

'He did have very poor eyesight. And since when did you object to anyone's dodging the draft?'

'Pfui,' said Ann, and went back to Nero Wolfe.

I confess that I love White Beeches mostly for themselves alone but also for the name they bear. The verdict of history is mixed. Leichhardt will remain an enigma. His last expedition will continue to seem criminally suicidal but nothing can distort the sensibility that informs his writing.

Nowadays if Leichhardt's beech is planted at all it is likely to be as a street tree. Its neat round-headed habit, its straight smooth trunk and tidy bole, together with its moderate rate of growth, are positive advantages when it comes to being planted in pavements close to walls and buildings. When I see the White Beeches along the boulevards of the Gold Coast, marooned between roaring carriageways, buffeted by fume-laden draughts, far from their in-dwelling invertebrates, their phalangers and parrots, their festoons of vines and garlands of epiphytes, I pray for them to disqualify themselves for such ignominy by dying soon, but instead, dwarfed, filthy and ragged, they suffer on.

The baby beeches were planted out in 2006. Some are already quite big trees, others are holding their breath, but they are all established. None has actually died. Having acquired their complement of invertebrate species, they are already full members of our forest community. As I walk under the canopy of our baby forests, my heart quickens with the sense of adventure. Like Leichhardt rambling over Australia, I don't know where I'm going. Like him I struggle to comprehend what I observe, with every ounce of brainpower I have left. Hordes of unfamiliar insects appear and lay billions of eggs on trees too small to survive the infestation. What should I do? The answer comes: watch, wait, live, learn. The forest is not just the trees, it is everything that lives in and on the trees, every fungus, every bug, every spider, every bird, every serpent, every bat. As a newcomer to this community, I cannot delude myself that I should or can control it. I am glad to be the forest's fool.

EDEN

If I know anything at all about botany it's because my younger sister taught me. For years we went together on botanising holidays. She taught me how to key plants out, something I'm still not very good at, partly because I tend to rely on my photographic memory and leap to an identification without going through the steps, from family, to genus, to species.

'No,' she would say, 'go back to the beginning. Is it rutaceous or myrtaceous?'

'It's a Kunzea,' I'd say, 'so it must be myrtaceous.'

'Wrong way round,' she'd say. 'What are the distinguishing characteristics of the Myrtaceae again?' She pronounced it 'mertacey', which is a sign that she is a properly trained Australian botanist. A non-botanising academic like me should pronounce it 'mertaycee-ee', but now I say 'mertacey' too.

'Um, sclerophyllous' – which means woody – 'simple leaves, without stipules, oil glands present, aromatic—'

'How can you distinguish Myrtaceae from Rutaceae?'

'By the smell?'

'Which is?'

'Rutaceae smell like citrus, sort of?' This was a sore point, because I thought some of them smelt like kerosene.

Jane taught me to use a loupe to look for oil dots and to search for tiny variations in flower form, so that I could be quite sure of my identification. This is the really nerdy part of botanising, but pernickety drudgery is an essential part of any scientific discipline. At the end of a day's rambling, after we had picked the ticks off each other, Jane and I would sit with a pile of specimens spread out on a tabletop and she would take me through them one by one.

Jane went to work when she left school, and didn't get to university until she had raised her two sons. Then she was treated as mere ballast in the class, until they belatedly recognised how serious and how gifted she was, and began to pay more attention to her searching questions, about the hypothesis of parallel evolution, for example, and to look more closely at her practical work. She could have gone on to do an honours year, but she had no interest in academic research. She went to work again, as a practical botanist, to do what she could to preserve what was left of the biodiversity of the Mornington Peninsula where she lives. Now she has a busy practice, carrying out vegetation surveys for clients private and public, identifying plant communities that need to be protected and designing planting schemes that are consistent with the indigenous vegetation. Her own garden, with its murmuring veils of Casuarina trees standing ankle-deep in their fallen needles, its tossing sedges fringed by Coast Banksias and cloud-shaped Moonahs, and massed plantings of Correas, not to mention its lawn of Wallaby Grass that grows like green fluff and its drifts of Greenhood Orchids in the spring, is deservedly famous.

It was Jane who taught me about the perils of Australia's steadily rising water table, which is bringing to the surface the salts deposited over millennia by the buffeting ocean winds, and carrying the spores of the Cinnamon Fungus (*Phytophthora cinnamomi*) that is destroying the vascular system of woody plants all over the island continent. Together we have examined the changes in vegetation that signal increased salinity, and gazed in despair at the glittering expanses that are the ulcers caused by salt. Jane is one person who is not afraid to sit beside me as I turn off the metalled roads and plunge down farm tracks and service roads, looking to see what is really going on in the great south land, counting the dead and dying trees, photographing the skeletal branches that crop out even in the greenest forest, and the new sand dunes that are travelling across the wheatbelts as the wind rakes the treeless land.

Jane, like most Australian botanists, is very interested in the uses of fire. One possible solution to the creeping death carried by Cinnamon Fungus could be fire. Many of the native species are adapted to fire, which alone

will split the woody capsules in which their seeds live. They have a history
of repeated exposure to fire, but the fire that would kill the fungus would
need to be much hotter than usual, and might burn seeds and all, or broil
the roots of trees that would normally spring into epicormic growth after
fire. In most cleared districts there has been little or no fire for a century;
the accumulated fuel load is enormous and tinder-dry. Some of the
national parks in some of the states have instituted controlled burning
programmes, which have an unfortunate propensity to get out of hand
and incinerate valuable real estate. Jane's house is on the edge of publicly
owned Moonah Woodland which desperately needs to be burnt if it is
not to choke in its own rubbish. One day, possibly quite soon, it will
burn. When it does Jane's beautiful house and garden will burn with it.
She will do nothing to prevent nature taking its course, even if it leaves
her without a roof over her head. In our botanising rambles we have
learnt the value of burnt ground, for it is there that we have found the
greatest diversity of native plants, bursting from the blackened earth with
new vigour. The first one to sight an outcrop of blackened branches in
the distance will yell 'Burny bit!' and off-road we will go until we get to
it. We crawl through the charred twiggery until we are black from
head to foot, photographing orchids, Waxflowers, Trigger Plants,
Lechenaultias, Dampieras, Beard-heaths, Dasypogons, creeping Banksias.
It is all the more remarkable then that I have ended up with responsibility
for a parcel of land where even a whiff of burning would be lethal.

It is because of my sister that I have been looking for a piece of land
in Australia, something we could work together to manage, to
protect or restore, a project we would have in common. So when
one of my oldest friends sent me pictures of a property on the south
coast of New South Wales, it made sense that we went off to see it
together. We used to enjoy these driving marathons, fuelled by bags
of fruit and aniseed jellies, with regular stops for a beer and a pie. The
pies get better the further away you are from suburbia, as all the other
food gets worse. Nothing tastes better than a cold beer and a hot pie
at Woollabookankyah or the Black Stump.

We drove eastwards from Melbourne along the coast, past sleepy
estuaries where pelicans rose and fell on the tidal swell, up through
the old-growth forests of East Gippsland, gloating over the cycads

and the tall sedges and the grass trees, as we dodged in and out among the logging trucks. We were heading for a place just south of the old fishing town of Eden, which stands on the north arm of Twofold Bay just over the border in New South Wales. From my first visit to Eden forty years before I remembered the gold of the sand bars, the ultramarine of the ocean surge, and the green-on-green of temperate rainforest, a typical holidaymaker's vision. From the second I can remember only the man I was with. What I would make of the area now that the scales had been carefully removed from my eyes by my little sister, I couldn't tell, but I wasn't optimistic.

It was dark when we turned off the dirt track that took us from the main road to the friend's house where we were to stay. The headlights picked out a gate with two signs announcing 'Wild Life Refuge'. On the bigger sign, beside a fetching logo featuring a male Lyrebird in full display, was the statement:

This property has been declared a wild-life refuge under the National Parks and Wildlife Act 1974 to conserve wild life and natural environments. All native plants and animals are protected.

I ground my teeth.

'What's the matter?' asked Jane.

'What can this mean? That we can't come in and kill things? It's the old Leopard's bane story.'

'Explain.'

'If you plant Leopard's bane, *Doronicum orientale*, you won't be troubled with leopards. The plant is endemic to south-eastern Europe so no leopard has ever been seen anywhere near it. Leon's valiantly fighting off plant nappers and bounty hunters who don't exist. Making a virtue of doing nothing. It pisses me off.'

Jane was puzzled. 'What is this National Parks and Wildlife Act 1974? Leon's a lawyer remember. We may be missing a trick.'

On the second sign it said:

Wildlife habitats within this property are being managed for the conservation of wildlife. All flora and fauna protected. Maximum penalty for an offence $1000.

The property had been give a number, and a caretaker's name and
telephone number appeared alongside.

'What would an offence be?' asked Jane. 'Picking a flower?'

'Certainly not planting a weed,' I said, as the headlights picked up
long lines of Agapanthus.

(A short digression: *Agapanthus africanus*, under its older name *A.
umbellatus*, was introduced to Australia by Robert Henderson of
Surry Hills, who won first prize with it at the second meeting of the
Sydney Floral and Horticultural Society in the saloon of the Royal
Hotel in George Street on 13 February 1839. The genus having
undergone some revision, we cannot now be sure which species
Henderson offered in 1839; the Agapanthus that is a major weed in
the Blue Mountains and in coastal Victoria is now called *A. praecox*
ssp. *orientalis*. In the north island of New Zealand it is known as
'motorway weed'.)

Conservation in Australia is largely a matter of pious intentions.
Badges and slogans and dedicated days abound but, with neither stick
nor carrot to drive or draw it forward, no progress is made. People
are neither constrained by law to care for land nor encouraged and
rewarded for doing it on their own initiative. Signs crop up everywhere. Landcare! they trumpet. Land for Wildlife!

Land for Wildlife as run by the New South Wales National Parks
and Wildlife Service is supposed to support landholders who provide
habitat for native wildlife on their land. The support is for the most
part anything but practical. All the landholders get is information,
links and contacts with like-minded people, and access to education
programmes. Lots of people get to tell you what to do, but no one
gives you any help in doing it, not even a tax rebate, but then you
don't have to do much. All you have to do to get the sign to put on
your gate is promise not to develop, that is devastate, your land any
further. You can keep farming, insecticiding, herbiciding, planting
with exotics, raise llamas or ostriches or whatever, as long as you
don't actually clear any more land than is already cleared. When you
sell the property, the commitment ceases. It struck me (and still
strikes me) as far too little much too late. To slow the rate of extinction of Australian species much more than this half-hearted
commitment will be necessary.

'What's eating you?' asked Jane, as I stomped into the kitchen.

'It gets me that people can take credit for what they're not doing, when the situation is so grave. It's like Landcare and Greening Australia. Australia isn't supposed to be green, for godsake. They should have called it Browning Australia.'

Jane laughed. Then she said, 'Landcare do some good work.'

'Do they now?' I sneered. 'It never seems to occur to anyone that European-style farming in Australia should just stop. You can't have, say, a competitive cotton industry and biodiversity as well. If you do for the environment only what will "increase your bottom line", you'll end up doing worse than nothing. As long as people keep pretending that this is the way forward, we'll keep on destroying our own heritage. There's more to this than T-shirts and stubby holders bedizened with good intentions, and giving each other awards all the time. Six hundred people turn up on the weekend for a few hours volunteering and they're given credit for controlling coastal erosion, creating wildlife corridors, restoring woodland and darning the hole in the ozone layer. It's bullshit. It creates a fog of good intentions and phoney positive thinking that allows the government to keep ignoring the real gravity of the situation. Rivercare requires coordinated planning, not a gaggle of well-intentioned locals weeding a hundred metres of river bank. And farmers shouldn't be helped. Only a handful of them are making any money anyway. They should be told to fuck off out of it.'

'Well, I'll go on working with Landcare,' said Jane. 'If only because it raises awareness. People can do conservation in their own backyards; if they can't then I'm out of a job. But they need someone to give them a steer.'

'A bum steer,' I said grumpily, as I took a short fat bottle of freezing 'lite' beer out of the fridge, pushed it into a stubby holder with 'Save the koala' written on it in fluorescent yellow and put it in her hand.

Jane looked serious. 'The best thing about Landcare is that they attract funding from corporate sponsors. Without serious funding from large corporations we'll never get anywhere, and you have to fly a flag that they'll rally to. Landcare sounds safe and cuddly, and they go for it.'

Landcare's logo is a pair of green hands cradling a shape that resembles the outline of Australia.

'If I thought I'd have to get into bed with Rio Tinto and Alcoa I'd cut my throat. This is exactly what I mean. A set-up like Landcare gives ruthless corporations the chance to pass themselves off as benign. And a cheap chance at that. Volunteers cost a lot less than advertising agencies.'

'If the Landcare deal wasn't a bargain, the corporate sponsors wouldn't go for it,' Jane said.

Before I was fully awake next morning I was aware of the endlessly reiterated chinking sound of bellbirds. As we breakfasted on toast and tea on the verandah, Jane pointed out, on the other side of a few acres of degraded pasture, a bedraggled stand of eucalypts.

'See those dead branches topping out there? That's dieback. Probably Bell Miner Associated Dieback, judging by the noise. Drink up your tea and we'll go and see.'

The homestead stood on a knoll, in a bend of the Towamba River which rises in the Great Dividing Range, plunges over the coastal scarp and dawdles to the sea. Its glimmering reach surrounded us on three sides. We could see shifting banks and beaches of fine pink sand, some supporting an evanescent population of Hop-bushes and Cherry Ballarts, interspersed with wonderful blond Stipas with fronds that swung about in the onshore breeze like hair in a shampoo advertisement.

'The river must be still salt up here,' said Jane. She pointed to glassworts and saltbush growing in an inlet.

The land, all but a few acres, had long ago been cleared for sheep. We were walking through waist-high thickets of overgrown pasture grass, amid bursts of sweetbriar, bulrushes and thistles, where the odd sheep still mooched.

'This really is the most terrible mess. What d'you reckon was here before they cleared it?' I asked.

'Depends,' said Jane. 'Down here in the river sand I reckon would have been some kind of saltmarsh, which must have been drained to provide pasture. As the ground rises you get different assemblages, different kinds of woodland. This is the driest and windiest part of the New South Wales coast. It's in a rain shadow, because the sou'westerlies dump all their rain on the Dividing Range before they get here. I can see one familiar tree.' She pointed to a eucalypt. 'That's Coast Grey Box, *Eucalyptus bosistoana*. I think that over there must be Silver-top Ash, *Eucalyptus sieberi*. Can you see how the mature leaves shine sort of silver? There's at least one kind of stringybark and an ironbark, and I think those must be woollybutts, *Eucalyptus longifolia*. I'm guessing about the gums but this Black Wattle is a species I know really well.' She pulled off a twiglet and handed it to me. '*Acacia mearnsii*. See how it's got bipinnate leaves instead of phyllodes?'

'Typical. I've no sooner learnt that wattles have phyllodes instead of leaves than you show me one that has leaves instead of phyllodes.'

'What's this?' Jane had stopped by a knee-high set of rangy stems growing up from a basal rosette.

For once I knew it. 'That's Sea Lavender. Limonium.'

Jane was used to my knowing European things. 'Exotic.'

'I don't think so. It looks different. I think it's a native version.' When we came to look it up it turned out to be *Limonium australe*, the native Sea Lavender.

'Limonium's a saltmarsh genus. That'd be a lark, wouldn't it? Turning the run-down pasture back to saltmarsh?'

'Maybe all you'd have to do would be to let the river inundate it regularly. That'd kill the pasture, and the introduced weeds, and then things like this would take over.' She was pointing her boot at a clump of Sea Rushes. 'That's our native Sea Rush, which is pretty special, because it's being pushed out of most marshland by the exotic Spiny Rush, *Juncus acutus*. You should end up with more of those fabulous Stipas as well. *Austrostipa stipoides*. That's a Gahnia over there, *Gahnia filum* probably. The local paperbark would probably grow here too, at least where it wasn't too salt. This is another ballart.'

She was holding a branchlet of a needle-leaved bush that had upside-down fruit on it, with a blue-black kernel hanging below white semi-transparent flesh, and gesturing with her other hand to the cypress-like bushes around it. 'Those are Cherry Ballarts, *Exocarpos cupressiformis*, with fruits like this but red. They grow on eucalyptus roots, but this is different. This is *Exocarpos strictus*. I'm surprised to find it growing here, I must say.' We were standing on one of the sandbanks that formed the river beach.

'Coastal saltmarsh is an endangered ecosystem. I should say a group of endangered communities, because saltmarshes are all different, but they tend to get lumped together in conservation-speak. Wherever they are, they're in constant danger of being "reclaimed" and built over. And they're really essential elements in the mosaic.'

There was no need to explain. We both knew that saltmarsh is the habitat of a raft of species from the tiniest molluscs to the crustaceans and birds and fish that feed on them and on each other. They are the places where bats come to hunt insects, where baby fish find shelter from predators, and where migratory birds come to rest and refuel. For years Jane had been one of a group of dedicated workers trying to protect Hooded Plovers nesting on the back beach at Sorrento from the impact of humans and their dogs. If we were managing saltmarsh of our own Jane would have been able to create asylum for her plovers, and for Godwits and Sandpipers, not to mention the Black-winged Stilt and the White-fronted Chat.

'Then again,' Jane went on,' you mightn't have to do anything. If the sea level rises as they think it will, then this land will be regularly inundated anyway.'

We had walked on to a tongue of higher land between the pasture and the river. Jane pounced on a fluffy spike growing out of a clump of grass and pulled the inflorescence apart with her nails. 'Wallaby Grass! The hardest thing about reinstating native grasses is finding the seed. There's none in commerce, as far as I know, and here it is.' She waved the flower spike and the seed lifted off like smoke.

Jane's Wallaby Grass lawn is famous. Every year she collects the seed with a vacuum cleaner and sows a new area. I love Wallaby Grass because, even without macropods keeping it down, it never needs mowing. Lawn-mowing was the bane of my suburban childhood.

'It would make headway only if you extirpated the exotic grasses. See this' – she snapped off a tall frond, and pulled back a blade to show the ligule – 'this is African Lovegrass, *Eragrostis curvula*. It's virtually annihilated its less vigorous Australian cousin, *E. leptostachya*.' As we walked she showed me Serrated Tussock (*Nassella trichotoma*), Pampas Grass, Chilean Needle Grass and Rat's Tail grasses.

'These are all scheduled as weeds because they degrade pasture. Half the native grasses are classed as weeds for the same reason. If you wanted to do serious conservation here, you'd have to deal with both exotic weed grasses and pasture grasses. And the exotics would be continually reseeding from the adjoining properties. Hopeless really.'

At first I had quite liked the Bell Miners' incessant tinkling, but as we drew nearer the stand of devastated gums it seemed to bounce off the morning sky and fall on our ears like lead shot.

'God,' said Jane, 'the bloody Anvil Chorus.'

The eucalypts were so defoliated that there was no way of identifying them for certain. Though the trees looked different from the Manna Gums that grow on the Mornington Peninsula, Jane thought they were probably the same species, *Eucalyptus viminalis* (and she was right). When we came under their ragged canopy, we could smell the Bell Miner colony. A sticky debris of leaves and twigs lay about our feet. The noise had become deafening.

'Tell me about Bell Miners.'

'Miners are related to honeyeaters; they've got the same sort of tongue, with a brush-tip, but they have a more complex social structure. They live in large groups, and mate promiscuously, and their young are fed indiscriminately by all adults, I think, certainly by other members of the colony besides their parents. They're very aggressive in the defence of their territory and drive off all other species that try to share their food source. It seems that males far outnumber females in the colony. Which figures.'

'Do they live on nectar?'

'No. That's the problem. Bell Miners eat lerps.'

'Lerps?'

'Lerps are the sugary coats that the nymphs of sap-sucking psyllids build for themselves. Pardalotes and other insectivorous birds pull the nymph out from under the lerp and eat that. If Bell Miners move in to eat the lerps the other birds leave behind, they drive away the insectivores and prevent them from finishing the job. Some people think the Bell Miners actually farm the lerps to get their sugar fix.'

'Surely they've always done that. Why has it become such a problem now?'

'Nobody knows for sure. In 1999 Bell Miners were removed from an area of infestation; there was an immediate influx of insectivorous birds who brought the population of psyllids down, but after ten months the trees showed no sign of recovery. The scientists involved in the experiment concluded that the real cause of the trees' death was probably the destruction of their vascular system by guess what?'

I groaned. 'Cinnamon Fungus.'

This was so depressing a thought that we were both silent as we walked on down to the river, where the eternal clangour of the birds followed us, echoing off the water. When we sat down in the warm sand Jane told me more about Bell Miner Associated Dieback.

'BMAD is a huge problem, and getting worse. It's official now that in northern New South Wales more than 20,000 hectares of sclerophyll forest are affected by BMAD. And the problem extends right down the Great Dividing Range as far south as Melbourne. Our state bird, the Yellow-tufted Honeyeater, has been driven to extinction by the Bell Miner takeover of its habitat.'

'Why is it spreading so fast?'

'Probably because the trees are already under stress. When the trees die, the Bell Miners simply move on to another stand and start the process all over again. They're gradually reducing the habitat available for other birds. Some conservationists think that the increase of drought stress as a consequence of global warming is weakening the trees, making them more susceptible to insect attack, and that the Bell Miners are merely opportunists. Others believe that "controlling" Bell Miners is the way to go. Others want to eliminate the psyllids. If it's Cinnamon Fungus that's really to blame for BMAD, it doesn't matter much what they do or if they do nothing.'

When Leon arrived that evening, we asked him what he was doing about his case of BMAD and he was doing exactly that, nothing. In his eyes nature could do no wrong, and everything out there was nature. There would be no killing or burning on his patch.

'Leon, the Bell Miner population is out of control. There's little enough natural vegetation left around here. You can't afford to lose what old-growth forest you've got.'

But the conversation had moved into a more diverting channel. The Cassandra in the corner went unheeded.

The next day we were taken upriver to see the property that was for sale. As we moved out of the tidal reach the vegetation changed. The riverbank on both sides was now hidden by a thick fringe of willows. Jane, who expects me to know European species better than she, asked me which willows they were.

'They look like Crack Willows,' I said, '*Salix fragilis*, which is bad news because crack willows drop terminal twigs even in a slight wind, and they readily root downstream. In England Crack Willows are among my favourite trees; I've planted lots of them. These are a bit different. I think they must be hybrids.'

As we were stepping out of our flat-bottomed boat, stooping to pass under the willows, I tripped and fell headlong into the mat of *Vinca major* that was all the streamside groundcover there was. Surefooted Jane was having trouble too, for no matter how high she stepped the interlacing strings of the Periwinkle trapped her boots.

'This is a bugger of a weed,' she said, 'because it allows absolutely no competition. Worse, it will thrive in deep shade and sheds its fronds which get carried downstream.'

'Just like the willows.'

'Yep.'

As it turned out our journey was pointless, for the owner of the property was interested in selling only if he could get an exorbitant price. He thought he might sell half of it, which would have meant that we had to share access and would live so close together that we could hear each other break wind. He was immensely proud of a huge oak tree that overshadowed his house.

'What would you do with the property if it was yours?' he asked me.

I didn't say that I would fell his monster oak. 'I'd get rid of the cattle,' I said.

'Oh, you couldn't do that,' he said. 'You need the steers to keep down the grass.'

I didn't tell him that I would poison the grass, but drank up my tea, paid my respects and withdrew. Leon was disappointed. He wanted to know why I hadn't stayed to bargain.

'Because I didn't want it. There'd be no way I could restore it, because every time the Towamba came in spate, I'd get all the riverine weeds back again.'

'What weeds?'

'Willows for one.'

'What's wrong with willows? Willows are lovely.'

'What's wrong with willows is what's wrong with all weeds. They're plants in the wrong place.'

Jane raised her eyebrows, interested to see how much I had understood of all her careful teaching. I ploughed on.

'The willow in Australia is not part of a plant community. It has no competitors and supports no suite of invertebrates or fungi or whatever. Its growth and reproduction are not limited by natural factors, so the willow can overwhelm all the niche plants growing in local ecosystems. Like lots of our worst tree weeds, it originally grew from cuttings imported by homesick settlers.'

'They probably needed cricket bats,' said Leon. 'Without those willows we'd never have won the Ashes.'

'Bat willow is a variety of *Salix alba*. It seems more likely to me that the early settlers thought they would need osiers, for baskets, and brought cuttings of *S. fragilis*. The worst willow in the Australian situation is *S. nigra*. It's beyond belief that *S. nigra* was imported from America as late as 1962, as part of the effort to combat erosion.

'The willows've been hybridising across the clones for a couple of hundred years. In their native habitats this kind of interbreeding would have been prevented by natural factors, geographic distance, different flowering times, and genetic incompatibility. In Australia bastard willows can breed with any other willow growing within a kilometre radius. And the hybrids can tolerate a vast range of cultural conditions. When they take over an area they obliterate biodiversity and flourish as a hugely prolific monoculture. Within a very few years of their introduction into Australia willows had spread through the south-eastern river systems, changing their patterns of flow.'

'Can they be controlled?' asked Leon.

'Not easily. Any frond breaking off and falling into the river will root downstream. Fronds washed onto a bank will get a foothold in the mud. Seeds too are carried downstream, as well as on the wind. In huge quantities. Even if we ripped out or poisoned all the willows on the lower Towamba, within a year or two the willow population would be back close to maximum density. Eventually willows would immobilise the sandbanks and obstruct the course of floodwater when the river is in spate, increasing erosion.'

'You made the willow problem seem insoluble,' said Jane, as we undressed for bed.

'I didn't tell him the half of it. I didn't talk about loss of habitat for native species, or what happens when billions of leaves are dumped in watercourses when willows deciduate, or about the loss of sub-terranean water in drought seasons. Anyhow, Leon wasn't listening. He thinks it enough that he doesn't turn the property into a golf course or a marina.'

'I feel like going out there right now and setting fire to the Manna Gums with the Bell Miners in them,' said Jane.

'You wouldn't dare.'

'You're right,' said Jane and turned out the light.

Leon even liked the Bell Miners. One thing he was sure about: no wild creatures would be shot or poisoned on his watch. No fox. Not even a rabbit. His property had been cleared more than a hundred years ago. It was more than he could do to unclear it now. So he ran a few sheep, brought friends down from Sydney for restful weekends and did a little fishing at the mouth of the shimmering Towamba, where oysters grew on the rocks. If the wedgetails took his newborn lambs he blessed them. When I clicked my teeth because the only wildflowers in the pasture were Yellow Sorrel and Capeweed from South Africa, he accused me of rabid nationalism.

'I'm an exotic,' he said, 'Purebred from Bialystok. And you're a hybrid from everywhere but here. You might as well say we've got no right to be here.'

'I have said that.'

'Don't be silly,' said Leon.

The next day we went downstream in the tinny for a look at a parcel of land that Leon was willing to sell. This was unimproved old-growth forest, opposite Boydtown, one of the few sites on the south coast of New South Wales that Aboriginal people have been able to repossess. The site, overlooking the mouth of the Towamba, was bordered with rocks encrusted with delicious oysters that I would have been happy to live on, if only the walk up and down from the river's edge had not been quite so steep. That steepness gave me a vantage point from which I would have been able to watch the whales that visit the bay in October–November. The forest was healthy, though not undisturbed. The only serious infestation I would need to get rid of was *Pittosporum undulatum*, an Australian native that is classified as a noxious weed in California, Hawaii, New Zealand, South Africa, Lord Howe Island and Norfolk Island, as well as in much of eastern Australia. It was outside its range in this dry grass forest understorey, where it had become dominant because of changes in the fire regime. Controlling it would have been a doddle. But there was another problem. Under pressure from the insurance industry, new regulations for fire damage limitation have been brought in all over Australia. The New South Wales government would have required me to undertake to clear the forest for a radius of fifty metres around any house I intended to build, before planning permission would be granted. I wanted a house surrounded by native vegetation; there was simply no way that I would buy a piece of forest only to destroy it. The case probably could have been argued, specially as I wanted to build a fireproof house, but there were other, equally weighty reasons for not going ahead.

I couldn't make Leon see that the serious environmental weeds, the willows, the Smilax, the blackberry, the sweetbriar, the pines, the exotic grasses, had to be tackled. He thought it was enough to plant the occasional tree. A free load of whips had been supplied by some agency or another, and planted directly into the rough grass in front of the house, where they languished for lack of the water necessary to get such little trees started. If the tags that still fluttered on them were any guide, few of them were true natives of the area. No botanical survey had been done of Leon's properties, nor could one have been particularly helpful, for practically every form of vegetation on most of the properties was a feral exotic. Some of the native species he selected would become feral in their turn. I tried to make him see the beauty of the Cherry Ballarts growing on the undisturbed sandbanks at the river mouth, and the cloud shapes of the Melaleucas along the low shore, but he was not inspired to act. I talked to him about endangered dry grass forest communities and the importance of keeping robust competitors out until the trees and the grasses have had a chance to re-establish, but he didn't listen. It would have taken hard work, a lot of money, and rigorous mental discipline to have restored even a modicum of the biodiversity of his consortium's string of bits of land; without consensus we couldn't even begin. Meanwhile, beyond the boundaries of the property, the area was losing its amenity with every day that passed.

Twofold Bay has been in trouble ever since it was visited by Bass and Flinders in 1798. In July 1803 Her Majesty's armed tender *Lady Nelson* fired cannonballs into the cliffs for no particular reason. Sealers who used the bay to flense their catches had no scruples about removing the Kudingal women for their own use and shooting Kudingal men who presumed to object. Such is the reverence felt by Australians for their own brief history that the old whaling station, where the fat was boiled off the great beasts, so that the stench of rotting whale meat hung over the bay and decaying matter choked it, is now a carefully manicured tourist venue. The town of Eden popped up on the shore when more and more hopefuls arrived by boat to try their hand at panning alluvial gold at Kiandra in the 1850s. There were grandiose plans for a city, but by 1866 the gold had petered out. At one point the citizens of Eden got very excited when their town was considered as a possible site of the Federal Capital, but Canberra was chosen instead. Eden remained a backwater, logging for railway sleepers and fish canning its only industries. In 1999, after fifty years of operation, the Eden fish cannery was finally closed because it was not 'globally competitive', throwing 12 per cent of the total population of the town out of work. Eight months later the site was sold, for the building of a tourist resort. Meanwhile the beauty of the bay had not been advanced by the building of a fuel storage depot on Lookout Point, smack in the middle of the two lobes of Twofold Bay.

Eden has been described as a town forever waiting to be saved by the next major development. In 1970, when the Daishowa Paper Company of Japan, which had been logging in the old-growth forests of south-eastern New South Wales and Gippsland, opened its woodchip mill on Munganno Point, most of the citizens of Eden were convinced that prosperity would follow. Opposition to the demolition of the forests came from outside, from middle-class greenies who lived in the cities, who became more vocal as more and more old-growth forests were logged. The state government's only response was to guarantee 'resource security' to Daishowa; each year the quotas were increased and the royalties reduced, to offset raised transport costs as Daishowa had to go further afield to find the trees to fell.

Conservationists hoped that the chip mill would close in 1997. When it showed no signs of doing so there were public demonstrations which resulted in its temporary closure in 2000. Harris-Daishowa, since 2003 called South-East Fibre Exports, is once more running full-bore, though in June 2005 work stopped for a day when activists entered the mill and lashed themselves to the conveyor belt between the chipper and the stockpile. In 2004 observers from the action group Chipstop counted the number of trucks bringing timber to the mill, an average of 163 per day; 79 per cent of the loads contained old-growth trees, many of such girth that they had had to be split before loading.

I wondered whether it might not be my destiny to be caught up in the struggle to preserve the forests of the south-east. It wasn't as if I could ignore it, if I became a landholder in the area. The mill and its wharf and the container ships are visible from all round the bay. The noise from the mill carries way up the river, augmented by the constant noise of the timber transports turning off the main road and along the purpose-built road through the bush. Not to fight against the destruction of the forests would be tacitly to support it. I couldn't see the activists letting me stay out of it, come to that. I didn't have the stomach for so hopeless a fight.

There was even worse in the offing. In 1999 it had been announced that Twofold Bay was the site chosen by the Australian government for a new naval munitions wharf and storage facility. A 200-metre-long wharf in East Boyd Bay was to be connected to the shore by a jetty seven metres wide; the bay would be dredged to a depth of 10.5 metres to provide the berth and turning space for the munitions ships. A new access road was to be built from the shore to the roadway and on to a storage depot fifteen kilometres away in the state forest, amid fire-prone sclerophylls. The Nature Conservation Council of New South Wales objected to the proposed construction, citing the effect it would have on the protected seagrasses, and on the rare

Weedy Seadragon (*Phyllopteryx taeniolatus*), on the likelihood of polluted run-off and the importation of sea pests, the change in patterns of tidal flow, deposits of sediment and erosion. They could have made a more convincing case if they had been given time, but it would have made no odds.

The port, which in my innocence I thought would never be built, opened on 17 October 2003. All arguments against its siting in Twofold Bay had failed, mainly because all the other suggested sites were too close to centres of habitation. One of the benefits of the remoteness of the area and the depression of the rural economy was that local opposition was minimal, and apparently further afield nobody cared. The local MP Gary Nairne declared, 'The Navy Wharf project has been an enormous boon for the Eden and Bega Valley Regions, creating 112 local job opportunities and potentially attracting millions of dollars of private investment to the region.' Whales may no longer play there, and the oysters on the rocks may be too dangerous to eat, but everyone will be, potentially, richer.

Environmental degradation spawns its own inevitability. When it was suggested that Eden's mussel farm be extended from twelve hectares to fifty, it was argued that fifty hectares of bobbing buoys could hardly detract more from an area of great natural beauty than the chip mill, the fuel tanks on Lookout Point, and the munitions wharf already did. On 4 April 2004 a toxic bloom of the dinoflagellate *Dinophysis acuminata* was discovered in Twofold Bay. This organism infects shellfish, rendering them toxic at very low concentrations. Not for the first time, oysters, pipis and mussels from Twofold Bay were declared inedible. Yet in 2005 the state government signed off the permission for the mussel-farming project to proceed to its second stage. This may not be as stupid as it looks, because one way of reducing the overabundance of nitrogen that favours the proliferation of mixotrophic algae is to have mussels filter it out of the water. If I had bought Leon's parcel of forest, I'd have had a munitions wharf and storage depot, a chip mill working twenty-four hours every day, and 163 timber lorries a day, and fifty hectares of mussel farm to look at and listen to, as well as several losing battles to fight.

Before I left the south coast I made one last attempt. The local estate agents had a 'historic' homestead on the books, so Jane and I went to see it. Our way up into the pastoral district of the Monaro took us on zigzag timber roads over the coastal scarp through the higher-altitude sclerophyll forests, where far too often we could hear the cling-clang of the Bell Miners. As we got further inland the native forest gave way to huge dark plantations of Monterey Pine. The road fizzled out and navigation got harder, as we wove our way through the crisscross logging tracks. We seemed to be driving for hours without getting anywhere. I was convinced that in my obsession for travelling cross-country I had finally succeeded in getting us properly lost when the five-barred gate of the station was suddenly in front of us. I jumped out, stepped up to unhook the chain and open the gate, and froze. Beyond the gate the broad, undulating pasture lay grey and dry, watched grimly by the distant pines. In the birdless, terrible quiet, nothing moved. The sky too seemed drained of colour. It was as if my vision had gone from colour to black and white.

'What's wrong?' asked Jane.

I didn't know. 'I don't want to go in,' was all I said. My hands were cold. My sister studied my face and said nothing. We'd been driving for more than three hours to get to this place, but she didn't ask even to stretch her legs. I got back in the car, turned it around and drove the three hours back again. I apologised for my strange behaviour. Jane shook her head.

'You didn't see yourself. Your face was grey.'

It was many months before I found out that the property we went to see was the very station where, sometime in the 1840s, a whole Aboriginal community was murdered. The story, which has been passed down by one to another manager of the station ever since, is that the Aboriginal people used to sneak into the dairy at night and lick the cream off the top of the milk in the separating dishes. Nothing was simpler than to lace the milk with strychnine. Somebody must have bought the station ultimately, for I see it's operating once more, but I'm glad that someone wasn't I.

Thus ended my search for a place in New South Wales.

DESERT

What I really wanted was desert. For twenty years I had been roving back and forth over central Australia, hunting for my own patch of ground. Whether stony, rocky or sandy, pink, vermilion or blood-red, whether bald, furred with native grasses, or diapered with saltbush and spinifex, I wanted it. For years I have gorged on the life that pounds within what we were taught to call the 'dead heart', from the sudden glitter of dawn, when kangaroos sprang in front of me and emus loped beside me, with my ears tuned to the electric sizzle of the finches' song against the limitless silence, to the creeping violet fingers of evening. The white heat never seemed all that hot to me, because the desert winds freeze-dried the sweat on my body. Zero humidity and I were made for each other. The more I saw of semi-arid Australia, the more I yearned for it.

This falling in love began when I first drove the Birdsville track from Bourke to Alice Springs in 1970 and camped in the deep warm pink sand of the dry Todd River. I had never had an Aborigine's-eye view of my country before, and what I saw I loved, until the police raided the beer garden of the Alice Springs Hotel and took most of my fellow campers to jail. After I had followed the sequence of injustices through the magistrate's court on Monday morning when all my new friends, who had committed no offence, were given custodial sentences, some of them as long as six months, there was no time to venture out of the town and discover the inland for myself. I flew back to Sydney and eventually back to England, but the feel of that warm sand in the dappled shade of the river gums under the cobalt sky never left me. Whenever I found myself in Australia, I took every opportunity to escape from the endless sprawl of suburbia into the vast blue yonder.

Literary description of semi-arid Australia always dramatises its pitiless emptiness. Nicolas Rothwell, who followed the tracks of the explorers for his book *Wings of the Kite-Hawk*, recycles all the clichés. Why do I not feel 'the stillness of the bush, pure and uncaring', or the 'dull monotony of tree and scrub', in this 'inhuman', 'unnatural', 'alien' 'world of suffering, exhaustion, danger and death', 'the cruellest and most inhuman world that it was possible to conceive' under the 'empty blueness of the sky'? I don't feel the desert as an 'empire of formlessness and death'; what I feel in the desert is deep comfort. Only in suburbia do I begin to feel frantic and hopeless, suddenly back where I was in my teens, imprisoned, heartsick, revolted by the endless roofscape, desperate for life to begin. Maybe the claustrophobia I inherited from my father, that has disqualified me for life in the brick veneer bungalow on its quarter-acre block, hemmed in by fences on all sides, is quieted only in the desert, where I can wrap myself in the same kind of euphoria that lures divers to their deaths at the bottom of the sea. I am never frightened in the desert, not even when I'm well and truly lost, and God knows I should be. A silk dress and a car key are unlikely to get you out of trouble, should you strike it, but I take a delight in following the example of my forebears who went bush during the Great Depression, with nothing but the clothes they stood up in and a bicycle. If Aboriginal people can get around the bush without four-wheel drives and spare fuel- and water-tanks and air conditioning and roo bars, then so can I. I have never felt that the country was harsh or unforgiving. Whitefellas have always seemed to me the most dangerous animals in it.

When you travel all day through the ranges you become aware that with every minute change of light and orientation the character of the country changes. Different elements become visible and others fade or are burned out. Fissures in rock can turn from blue to purple to black. Depending on the time of day the very colour of the air changes, from magnesium white to misty blue or honey gold or peach pink. When it rains everything is transformed. I have seen Uluru in rainy weather, and it was blue. One of my fantasies has always been to lie in my own bed and watch the desert landscape slowly turn violet while fat yellow stars pop out in the inky sky and owlet-nightjars shake the still-warm sand through their tawny feathers. Or to watch the storms as they ride over the scarps, sending their white-hot feelers raking down the ridges and exploding in sheets of coloured light. I have driven the backroads of the Pilbara when flames were popping all around, and the saltbush and scribbly gum were bursting in showers of sparks that fell in front of my tyres, and still I wasn't afraid. It's not that I trust the desert not to kill me; it has killed better people than I. It's more that I don't mind if it does. Better a swift agony in the desert than my mother's long twilight in a seaside nursing home.

Thousands of other people too find the desert comfortable, and far safer than the town. Anmatyerre women will take off barefoot for a day's hunting, with no more protective gear than wash-cotton dresses plus the full complement of respectable underwear, armed with nothing but a crowbar and a hatchet, with their children and dogs gambolling around them. No boots, no hats, no sunblock, no sunglasses. I was lucky enough to spend a day hunting with them once, because my hired four-wheel drive was just what they needed to get them far enough out in the scrub to find a big goanna. Goanna fat is the essential bush cosmetic; it is the basis for the scented unguents that the women use to keep their skin soft and supple and the insects at bay. To help me recognise the goanna's track one of the women drew it for me in the sand. She tucked three fingers under her palm, and as she pulled her hand across the sand she rocked it, so that the thumb and little finger made the marks of the scurrying feet on both sides of the trace of the dragging tail.

The Anmatyerre women were as much at ease in the 'inhospitable' landscape as if they were grand ladies presiding over their tea tables. They picked clear gum off a small mulga tree and gave it to me to chew, with as much grace as if they were handing around the cucumber sandwiches. 'Bush lolly', they called it. It had a faint aromatic sweetness that was enormously refreshing. We dug up the roots of the witchetty bushes and extracted the fat white grubs that are the greatest of all bush delicacies. One of the women used her hatchet to cut an oval of bark to use as a coolamon, sealing it off at the edges with red mud so that the harvested grubs wouldn't fall out. The children could hardly be dissuaded from wolfing the grubs raw. We followed the flight of native bees to their holes in the eucalypts, and stole their honey with impunity because they have no stings. To me the native bees are a perfect emblem of the gentleness of a country that, instead of lions and tigers, has kangaroos and koalas. Not for the first time I asked myself why the white explorers had felt it necessary to 'discover' a country that its inhabitants already knew like the backs of their hands and could manage with minimum effort.

I had met up with the women at Alhalkere on what used to be Utopia Station. When I first heard of Utopia the Aboriginal people had just acquired the leasehold with the help of the Aboriginal Land Fund Commission. I asked an old Aboriginal stockman in the Alice Springs Hotel how the Aboriginal people were getting on with their cattle. He looked at me with narrowed eyes.

'Ate 'em.'

I was shocked. That was twenty years ago. I wouldn't be shocked now.

Utopia came to the attention of the rest of Australia in the Seventies when the Anmatyerre women began producing silk batiks. In 1990 or so I went there to see their work for myself. When I got to Alhalkere the people had all gone bush, so I hung around for a bit, hoping that they'd come back. It was while I was cooling my heels that I realised that I was surrounded by a breast-deep sea of silky blond grass with feathery tops that swung in the slightest breeze, the like of which I had never seen before. Nowhere else in the Northern Territory had I seen unmunched, untrodden vegetation or clean waterholes where people could drink, rather than acres of trodden mud. Then I knew why the people had killed and eaten all the cattle. In the paintings by the women of Utopia you will see again and again the streamer patterns of the sacred grasses that are the glory of the place. The Anmatyerre are now the freehold owners of their land, and even the hundred or so head that Cowboy Louie Pwerle used to run for his own pleasure are no more. From the Anmatyerre I learned what I would do with any piece of central Australia I might get my hands on. I would leave it to recover from nearly two centuries of misguided exploitation.

Some graziers in the Northern Territory have agreed to set aside small areas of their lease for Aboriginal people to use as campsites; I wondered if Aboriginal people might not do as much for me, but as far as I could see no precedent had ever been set. As freeholders the people of Utopia should be allowed to sell any part of their 180,000 square kilometres, but whether they would be wise to do so after the long struggle they had to acquire it is another matter.

Again and again Aboriginal people showed me the beauty of country. In 1982 I had just wandered out of Port Hedland, going north on the one and only sealed road, the two-lane blacktop that rejoices in the name of the Great Northern Highway, with the intention of observing the mining operations in the Pilbara, when I came across two Aboriginal girls hitching by the side of the road. They said they wanted to go to Derby, but after a while it turned out that they really wanted to go to Marble Bar, where somebody who was important to them was in the lockup. I was only too happy to turn the rental car off the highway and plunge off ahead of a two-kilometre plume of blood-red dust on the unsealed road to Marble Bar, famous for generations as the hottest place in Australia. The girls were as reticent as Aboriginal people usually are. Most of the little they said to each other was murmured in language, but I eventually learned that they were supposed to be at school at a Catholic mission near Cap L'Eveque.

'Do they know where you are?'

'Nuh.'

'Didn't you tell someone?'

'Nuh. Just shot through.'

Fleeing from Catholicism. I could certainly relate to that.

We were eighty or ninety kilometres down the unsealed road, at the point where the Marble Bar road crosses the Coongan River, when the girls asked me to pull over. Without a word they jumped out and ran fully dressed into the mirror of water which burst around their skinny dark figures in cascades of opaque turquoise flakes. Nothing I had ever read about inland Australia prepared me for the radiance of that water reflecting the white colonnade of great River Red Gums, or for the dance of the light prisms that veiled the girls as they busily washed their legs and arms, drank thirstily from their cupped hands and tossed the water sequins over their heads. I felt as if I could have broken out my swag and camped on the red rock-shelves under those ancient eucalypts for the rest of my life.

It was inevitable that, with all avenues on the south coast of New South Wales exhausted, I would give in to my deepest longings, and fly to Alice Springs. There I took a charter plane northwards to Delmore Downs, to visit the Holts. If there was anything for sale in the Northern Territory they would know about it. They might even be prepared to let me buy something of theirs, but it was a slim chance. Don and Janet Holt have been important facilitators of the artwork of Utopia and principal patrons of the late Emily Kame Kngwarreye. Don laughed when I asked him whether he thought his daughters would marry the kinds of men who would choose an uncertain livelihood in the cattle industry.

'I'm a cattle-breeder. I want to keep my own progeny by me and I will if I can.'

'Are you going to restore the house at Delny?'

Delny was the title of another of the Holts' leases; it had belonged to Don's grandfather who had begun to build there one of the first concrete houses in Australia. The house was never finished. When their youngest child died of gastroenteritis, the family threw in the towel. I'd seen the half-built structure every time I'd driven the sand track up to Delmore, and something about it attracted me, its uncom-promising rectangularity perhaps, its huge windows. It didn't have to remain an emblem of defeat, or so I thought.

'Restore Delny? I don't think so. Why?'

'I thought I might have a go. You could sublet it to me maybe.'

'Why would you want to?'

'I'm looking for a good place to put my archive. Somewhere dry and not too weedy. Somewhere I could manage as a nature reserve. I'd only need ten hectares or so.'

Even as I said it I could feel the feasibility drain out of the idea. This was cattle country. There were still a few native animals about but an isolated ten-hectare reserve wouldn't be much good to them.

'Jeez, Germaine, that hardly makes sense. You'd be in the middle of cattle country, hundreds of ks away from any other wildlife reserves. The only wildlife you'd come across would be reptiles.'

'I don't mind reptiles. But it's the vegetation I'd be concerned about. I'd like to restore the original plant associations. If possible.'

'Even that might be difficult,' said Don. 'For one thing, the native grasses are gradually dying out. We've never seeded this property with buffel grass but buffel grasses are taking over, and just as well, because you'd never grow cattle on the native stuff.'

The first buffel grasses to come to Australia arrived in the 1870s as packing in the saddles of the camels that were the first mode of transport available in the inland. Botanists now disagree as to whether buffel grass is a burr grass in a separate genus Cenchrus or whether it should be included in the genus Pennisetum. It is thought that some of the grasses spreading across the Northern Territory now are the Afghan species, *Cenchrus pennisetiformis* and *C. setigerus*. *Cenchrus ciliaris*, native to Africa and south-western Asia, was imported in quantity into Australia in the 1950s to provide superior forage in areas of low rainfall, and also to stabilise soils destroyed by overgrazing. The United States Soil Conservation Service began experimental seedings of buffel grass in the 1930s to control erosion; they began to spread in the 1980s and buffel grasses are now serious weeds of the Sonora Desert. Now that buffel grasses have spread across more than half of the Australian continent, where they have all but overwhelmed the native grasses, it is far too late to attempt to control them. In the sandy gidgee country north of Alice, they thrive as nowhere else. Although buffel grasses have been identified as major environmental weeds in the Northern Territory, there is nothing to stop graziers seeding the new varieties that appear on the market every year. Cattle prefer to graze on immature buffel grass; the mature tussocks that are often left standing have a larger, tougher and deeper root system than native grasses. As a consequence when grass fires come through, the buffel grass tussocks burn much hotter and for much longer than the native grasses, with serious consequences for other types of vegetation. Buffel grasses will regenerate after such hot fires; the native vegetation will not.

'Buffel grasses are the most drought-tolerant pasture grasses in the world. And they're damn' good fodder as well,' Don went on.

'But what if the ecologists are right? They're saying that because buffel grasses burn so hot and so long, the soil heats up to a considerable depth and mulga and witchetty are killed. The River Red Gums that have survived millennia of grass fires won't survive the scorching of their root runs.'

At Delmore visiting blacks camped in a dry channel of the Bundey River, under huge River Red Gums. Don had grown up around that camp and under those trees, and I knew he'd be distraught to lose them. I didn't want to play the prophetess of doom, but the case had to be made, so I forged on.

'Once we exclude the cattle and control the buffel grasses, we'd probably get hundreds of species coming back. You wouldn't know till you got a botanist to do a survey.'

Don was unimpressed. 'Well, you'd have mulga, gidgee, witchetty bushes, Bush Orange, Bush Plum, Corkwood, She-oak, Cypress Pine maybe. Nothing special.'

'I don't want special. If I managed to get all those acacias to re-establish, we'd get some nitrogen back in the soil, and you'd start to see the wildflowers coming back again.'

Mulga, gidgee and witchetty are all acacias, fabaceous plants which with the help of associated bacteria fix nitrogen in the soil. Mulga is the common name for a group of Acacia species including *Acacia microneura* and *A. aneura*, not imposing trees but remarkable ones, that can live for a hundred years before achieving their full ten-metre height. The gidgee is *A. cambagei* and the witchetty is *A. kempeana*. I thought there might be a few more Acacia species as well, maybe Ironwood, *A. estrophiolata*, and Cooba, *A. salicina*. To minimise water loss through transpiration most desert species have greatly reduced leaves or phyllodes, more like needles or spines than leaves. Others have waxy coverings that reflect back the sun's radiance, or silvery fur, or turn their leaves side-on to the sun. Whatever the strategy the result is very little in the way of shade; rather than block the dazzling light the desert vegetation filters and patterns it. Most elegant among the desert trees is the She-oak, *Allocasuarina decaisneana*, that tends to grow with no other trees but its own kind, making a forest full of light. The White Cypress Pine, *Callitris glaucophylla*, which is actually blue, is rather less translucent than the She-oaks but much more so than the other species in the genus. If I acquired a strip of central Australia I would have them all, as well as the Honey Grevillea,

Grevillea juncifolia, ssp. *juncifolia*, that drips nectar in golden strings through its narrow leaves. Its flower is a loose burnt-orange affair; its big sister G. *striata*, the Beefwood, may provide less in the way of nectar, but has ten times as many flowers, almost more flowers than leaves, and they are white. After every trip to the centre I planned and unplanned my bush garden, crammed it with woody Hakeas, known in these parts as Corkwoods, and Mallees, Emu Bushes, Saltbushes, every shade of silver, jade and turquoise borne on purple shadows against the blood-red ground under the black-opal sky.

'Once you had the acacias, you'd get the dedicated butterflies, and the mistletoes, and with the mistletoes the Mistletoebirds. And all the other birds. And the wildflowers.'

For years I had been photographing Northern Territory wildflowers, Boobiallas, Everlastings, Mulla-mullas, Scaevolas, Potato Flowers, Desert Roses, and a good many weeds as well, and I still hadn't found time to identify them and label my photographs. With a sliver of land I could study the plants and their associations properly, instead of just taking their picture in their party dress and moving on.

'And the native grasses, like Lemon-scented Grass, Kangaroo Grass and, best of all, spinifex.'

'That's the last thing we need,' said Don. 'More bloody spinifex.'

I've never understood the hatred of spinifex that seems almost universal in white Australia. The pioneering botanists, who couldn't decide if the genus was Plectrachne or Triaphis or Triodia, or what family it was in, gave the species contemptuous names, *pungens*, *irritans*, *hostilis*, *molesta*, *inutilis*. Even now botanists cannot make sense of the exclusively Australian genus which at the present count consists of sixty-seven species. Admitted, spinifex is nothing like lawn. You can't play croquet or cricket on it and it's no good as pasture, but it is the characteristic dapple that softens the scarps and the sandhills of a fifth of the Australian continent. It is the dot in dot painting. Its name sounds aggressive, and you can't actually sit on it or run over it barefoot, but spinifex doesn't grow in dense swards. The hummocks don't connect up and in the sheltered spaces between live hundreds of ephemeral wildflower species. As the hummocks age the centres die out and the domes become rings; tree seedlings that sprout within a spinifex ring are the only ones in most parts of Australia that will be safe from introduced rabbits. Spinifex provides the habitat for the world's richest lizard fauna, and for tribes of tiny mammals. Aboriginal peoples pounded its seeds and baked the paste in the coals to make nutritious bread. Its resin, which was melted and used to glue together weapons and tools, was traded up and down the continent. The rhythm of spinifex hummocks growing up and over sandhills or carpeting the plains is the heartbeat of Australia.

When conditions are right the Delmore spinifex makes an apple-green dome of quilled leaf sheaths out of which radiate thousands of fine silver flower spikelets, in a shimmering nimbus, like the guard hairs on some precious fur. There would certainly be space for it on any land of mine.

'Look,' Don went on, 'I run cattle at very low density, probably not much more than one beast per square mile. This land, compared to the Barkly Tableland, for example, is clean. We don't have Parkinsonia; we don't have Noogoora Burr or Mesquite or Prickly Acacia. So we're ahead of the game.'

Parkinsonia, Mesquite and Prickly Acacia are thorny shrubs and trees that were deliberately introduced into Australia to provide shade and control erosion. All three will form impenetrable mono-specific thickets that greatly reduce the carrying capacity of the land, and obstruct the watering and mustering of cattle. Sheep straying into these thorn thickets are likely to be trapped by their wool and will die. *Parkinsonia aculeata* was introduced into northern Australia from central America as a hedging plant in the late nineteenth century and has now taken over more than 800,000 hectares. Mesquite or Prosopis is the dominant genus in the vegetation of the semi-arid south-western United States, where its seeds formed the dietary staple of the indigenous peoples. The species that has colonised huge tracts in the Northern Territory is *Prosopis pallida*. Like the other Mesquite species, it is long-lived, with a taproot twenty metres long, and tolerates an enormous variety of cultural conditions. Prickly Acacia (*Acacia nilotica* ssp. *indica*) from Pakistan has spread from Queensland across northern Australia as far as the Kimberley. Cattle and most other herbivores readily eat the pods of these three species and excrete their seed undamaged; the occasional flooding that is typical of the Australian inland climate carries the seeds to every watershed in the top end.

Noogoora Burr, a species of Xanthium, is an exotic prickle bush that in its immature phase is poisonous to stock. It probably came to Australia in the 1870s as an accidental contaminant in shipments of cotton seed from the Mississippi delta; its common name recalls Noogoora Station in Queensland, where in 1897 200 hectares were found to be infested. If Don hadn't found Noogoora Burr on his land in 2001 he may well have found it since, as it has travelled further along the watercourses deep into the territory. To control its spread in the Kimberley, all pastoral leases along the Fitzroy River, from Fitzroy Crossing to the river mouth, have been quarantined. Any traveller found ignoring the keep-out signs may be fined up to $1,000.

'Don, you're lucky not to have these weeds yet but, if Australians don't wise up to what's going on, you soon will. Landholders become conscious of these infestations only when they destroy the profitability of the land. By the same token, they're not fighting them in places where the cost of eradication would exceed the production value of the land, which ultimately means that the weeds must win. We know that a handful of introductions can end up taking over millions of hectares, yet we think that destroying a few plants in one place while millions thrive elsewhere will somehow contain the problem. There's no awareness that Australian biodiversity is in jeopardy.'

Don frowned. 'What's so good about biodiversity? Species that are better adapted to survival will replace species that aren't. That's how nature moves ahead surely. I don't run dozens of different breeds of cattle, because there's no point. I stick with the one breed that is best adapted to my conditions. Droughtmasters are quiet; they tolerate the heat; they're highly fertile and calve easily. They inherited the best characteristics of the breeds that went into them, so I stick with them.'

'That's just it,' I said, feeling a good deal less certain than I sounded, 'you need the other species to get your hybrid. The Droughtmaster's what? Brahman and what?'

'Brahman gives you the heat- and drought-tolerance and Shorthorn or Devon and Shorthorn give you the other characteristics, more or less. The selection of the best strains goes on continually.'

I was a bit unsure of my ground, because these are breeds rather than species. 'But you do see that you need to keep all that genetic variability or you'll have nothing to breed from.'

'The whole Devon breed is descended from one red bull and three red heifers that were taken to New England by the Pilgrim Fathers,' said Don, with a grin. 'If buffel grasses replace native grasses, it'll be because they're better grasses. Just as beef cattle replaced the bison. If spinifex tries to fight it out with buffel grass, buffel grass will win.'

I was silent, thinking about a valiant revegetation project that had been undertaken by schoolchildren just outside Alice. They had cleared a degraded road verge and planted a selection of native grasses and woody shrubs on it; a year later the whole site was supporting only two species, a buffel grass and Ruby Dock.

The next morning Janet and Don took me to see Delny. In the paddock between the house and the road, there was an old wooden mustering yard bleached silver by the sun, as well as a good deal of machinery quietly rusting down into a sea of overgrown buffel grass. The house stood on a distinct rise, which the floodwaters of the Bundey River never reached, judging by the soundness of the reinforced concrete shell that had been built around the original one-roomed stone house. In its time, the house design had been revolutionary. Rather than the ubiquitous pitched galvanised iron roof that would collect rainwater and channel it into freestanding tanks, the house had a flat roof that was dished so that rainwater would run into a shallow rectangular concrete tank built into the ceiling. Even without any glass in its tall louvred windows and without any water in the roof-tank, the house was cool and spacious, and full of the red mud nests of martins. I could see at once how you could extend it with open colonnades and enclosed courtyards, that would connect in a series of versatile breezeways, so you wouldn't need air conditioning. There was ample scope for solar power, which Don was already using to run the bore pumps for his cattle troughs. The trees around the house were few and scrawny, a Hakea or two, a Mallee here and there, and something else growing out of what must once have been a septic tank. At first I thought it was a She-oak, but it was darker, denser, different. Beyond it, between the house and the invisible river, there were more.

That evening I e-mailed Jane a photograph of the mystery trees, and asked her what they were. She called back at once.

'Tamarisks,'said Jane. '*Tamarix aphylla*, one of Australia's worst tree weeds. You'd have to get rid of them.'

'What's wrong with Tamarisks?'

'Everything. They put down a massive taproot that doesn't branch until it reaches the water table, and then sends out hundreds of laterals, to suck up all the underground water that supports the native vegetation on our old watercourses in the dry season. They also absorb salt from the soil and then excrete it through their leaves. As the leaves fall the salt builds up on the surface of the soil. And they're fire-prone. They're a bloody disaster.'

'Aren't they some sort of pine?'

'They look it and they're sometimes called Athel Pines. Americans call them Saltcedars, but they're angiosperms, in a family of their own, the Tamaricaceae. What look like needles on these ones are actually very small leaf-scales, which is why their species name is *Tamarix aphylla*. In 1930 somebody imported *T. aphylla* into Whyalla, for shade trees or something. At first it seemed ideally adapted to Australian conditions, so they planted it round Alice – for erosion control, I think. Now it's infested 600 ks of the Finke River. The salinity of the water has increased twenty-fold.'

I told Don about the Tamarisks and the Finke River. He was silent for a few minutes. The Finke River is possibly the oldest water-course in the world, and the Tamarisks are well on the way to killing it. At length he decided to reject my gloom and doom.

'Well, what's wrong with that? If the river gums can't compete, it means they're unfit. They won't survive.'

I was aware that I was beginning to make a nuisance of myself. If I wanted Delny this wasn't the way to get it. My face grew hot. I began unsteadily.

'Fitness applies to a whole ecosystem, rather than a single species. If any single plant species becomes a monoculture, it becomes vulner-able. You only have to think about what happens in plantations. Without a very high level of disease-control inputs they collapse. If plant relations are out of balance with other factors, the eventual result will be a rampant monoculture and then annihilation by a combination of pathogens.'

'And another species steps into the breach. That's life.'

'I don't believe that biodiversity must inevitably be reduced. I don't think that the end product of evolution will be the destruction of most species.'

'What would you do about the Tamarisks?' asked Janet.

'I'd poison them.'

'You can't spray them because they're on a watercourse.'

'I know. I'd inject them, so they died nice and slow.'

'Inject them?'

'You drill into them just far enough to reach the cambium and then you put in the poison, undiluted glyphosate or maybe something nastier, whatever it takes. If we leave the trees to die and then gradually rot, we avoid causing more disturbance and destruction. But you'd have to be prepared to do it again and again, because Tamarisks will resprout if the huge root system is not entirely dead. And if the Tamarisks have caused salination, native vegetation might not be able to re-establish. We'd probably need a few good rains to wash the accumulated salt away.'

There was no time for further talk, because the helicopter had radioed that the cattle were coming in and it was all hands to the drive. The jackeroos and Don's daughters were revving the engines of their trail bikes. Don was at the wheel of the Land Rover. I hopped in beside him. As the cattle came swinging through the trees we had to direct them towards the chute and into the muster yards, where they would be guided down different alleys into separate enclosures to be held until they were branded or branded and castrated. Dry cows went to one pen, to be eventually trucked away for slaughter, unless they were pregnant, when they stayed with the wet cows; unbranded steers went another way; branded ones were either let go, or sent to a holding pen to be collected when the cattle train came by. It was Don's job to drive the Land Rover flat out through the scrub to head off any bulls that took it into their heads to lead their harems away from danger. I had barely time to strap myself in before we wheeled and went rocketing through the scrub after a huge brown bull. The transparent screen of vegetation fell before the four-wheel drive with little more than a creak and a sigh, as hootin' and hollerin' we came alongside the big bull and, sliding with all four wheels, broadsided him back into the drive. The kids on the trail bikes with their bandannas tied across their noses under their sunglasses to protect them from the dust shot in and out, yelling to us to follow on the track of the runaways. I found myself hanging out of the window, pounding on the side of the Land Rover, yelling 'Come ORN' to the white-eyed animals that snorted around us. It was great fun, I have to say.

What came next was not so much fun. One by one the unbranded steers were pushed along a narrow alley that ended in a sliding gate. The boys liked to get the frightened animals to move forward by twisting their tails up tight; the girls got the same result without. When the gate was slid back and the end steer popped out, he stepped into a steel clamp that was locked shut and lowered onto its side, so that the branding iron that was heating in the fire could be applied. As the red-hot iron hissed on its flank, the animal would scream in shock, terror and pain and all the others would join in. A smell of scorching skin and hair filled the dusty air. While the steer lay helpless amid the din and panic, one of the girls would slip up with a small sharp knife and swiftly remove its scrotum. Then the clamp was righted, the beast released and shooed off down another alley. I was taking all this in good part, because after all I am partial to Northern Territory beef, when a calf who was too small for the clamp to hold darted straight through it. The kids grabbed him. He flung his small brown body about so wildly, fought so hard and broke free so often, that they eventually gave up and let him go, a cleanskin, to be branded and castrated next time. Over and above the clamour of the branding came the cries of the wet cows, calling for their babies. They would go on uttering those terrible cries all night. One of the factors I had to take into account was that the Delny house stood within earshot of the mustering yards.

The next day I drove back to Alice with one of the girls who was going in for supplies. Just as we came up to the bend in the track at Delny, we caught sight of something hanging on the fence. It was a young kangaroo. She had caught a toe in the top strand of barbed wire as she was trying to leap over it; her body had swung down and smacked into the fence, while her weight twisted the top strand of wire round a lower one, trapping her by the foot. She had hung there upside down until she died. I'm not superstitious, but the kangaroo hanging crucified upside down like St Peter added to my impression of Delny as a difficult place for any animal, including me. By the time the four-wheel drive had left the sand track and climbed up onto the highway, I had decided that, regardless of any deal the Holts might offer, Delny was not for me.

Fresh out of ideas, I wandered into a real estate agency in Alice Springs, to ask one last time if they had any rural properties on the books.

The person who dealt with rural properties was Maureen O'Grady. 'Well, there's a mango farm up at Ti Tree,' she said.

I knew about the mango farm, which had been on the market for months, with less than ten hectares and 1,000 mango trees for $260,000. The owners' reason for wanting to sell it, that you can't make money out of growing mangoes in central Australia, was everyone else's reason for not wanting to buy it. Because the property had been 'improved', the price per hectare was exorbitant. There would have been no point whatever in paying such a high price for a piece of land only to turn it back into spinifex and sand.

'Anything else?'

She shook her head. I wasn't surprised. When graziers decide to surrender their leases the word is out on the bush telegraph long before any real estate dealer can get to hear of it. The agency, which had offices all over Australia, dealt in suburban properties, in brick veneer, manicured lawns, swimming pools and carports. The occasional hobby farm might show up from time to time, but that was it.

I was almost out the door when Maureen came running out of her office.

'The lucerne farm! I forgot the lucerne farm!'

She thrust a prospectus into my hand. 'Hugh River Holdings' it said on the cover.

I knew the country well. The Hugh River is a broad channel of deep red sand between a double file of old Ghost Gums that crosses the Stuart Highway about ninety ks south of Alice Springs, at a place called Stuart's Well, between the James Range and Chandler's

Range. Sometime in the Seventies a man called Noel Fullarton set up, just off the highway on the north bank of the Hugh River, what he called a 'camel farm', which became a must-see for passengers on every tourist vehicle travelling north or south. On the south side of the river is Jim's Place, where you can get a snack and fuel or a room or a campsite, and enjoy the performance of Dinky the singing Dingo. Nobody ever mentions the chainwire-fenced enclosure or 'sanctuary' where trapped emus, wallabies and kangaroos wait for death, while the tourists video and photograph them. Australian animals react badly to captivity. The life expectancy of kangaroos and wallabies in cages is no more than a few weeks.

I slid into a seat in a pavement café, ordered a coffee and started to read the prospectus. The lucerne farm was directly opposite Jim's Place, on the other side of the highway, behind an electric kangaroo-proof fence. What the owners were trying to sell was their business, which was raising boom-irrigated lucerne for fodder. The land had been acquired as an excision from the lease of the surrounding Orange Creek Station. Originally the owners had tried to grow the lucerne over two circles, but the existing bores didn't draw down sufficient water for two circles so one had been shut down. By dint of being harvested twelve times a year the remaining circle produced 30,000 bales a year, to be sold at $8 a bale more or less, with production costs about half that. The prospectus made reference to 'partnership problems' and 'lack of capital for further development'. What interested me was that the cultivation used only 32.4 of the property's 135 hectares. I could buy the property, so solving the owners' cash-flow problem, and lease the farm back to them. They could go on growing their lucerne, with me and my archive safely housed up the back in the foothills of the James Range, within an hour's drive of Alice Springs airport. The asking price was $400,000, with a four-bedroom house, a large hay shed, an implement shed and various pumps, booms and what have you thrown in.

I tore down the Stuart Highway for a preliminary recce and then called Maureen. 'Let's go see them tomorrow morning, early, because I've got a flight out in the afternoon.'

We were at the farm for breakfast putting my proposition to the owners, who probably thought I was mad. Why anyone would sink so much money in a farm and then not farm it was a conundrum they couldn't solve, but at length they understood that I was serious. Back at the office I made an offer, $350,000, cash. My flight to Darwin took off to the south; as we banked to turn northwards I could see the deep emerald-green disc of lucerne beyond the jagged crests of the James Range.

When I had finished reading the documents included with the prospectus I understood the situation rather better. The enterprise had been set up in 1982–3, when the property was still part of Orange Creek Station, and from the beginning it had been a struggle. The owners' licence to extract water from the Mereenie Sandstone Aquifer originally covered four bores, each ninety metres deep. One had sanded up. Another was a 'crooked hole' in which a pumpshaft had broken off; both bore and pumping gear had been abandoned because the cost of retrieving the gear was uneconomic. The third bore was working; it was driven by a six-cylinder diesel motor housed in a steel shed which was open on one side. The fourth bore was pumped out by an identical motor, housed in a shed that was missing two sides. This was beginning to sound like a lot of noise battering the desert silence, and that was before I realised that the pivots were run by another four-cylinder generator that also served the house, a total of sixteen cylinders thudding away day and night. Twelve times a year there would have been the added commotion of the cutting and turning and baling of the lucerne, a fifty-four-hour process. The real reason the second circle was not being cultivated was because in 1991 the central pivot irrigator had been blown over and smashed, and the owners hadn't had the money to repair it. As soon as they had money, it was London to a brick that the pivot irrigator would be repaired and the second circle brought into action. The thirty-three or so hectares under cultivation would become sixty-six. Or more.

The owners accepted my offer. Their lawyers immediately set about drawing up their lease, which was to be granted at the same time as I acquired the freehold. If I had been more clued up I'd have insisted on vacant possession, and then agreed the lease separately. In the meantime the situation had changed. Massive flooding in the channel country had suddenly increased the demand for hay, and prices had soared. The pressure was off the owners who began playing hard to get, and refused to reduce the area of land they would reserve for their own use. In September I came back to Alice to clinch the deal but it was already falling apart.

When I met Jane at the airport, she read my face.

'You didn't really want a hay farm, did you?'

'One of the problems is that the back portion of land doesn't extend far enough into the range. If I could get tucked into the hills I mightn't hear so much of their noise; the way it is I reckon I'd get double the racket. I'd hear it first-hand and reflected back by the scarps as well.'

Jane nodded. 'Thing is you'd be paying top dollar for the least valuable land, and at the same time you're making it possible for the owners to extend their operations and further reduce the amenity. There has to be a better way of spending $350,000.'

Ever mindful of my sister's common sense, I dropped the idea of the lucerne farm there and then. I was back where I started.

'Can we do some tourist things? And some botanising?' asked Jane.

We drove the Tanami road north to Yuendumu, came back and took the back road west to Haast's Bluff. We did the gorges, Glen Helen, Redbank, Ormiston and Serpentine. We took Larapinta Drive to the Mereenie Loop and King's Canyon. We drove down to Erldunda and turned west along the Lasseter Highway, past the carcass of a huge black steer that the night before had been standing in the middle of the unlit unpaved road, invisible to the woman driver who was approaching at speed. She died on impact. I renewed my vow never to drive unfenced cattle country by night as we made our way to Uluru.

When I first came to Uluru it was called Ayers Rock. In 1985 the Pitjantjatjara and Yankunytjatjara peoples (nowadays more often called Anangu) were granted the freehold of what had been an Aboriginal reserve; because they realised how many tourists were already visiting the site, the elders immediately leased it to the Director of National Parks and Wildlife, while they retain the right to live unmolested nearby in the Mutitjulu community. Because the site is important to many Aboriginal peoples who visit it periodically for special ceremonial observances, the elders have moved to limit the amount of intrusion. Some parts of the rock may not be photographed and others not visited by the uninitiated, but the elders have not yet felt able to forbid the climbing of the rock. Long ago steel posts were drilled into it to carry a chain handhold. Signs point out that the traditional owners would rather that tourists did not make the climb; others commemorate the people who have died on the rock, which for Aboriginal peoples is the worst desecration imaginable.

Jane and I walked the base of the great monolith, which always strikes me as one of the holiest places in the world. At its foot we found native grasses aplenty, Cymbopogon and Tripogon species, sedges of different sizes, spinifex, Emu Bushes of different species growing side by side, as well as different kinds of Cassias, Acacias and Eucalypts, depending on the soil type. Every aspect of the rock displayed different associations. As I walked along in the lee of the great rock I prayed through clenched teeth to the tutelary spirits for country of my own, but I knew even as I did it that there is no country in Australia that I could ever really call my own. I was knocking on the wrong door. I relieved my feelings by pulling out a clump of Ruby Dock. Some tourists, who saw me do it, protested loudly.

'This is a weed,' I said. 'Pretty, if you like that sort of thing, but a weed.' Just about everywhere the soil is disturbed in the inland, Ruby Dock, *Acetosa vesicaria* (better known to older botanists as *Rumex vesicarius*), moves in and takes over. In 1999 a group of mining companies invested $80,000 in developing a Ruby Dock management scheme, but I never heard that they got anywhere. I have seen Ruby Dock thriving along the track of the Trans-Australian Railway all the way across the Nullarbor, all through the Pilbara and in the heart of the Simpson Desert.

Back in Alice we visited the Desert Park, where for the first time I met Bush Stone-curlews (*Burhinus grallarius*) and wondered how well-behaved you would have to be to be allowed to live with such beguiling creatures. We checked our botanical identifications at the Botanical Gardens. We went down the old track of the Ghan, past the ruined stations of Polhill, Ooraminna and Rodinga, and took the sand track to Chambers Pillar, through some of the most floriferous uplands I have ever seen anywhere. For hours we photographed Isotomes, Wahlenbergias, Indigo, Smoke Bushes, Butterfly Bushes, Satiny Bluebushes, Smooth Spider Bush, Milkmaids, Parrot Peas, Sea Heaths, Parakeelyas, Olearias and Mint Bushes. The more we saw of the centre the more I longed to protect such brilliant galaxies of niche plants from the onward march of the exotics.

Back at our hotel I complained to Jane. 'I think I'm just going to have to give up. We've been hunting for some land for me for more than two years, and there just isn't any.'

'How about one last shot?' asked Jane.

'Like what?'

'The James Range is the sort of country you want, isn't it?'

'That, or something like it.'

Jane brandished the prospectus, where she had found an account of the original rescission of the lucerne farm from the parent property. 'The James Range bisects the Orange Creek property. They've got a total of 560,000 acres, and they're only running 3,000 to 3,500 head, so they're certainly not using it all. Maybe they'll let you have a bit.'

Jane made some calls; we drove back past Stuart's Well for the umpteenth time, to the Orange Creek homestead. The muster helicopter was standing by, so they let the pilot take me up for a good look at the range. As we pulled up and away from the red-earth helipad, the livid green disc of the lucerne farm slid beneath us, and I breathed a sigh of relief that it wasn't mine.

'What did you think?' asked the grazier when I got back.

'I love it.'

'It's a bit rugged.'

'Rugged is good.'

'You'd need to make an access road, and it'd have to be properly engineered. That comes out expensive these days, because you have to observe all the environmental regs about drainage and dust and run-off. A single kilometre of graded road costs thousands and you'd need a lot more than one, because you'd have the easement to do as well. If you want to stick a house in the range somewhere you have to think about availability of water and power, and getting someone to build it for you, way out there.'

Graziers' houses are built as close as possible to main routes; only
Aboriginal people deliberately choose outstations hidden in the hills.
My mountain retreat would be the only thing of its kind in the
centre.

'I've got a builder who's game.'

'The real problem,' said the grazier, 'is getting land excised from
the lease for your use. We could sublet to you, in theory, but you'd
be mad to spend a lot of money improving land on my leasehold. I
don't want a house out there in the hills, so when your lease was up
or when you wanted to move on, all your hard work and energy
would just be left to rot back into the ground. I wouldn't let you do
it, even if I could without infringing the conditions of my lease.'

'So what if you managed a freehold excision from the lease, the way
the old owners of Orange Creek did with the lucerne farm?' asked Jane.

'That was for horticulture. The government is mad keen to
develop horticulture in the centre. There's a plan to make lots of
freehold excisions of ten hectares each along the Finke and the Hugh,
because there's underground water really close to the surface, but the
prices are going to be somewhere round $10,000 a hectare.'

'That's a lot of watermelon,' said Jane.

I'd been told that the grazier had acquired his lease for less than $3
million.

'What do you as the landholder make out of this?' asked Jane.

'Nothing. We water the cattle with bore water anyway, so we
don't really need the river frontage, and we can't expect much in the
way of compensation. We'd rather just hang on to the land, for
conservation reasons apart from anything else.'

'Would it be really expensive to arrange for an excision of really
arid land, like the rangeland? That wouldn't be anything like $10,000
a hectare, would it?'

'What you have to understand is that for a freehold property to be
created on land at present covered by crown leasehold, the lease has
to be rescinded, while the boundaries are resurveyed and redrawn.
It's not worth doing, unless there's a fair bit of money involved,
because the legal costs will be high. You won't find leaseholders
prepared to do it at all if the potential winnings aren't high, because
there's a risk involved.'

'Native title,' said Jane.

'Exactly. As soon as a crown lease is rescinded, the land becomes vulnerable to a native claim. It wouldn't necessarily be successful, but it's practically certain to be made and defended. The lawyers have a field day. It costs everyone money, and you could end up with nothing.'

In the car on the way back to Alice, Jane said, 'You wouldn't contest the validity of any Aboriginal land claim, would you?'

'No.'

'Never? No matter what?'

'Never. No matter what.'

'So that's that?'

'That's that.'

And that was that.

THE BIRD

Logan City lies twenty-five kilometres or thirty minutes south of the Brisbane Central Business District. Described as 'young, dynamic and booming with growth', it has sister city and friendship agreements with cities in China, Japan and Taiwan. Many immigrants disembarking for the first time on the shores of the lucky country wind up in Logan. They bring with them all the baggage of the uprooted – disorientation, grief, confusion, anxiety, exhaustion. Their suffering is compounded by the difficulties they encounter, in finding decent work, in gaining decent pay, and in accommodating and adjusting to the Australian way of life. Deracination is felt most keenly by women who are too often housebound and bereft of female kindred, entirely dependent upon the whims of their husbands as their mothers were not. The extent of physical and psychological illness experienced by first-generation migrant women is massive and largely undeclared. In 1992, with no funding from state or federal government, feminist activists in Logan set up a women's health centre to be run by women for women. In 2000, desperate for cash, the organisers contacted me, asking what I would charge for a lecture that they could run as a fundraiser. I wrote back and said, 'Nothing. Hire a hall, sell tickets and pocket the profits.' When the desert project fell over, it was time for me to make my way to Logan, to fulfil my part of the bargain.

It was a great night, as we say. As we were chatting afterwards, I told the organisers how I had been searching for a house in the centre. Many of them had worked with Aboriginal groups and many more knew careworkers in the centre. They promised to send a message on the bush telegraph asking if anyone out there could help me find a bit of land. Then someone said, 'What about Ken's place?'

'You mean Ken's mother's place.'

'Yeah. Ken's really keen to sell that. It might be what you're looking for.'

'Where is it?'

'About an hour away, mebbe a bit more.'

Ken is Ken Piaggio, a psychotherapist who worked at the women's health centre. Next morning he and his wife Jane-Frances O'Regan turned up at my hotel, to take me to see the property. I hadn't asked where it was. I hoped it was out to the west, beyond the Dividing Range, in the Darling Downs perhaps, but we were driving south, down the Pacific Highway towards the Gold Coast. My heart sank.

At Nerang we left the highway, crossed the Nerang River and headed south-west through aspirational suburban developments towards the hinterland. The houses became fewer as the road began to climb into the hills, through fire-scarred sclerophyll forests. As we skirted a cutting Ken pointed out the high-rise buildings of Surfers Paradise, clearly visible against the grey-blue ocean. We passed a signpost that said 'O'Reilly's Plateau'.

'O'Reilly's? Is that Green Mountains up there?'

Green Mountains was a set book at my convent school. I read my copy to pieces, longing to experience the country it described. It was written by Bernard O'Reilly, the man who in February 1937 set out alone from the family farm on the Lamington Plateau in search of a missing aircraft, convinced that it had to be where his sharp eyes had identified a single burnt tree amid the dark green of the rainforest. The story of how he picked his way through rugged jungle to find the crashed plane, with the two out of seven men aboard who were still alive, has gladdened the hearts of generations of Australian schoolchildren.

'Yep. But it's a long way round. O'Reilly's is due west of where we're going, only a few ks away as the crow flies. Door to door the trip's about 100 ks.'

So maybe the country we were heading for wasn't sumptuous like Green Mountains at all. I could see caravans and parkhomes on a site above the road.

'That's the new Advancetown. It used to be down there,' Ken gestured with his left hand, 'where the original track down from Beechmont met the old Numinbah Road. In 1970 or so it was decided that the dam on the Little Nerang River would have to be rebuilt on a far bigger scale to ensure a reliable water supply for the expanding Gold Coast, and so the valley was flooded and Advancetown went under water. A timber-getter called Ernest Belliss built a pub there. For eighty years the old bullockies who hauled the timber out of the hills used to meet and do business in the Bushmen's Bar. It was an early slab-built structure, a really important part of local history. Belliss invented the name Advancetown and donated land and money to build a school. All gone now.'

A sign high on the steep verge advertised the Advancetown Hotel.

'Is that the same building?'

'No. They did bring the Bushmen's Bar up here and set it up behind that new building, but they soon sold it. It's on private property somewhere, I think.'

I know now that Belliss was an Englishman, from Shropshire, who came out to Australia in 1866. He is also the man who is believed to have plied one Aboriginal group with liquor and egged them on to attack others who had settled on land on the lower Nerang that had been set aside for an Aboriginal Industrial Mission. According to local man Carl Lentz, Belliss lost no time in getting up 'a petition with a request to the Lands Department, he got plenty of signatures, to have the Natives reserve thrown open for selections . . . It was divided up in smaller portions and selected in quick time. Belliss selected a big share with plenty good hoop pine and other timber on it, and built a sawmill adjoining the mission station.' For this estimable service a tributary of the Nerang now rejoices in the name Belliss Creek, if you're driving one way, and Bellis Creek if you're driving the other. Nothing remains to indicate that a gallant band of German missionaries had once moved heaven and earth to keep a foothold for Aboriginal people on the Nerang River.

We passed another sign. 'The Hinze Dam. Who was Hinze?'

'Russ Hinze was Joh Bjelke-Petersen's local government minister,' said Ken. 'Not a local hero, as you might imagine. A lot of people had to move when the valley was flooded, and the people living above the lake had no way of getting to the coast when the road went under water. The dam's been raised once and it's due to be raised again. By 2010 the Advancetown Lake will cover 1,640 hectares. The upside is that the catchment can't be zoned for development. You can fish here if you like; they've stocked it with bass, perch, Mary River cod, Saratoga, stuff like that. But you need a permit.'

'I'd rather get me a flathead out of the ocean.'

'Me too,' said Ken. 'The old Numinbah Road ran along the river, which had its disadvantages because it went under water fairly regularly, but it meant there were plenty of fishing holes and picnic spots. Not to mention all the old pioneer homesteads that were swallowed by the lake.'

East of the road a knob-like head reared itself. 'That's Page's Pinnacle. It used to be called Pine Mountain, but once the pine was logged out, they gave it a new name. The old name was already being used for a place near Ipswich.'

'Who was Page?'

'Sir Earle Page, the politician. He took up land round here, took the timber off it and then sold it.'

A Harley Davidson motorbike swung around the bend ahead and came roaring towards us at high speed. A dozen more followed it, all ridden by men with beards and long grey hair, tricked out in full leathers, gauntlets, helmets, goggles and boots.

'Bikies like this new road because there's so many curves and so much reverse camber. Nobody else likes it much. They say it was designed and engineered by computer and the computer got it wrong. You might have noticed the crash zone sign? Bikies come to grief here fairly often. Just makes it more popular.'

I had already noticed several wayside shrines to fallen bikies, bedizened with plastic flowers, beer cans, and T-shirts. I peered through the trees for a glimpse of the dam. The vegetation was a mix of eucalypts, Forest Red Gum, Grey Gum, Grey Ironbark, White Mahogany and Pink Bloodwood. The eucalypts seemed greener than I was used to and the understorey was grassier. Two of the grasses were native, Kangaroo Grass, *Themeda australis*, and Blady Grass, *Imperata cylindrica*. Casuarinas, that like to grow in lines along creeksides, had colonised the road cuttings. The country grew more rugged; the road straddled narrow gullies and the curves had got sharper. Some of the gullies were named.

'Does Black Shoot Gully mean what I think it means?'

'It's nothing to do with shooting blacks,' said Ken. 'A "shoot" is actually a chute. The timber-getters would send the cut timber straight off the mountain down a chute which they dug out and sometimes lined with felled timber. Back in the day the Black Shoot was the main way of getting from Beechmont to Advancetown. I have heard that when the kids from the valley had to go to school up on Beechmont, this is how they got there. Apparently the school bus used to get up and down this way, but it's hard to imagine.'

We had entered the Numinbah Valley, as the valley of the upper Nerang River is known. We crossed it by the new Pine Creek Bridge, with not a Hoop Pine to be seen, and entered the Numinbah State Forest, 'of a thousand uses'. A sign by the Numinbah Environmental Education Centre featuring sweet-faced forest fauna asked us not to litter the valley. 'The locals are watching you'. Further on was a 'Forest Park' with toilets and picnic tables.

'That'll be drowned after they raise the dam,' said Ken. 'They'll need a new bridge for the Pocket too.'

'What is the Pocket?'

'It's the area between the Nerang River and the scarp of the Lamington Plateau. One way in, same way out, hence the Pocket.'

We passed through what would once have been known as a township, and is now called a village on its signage and a suburb of Gold Coast City everywhere else. The locals knew it as Upper Nerang; the authorities named it Numinbah Valley. The most imposing building in it is the School of Arts. In 1925 subscriptions were taken up and free hardwood was supplied to build a cultural centre for the residents of the Upper Nerang Valley, where concerts, lectures, performances and dances could take place.

'This is Priem's crossing. Karl Priem was the first man to grow wine in the valley,' said Ken. 'And possibly the last.'

A spectacular volcanic plug had popped out of the river flat on the west side of the road. 'That's Egg Rock. During the war airmen trained there for survival in the New Guinea jungle. That scarp beyond it is Ships Stern.' (Ships Stern, a rhyolite rampart hanging off the side of the Lamington Plateau, used to have an apostrophe. You wonder why the Geographic Names Board didn't eliminate the 's' as well as the apostrophe. Ship Stern makes more sense than Ships Stern.)

On the other side of a single-lane bridge was an imposing timber gate. Signs warned visitors to announce themselves to reception. 'What's that?'

'That's the prison farm. Her Majesty's State Farm Numinbah. Or the Numinbah Correctional Centre.'

'Why does everything round here have two names?'

'More,' said Ken. 'It used to be called Whitinbah State Farm for some reason.'

'Villages in Britain still carry the Norse names given them by the Vikings eons ago. Here in Queensland names seem to change every five minutes.'

Ken laughed. 'It gets worse. This is Natural Bridge. It used to be called Upper Numinbah, but they changed it to avoid confusion with the Numinbah on the other side of the border.' As I was to discover, that Numinbah and this Numinbah were two parts of the same place. A small park appeared in a loop of the river on our right. Ken explained. 'This is where kids used to go for the big splash off a big old river gum, but that's gone now. The shire council took the place over in the Seventies and shmicked it up with toilets and barbecues and garbage bins, and called it Bochow Park.'

The air was growing humid and the vegetation had changed. On the roadside only the Camphor Laurels stood proud and unencumbered, wrapped in their own toxic vapours, while the native trees suffocated under curtains of Balloon Vine and Morning Glory. Around and between them Scheffleras, Jacarandas, Coral Trees, Traveller's Palms and Cocos Palms vied with every kind of gaudy suburban garden escapee. The Scheffleras are *Schefflera actinophylla*, native to the Australian wet tropics. In their native plant community they are held in check by competition; in south-east Queensland they are an aggressive intruder. Their umbrella-shaped inflorescence is loved by native birds who drop its seeds everywhere.

Everybody loves Jacarandas, which flower in violet-blue panicles on their bare branches. As soon as the Jacaranda was introduced it was an absolute must-have for Australian gardeners. The gardening correspondent of the *Sydney Morning Herald* (3 December 1868) waxed lyrical in its praise:

> This most beautiful flowering tree is a native of Brazil, and no garden of any pretentions can be said to be complete without a plant of it. The specimen in the Botanic Garden is well worth a journey of 50 miles to see. Its beautiful rich lavender blossoms, and its light feathery foliage, render it the gem of the season . . . the difficulty of the propagation . . . overcome, Jacaranda mimosifolia, instead of being rare and scarce, will now be within reach of all who love a garden . . .

In Queensland, Walter Hill, curator of the Brisbane City Botanical Gardens, was the first person to show a specimen of Jacaranda, at the Queensland Horticultural and Agricultural Society Exhibition in October 1865 (*BC*, 26 October). The Jacaranda he showed was described as a shrub; over the years it would have grown to about thirty metres in height and produced copious quantities of seed. A hundred and fifty years later Queensland has woken up to the fact that *Jacaranda mimosifolia* is an invasive species, which doesn't mean that nurserymen have stopped selling it or that gardeners have stopped planting it. The town of Grafton on the Clarence River has all its streets lined with Jacarandas so that for six weeks every year the whole town turns purple. The same massive error of taste has been repeated in the town of Ipswich, south-east of Brisbane. In its home range of north-western Argentina and Bolivia the Jacaranda is now listed as vulnerable.

In the same show in 1865 Hill also presented 'four specimens of the coral tree, which has a large drooping-red flower, shaped something like a fuchsia'. The genus, which was named Erythrina by Linnaeus in 1753 with the annotation 'corallodendron', has a Gondwanan distribution. Australia has a number of native species, but the specimens shown by Hill were almost certainly examples of the South American Cock's Spur Coral Tree, *Erythrina crista-galli*, the national flower of Argentina and Paraguay. Around the turn of the century a now forgotten plant breeder produced a new hybrid Erythrina and presented it to the Brisbane Botanical Garden, where it grows to this day. Its parentage is unknown, but it is thought to be a hybrid of the American *E. coralloides* and the African *E. lysistemon*. It was not until the 1960s that a botanist called William Sykes, who saw the same Coral Tree growing all over New Zealand, identified it as a hybrid cultivar, hence its current name *Erythrina* x *sykesii*. Though the hybrid does not set fertile seed, it has now joined *E. crista-galli* as a serious weed of rainforest in Australia because, even after it has been poisoned and is apparently dead, the fallen branches are capable of rooting and regenerating. Both Coral Trees are beloved of suburban gardeners for the crowded hands of bright red flowers that appear before the thick, dark, leathery leaves. It took us five years to eliminate them from the CCRRS rainforest.

The latest count by Tony Bean of the Queensland Herbarium yields five native Erythrina species, which the early nurserymen might have collected and improved. The local version of *E. vespertilio* has flowers of burnt orange shading to espresso brown-black at the base. Another local species, now called *E. numerosa* (it was *E.* sp. Croftby), is peach-pink, with its protruding anthers stained rose-madder. You will see blood-red Coral Trees in their millions in north-east New South Wales and south-east Queensland; you are most unlikely to see any of these slower-growing and more elegant natives.

The pattern was early set: Australian nurserymen would not bother to propagate or improve local species; instead they would import seed and specimens of exotic species. It's hard to believe that the same settlers who tore out, knocked down and burnt the hundreds of species of trees that grew naturally in south-east Queensland were happy to spend proper money on half-a-dozen species of exotic trees to plant around their houses. Anyone who didn't plant a Coral Tree and a Jacaranda in the front garden was deemed insensible to beauty.

Native groundcovers were weeds by definition; they too were uprooted and burnt, to be replaced by long avenues of Agapanthus. Attempts to prevent the sale of Agapanthus varieties in Australia have been strongly resisted by the horticultural industry. Australian gardens are still full of them, as well as thousands of other exotics many of which have serious weed potential. Various Heliotropes, Gladioli, daisies, lilies, Oxalis, Honeysuckles, gingers, Verbenas, Vincas, Gazanias, Morning Glories, Moth Vine, Mother-in-law's Tongue and Watsonias are declared weeds already, and there are more where those came from. The situation was summarised in 2005 for the World Wildlife Fund by CSIRO botanists:

> The gardening industry is by far the largest importer of introduced plant species, being the source for the introduction of 25,360 or 94% of all new plant species into Australia. Garden plant introductions are also the dominant source of new naturalised plants and weeds in Australia. Of the 2,779 introduced plant species now known to be established in the Australian environment, 1,831 (or 66%) are escaped garden plant species. (Groves *et al.*, 7)

Not so long ago, I was as insensitive to the beauty of Australian native vegetation as anyone else. As a child I had longed for the flowers that starred the Alpine meadows where Heidi grew up, for Edelweiss and gentians and daisies. In coastal Victoria the only daisies I had to make chains with were not silver-white with golden centres, but dull yellow with dirty grey disc florets; they were Capeweed, *Arctotheca calendula*, from South Africa. I used to climb up into the tea-trees in the beachside park and sit there with yellow Capeweed flowers wound round my head, pretending to be Ophelia.

I studied European wildflowers for years before I paid any attention to the wildflowers of the great south land. Recognition of the beauty and subtle symmetry of natural plant associations in Europe prepared me for more sensitive observation of Australian species. If I look for a Eureka moment it seems to be a TV programme on Australian flora presented by David Bellamy. Nobody had ever explained to me why Australian flowers were the way they were, and how fascinating their difference was. What Bellamy projected as he explained the structure of all kinds of Australian flowers, from the spectacular to the insignificant, was his wonder and intellectual excitement. By the time the credits rolled I had stopped wishing Australian blooms were like flowers in manuscript illumination and Dutch painting and I was ready to give them my full attention. I didn't fall in love with native Australian vegetation until I was middle-aged, and then I fell hard, as middle-aged women do.

As the road crossed the river and followed its left bank high into the hills, I began to notice that, though the canopy trees in the native woodland were the usual, the grassy understorey had been replaced by wattles and geebungs. As the road wound higher the forest changed again. Dark green saplings had begun to colonise the forest floor. The emergents changed; I was now looking at big specimens of Brush Box, Flooded Gum, Tallowwood and Turpentine. Along the river I could see different River She-oaks and red Callistemons. We passed an almost full-grown Lilly pilly, and then I understood. The eucalypts I was looking at were not virgin forest but regrowth. Before white settlement this part of the valley must have been clothed in rainforest. Ever since it was cleared, it has been colonised by pioneer myrtaceous species that grow much faster than the original vegetation, which was and is still struggling to reclaim its territory. The struggle is hopeless, because the sclerophylls regularly burn, either spontaneously or because of deliberate backburning. They survive the conflagration, but the rainforest saplings do not. What I was seeing was a practical demonstration of how it was that the rainforest that once clothed Australia was corralled and driven back by the collaboration of eucalypts and fire, until it was no more than a chain of remnants down the east coast of the continent. What I didn't know then and could hardly have imagined was that when rare rainforest trees were removed from state forests, they were replaced by fast-growing eucalypts, as a matter of government policy.

There was not much to like about the regrowth forest; in the cleared areas the cattle looked hot and cross and the horses on the hobby farms were wearing masks and capes to protect them from the stinging flies. The road wound higher. The spectacular views of the scarps of Springbrook Plateau to our left and Lamington Plateau to our right were closed out as the valley narrowed. The road climbed out of the river valley, crossing a rocky creek making its way to the Nerang. The name on the sign was Cave Creek.

We passed a half-rotten house buried in unkempt vegetation and surrounded by parked cars.

'What goes on there?'

'Meditation, I think. The bloke does a roaring trade. Something to do with anagrams.'

'Holy shit.'

We turned left into the entrance of the Natural Arch section of the Springbrook National Park and everything changed. Massive watervines curtained the road. Cordylines and Lomandras bordered the tarmac. Huge pea pods and strings of nuts hung in the trees. Tree ferns and palms patterned the understorey. A black Brush-turkey, with bald red head, chrome-yellow cravat and a tail attached vertically instead of horizontally, fled at our approach. The narrow road divided and then turned into a car park, which was full of people, most of them in bathers. A sign said 'Thieves are active in this car park. Do not leave valuables in the car'. The scatter of glass fragments on the tarmac told its own story. Most of the people I saw were carrying nothing but beach towels and water bottles.

'What's going on here?'

'They've come to see the Natural Arch.'

'A rock formation,' I scoffed. 'Australians are the only people in the world who will drive for hundreds of ks just to see a funny-looking rock.'

'This is a pretty special rock,' said Jane-Frances. 'The creek has worn a hole in a massive rock-ledge and falls through into a cave that's been carved out by water action underneath. The formation used to be called Natural Bridge, like the township, but they decided that too many people were getting hurt when they tried to cross over it. So they changed the name to Natural Arch, and tried to fence it off. Visitors aren't supposed to swim there either, because it's very dangerous, but most people do. People who come in the daytime that is. A whole bunch of tourists come at night, to see the glow-worms. Asians mostly.'

Twenty-four-hour tourism. So much for tranquillity. And that's without the accidents. For years Natural Bridge was the place where Surf Lifesavers came to celebrate the completion of their training by jumping through the hole in the cave roof. Others did not even have their excuse, having merely downed one stubby too many. In 2005 a British tourist dived into the pool and didn't surface. The downward force of the waterfall had pushed him under a rock-shelf. It was not until the next day that rescuers succeeded in recovering his body. An earlier visitor who slipped when cavorting on the bridge was so badly injured that he remains paralysed. Now signs warn visitors that swimming in the creek will incur a heavy fine. As the park has too few staff even to keep an eye on the parked vehicles, the signs are ignored.

We drove to the end of the car park, past the toilets and the information kiosk, and bore left, where a sign said 'Pedestrian access only'. We kept driving, athwart a steep slope, between rainforest on the upper side and a dense stand of Hoop Pines on the lower, through an open gate, and several acres of Lantana.

'This is it,' said Ken, as we crossed a concrete causeway over a creek full of Mist Weed and Busy Lizzie. I could see Bird's Nest Ferns and Staghorns hanging in the trees. We kept going under the trees, past a single-storey house sagging on slanting piles to a gate and open fields. Beyond stood rather surprised cattle, hock-deep in lush Kikuyu Grass. When we opened the gate, they retreated to a safe distance and stood watching and ruminating. Ken pulled up short of the main house, just in case the tenants were home. A utility truck was parked under a massive Jacaranda.

Once out of the car I could see that the property nestled within a half-hoop of bare weathered scarps cropping out above the forest that foamed up in deep green waves from the cleared area where we found ourselves. Even though it was the middle of the day and the sun stood directly overhead, bleaching out colour and turning shadows black, the effect was spectacular. We walked past the house and on, past muster yards and a milking parlour and a hay shed, up the main track, past Blackwoods and Silky Oaks and other trees whose names I didn't know. Ken pointed out the course of the creek below us, and the tributaries coming down from above. I felt blank. Bewildered. Rainforest. I had never thought of rainforest. It was hot, but not dry hot like the desert, sticky hot.

'A hundred and fifty acres,' Ken was saying. 'We bought it for my mother, so she'd have something for her retirement. She's worked all her life in the public health service, so she's not got much to retire on. We were hoping we could make money from this place, you know, give her some extra income, but in the end we've just got to get the capital back out of it. She needs the cash. It's been on the market for a while, but there's been no interest whatsoever.'

'How much d'you want for it?'

'I won't bullshit you,' he said. 'We'd settle for half a million. Mum's not too well. I feel as if we're running out of time.'

It was the same old story. The investment that wasn't. They had tried just about everything. It was probably a mercy ultimately that they hadn't had the capital to develop the property. Any money they'd spent on it would have been lost.

Ken went on. 'You can't get anywhere with a property this size unless you live on it. You don't make enough to afford wages, to begin with. If you live here, and you work from first light to last, you might break even – if you're lucky. Otherwise you're in hock to the bank and anything you make they take in interest. Doesn't seem right, them making more money out of lending you money than you do for doing the work.

'We spent a bit of money getting someone to draw up a plan for an eco-tourist development, and we got outline planning permission for it too, but we couldn't find a buyer and the permission lapsed.'

Ken fished in his windcheater and brought out a newspaper clipping. The sale advertisement for the property, dated two years before. The asking price was a million.

'We'd have taken less, but we never even got an offer. Not a single one.'

I said nothing. I felt nothing, beyond a twinge of embarrassment. I was rehearsing how to tell these two good people that, after all their trouble, I wasn't interested either. Ken thought it might be nice to walk down to the creek. He walked across a paddock and into a stand of rainforest. I stepped after him into the forest twilight. Something invisible clawed at my cheek and hung on. I tried to pluck it off without ripping the skin, only to be snared by the elbow.

'Lawyer Vine,' said Ken. 'There's a lot of it in here.'

There was too. I backed off and looked at the plant carefully. It was a scrambling palm, that hoisted its great snaky canes up into the trees by dint of snagging them with fine backward-hooked whips set opposite each compound leaf. I peeled off the one that had latched onto my cheek and felt blood sliding after. The growing ends and leaf nodes of the canes were trimmed with fringes of fine brown spines; the leaf edges and stalks were spiny too. I had no stick to hold the Lawyer Vine back with, and there was no way of pushing through it.

Ken looked back and saw me twisting and turning to find a way through. 'Look out!' he yelled. 'See that thing on your left there? No, don't touch it!'

I didn't. 'What is it?'

'I think,' said Ken, 'it's a Shiny Stinger. I'm never really sure exactly what they look like. If there's a Shiny Stinger, there's usually an ordinary one not too far off. See.'

He pointed his stick over my shoulder towards a velvety apple-green sapling. 'That's a Stinger.'

This was definitely not my cup of tea, a closed forest, steep, rocky ground, and malicious plantlife to boot. And we hadn't even got to the snakes and spiders yet. Ahead of me Ken was in trouble. The terrain had gradually degenerated until it was nothing but a tumble of rocks, and still no sign of the creek, which we could hear gurgling somewhere underneath. Clambering down into the gully would be asking for trouble.

'I thought there was a path here,' said Ken, 'but there isn't, obviously.'

We turned tail and walked back through the forest. The curious cattle were waiting for us at the edge.

'Whose beasts are these?'

'Not ours. We let a neighbour keep them here in return for a bit of spraying.'

'What's to spray?'

He gestured, 'Fireweed, Wild Cotton, Mist Weed, Crofton Weed, Castor Oil Plant, thistles. You have to have the cattle regardless, because you need them to keep the grass down. It's dangerous having the grass too high, especially near the house.'

'Snakes.'

Great.

Jane-Frances suggested that we go to Angela's for lunch. Angela's was a colonial-style pseudo-farmhouse with a curving drive bordered with Agapanthus, shaded by the usual partnership of Coral Trees and Jacarandas. According to her signage, Angela sold hot pies in inverted commas, snacks and craft. Jane-Frances and Ken introduced me as 'Germaine'. 'I hope you're nothing to do with that bloody Germaine Greer,' said Angela, as she led us between shelves laden with hand-made forgettabilia.

On the ride back to Logan I didn't say anything about the property.
We talked about other things. I said I'd be in touch. On impulse, as
I was passing the hire-car desk in the hotel lobby, I decided to rent a
car and drive to Sydney instead of flying. Then I rang a resort I had
noticed on the way up from Nerang and booked accommodation. I
checked out of the hotel, wheeled the rental car out onto the highway
and raced back the way I had come. If I had calculated correctly, I
would be back at Natural Arch before sunset. I felt that I owed it to
the Piaggios to give their property another chance. In the hot middle
of the day the Australian bush is silent; to understand the place I had
to see it when it was coming alive, when the indigo mists well up
from the gullies.

I parked the car under the Jacarandas, and walked up the track,
between tall stands of feral Verbena and Wild Cotton. The cooling
air was full of what I knew from my time in Oklahoma as Monarch
butterflies, *Danaus plexippus*, known better in Australia as Wanderers,
some copulating in mid-air. The story of their presence here was
partly known to me; the first Monarch butterflies appeared in
Queensland in 1870 or so, and the belief is that they migrated there
from northern Brazil under their own wing-power. However they
pupate on Wild Cotton, *Gomphocarpus fruticosus*, which is also their
larval food plant, and it would seem more likely that they and it
were imported together – if only the Gomphocarpus, sometimes
called Cape Cotton, were not indigenous to South Africa. Wild
Cotton had spread 'rapidly in different parts of the colony' by 1856
(*SMH*, 26 November). A related plant, *Asclepias curassavica*, is also
called Wild Cotton and I could see it too growing in the tangle
alongside the track. In 1879 it was already 'common around
Brisbane, and unfortunately, throughout the colony.' (*Q*,
22 November)

I turned off the track and struggled over rocks hidden by the long
grass downwards towards the creek. From the forest on the slopes
above me came a noise like fighting tomcats. Possums, I thought.
(Catbirds, actually.) Tiny jewelled birds were bouncing about in the
Lantana. Big brown pigeons were gorging on the fruits of Wild
Tobacco. I perched on one of the biggest of the rocks and

contemplated the forest edge. Half a million dollars for a run-down dairy farm. I didn't think so.

Out from the clumps of Native Raspberry at the forest edge stepped a bird, a sort-of crow in fancy dress. He was clad in a tabard of a yellow so intense that it seemed to burn, and a cap of the same yellow with a frosting of red on the crown. He walked up to within a few feet of me, fixed me with his round yellow eye and began to move his black rump rhythmically back and forth. There was no doubt about it. He was dancing. Up and down bobbed his gaudy head, in and out went his hips, and all the time he kept a golden eye fixed on my face. Something, a wallaby I thought, thudded through the unseen gully below me. I turned my head to follow the noise and the bird sashayed after, keeping me in his sights. And all the while he kept dancing.

'What do you want with me, birdie?'

More dancing, a little faster if anything.

Dusk in these latitudes is momentary. The pinkness of the sky above the purple scarps had drained to a phosphorescent green.

'Birdie, I have to go, or I'll be caught here in the dark.'

More dancing.

I stood up.

'Bye bye, birdie.'

The black and gold bird made a little bow and disappeared among the raspberries.

As I came in sight of the house, a man was leaning on the verandah rail.

I said, 'Hi.' What I thought was, 'Sorry, mate, I'm gunna buy your house.'

I came back at dawn the next day and spent a little time wading through the soaking grass, but there was no need. The decision had been made the night before. As I drove back out, a flock of Red-browed Finches flew up beside the car. I felt blessed, excited and frightened, all at once. The place was amazing, bursting with life, to be sure, but so battered! Battered by clearing, by logging, by spraying, and worse. The heraldic bird had thrown down the gauntlet. Was I game to take on the challenge? Could I rebuild the forest? The job was immense but I felt sure that it was doable, just about, if I lived long enough.

I stopped on the causeway to empty a boot. My white sock was sticky with blood. I peeled it off and shook it. Out fell a sated leech. Vital substance of mine was already incorporated in the Cave Creek biomass. Around me the ground was covered with royal blue flowers, like miniature Tradescantias. With a big toe still bleeding copiously I got back into the car and drove south to the Numinbah Gap. As even Queenslanders don't know where it is, I will use the account provided by Jack Gresty to the Queensland Geographical Society in 1947 which in a few words conveys the grandeur of the place.

> The Numinbah Valley lies between high spur ranges of the McPherson Range . . . to the west is the Beechmont Range and to the east the Springbrook Range or Plateau. At the head of the valley there is a steep declivity in the McPherson Range forming a low divide between the Tweed and Nerang Waters and known as the Numinbah Gap. On either side of the Gap the McPherson Range rises to a height of over three thousand feet.

The road from Nerang to Murwillumbah makes its way up towards the headwaters of the Nerang River on the north-facing slopes of the McPherson Range. As it climbed toward the crossing point the roadside weeds proliferated, with impenetrable stands of Buddleia and bamboo to add to the usual garden escapes, while the broad river valley below was all but treeless and chequered with cattle-pads. Even on the higher slopes the rainforest had been stripped away. As the car slid past the tick gate and into New South Wales, regrowth eucalypts gave way to Camphor Laurel, along the fence lines, along the creek banks and along the road. I passed roadside stalls with a few bunches of bananas for sale, an occasional avocado plantation, acres cloaked in deep blue Morning Glory, and even a row of weed eucalypts planted by the local council. I began to wonder if the vivid image of a deep green native forest had been a hallucination.

I was scanning the magazine rack in a lounge at Sydney airport, filling in time before the flight back to England, and there he was, the bird, on the cover of a nature magazine. The caption read 'Regent Bowerbird'.

The Regent bowerbird (*Sericulus chrysocephalus*) only descends from the rainforest canopy when he is in search of a mate; then he builds his bower and displays to any likely female, spreading his tail and beating his wings, all the while uttering his wheezy call.

My Regent Bowerbird was quite silent, and didn't display his wings and tail, so he hadn't taken me for some outsize mate. He pranced and twisted, but didn't prostrate himself in front of me with his tail fanned and his wings spread, so his wasn't a mating display. I may have been close to his bower; in such a case a bowerbird will usually fly up into a tree and vocalise loudly to distract attention, rather than trying to dance the interloper away. I didn't know when this famous cover-bird came high-stepping out of the raspberries that he had been on the 35-cent stamp or that he was the trademark of the Lodge at O'Reilly's where the bowerbirds are so tame that tourists can get them to feed from their hands. The forest knew what it was doing. It could hardly have chosen a better envoy to help me understand where my future lay.

I dropped the letter with a cheque for the deposit into the airport postbox. The die was cast. For better or worse, the forest has me till death do us part.

THE FOREST

When the paperwork for the purchase was nearly complete, I rang Jane.

'I've bought something. Sixty hectares.'

'Where?'

'Gold Coast City.'

'You're not serious.'

'I am.'

I was. As you come over the border from New South Wales into Queensland on the Nerang–Murwillumbah road, right by the tick gate, through which Queensland cattle may not pass southwards into New South Wales, a sign welcomes you to Gold Coast City. Anything less citified would be hard to imagine.

'You're losing it, girl. Why would you buy something on the Gold Coast? You don't even play golf.'

'It's in the Hinterland.'

'Let me guess: horsiness, fake villages and avenues of Cocos Palms. The food and wine trail. Bad food and worse wine.'

'No. It's rainforest. Or abandoned dairy farm. It depends which way you look at it.'

'You're the only person I know who would spend two years shopping for desert and come back with rainforest. When am I going to see it?'

I arranged a stay for Jane, her husband Peter and myself at one of many expensive rainforest retreats, which didn't look terribly far away from Cave Creek on the map but was. We got there late after driving for an hour through blinding rain, the only guests in the place. The kitchen was closed. Morning revealed that we were mere feet away from a just-about-still-working avocado plantation full of angry bees. The 'ancient' rainforest our rooms overlooked was actually a mess of tangled regrowth, the only mature trees to be seen in it immense Flooded Gums. I found one luxuriant plant, a rambling passionfruit with pure white flowers, and took its photograph. I now know it only too well as *Passiflora subpeltata*, one of the most invasive weeds in disturbed forest.

Over breakfast, consisting of a variety of boxed cereals and DIY raisin toast, we worked out where we were, which was Mount Tamborine, and where we were going. Mount Tamborine stands on the eastern extremity of the Albert River catchment. Between it and the Nerang River lies the Coomera River catchment. Both these rivers rise on the Lamington Plateau, deep within the trackless confines of the national park, and flow northwards. The range that divides the two catchments is the Darlington Range; the western boundary of the Nerang River Valley is the Beechmont Range which runs at right angles to the McPherson Range, which extends all the way from the sea at Point Danger to Wallangarra, 220 kilometres inland. In the angle between them lies the Lamington Plateau. The movement to turn its 20,590 hectares into a national park was initiated in 1896 by a grazier called Robert Collins, who invited Lord Lamington, the then governor of Queensland, to visit the area. (Lord Lamington, who was more used to visiting his British friends to shoot on their country estates, took the opportunity to shoot a koala.) The eastern boundary of the Numinbah Valley is another national park, the Springbrook Plateau. The only way to get back from Mount Tamborine to Cave Creek was to drive down to the coastal highway and back up the Nerang. Even though Numinbah lies within a few minutes of the Lamington Plateau and Springbrook as the crow would fly, both are hours away by road.

As we drove through the devastated hinterland and along the six-lane Pacific Highway Jane uttered no more than the occasional sigh. The road up through the regrowth forests seemed longer and drearier than usual. Never was I more grateful for the dramatic entrance through the national park. Jane was stunned by the sheer variety of unfamiliar plants. We slid past strings of nuts hanging from the Macadamias and the huge pods dangling from the Black Beans, and down into the alley between the rainforest and the Hoop Pines.

'Are these yours?' asked Jane, looking at the rows of Hoop Pines.

'Not now. They're the remains of a plantation that was grown on the property before that bit of it was ceded to the national park, and now of course they can't be harvested. They should be taken out for timber and the park should spend the proceeds on some extra weed control, but there's no chance.'

We came to a lopsided gate. 'This is where my property begins.'

On the left a steep slope clothed in Lantana, on the right the other half of the same. Jane was unimpressed.

'Bit of a challenge,' said Peter.

That bit was, if I had known it, but a thousandth part of the challenge. There was Lantana all along the forest edges and in every gully, and wherever the land was cleared but not put down to grass. Way up in the forest there are still, ten years on, fifteen hectares that were cleared for bananas that are now full-on Lantana. And Lantana was not the worst of it.

We crossed the causeway over the creek.

'This is Cave Creek. It's one of the headwaters of the Nerang River, which rises a bit further up and a bit further south-west, on Mount Hobwee.'

I drove on under a huge cedar dressed from head to foot in Staghorns, Bird's Nest Ferns and an enormous King Orchid, and on to a second gate. Grazing cattle raised their heads and stared as Peter got out to open and shut the gate. They kept staring as we drove on up to the house, a Queenslander of sorts, standing on cement columns topped with old hub caps, which were meant to stop termites from travelling up into the wood of the house. The key I had been given didn't fit the lock of the flimsy front door. Before I could kick it in, Peter pried open a window at the end of the verandah, climbed through and let us in.

'How can people live like this?' asked Jane as she stepped into the kitchen.

The walls were filthy, but not as filthy as the doorjambs, which were black with grimy handprints. The boarded ceilings sagged, and brown dirt had sifted down through the cracks to gather on every horizontal surface. The windows were curtained with spiderwebs inside and out. The floors were covered with several layers of cheap carpeting, most of it rotten, all of it black with dirt. Three of the internal partitions were so eaten out by termites that you could put your hand through them. The floors of the bathroom and neighbouring lavatory sloped downwards; both were hanging off the side of the house because the joists had rotted away. The septic tank had a young Red Cedar growing out of it. Jane went to see if the lavatory was usable. I heard her lift the top off the cistern and force it to empty. When she ran the water to wash her hands it scalded her. I touched a switch and the light went on.

'Could be worse,' said Peter.

'I'd get rid of all of this,' said Jane, pushing her toe into the soggy carpeting. 'And then I'd gurney the whole place out.'

Jane never goes bushwards without the wherewithal for making tea. As she put her little kettle-cum-teapot on the filthy hob she asked, 'What's the plan?'

'To restore the forest.'

Jane tipped leaf tea into the holder in the top of the pot. 'That's obvious. But how?'

Peter, as usual, said nothing.

'I have no idea. You can help me.'

'You reckon. I don't know anything about this vegetation. It's all I can do to keep abreast of the systems on the Mornington Peninsula. I don't even know the genera that grow here, let alone the species. Rainforests are the most intricate systems on earth. That's why when they're disturbed, everything goes haywire. You might think you're restoring what was there, but in fact you're just another interloper, doing more harm than good.'

I took a deep breath. 'I can learn. We can learn, together.'

That was part of the idea, but typically I hadn't consulted her.

Jane, who will no more countenance the drinking of tea out of mugs than the use of tea bags, put a cup and saucer beside me. 'You don't get it, do you? There are no teachers.'

Peter said, 'The soil looks pretty good. Basalt, isn't it? What's the rainfall?'

'About two metres a year.'

'Must be worth a try.'

We drank our tea and talked of other things. A Butcherbird hopped onto the verandah rail and sang a canzonetta composed for the occasion. Behind the house King Parrots were whistling. In the pasture Crimson Rosellas were swinging on the heads of seeding grass. Wanderer butterflies sailed past in airborne coitus. The tea things stowed in their basket, we went for a walk up the main track. I was praying for something special, the bowerbird maybe, to win my sister over. We trudged uphill and came to a broad clearing where Jane stopped dead. She was gazing up at the bare rhyolite precipice that topped out above the forest like the battlements of some huge prehistoric castle.

'Now that I do understand. That is fantastic. Can we get nearer?'

The forest edge was a mass of Lantana, with no visible opening.

Jane studied the tumbled mess of rocks around us. 'These aren't geologic. They're all out of position. Just heaped and pushed about – to make the pasture, I guess.'

She was right as usual, but the truth was sadder than her guess. In these parts the farmers didn't simply roll the rocks aside to create level tracts of pasture; they dug them up to sell. It took me months to realise that the forest had not been abused just as a farm. From 1985 the upland portion had been one of the four quarries on Numinbah Valley farms that supplied 50,000 tonnes of rock to build the seafronts of the artificial waterside suburbs that stretch from Byron Bay to Noosa and points north. The figure is merely notional; the total may be many times that much. The farmers have no weigh-bridges and there is no one overseeing the traffic. The rock merchants don't care; the farmers don't care; nobody cares. Rocks too irregularly shaped to be usable were bulldozed out of the way into creeks and gullies. Of the natural contours of that part of the northern lip of the Mount Warning caldera almost nothing remains.

The forest takes this devastation in its stride. The valiant workforce has planted into the worst heaps of spoil, and the trees have shot up just as if they were standing in deep loam, spreading their roots across the rubble, holding it all together. The answer to everything, to the instability of the land, the slumping, the landslips, the pugging and the waterlogging, is to plant more trees. Under the protection of the canopy the land heals.

In the blitheness of my innocence I pitched the project to my sister. 'The way I see it, the pasture is an ulcer in the healthy tissue of the forest. What I have to do is to draw the healthy tissue in, little by little, till the ulcer is gone.'

'What if it's a rodent ulcer?'

'It isn't. See, the Lantana can only grow in sunlight, on the forest edge. The forest isn't retreating from the pasture, it's drawing in wherever it can. What I have to do is to remove some of the obstacles and the forest will do the rest.'

Jane sighed at my ignorance. 'You're going to have to learn about succession, my girl. And that won't be easy, because nobody really knows how it works. To restore your forest would take about eight hundred years.'

'I'd better not die then.'

The next day, at Mount Tamborine, we found a little information centre and in it a copy of the famous Red Book, with its original title, *Trees and Shrubs in the Rainforest of New South Wales and Southern Queensland.*

'Here you are,' said Jane. 'Page six, Subtropical rainforest.' She read out:

– 2 or 3 strata of trees
– diverse: 10–60 species in canopy
– leaf size large: notophylls and mesophylls common

'What are notophylls and mesophylls?'

'It's a fancy way of indicating leaf size. Notophylls are leaves between about three inches, say eight centimetres and about five inches, thirteen centimetres. Mesophylls are bigger.' She went on reading:

– leaves often compound—

I interrupted her again. 'Meaning?'

'Hm. That's not so easy to explain. A simple leaf has a single blade, yes? And a simple leaf can have indentations in its outline, like a maple leaf for example? If those indentations go right to the main vein, and the bits between form separate leaf blades and the main vein becomes the rachis, you've got a compound leaf. The separate leaves or, more correctly, leaflets may have stalks connecting them to the rachis or not.'

'How can you tell if you're looking at a leaf or a leaflet?'

'That's easy. Leaflets don't have axils, or rather, there are no buds in the axils, no leaf buds or flower buds or stipules. The real axil will be way back where the rachis joins the branchlet. Leaflets don't fall separately either; the compound leaf tends to drop as a whole.'

'So if I'm not sure, I can look for a fallen leaf?'

'Yes, but you won't need to do that, I reckon. You'll get used to it pretty quick.'

Jane was wrong about that. Taking a leaflet for a leaf is one of the commonest mistakes made by the amateur dendrologist. It was to be many months before I could distinguish more than a very few species. For too long it seemed to me that I forgot more than I learned, that I was learning the same names over and over again. And then one day I found myself recognising trees at a distance, and even their saplings, and then their seedlings, which were often very different from the adult tree. I have still to master the art of recognising trees from their trunks when the canopy is out of sight, but I'm getting there.

Jane read on:

– Leaves often compound, and mostly with entire margins—

'Entire margins?'

'Without serrations or indentations. Not toothed, angled or lobed.' She went on:

– stranglers (figs) often common
– palms often common
– plank-buttresses often common
– uneven, non-uniform canopy
Vines – large, thick-stemmed vines common and diverse
Large epiphytes – (orchids, ferns, aroids) common and diverse
Special features – large-leaved herbs and ground-ferns common

'Most authorities divide rainforest into more than four types, actually. I'm trying to remember my Tracey and Webb; they divide rainforest into more than a dozen types, I seem to recall. Your kind of subtropical rainforest is this one, Complex Notophyll Vine Forest.'

Jane and Peter went home to Victoria and I was left to contemplate my folly. First of all I tramped down to the creek, and picked my way along it. It seemed preposterous to me that anyone could own anything like it and yet it was legally mine. Though the creek was full of weeds, red, pink and white Busy Lizzie, Mist Weed and Elephant Grass, it was equally full of promise. On the flat top of a rock in the creek I found a little heap of crayfish claws, indigo-blue, edged with vermilion, left there by the Azure Kingfisher. Many of the trees had snaking buttress roots, and within the curve of one of them, amid the bright blue fruit shed by the quandongs, I surprised a Noisy Pitta. I found a way into the forest and ventured into the twilight under the canopy where giant mosses and lycopods grew, and gushes of scented blossom swung down. The canopy, fifty metres above my head, was a total mystery to me.

The first thing I needed was a flora survey. I had been given the name of a self-trained local botanist called David Jinks. He was famous because he had already fulfilled the botanist's dream. Scrambling in a gully above Natural Arch he came upon a new tree, which he identified as a Eucryphia. This was no mean feat. Eucryphia is a small Gondwanan genus of only seven species, two in Chile and five (counting the new one) in Australia. The new Eucryphia is called *Eucryphia jinksii*, and academic botanists have had to make space for David in their hallowed company. He was quick to put together a tree survey for me, and to tell me that my sixty hectares had some of the highest biodiversity to be found anywhere outside the wet tropics. He explained that because we had different soil types, rich basaltic soils and krasnozems striped with sandstone, and a constant supply of moisture percolating down from the higher scarps of the McPherson Range, the Cave Creek forest was both montane and riparian, with odd dryer spots and patches of alluvium. Add the range of altitude, from 250 to 500 metres above sea level, plus the different aspects of these steep slopes, and you had niches to suit just about everything that could grow in any high-rainfall forest within two hundred kilometres.

So I had little plastic signs made, screwed them onto star pickets and had them put up all along the unfenced boundary. 'Cave Creek Rainforest Rehabilitation Scheme' they said, and warned passers-by that anyone removing material of any kind from the property would be prosecuted. The name may seem odd, but a lot of thought went into it. Revegetation was the wrong word for what we were doing because it didn't suggest the element of specificity; we weren't just stopping erosion, we were replanting a forest. Restoration wasn't the right word either because it made the trees sound like furniture. I went for 'rehabilitation' because it suggested the role that the forest would play in rebuilding itself. So CCRRS it is. The nearest thing to a logo we have is the image of the remarkable inflorescence of the small Bolwarra, *Eupomatia bennettii*. This is a true Gondwanan survivor, one of three species in the single genus of the family Eupomatiaceae. It was ten years before we succeeded in propagating this very special plant. Because the forest frugivores always stole the fruit before it was quite ripe, we finally decided to put a cage over the next fruiting plant we found. After watching the single fruit develop for a whole six months, waiting with increasing impatience till it was truly ripe and ready, we ended up with some hundreds of seedlings.

David discovered galaxies of rare plants, *Ardisia bakeri*, *Rhodamnia maideniana*, *Tapeinosperma repandulum*, *Quassia* Mt Nardi, *Neisosperma poweri*, *Cupaniopsis newmannii*, *Lepiderema pulchella*. On basalt benches under the canopy on the north edge of the property he found many examples of the Southern Fontainea or *Fontainea australis*, recognisable by its oddly jointed leafstalks and the two oil glands on the underside of the base of the leaf. *Syzygium hodgkinsoniae*, Miss Hodgkinson's lilly pilly, more commonly known as the Rose Apple, like the Fontainea listed as vulnerable, grows profusely all over CCRRS, much to David's surprise. I had every intention of rebuilding the forest that should have been covering the cleared acres; to discover that by restoring that habitat I would be multiplying the numbers of individuals in threatened, endangered, vulnerable or rare species was an utter bonus.

David warned me to expect a visitor from the Queensland herbarium whose job it was to check that another very rare plant on the property, the Smooth Davidson's Plum, was still surviving. The consensus used to be that plants that survive only on land in private ownership were doomed. The three sites where this plant was then recorded are all privately owned. There was nothing the herbarium could do to stop me wiping the Cave Creek Davidsonias out of existence; they could only check to see if the record should be changed from 'endangered' to 'critically endangered' or even 'extinct'. The Smooth Davidson's Plum was first described by New South Wales botanists John Williams and Gwen Harden in 1979, and finally named by them in 2000, *Davidsonia johnsonii*, after L. A. S. Johnson.

The late Lawrie Johnson is the acknowledged master of Gondwanan botany in Australia, responsible for the naming of four new plant families, thirty-three new genera and 286 new species, for segregating Angophora and Corymbia from the genus Eucalyptus, and for beginning the research on the Proteaceae that is now coming to fruition. In the preface he wrote for *Flowers and Plants of New South Wales and Southern Queensland* in 1975, Johnson urged readers:

> On the local front, resist by all legal means the unnecessary fouling of gullies by residential or other development at their heads, leading to mineral enrichment and choking by weeds. Resist 'reclaiming' (a profoundly dishonest word) of swamps. Prevent building on headlands and unnecessary artificial revegetation of sand-dunes. Oppose clearing, mowing, planting of roadsides; let the native vegetation or even harmless 'weeds' grow – they will support a rich life of invertebrate animals and some birds and other vertebrates (though certain noxious weeds cannot be tolerated and harbour for rabbits must sometimes be destroyed). Keep even the smallest patches of native or semi-native vegetation – *the large reserves alone are not enough.* (Rotherham *et al.*, 7–8)

Lawrie Johnson would have understood what we are doing at CCRRS. I like to think that we have his blessing. We have since found other groups of *Davidsonia johnsonii*, and we have propagated it as well, so with us it is no longer rare.

David was drinking coffee on the verandah when I pointed to a small tree standing in the middle of the pasture and asked him what it was. He took one look and was off the verandah and bounding across the Kikuyu towards it. He came back bearing a twig.

'Unbelievable,' he said. 'This is *Corynocarpus rupestris*, the Glenugie Karaka. It's not supposed to grow anywhere in Australia outside the Glenugie Peak Flora Reserve.'

Glenugie Peak is the alternative name of Mount Elaine, a steep extinct volcano south-east of Grafton.

'Karaka. Sounds like a Maori name.'

'It is. The genus was first collected in New Zealand by the Forsters on Cook's second voyage. "Karaka" means "orange" in Maori; the fruit of the New Zealand species, *Corynocarpus laevigatus*, is orange. It was one of the few plants actively cultivated by the Maori, who used the kernels to make a special kind of flour. The Australian species was first collected by a worker in the Glenugie State Forest in 1956, but the specimen sat around for twenty-five years until Gordon Guymer took a look at it and wrote it up in *Flora of Australia* [22: 214–16]. The species is divided into two subspecies. *Corynocarpus rupestris arborescens* is found on a few Queensland sites, but this isn't it. You know it's the subspecies *rupestris* rather than *arborescens* because of these stem-girdling larvae that keep pruning the tree, so it never gets any higher. No doubt about it. This is the genuine Glenugie Karaka, *Corynocarpus rupestris rupestris*. Look at this.'

He showed me a sharp hooked tooth at the tip of a juvenile leaf. 'That's really primitive.'

He might as well have been showing me the wing of a pterodactyl.

'How do you suppose the Corynocarpus got here?' I asked.

'Birdshit?'

'The Glenugie State Forest is more than a hundred ks away. Can a bird fly that far between bowel movements?'

We've done our best since to propagate our Corynocarpus, which we have never seen to flower or fruit. It seems that this primitive tree is 'gender dimorphic' or 'gynodioecious'; though it doesn't have separate male and female inflorescences as such, in some specimens the female organs of the inflorescence are highly developed and in others the male (Brockie *et al.*). And it looks as if in certain circumstances, the inflorescence may change from one to the other. Whenever a branch falls, pruned by the in-dwelling larvae, we turn it into cuttings but so far only a very few have struck and they grow agonisingly slowly.

Perhaps more important than anything else David found for me were two young men who had worked for him when he had a rainforest nursery. Simon and Will were both experienced in regeneration work and in identifying plants in the wild. Simon had worked for me for less than a week when he found a Plum Pine (*Podocarpus elatus*) that wasn't on David's list, and a pair of giant Water Gums (*Tristaniopsis laurina*) growing on a rocky slope otherwise covered in Mist Weed. Hardly a week went by without one or other adding new species to our flora list. Deep in the forest they found *Ochrosia moorei*, an endangered plant known from the Springbrook National Park.

Besides endangered and vulnerable plants, there is another class of plants that are simply rare. Some species are so demanding of a particular suite of cultural conditions that they will never dominate in any plant community, like the Veiny Laceflower (*Archidendron muellerianum*), Ardisia (*Ardisia bakeri*), the Long-leaved Tuckeroo (*Cupaniopsis newmannii*), Smooth Scrub Turpentine (*Rhodamnia maideniana*) and Milkbush (*Neisosperma poweri*). It makes no sense to start trying to save a disappearing plant without dealing with the conditions that are causing its disappearance, and that requires restoration of the plant community of which the rare plant is a member. Plant the commoner members of the assemblage and in their own good time the rarer ones will turn up.

Next came Rob Price and Lui Weber, who found *Endiandra hayesii*, another vulnerable inhabitant. Rob and Lui are proper old-fashioned botanists who are interested in the whole forest assemblage. They teach me the liverworts and lichens, ferns and mosses, sedges and grasses, orchids and vines, thousands upon thousands of species. Every time they come by they find more tree species.

Sixty species in the canopy would have been the top of the predictable range; CCRRS had more than twice that. The point of restoring the forest was now reinforced. To let the Cave Creek forest reclaim its own would leave a living museum of genetic diversity that might even survive global warming, given its curious situation in a suspended drainage basin that could not dry out.

It was probably inevitable that I would begin the restoration of the forest by making a bad mistake. I employed a local contractor to clear the forest edge and cut access paths while I was away in England. I came back to find that his huge machine had ripped down, as well as the curtain of Lantana that blocked access to the forest, dozens of young trees and as many branches with their epiphytes and birds' nests, and had chewed out steep tracks that carved through root systems and gashed tender buttress roots. It had even run over a sleeping python. My friend Ann flew up from Melbourne to find me perplexed and uncertain. Will, who greatly disapproved of the heavy machinery approach, had been taking the workforce up into the corner of the property that was surrounded by national park and was teaching them to remove weeds by hand, following the method established by Joan and Eileen Bradley in the 1960s (*ADB*). He and his co-workers simply pulled out exotic soft weeds by hand, one by one. The soil was far too moist and fertile to remain naked for long; the area was no sooner cleared than it was time to clear it again. Will's instinct was to leave all native vegetation; Native Raspberry, Kangaroo Vine and Cayratia were allowed to spread unchecked. In his wisdom he left all and any native tree, including the pioneer species Bleeding Heart (*Omalanthus populifolius*) and Native Mulberry (*Pipturus argenteus*). It took more than five years to happen, but eventually the pioneer species that he protected formed a canopy dense enough to shade out the weeds. This corner of the property is now genuine rainforest, with a knee-high understorey of *Pollia crispata*, shining in the gloom like a rising tide of four-pointed green stars. Female Paradise Riflebirds love to perch in the branches of the Native Mulberries.

Back in 2003 it seemed that we were getting nowhere, slowly. We had yet to plant a single tree. The only place we had clear to plant was a half-hectare by the entrance gate that had been stripped by the excavator. It was fast filling up with Lantana again.

'You'll have to use herbicides, won't you?' said Ann.

I thought so. 'The excavator was too much, but we can't pussyfoot around either. We have to clear and plant, and then keep the competition down until the little trees start casting shade. What I don't know is whether the baby trees have to be shaded. Whether we should be planting them with nurse trees, pioneers that keep them shaded until they're tough enough to grow in full sun.'

We had plenty of nurse trees, mostly Blackwoods (*Acacia melanoxylon*). The conventional wisdom is that these 'nurse trees' safeguard natural forest succession, but I could see that the rainforest saplings that had germinated underneath them were holding their breath. Some of the land originally cleared at Cave Creek had become what seemed to be a monoculture of Blackwoods until you walked through it and found hundreds of Red Cedar saplings standing underneath the wattles. By the lichens growing on the leaves you could tell that the saplings had been there for generations, waiting in vain for the Blackwoods to collapse. Forestry researchers have found that when *Acacia melanoxylon* leaves rot down they generate sufficient toxicity to inhibit the growth of surrounding plants, a phenomenon known as allelopathy (González *et al*.). Another sinister aspect of Blackwoods is that their seeds need extreme heat to germinate, and they pop up everywhere after fire. Their ubiquity at Cave Creek is a direct consequence of the original settlers' use of fire to clear the rainforest.

'What I'm thinking is that the trigger for the saplings in the rainforest to grow is the opening of a gap in the canopy. The little old trees you see in the understorey are waiting for a look at the sky, waiting for a neighbour tree to fall. They don't want to be shaded. Being shaded will keep them small.'

Ann was puzzled. 'When you see rainforest trees in the open, they grow out instead of up, don't they?'

'Yes, but that's where the competition comes in. The trees that are heading for a gap in the canopy have to go up and up. They self-prune by shedding their lateral branches, because they have to make it to their place in the sun. The shaded lower branches die off and fall. What we'll do is plant the full suite of canopy trees at one-metre centres, and let them fight it out between them. The fastest-growing, the Macarangas and Bleeding Hearts and Polyscias, are also the shortest-lived, so when they fall over, the slow growers will get their chance.'

'What are you going to do about the cattle?'

'Everyone says that I need them to keep down the grass, but they get up in the forest and eat the young Native Ginger and all the fallen fruit. I think I'll have to get rid of them. I've tried electric fencing but it seems to malfunction all the time. Too much wet vegetation, I think. We can't stop the cattle peeing and shitting in the creek either. And they trample the pythons.'

'Does the bloke who owns the beasts actually pay you for letting them graze here?'

He didn't.

'So get rid of them.'

I did. It was a sad day, because there were two little steers that I rather loved. They had been household pets in their former home and knew how to get treats by being cute, but they got loaded onto the truck with all the others and away they went. I asked Garry to pull out all the barbed wire, wherever it was, and take it to the dump. We knocked over the hay shed, which was just a roof on posts sunk in 44-gallon-drums filled with concrete, and pulled down the dairy. The young Red Cedar that had been growing through the dairy roof threw up its arms to the sky. Borer had got into part of it, but we carefully cut the diseased part away and the tree never looked back. Someone collected the portable muster yard with its bails and rails.

'You realise that you're steadily reducing the value of this real estate,' said Ann.

'Mm. David thinks that revegetating land like this will one day be understood to enhance its value, but I'll be long dead by that time, supposing such a time ever comes.'

Almost without noticing I had taken over the project. David had been meant to direct it, but progress was too slow. It was all very well for me to draw up lists of tree species that I would plant; I had to find someone to grow them for me first. The Cave Creek rainforest trees were not the kind of thing you'd find in every neighbourhood garden centre. I found Charlie Booth of Bushnuts, who could already supply about half the species I needed, and was happy to collect seed at CCRRS and grow more. And so in May 2003 the first half-hectare was planted. To keep the weeds down and the soil around the baby trees moist, we had to use a thick layer of mulch. What we used were the fronds stripped off sugarcane at harvest, efficient but costly. Even with the mulch we had to spray herbicide, and twice we removed native vines that were intent on dragging the little trees to their deaths. For a year nothing much happened. The little trees were still only knee-high. I felt my heart sinking. Rebuilding a forest was proving much harder than I anticipated. And much more expensive. The costs per tree were shooting up while the trees remained the same size. Hours after we finished a second planting on the creek bank, a black curtain of rain came roaring over the scarp. Hour after hour, pulse after pulse, it kept coming. The creek rose and rose until the torrent overflowed into a side channel and tore out all the new little trees. When the fresh subsided Simon and I crawled through the detritus dumped by the creek, combing through it with our fingers to find the uprooted seedlings and replant them.

I went back to England with a heavy heart.

At a formal dinner at my college a woman sitting at my table asked me about the rainforest. Unwisely perhaps I began to tell her. The man on her right interrupted.

'Surely all you need to do is to lock up the forest and let it restore itself. What you're doing is just a very expensive version of gardening. If the rainforest can survive it will. If it can't, nothing you do will make any difference.'

I should have saved my breath, and let him score his point, but I couldn't. 'You could be right, but I don't think so. The forest can reclaim its own only if certain obstacles are removed. When old-growth forest is logged, apart from the devastation of trees surrounding the target tree, Red Cedar or whatever, the vines go berserk. One of the most reliable indicators of logging in the past is the proliferation of Kangaroo Vine which climbs right into the canopy and literally suffocates the canopy trees. Lawyer Vine too is an indicator of disturbance; when plants like these fill up gaps in the forest, it turns to scrub. Seedling trees and saplings can't cope with the sheer weight of the rampant vines. Add to that the fact that the biggest forest emergents are the slowest-growing, there's no way that the forest can rebuild itself without assistance.

'Then there are the pioneer species that volunteer to fill gaps in the forest. The idea that they aid the reconstruction of the forest community is just wrong, I'm afraid. No wild species is altruistic. All the forest volunteers are in it for their own species. The proteoid roots of Silky Oak, *Grevillea robusta*, excrete chemicals that bacteria turn into alumina. Eucalypts too tend to establish monocultures because the chemicals in their leaf litter inhibit the germination of other species. In Numinbah whole hillsides which should be supporting rainforest have been taken over by Brush Box. Brush Box, *Lophostemon confertus*, is myrtaceous, and like eucalypts in other ways too. It's supposed to be fire-retardant, a concept that makes no sense to me. I think it means that it burns more slowly than eucalypts, which surround themselves with highly inflammable vapour and literally burst into flame. Rainforest is fire-sensitive. Elsewhere in Numinbah Valley you can see rainforest saplings pushing up under regrowth eucalypts, Sydney Blue Gums and Flooded Gums. When the eucalypts catch fire, which they do every two or three years, the rainforest saplings are all killed.

'Then there are other pioneers, Kurrajongs, Polyscias, Bleeding Hearts, Macarangas, all quite capable of filling up spaces that are then not available to rainforest species. A worse problem is grass. When the land was originally cleared, the forest was clear-felled and burnt. The pasture grasses that were then sown either conked out or became rampant. Small trees can't push against Kikuyu, which is the dominant grass in the Numinbah Valley. It spreads incredibly rapidly, by stolons and by seed, and builds up great mats within months.

'Then you have to deal with the exotic trees that the farmers planted, of which the worst by far is Camphor Laurel. Not to mention the feral fruit trees that are all that remain of the local fruit-growing industry.'

The gentleman opposite had let me run on quite long enough.

'If the forest can't defend itself against these invaders there's no point in trying to restore it, surely.'

I have never trusted people who use the word 'surely' in argument and answered with more certainty than I felt. 'Oh, but there is. If we can rebuild the original plant community, it will be strong enough to fight off the competition.'

'And how do you propose to do that?'

'By gathering seed from the old-growth forest, propagating it, and planting it out on cleared land, and keeping the baby forest weed-free until it can fend for itself.'

The gentleman turned away, bored with the subject. The fatty lump of farmed salmon in front of me was cold. The waiter was waiting to take my plate, and the other diners were waiting for their pudding. As I toyed with my Tarte au Citron, I thought about the weeds that choke regrowth forest. Every year brings a new one, each worse than the last. I thought of Madeira Vine with leaves and fruit so heavy that it will reduce a mature rainforest tree to a pole, and grow away across the canopy dropping aerial tubers. I thought of Balloon Vine, and Moth Vine, and Morning Glory, and Glycine, and White Passionfruit, and Siratro and now, worst of all, Kudzu. All of them flourish in the subtropical rainforest. I thought of the Wandering Jew (*Tradescantia fluminensis*) that is blanketing the native groundcovers. We could extirpate them all, with maximum effort and expense. Was I mad to think it would be worth it?

As we were taking port in the senior common room, the woman who had raised the subject touched my arm. 'I'd like to help with the work if I can. Can I make a donation?'

A donation. I thought I couldn't accept a donation. The woman smiled. 'You need to set up a charity and give your forest to the charity. Then we can all help.'

The thought of giving up the forest made my heart hurt, but then I would have to give it up one day, wouldn't I? I was going to die, wasn't I? I put the idea in the too-hard basket, to be dealt with later.

When I next drove through the gate, our first planting was five months older and three metres taller. As I let the car roll slowly down the track, I found myself looking into brand-new forest, with a canopy, low to be sure, but a canopy that cast shade. I pulled up, hopped out of the car and walked under the young trees. The sunlight was no more than an occasional coin-dot on the soil which was already disappearing under mats of Commelina and Oplismenus. I walked to where Brush-turkeys had scraped all the expensive mulch into a huge new mound inside which their eggs were already incubating. All my anxiety ebbed out of memory. How could I have thought that I was in this by myself? I had helpers, thousands, no, millions of them, as well as five humans. Cave Creek wasn't just another anthropogenic biome after all. We were all working together, bacteria, fungi, invertebrates, reptiles, amphibians, birds and trees, plus the odd human. As I walked back to the car an Eastern Water Dragon ran ahead of me, upright on its back legs, its tail held high. Into my head came God's reassurance to Julian of Norwich. 'All shall be well,' I thought, 'and all shall be well and all manner of thing shall be well.'

THE TRADITIONAL OWNERS

When they learn that I was happy to hand over a wad of money for a piece of Australia, all the while saying that I wouldn't call Australia home until Aboriginal sovereignty was recognised, many thoughtful people will suspect that I have betrayed my deepest convictions. In my defence I can only say that I didn't buy a home. I bought a project. It would never have occurred to me that my whitefella freehold title endowed me with proprietorial rights. The first thing I did, once the documents were signed and the transfer completed, before I had spent a single night at CCRRS, was to go in search of the traditional owners. At the Minjungbal Aboriginal Cultural Centre at Tweed Heads I thought I would find somebody who could tell me the property's true name, and whom I should approach for permission to camp there. I even dared to hope I could find someone to perform a welcome ceremony for me. I in turn would have been more than happy to let Indigenous people use the land as they wished.

As soon as I opened my mouth, I knew I'd come on a fool's errand.

'I've just acquired the freehold of a piece of land at Natural Arch, and I'm really anxious to know its proper name. Its Aboriginal name.'

The two women behind the counter looked at each other, not at me, and said nothing.

'Aboriginal people must surely have known about it, well, some Aboriginal people at least, about the natural bridge, I mean, and the waterfall and the cave . . .'

What I needed was an elder, a senior law woman. The youngish women in front of me were behaving as if they had never heard of Natural Arch.

I struggled on. 'The place has been given many whitefella names but they don't stick. I'd like to get it right if I can.'

At this point the Natural Bridge was still gazetted under its new name of the Natural Arch, though the township originally called after it was still called Natural Bridge. Apparently the Place Names Board changed the name of the rock formation to the Natural Arch in 1982, at the instance of tour operators, and without consultation with local residents (Hall *et al.*, 161). After months of lobbying, the name was silently changed back to the Natural Bridge. The locals had never called the place anything else, but people living on the Gold Coast, most of whom have never been there, still call it Natural Arch. CCRRS is still in the telephone directory as Natural Arch Farm, despite repeated requests for deletion of the entry.

I didn't suggest a welcome ceremony. I wrote down my name and the postal address on a slip of paper and put it on the desk. Neither woman picked it up.

'Any help you can give me – I'd be very grateful.'

A year went past, but no word came from the Minjungbal Centre. I wasn't surprised or annoyed. It wasn't as if I had a right to their help. I kept asking around. Eventually (two years later) a magenta-haired woman selling hand-crafted wind-chimes at the Murwillumbah market told me that I needed to talk to the Bundjalung elders who would be at the next Wollumbin Festival. I Googled the festival. I wasn't sure that I was up for a multicultural celebration of 'the Indigenous connection with Mother Earth' that highlighted 'environmental awareness, healing and sustainable lifestyles' but, before I could put myself to the test, the festival collapsed.

A year or two later, when Ann was at CCRRS on one of her regular visits, one sleepy evening when I thought she was engrossed in another of the Nero Wolfe novels I had found in a second-hand bookshop at Southport, she came round the corner of the verandah to find me gazing glumly at my laptop.

'How is a woman expected to enjoy her book when you will keep sighing all the time?'

'Sorry. I've worked on the question of traditional ownership for months and I've got absolutely nowhere. Nothing about the ethnology of this region makes sense to me.'

The sun had long ago slid behind the western scarp. The bats were flying and I could hear the oom-oom-oom of the frogmouth. Cocktail hour. I got up to fetch a bottle. 'Red or white?'

Ann marked her place with a Crimson Rosella feather, and put her book away. 'Do you want to tell me about it?'

Ann is possibly the wisest person I know, and also the most patient. If anyone could help me solve the riddle of the traditional owners, it would be she.

I poured the wine, leaned back in my chair and did my best to begin at the beginning.

'The Tourism Queensland website, and all the websites derived from it, say that Natural Bridge is in the territory of the local Kombumerri people. They're supposed to be the traditional owners of the whole of the Gold Coast region, which includes the areas drained by the Logan, Albert, Coomera and Nerang Rivers and the Tallebudgera Creek. They call themselves a family of the Yugambeh.' (Best and Barlow, p. 9)

Since the 1980s, under the leadership of Uncle Graham Dillon, the Kombumerri have been recovering their cultural heritage. In 1984 Dillon organised survivors to campaign for the reburial of Kombumerri people disinterred between 1965 and 1968 from a thousand-year-old burial site at Broadbeach; the reburial of these remains in a dawn ceremony in 1987 marked a watershed for his people. The Kombumerri are now recognised as the dominant clan in the area covered by Gold Coast City which extends south to the border and the scarps of the McPherson Range. In 1996 a native title claim over the Gold Coast failed because the broader community did not support it; the same thing happened again in 1998. In 2001 Eastern Yugambeh Ltd made another claim which was opposed by a single clan. In 2006 Eastern Yugambeh Ltd joined forces with Jabree Ltd and one other and tried again. This time the claim extends south to the Tweed and west to Mount Tamborine and includes Natural Bridge.

Wesley Aird heads 400 families who claim to be descended from twelve 'apical ancestors', themselves descended from a mere six, a tiny fragment of a group that once numbered thousands, 'Joseph Blow, Coolum, George Drumley (Darramlee), Sarah Drumley (Warri), Jackey Jackey (Bilin Bilin), Mark Jackey, Harry Jackey, Nellie Jackey, John Alexander Sandy (Bungaree), Kitty Sandy (Yelganun), Slab and Kipper Tommy Andrews'. An Aboriginal man called Blow and his wife Kitty worked for the settlers on the Nerang in the 1890s and a George Blow who eventually went to live in Beaudesert was raised by the Mills family at Gilston; Drumley is the maiden name of the Kombumerri matriarch Jenny Graham; the Jackeys are all descended from Bilin Bilin, who persuaded his people to give up resistance and throw themselves on the mercy of the missions; Slab and his wife Suzan too were well known in Numinbah; Kipper Tommy Andrews is probably not the Kipper Tommy who figures in our story who was said to be Bullongin. The Gold Coast Native Title Group claims only procedural rights and only over vacant crown land. In six years no conclusion seems to have been reached, apparently because the families who lodged the first two applications refuse to accept the authority of the families now making the claim. Both sides are descended from the same handful of apical ancestors.

'What's the problem?' asked Ann.

'It doesn't add up. Descendants of a single small kin group can hardly lay claim to such a huge swathe of territory. What is more you won't find the name Kombumerri used for the people of the Nerang before 1913. They were first called Kombumerri by Bullum, whitefella name John Allen, who supplied Aboriginal translations of English words put to him by schoolmaster John Lane. Bullum's word list was published as an appendix to the Report of the Protector of Aboriginals in 1913. The name Kombumerri means "mangrove-worm eaters". Before Bullum gave them that name, the people of the Nerang were either known as the "Nerangballum" or the "Talgiburri". Archibald Meston always refers to the Nerang people as Talgiburri.'

In 1894 in a letter to the editor of the *Brisbane Courier* (21 July) Meston recounted how, in 1868, when he was seventeen, he made a pioneering journey up the Nerang and over the Darlington Range 'accompanied by a then well-known aboriginal called "Tullaman," one of the Talgiburri tribe, a fine, athletic specimen of a man.' Pioneer settler Edmund Harper responded to Meston's article, correcting his version of Tullaman's name, supplying it instead as 'Tulongmool', the 'Talgiburri' reference being allowed to stand (Q, 1 September, 410). Harper, who lived and worked with Aboriginal people, is supposed to have been fluent in a number of Aboriginal dialects. Unusually, he acknowledged a son, Billy, by an Aboriginal woman (BC, 28 June 1894). In a reply to Harper (Q, 22 September, 549) Meston repeated that Tullaman was what the Talgiburri man was always called by whites, and that, like many Aboriginal men, he worked for the cedar-getters; 'he was one of the best axemen in the district, and as a log squarer had no superior'. Meston refers to the Talgiburri again in one of the articles he wrote in 1923 for *The Queenslander* on the 'Lost Tribes of Moreton Bay' (14 July, 18):

> There were some fine men and women among the 'Talgiburri' and 'Chabbooburri' tribes of Nerang but today they are extinct. Among the Talgiburri at that time was a young Talgiburri black, about 20 years of age, very expert with the boomerang (bargann), the shield, and nulla.

This was none other than 'Lumpy Billy', so called because he had some kind of tumour on his face. He was also known as 'Yoocum Billy' because, as he spoke Yugambeh, he used the word 'yugam' for 'no'. His blackfella name was 'Dilmiann'. In the 1880s he eked out a living giving boomerang displays outside Brisbane pubs (BC, 2 October 1928 and 25 March 1931).

For months I puzzled over Meston's 'Talgiburri'. I was almost ready to give up when an interesting document turned up on line. It was called 'Turnix Report 179' and it dealt with cultural heritage issues involved in the potential development of Bahr's Scrub, which is part of Logan City. The report, written by archaeologist Eleanor Crosby, discussed what might be the identity of the traditional owners of the scrub, and how a group might call itself one thing, and be called another by its neighbours. The example she chose was that of the Kombumerri who called themselves in Meston's version 'Talgiburri' and in Margaret Sharpe's 'Dalgaybara', the people of the 'dalgay' or dry forest. It seemed obvious to me that Talgiburri (with a hard 'g') was cognate with Dalgaybara, the same word with slightly different voicing. Sharpe also thinks 'dalgay' means 'dry' as in 'dead', when I reckon the word is used the same way botanists use it now. Dry forest is sclerophyll forest.

I explained this to Ann: 'The Kombumerri called themselves people of the dry forest; Bullum called them mangrove-worm-eaters; they have since described themselves as "saltwater people".' (O'Connor) 'I can't find anything to connect them to rainforest.'

'Have you spoken to any of the Kombumerri?' asked Ann.

'When I met Uncle Graham Dillon Kombumerri at a Griffith University do, I asked him about Natural Bridge. He murmured the words "borderline" and "disputed" and then changed the subject altogether.'

Uncle Graham was then CEO of Kalwun Development Corporation, which is named for the Albert Lyrebird, that can live nowhere but in montane rainforest. The corporation runs twice-daily Paradise Dreaming Tours that take their clients to the Merrimac burial ground, to the Bora ring at Burleigh, then around the Burleigh Mountain to a midden and then to the Queensland Parks and Wildlife Service HQ to see a cultural dance. Natural Bridge is not on their itinerary.

'Every map I look at shows something different. This map was drawn by Faith Baisden for the Kombumerri Corporation in the 1990s.' (Sharpe, 1998, xiv) 'It's partly based on the map supplied with the vocabulary collected from Bullum in 1913. It's supposed to show "Yugambeh clan areas". I always thought Yugambeh was a language, but here it is being used for a people.'

'I realise that we don't use the word "tribe" any more,' said Ann. 'Is that just political correctness or what?'

'I think it's more just correctness. The Yugambeh peoples are exogamous, I think. They had to marry out of their own clans, so there was a constant interchange between clans. The clans are not in competition with each other, though they did stage stereotyped combats of different kinds on special occasions. So it's wrong to describe them as tribes. Still, lots of people do, including Aboriginal people.' (Powell and Hesline, 116)

I sipped my wine while Ann studied the map. She shook her head. 'It shows the Kombumerri on the lower Nerang, nowhere near

Natural Arch. Or Bridge or whatever the dickens it's called. We're here, right?'

Ann pointed to a dotted area on the map that extended southwards from the heads of the Nerang River and Tallebudgera Creek, deep into the Mount Warning caldera. It included the Natural Bridge and was labelled 'Birinburra'.

She went on. 'That's pretty straightforward. All you have to do is find the Birinburra.'

'If this map was correct the Birinburra would have to be leaping up and down the ring dykes of the caldera like chamois. Most of that country is downright uninhabitable. The people who were said to live on the south side of the northern rim of the caldera were the Tul-gi-gin. That's according to Joshua Bray, who arrived in the Tweed in 1863. I would have said Talgiburri are the same as Tul-gig-in, the root word is "talgi-" or "tulgi-", cognate with "dalgay", while "-gin" is a plural, and "-burri" is a version of "-bara" or "-burra". With Australian ethnolinguists, nothing is that easy. Margaret Sharpe persists in thinking "tulgi-" is the name of an unidentified species of tree, even though she lists Talgiburri as a version of Dalgaybara.'

'Who's Margaret Sharpe?'

'She's the acknowledged expert on the Yugambeh language. She began recording language at Woodenbong in the Sixties and she's been working on it ever since.'

Arthur Groom (*ADB*) who came to Numinbah in the 1920s used the name 'Brinburra' for the Kombumerri themselves. He wrote in 1949 that 'between the Wangerriburras and the coast, the smaller Nerang or Kombumerri tribe, sometimes known as Brinburra, was hemmed within a walled valley; but these people wandered round the foothills as far as the base of Mount Warning.' Groom would be very surprised to learn that his small Kombumerri group now claims the whole Gold Coast from the Logan to the Tweed.

'Here's another map, based on accounts given to a student called Hausfeldt in the Fifties by people from Woodenbong. The whole caldera and all the land east of the Nerang River is shown as territory of the "Nerangbul". The "Minyungbal" are shown as occupying all the land between the Nerang River and the Albert, and all the land

between the Albert and the Logan is labelled "Yukumbear".'
(Hausfeldt)

'What a mess,' said Ann. 'On the Kombumerri Corporation map
the Minjungbal are shown at the mouth of the Tweed, and on
Hausfeldt's map there are no Minjungbal, only Minyungbal way
further inland and way further north, right up to the mouth of the
Logan.'

'Which doesn't make sense because, according to Sharpe, the
Minjungbal and the Minyungbal are the same people.' (1998, 2)

'Did you say Sharpe started work in Woodenbong? The
Kombumerri Corporation map doesn't go that far west.'

'I know. These days the Woodenbong people call themselves
Githabul, and don't call their language Bundjalung or even
Yugambeh. Sharpe believes in a Bundjalung dialect chain, but the
Githabul emphatically deny that any such thing exists. Tourism
Queensland might say that the natural bridge is in the territory of the
local Kombumerri Aboriginal people, but I still don't know why
they think the Kombumerri are local.'

'So if the custodians are not Kombumerri what would they be?'

'North of the stateline you hear only of Kombumerri. They never
mention the Bundjalung and the Bundjalung never refer to them.
According to the Bundjalung Elders Council Aboriginal Corporation's
website, the Bundjalung arrived from far northern Australia
somewhere around 6000 BC and occupied the region extending from
the Logan River in Queensland to as far south as the Clarence River
in northern New South Wales and west to the Great Dividing
Range.'

Ann was astonished. 'But that means they both claim the Gold
Coast! The Kombumerri must be a part of the Bundjalung.'

'Which is why I toddled off to Tweed Heads to talk to the people
at the Minjungbal Centre. The people involved in reviving the
language of the Kombumerri now deny that Yugambeh is part of the
same language group even.' (Best and Barlow, 11)

'Wait a minute,' said Ann, who had Norman Tindale's map of the
distribution of Australian tribes at the time of contact unfolded on
the table. 'Tindale has the "Badjalang" much further down the coast.
Between the "Jugambe" and the Badjalang there are the "Arakwal",

the "Widjabal", the "Katibal" and the "Minjungbal", and their terri-
tories are all roughly the same size. Tindale certainly thought the
Yugambeh were just one tribe among many. The people he puts in
Numinbah are the "Kalibal".'

Tindale's Catalogue of Australian Aboriginal Tribes calls the
Kalibal 'a rainforest frequenting people' with a territory based on the
McPherson Range, extending north from near Unumgar in New
South Wales to Christmas Creek in Queensland, east to the Upper
Nerang Valley and south to Mount Cougal and the Tweed Range,
Tyalgum and the Brunswick River divide.

'So we're in Kalibal country. Where does that leave the Birinburra?'

'I think Birinburra has to be another name for the same people.
Clans have self names that they use for themselves, while other clans
call them by different names.'

For some time I had been really puzzled to find that the word
'birin' in various spellings kept turning up where I didn't expect it.
In his book *Wollumbin*, Norman Keats included among the
Bundjalung dialects and their speakers 'Birhin/Birhinbal'. To my
surprise these people turned out to be swamp-dwellers who lived
south-east of Casino, along the Summerland Way and westward to
beyond Rappville. Keats remarks ruefully, 'Little is known of the
Birhin people in general.' In L. P. Winterbotham's account of the
recollections of Gaiarbau, the last man of the Jinibara who was born
in Kilcoy way to the north, Gaiarbau lists 'the Jukambe (Jugambeir),
the Jagarbal (Jugarabul) and the Kitabel (Gitabal) tribes, who together
were known as Biri:n people'. Suddenly I knew what 'birin' meant
and why I would never find a clan calling itself by that name. It
simply meant 'south' or 'southern' (Sharpe, 1998). Among the people
called southern by the Queensland clans living north of the McPherson
Range were the Kalibal.

'What do we know about the Kalibal?' asked Ann.

'That they're sometimes spelt Galibal. That's about it. They're
supposed to have hunted pademelons, possums and birds, and used
Bangalow Palm fronds as water containers and the fibres of stingers
to make nets, but I don't know what the hard evidence is for that.
From the 1840s they were made to pick out the best stands of Hoop
Pine and Red Cedar for the timber-getters, but by the 1870s settlers

had driven them off the land altogether and they were reduced to living in camps. I reckon they'd see themselves as a clan of the Githabul.'

'So they're way to the west of Natural Bridge?'

'As of now their territory begins on the western side of the caldera and Natural Bridge is on the north face of the northern side, but Tindale, who worked on his map from the 1920s until it was published in 1974, gives the Kalibal the whole Mount Warning caldera and Numinbah.'

'Which means that Kalibal territory straddles the border,' said Ann, 'which is what you would expect, no?'

The area called Numinbah is shaped like an hourglass with the top in Queensland and the bottom in New South Wales and the Numinbah Gap at its narrowest part. It extends northwards from the north bank of the Rous River in New South Wales through the Numinbah Gap to the junction of Pine Creek with the Nerang River in Queensland. The single name certainly suggests a single people.

'What does Numinbah mean?'

'A blackfella called Numinbah Johnnie is supposed to have told Frank Nixon, the first white settler, that it meant place of devils. I reckon he was just trying to put him off.'

Numinbah Johnny, known to his own people as Bulgoojera, was real enough. He was said to be 'a smart fellow' who 'could do mental arithmetic to the astonishment and sometimes to the discomfiture of the white timber-getters'. Two of Bulgoojera's sons were fine athletes. The boys ended up at Deebing Creek mission station, where they died of tuberculosis (Gresty, 62). Nobody seems to know what became of their father.

'The Kombumerri Aboriginal Corporation for Culture says that in Yugambeh "Numinbah" means "shelter".'

'What does Sharpe say?'

Ann fetched the *Dictionary of Yugambeh*. 'She doesn't have any word meaning "shelter". She says "nyamin" means small palm tree or "midjim".'

'Midyim is certainly the Yugambeh name for the Walking-stick Palm, which is endemic to the Numinbah Valley. If that's the root of the name, it should be Nyuminbah.'

Ann worked her way back and forth between the word-list and the sources. 'It isn't Nyumminbah, is it?' She was beginning to sound testy. 'All this high-handed re-spelling is getting me down. The only source Sharpe gives is W. E. Hanlon, who collected words from pre-existing records and from Jenny Graham.' (Sharpe, 1998, 145, Hanlon)

'Everything and everyone is connected to Jenny Graham. She's a daughter of George Drumley or Darramlee. She seems to have borne her first child to Andrew Graham, a river pilot on the Southport Broadwater, in 1873; she married in 1898, and most of the Kombumerri claimants are descended from her surviving children. The entire Kombumerri Corporation for Culture are descendants of Jenny Graham.'

'Did she have any direct connection with Numinbah?'

'I can't see that she did. She grew up in Beaudesert, which seems to have been the last stronghold of the Yugambeh speakers. Then she lived in Southport. Died in 1945. The most authoritative account of the Numinbah Aborigines has to be the one given by Jack Gresty in 1947, and he says that the local aborigines had died out twenty-five years earlier.' (Gresty, 69)

Gresty, who worked for the Queensland Forestry Department, spent much of his time in Numinbah. He also had the benefit of information from William Duncan's sons who were brought up with the local Aborigines and spoke their languages. I foraged in a drawer and pulled out a file: 'This is Gresty's version, "The real significance of the word 'Numinbah' was that the aborigines believed that the narrow valley held the mountains tightly together. The tribe had two highly prized hunting dogs; one was named 'Numinbah' – 'hold him tight' – and the other 'Wundburra' ('Wunburra') – 'climb upwards'. " ' (Gresty, 60)

'Is there any support for that?' asked Ann.

'Sharpe lists a word "naminbah" as meaning "hold on", saying that it's derived from "southern dialects", and she gives two authorities as quoted in *Science of Man* in 1904, and doesn't notice the occurrence in Gresty. And she doesn't notice the geographical name either. Weird.'

I got up to put together the salad for our supper as Ann worked her way through Gresty's word-list, which she was trying to compare with Sharpe's. 'I think there is a significant group of words for which Sharpe has no authority but Gresty, which would be Numinbah words rather than Nerang words, but the spelling is so peculiar it's hard to be sure. Gresty is the only source for the names of some trees—'

I paused in the rinsing of the lettuce. 'Such as?'

Ann read from the notes she had made, 'Black Apple, Red Bean, Crow's Ash, Native Elm, Red Carabeen, Black Myrtle, Pink Tulip Oak.'

'Brilliant. All rainforest species, and none of them listed by any other informant. I've spent hours scanning the other Yugambeh/ Bundjalung word lists and there's only a few words that relate to rainforest. The trees they have names for are eucalypts, banksias, wattles; the animals are animals of the open forest.'

'Well you did say that the Kombumerri called themselves "people of the dry forest". That part makes sense at least.'

'The problem is that the rainforest vocab might be missing because the compiler didn't ask about rainforest species, not because the respondent didn't have names for them. Still. It's a clue. What's the word given for Crow's Ash?'

'Um . . . "bulbar" – that's Sharpe's version of Gresty's "bulburra".'

'Crow's Ash is a Flindersia; the usual name given for the Flindersias is "cudgerie", supposed to be from the Bundjalung "gajari". Gresty's word is completely different.'

Ann hunted through Sharpe as I laid the table.

'Found it! Sharpe routinely changes "g" to "k". She's got an entry "kadhir", which she says is a location name from a type of tree, "cudgery tree". Her source supplies "Cudherygun where the cudgeree trees grow". She expands that saying that it grows on a clear hill above Tyalgun, Murwillumbah area.'

'Tyalgum, she means. Gresty gives her that word, for a fighting chieftain; she changes it to "dayalgam" and then says that "kayalgam" is the more likely form.'

'And then spells the gazetted place-name wrong.'

Ann closed the book with a snap and we sat down to supper.

Early the next morning I brought Ann her morning cup of hot water and lemon, and asked her to come with me to the Natural

Bridge. We left the car by the causeway, walked up through the rainforest along the creek, where in the dawn twilight we surprised a pademelon and her joey feeding on fallen fruit. At every step the roar of the water plunging through the hole in the roof of the cave grew louder. The air was clammy and dank. As we climbed up the path leading to the cave we could feel the ground shuddering beneath our feet. We stepped into the gloom of the cave. Ann wrapped her arms across her chest. I zipped my body-warmer up to my chin. We had no desire to creep under the guardrail, but stood motionless, awed by the white column of falling water and its reflection trembling on the black waters of the pool. The energy contained within the space is massive and utterly intimidating. Tourists however are seldom intimidated. As far as tourism is concerned the place is a mere curiosity.

As we walked out of the roar of the falling water and back down the creek, Ann shivered.

'Disturbing, isn't it?'

'Definitely,' said Ann.

I turned off the track and led Ann into the forest. I cautioned her to be careful round a group of young stingers. 'See that?'

I was pointing at an anvil-shaped rock, with a smaller rock sitting on top of it. Ann picked up the smaller rock. A black spider ran for its life.

'It's got a hole in the side that my thumb just fits into,' she said. 'And it's dead flat.'

'Rub it across the stone.'

She did, and a bright red streak was suddenly uncovered.

'Ochre,' she said. 'Is there ochre round here?'

'There is, but not this close to the creek. I've known about this stone since the first week I was here. Every time I come here I check it, and it's always undisturbed. The black spider is always under the pestle.'

Ann stood up. 'You think it's a mortar and pestle. For grinding ochre. Body paint.'

'The way I see it there's simply no chance that Aboriginal people didn't know about the waterfall, the cavern and the pool, or that they hadn't invested the place with special significance. Groom says

"The natives knew the place well and kept away from it." [66] Deep as it is in the creek gorge, it would have been easy to keep secret from all but the initiated.'

'Why would it need to be secret?'

'Because it would have to be sacred. Think about the topography, the deep gorge, the joining arch of rock, the wide, low cavern, the thunderous shaft of water. It's like an image of titanic intercourse.'

'Or something,' said Ann, looking back to the creek.

> But oh! that deep romantic chasm which slanted
> Down the green hill athwart a cedarn cover!

She chanted, and I joined in:

> A savage place! As holy and enchanted
> As e'er beneath a waning moon was haunted
> By woman wailing for her daemon lover!

'Coleridge would have got it,' I said.

'Coleridge was a junkie,' said Ann.

'I still reckon this is a sacred site,' said I stubbornly.

I didn't utter the words that were uppermost in my mind. 'Secret women's business' are the most ridiculed three words in a nation given to ridiculing anything it cannot understand. In 1995 the struggle of Ngarrindjeri women to prevent a bridge being built from the mainland to Hindmarsh Island at the mouth of the Murray River was quashed by the finding of a Royal Commission that the evidence of the women was fabricated. In 2001, when the developers sought compensation for the cost of delays in building the bridge caused by the Indigenous people's opposition, a Federal Court found for the women, who claimed that the island had a special significance as a burial ground. Then in December 2002 workmen laying cables for the redevelopment of the wharf at Goolwa dug up the skeletal remains of a Ngarrindjeri woman and her daughter. The secret was manifest in the topography if only the developers had had eyes to see. The last time I was there, there was no water under the bridge the whitefellas had been so desperate to build. The pleasure craft moored under it were locked in dried mud.

Ann was on to me. 'You're thinking women's business, aren't you?'

'Yep. If you'd been a man I wouldn't have shown you the mortar. My guess is that the cave was a place of serious women's business, even of pilgrimage in time of special need. Infertility. Unwanted pregnancy. Maybe even infanticide. That's why I made you get up early. I never go to the Natural Bridge unless I can be fairly certain the tourists aren't there.'

Later in the day, when Ann had gone back to the lounger and her Rex Stout mystery and I was once more scowling at my laptop, I threw myself back in my chair.

'There's something odd about the way the natural bridge was found.'

Ann left her book on the lounger and pulled a chair up next to me. 'Such as what?'

'Whitefella history says that the natural bridge was "discovered" in 1893 by a white man called "Sandy" Duncan. He and his mate "Din" Guinea were cutting cedar round here. With them was a Bullongin man called Kipper Tommy. Duncan is supposed to have scrambled down to the creek for water for the billy and come upon the stone bridge by accident.'

'So what's the problem?'

'Guinea and Duncan have employed Kipper Tommy, right? So what's his job?'

'Well, he picks out the cedar, and brushes the tracks to get to it, stuff like that.'

'One of the things he definitely does have to do is to find drinking water.'

'So?'

'So why did Sandy Duncan end up scrambling down a steep rocky slope to fill the billy?'

'OK. I'll play,' said Ann. 'Why did Sandy Duncan have to go look for water himself? Because Kipper Tommy wouldn't?'

'Exactly. He probably said something about bunyips or devils or something.'

'Because – why?'

'Because he knew the place was sacred. That it was secret. That would be enough, but it may also have been something that was death for a man to look upon.'

'But how would he have known?'

'That would depend on how far he'd got in the initiation process. The name Kipper refers to the initiation ceremony. Jack Gresty says that "kippera" was the local word for a youth, "between boyhood and manhood" [64]. Tommy was known as Kipper Tommy all his life. "Kipper Tommy" is one of the condescending nicknames that whitefellas bestowed on Aboriginal men indiscriminately, so we can't assume just on that evidence that his initiation was never completed.'

Everybody in the Numinbah Valley knew Kipper Tommy, who eked out a living doing odd jobs for various white settlers. A correspondent who calls him 'head of the Coomera tribe' provided the following reminiscence to the *Gold Coast Bulletin*:

> On a wet morning when us children went downstairs for breakfast, our old Aborigine friend Kipper Tomy would be there at the warm end of the kitchen . . . One Sunday morning my brother George and I . . . called at Tomy's camp. His living quarters were a couple of sheets of bark leaning up against a log.
>
> He was sitting by the fire with his two dogs, Carum (meaning a fast dog) and Trampum (meaning a slow walker) and cooking a goanna . . .
>
> Not long after seeing him in the camp he called at our home limping badly and showed Dad a big growth on his groin and he had a sharp piece of broken glass with him to open it. He would not let Dad take him to a doctor, and we never saw him any more, so it had to be goodbye Kipper. (Hall *et al.*, 34)

Numinbah farmer Tom Cowderoy, who calls Tommy 'King of the small Coomera tribe', is clearly talking about the same person.

> His wife was called Ginny and they were both very fond of tobacco. They carried their pipes along in the hope of being able to beg some tobacco. If Tommy should happen to be given any, he would have to give Ginny her share. They had a son called Peter. Kipper also had two dogs called Corum and Trampum.

Occasionally he would make a friendly visit to the Numinbah blacks with his tribe and then there would be great feasting on the plentiful supply of Queensland nuts, the fish and wild game that was abundant in the valley in those days. (Hall *et al.*, 54)

The Bullongin of Coomera were a clan rather than a tribe, and did not have a 'king'. A 'Kipper Tommy' is mentioned in one account as one of a group of six Aboriginal boys who were kidnapped and taken by the Native Police to Port Douglas to be trained as trackers. The boys eventually escaped, walking all the way home (Gresty, 64). Other versions of the story identify the place as Port Denison, and do not mention a Kipper Tommy. The Numinbah Kipper Tommy is thought to have died in about 1904. He and his wife are said to have been buried 'at the back of Nerang Cemetery' but no trace of their graves can now be found (Hall *et al.*, 28, 31–2, 54).

'We don't have any evidence that Aboriginal people avoided the Natural Bridge, do we?' asked Ann.

'There is a bit. Gresty says that Aboriginal mothers told their children not to hang round near the cliffs.' In Gresty's own words, ' "Do not go near the cliffs," they would say, "for if you do, Koonimbagowgunn will roll rocks down on you." . . . When a boulder, loosened by rain or weathering, would be heard in the camp, especially at night, coming down with a tremendous roar and a thump, mothers would say to the little ones, "There's old Koonimbagowgunn again! . . . Remember to keep away from the cliffs, so that she cannot roll one down on top of you".' (67)

Koonimbagowgunn, spelt 'kunimbuggaugunn', turns up in Bullum's Wangerriburra vocabulary (Allen). And Steele, who says the name means 'widow', claims that Koonimbagowgunn's realm was the cliffs between Dave's Creek, which is directly opposite CCRRS on the other side of the Nerang River, and Ships Stern (Steele, Sharpe, 122, cf. Gresty, 67); a map of Lamington National Park printed in 1982 shows a part of the west face of Ships Stern actually labelled 'Koonimbagowan'. In 1890 a series of huge landslides following months of heavy rain totally transformed the cliffscape between Turtle Rock and Nixon Creek. Tom Cowderoy's father told him that he used to be woken up at night 'by the noise of these landslides – great boulders, some as big as a house, giving way after the heavy rain and thundering down the cliffs' (Cowderoy).

I went on thinking aloud. 'It's odd that Aboriginal people haven't claimed any connection with a natural feature as conspicuous as the Natural Bridge. I see hundreds of tourists every time I go in or out but never an Aboriginal person. I mention the place to two Aboriginal women in an information centre and they blank me. I've lost count of the number of Aboriginal people who've said they would ask their grandparents and didn't get back to me.'

'But didn't Aboriginal people travel through here?'

'I don't think they did. You remember Meston's account of being taken over the mountains by Tullaman? It's only just struck me that Tullaman didn't take him through Numinbah.' In the account of this excursion which he sent to the editor of the *Brisbane Courier* in 1894, Meston says that he and Tullaman crossed the river where Nerang now stands and followed a branch of it to where it ended 'in a beautiful waterfall wreathing its flashing waters over dark basaltic rock', from which point they climbed up to the 'top of the Darlington Plateau' which had not yet been named for Lord Lamington, and turned westwards, ending up on the summit of a bare mountain at the head of the Tweed.

We are now slowly beginning to understand that Aboriginal peoples put a great deal of effort into managing their lands, by keeping certain areas clear by the use of fire, so that fresh grass attracted game. People travelling through their territories had perforce to hunt and kill the same game for themselves and so had to seek permission from the traditional owners. They had also to stick to specified routes. To travel from the caldera to the Bunya nut festival, for example, the Githabul crossed the range using scrub tunnels running along a spur of Mount Durigan and then travelled north down the Albert River (Steele). The peoples of the Nerang and the Tweed travelled to the Bunya feasting northwards along the beaches to the shores of Moreton Bay before turning inland.

There used to be a corroboree ground near the Pine Creek Bridge on a flat called Tagaballum. A huge number of Aboriginal artefacts, stone blades, axeheads and stone fragments has been found nearby. What this could indicate is that groups gathering there mounted large-scale hunts where pademelons, a favourite food source, were driven from the edges of the forest into waiting nets or on to waiting spears. More important probably is the bora ring described by John Shirley in 1910 as 'at Munninba, between the selections of Hon. J. G. Appel and Mr Alexander Duncan'; 'Munninba' is a mistake for Numinbah. In 1910 the Duncans owned Portion 10v adjoining Appel's Portion 56, a mile upstream from the junction of Nixon Creek and the Nerang. The earthworks nowadays called bora rings served as sites for all kinds of public gatherings besides the initiation ceremony or 'bora' – 'kippera' in Yugambeh. The presence of earthen rings in Numinbah implies that it was a centre of clan activities.

'Tullaman must have taken Meston up a track well north of the Numinbah Gap because they ended up on the Lamington Plateau.' Meston says Tullaman took him 'south along the tableland towards the Macpherson Range, through dense scrub and rich basalt soil, dining on turkeys, wongan, bandicoots, carpet snakes, tree grubs, yams, young palm shoots, paddymella and turkey eggs' (BC, 21 July 1894). What this tells us is that the Talgiburri knew how to use rainforest game and foodstuffs. Generally speaking these foods are taken at the forest edge rather than in the deep forest, while carpet snakes and bandicoots can be found in the dry forest as well as rainforest. Some caution must be exercised with Meston's account. Meston was a promoter and a self-promoter, who was extraordinarily careless with his facts. His dates, names and places are often misremembered, and there is now no way of checking them. He was wrong about the year he crossed the Darlington Range, and wrong about one of the two men who went with him. He may also have been wrong about the way they went and what they ate. He does not include flying foxes, for example, which were typical rainforest game, and very easily taken.

'Meston said in 1928 that the Talgiburri and the Chabooburri were extinct. What happened to them?'

'The original smallpox epidemic in 1789 is thought to have killed half to seventy per cent of the Aboriginal population around Port Jackson; it is also thought to have extended far beyond the original area of contact [Mear]. We may assume that old people were more susceptible, and that's your Dreaming, your knowledge, your culture annihilated right there. Three further epidemics are recorded – smallpox in 1831, influenza in 1858 and dysentery in 1865. Measles would have been a killer too, and whooping cough was around as well. Such disasters cause clans to collapse and force them to amalgamate. Besides, dispersal was a deliberate policy of the whites. Timber-getters made a point of employing non-local Aborigines who could not conspire with their clansmen against them. Generally coastal groups of hunter-gatherers are semi-settled but this is a period when Aboriginal people are being driven from pillar to post and back again, ending up all over the place, anywhere they can find a livelihood. And it's worse than that. Untold numbers of Aboriginal people were simply murdered. Even Gresty, who was a government employee, refers to "deliberate measures for their extermination, with either official sanction or connivance" [69]. If the blacks "got bad", which is how the settlers referred to resistance to expropriation, it was legitimate to eliminate them. The settlers either killed the Aborigines themselves or got the Native Police to do it for them [Lumholtz, 53–4, 262]. It was no secret. Did you ever hear of the Hornet Bank Massacre?'

'Isn't that where the Aborigines were given poisoned Christmas puddings?'

'Yep. The Frasers also shot eleven of the local Yeeman people for spearing cattle, and they interfered with the Yeeman women. The Yeeman waited until the Fraser menfolk were away to take a horrifyingly brutal revenge. The son and heir, William Fraser, then embarked on the extermination of the whole Yeeman clan, plus any other Aborigine who got in the way. He's supposed to have killed three hundred people, most of them before witnesses, in broad daylight. A year later, 1858, the Yeeman were said to be extinct.'

'Was Fraser ever brought to trial?'

'No. Aborigines couldn't be bound by an oath on the Bible, so only evidence from a white man was admissible, and no white man would give evidence against him. Mass killings of Aborigines had been happening for years. There was no comeback. And no denying what had happened. It was in fact systematic extermination.'

The Hornet Bank outrage was by no means the first. There was a mass poisoning of about fifty people in the Brisbane Valley in 1842. In the same year, when one of the Gössner missionaries at Zion's Hill was told that fifty or sixty Kabi Kabi people had been poisoned by flour given to them at Kilcoy Station, a hundred kilometres or so north-west of Brisbane, he confided the matter to his journal until he could safely reveal it. The Aboriginal people meanwhile spread the news of the atrocity far and wide. Flour left in shepherd's huts was so apt to be poisoned that the Aboriginal people who helped themselves to it ate only enough to see whether fits came on, and if they did drank salt water until they saved themselves by being sick (Petrie, 208–9). When the Kilcoy massacre became known to the authorities, the attorney-general threatened prosecution but no official complaint was ever lodged and the perpetrator was never apprehended (Kidd, *passim*).

Word of the slaughter of Aboriginal peoples had already reached London, where the newly founded Aborigines' Protection Society had in 1838 published the findings of a Select Parliamentary Committee as *Information Respecting the Aborigines in British Colonies*. From 1847 it published *The Aborigines' Friend or Colonial Intelligencer*. The members of the society were quite clear that Aboriginal peoples had rights under common law, including the right to territory, and that the expropriation of the Australian Aboriginal peoples was illegal. However there was little they could do to protect the rights of indigenous Australians. When seven of the eleven men responsible for the Myall Creek massacre at Inverell in northern New South Wales were found guilty and hanged, the settlers adopted a code of silence. Meanwhile it was relatively easy to make a case for justification when Aboriginal people were gunned down. Without modern weapons Aboriginal people could offer little resistance; if they stole weapons, which was the only way they could obtain them, they could be pursued and killed with complete impunity.

The poisoning at Kilcoy Station was in the news again in the 1860s when general concern about the decline in the Queensland Aboriginal population began to be expressed. In 1861 Lieutenant Wheeler of the Native Police was happy to assure an official inquiry that he had dispersed the Moreton Bay blacks (Rowley, i:167); what he meant was that he and the Native Police under his command had killed them. The *Colonial Intelligencer* for March 1868 reported 'that if the native police . . . had been properly organised for the purpose of extirpating the aborigines, they could not accomplish that object more effectually.' The *Daily Guardian* reported on 8 August 1863:

> The old Brisbane tribe of blacks which once numbered over 1000 fighting men is now nearly extinct. Their language has disappeared, and they are now compelled to have recourse to the dialect of the Wide Bay natives, who have poured in to occupy the hunting grounds left vacant by the speedy decrease in numbers of the Brisbane tribe. Six years ago, 1500 blacks might be seen at a corroboree. Now however it would be a difficult matter to muster 500. These results cannot be wholly ascribed to natural causes; they must be the effect of some process of extermination that has risen to the rank of an established institution among us. Not many years ago half a tribe of blacks was destroyed by arsenic, generously administered to them by a squatter, through a present of flour.

The Aborigines Protection Society reported in 1868 that 'the aborigines of Australia have, in many districts, been exterminated by the combined agency of strong drink, imported diseases, and the squatter's rifle'. Nowhere was this combination more effective than in south-east Queensland.

Ann headed back to Melbourne, and I went on struggling with the contradictory history of the devastated peoples of the Gold Coast hinterland.

Meston does not mention encountering any indigenous people on his safari through the rainforest. Tindale was not the only person who believed that they would have been Kalibal or Gilibal, who spoke a variety of the Bundjalung language called Dinggabal. When Arthur Capell visited Woodenbong in 1960 to make recordings of spoken Dinggabal, he described the language as Yugambeh/ Yugumbir. The Kalibal may also be the same people as the Dijabal, the Kidabal, the Kitabool, the Kitabal, the Kuttibal, the Galibal, the Gidabal, the Gidabul, the Gidabhal, the Gidjabal, the Gidjubal, the Gilival, the Gulivul and the Githabul. What nobody is very clear about is whether they are Bundjalung. The question is material.

The Bundjalung Council of Elders Aboriginal Corporation, based in Lismore, is one of the first such councils to be incorporated, as long ago as 1989. As incorporated representatives of the Indigenous population the elders' council is eligible to receive grants from a variety of sources, for a vast range of activities, acquiring land, developing educational and health programmes, staging events, raising the profile of the group, providing legal assistance where necessary, developing infrastructure, promoting art, performance and music, developing cultural media and educational material, recording and teaching languages, accumulating and keeping records, protecting and managing sacred sites and artefacts. An Aboriginal Corporation can be a source of considerable wealth to a comparatively small self-selecting body of people.

The Bundjalung claim Mount Warning by default because, they say, 'the Wollumbin tribe was massacred back in the 1860s'. According to the website of Wollumbin Dowsing there was a massacre:

> where the bodies of the men women and children had been mutilated and hacked into pieces which so distressed the people who discovered the massacre that they lit up beacon fires all around Mt Warning to call in all the clans to come to this place and to perform funeral rites to try and restore dignity for the victims . . . all the clever men also known as men of high degree of initiation, were assembled and sat down for 3 days and 3 nights to sing a curse into the land that would last for all time . . . The death song or curse is still being sung today from the spirit world and can be discerned by anyone who is into their listening and dowsers will find 5 metre squares of discharging energy all around.

There is no record of any such massacre in the 1860s, which cannot be taken to mean that no such thing happened, but from this description the killing must have been done with axes and clubs, which does not suggest an outrage perpetrated by Europeans. Though developers are nowadays required to consult heritage experts before applying for planning permission for new developments along the Tweed, no objection was made to a new luxury lifestyle 'Nightcap Village' development at Mebbin Springs on the exact site of the purported massacre (*Koori Mail*, 29 January 2009).

Aboriginal survivors who have consulted both government archives and their own elders are now demanding withdrawal of rights and privileges from groups claiming to be Bundjalung and the restoration of their traditional lands to the distinct peoples of the caldera. Chief among the peoples now claiming their birthright are the Githabul, some of whom accuse the Bundjalung of cultural genocide, claiming that the '(Ngarakwal/Githabul) and the other distinct peoples of the Northern New South Wales, South East Queensland region are being subject to forced assimilation as Bundjalung'. The Githabul are now emerging as the dominant clan group along the Border ranges, with law and history on their side.

In February 2007, the Federal Court of Australia found for the Githabul people against the crown, and recognised their title to 1,120 square kilometres of national parks and state forests in northern New South Wales. The Githabul were represented by Trevor Close, who had been given financial and legal assistance in training as a native title lawyer and presenting the claim by the Canadian government. It was the first time any native title claim had succeeded in New South Wales. The Githabul won because they passed the state government's 'credible evidence test'. They were able to bring forward not only their language, which is still spoken, but also continuous family histories supported by documentary evidence from the United Aborigines Mission. As well as lands in New South Wales the Githabul claimed the summit of Mount Lindesay, which lay beyond the border in Queensland. In September that year the Beattie government recognised that claim as well. On 29 November 2007, on Woodenbong Common, Justice Catherine Branson signed the Indigenous Land Use Agreement that recognised the Githabul title.

When it happened I rang Ann and gave her as good an account as I could of the Githabul negotiations, because she has a lifetime of training negotiators behind her and I knew she'd be interested.

'Close didn't claim any private property, not even crown leasehold. Apparently native title claimants may not lay claim to freehold land or even to crown land in current leasehold, which seems unfair, to say the least.'

'How near did they get to Cave Creek?'

'They got a chunk of the Border Ranges National Park which brings them to the western edge of the Lamington plateau. I don't think they'll stop there, because they claim the Ngarakwal/

Ngandawul as a moiety and that gives them an interest in Mount Warning.'

The success of the Githabul claim is by no means the end of the story. On August 31 2009 Ngarakwal/Githabul activists made a submission to the Tweed Shire Council protesting against the perpetuation of the Bundjalung myth, the misuse of information from Indigenous elders and the lie of the dual identity of Mount Warning. According to Githabul elder Harry Boyd, Mount Warning is not Wollumbin the cloud-catcher and has nothing to do with any warrior king. The whole caldera is Wulambiny Momoli or 'scrub turkey nest', a 'djurebil' or increase site where hunting is forbidden so that Brush-turkeys may replenish their numbers. He and his supporters denounced the 'Bundjalung nation' as a white fiction. 'There is no Bundjalung nation, tribe, people, language, culture, clan, nor horde. No Bundjalung anything.'

It was my turn to visit Ann in Melbourne, where I gave her a progress report.

'The Ngarakwal, Tindale's Arakwal, now say that the real Bundjalung are the Clarence River people; they also say that the Tweed Bundjalung are well aware that they are descendants of Islanders, and not Aboriginal at all.'

'Is that true?' asked Ann.

'Who would know? These days you daren't even ask the question. Most people would say it's immaterial. Islanders lived with Aboriginal people and married into the clans, so they are entitled to self-identify. Besides the Torres Strait Islands are Australian.'

Ann frowned. 'People were blackbirded from all over the South Seas. They weren't all Australian by any means. Still. What next?'

'Uncle Harry Boyd says he's preparing a title claim that will cover as far as Nerang.'

Ann laughed. 'Well, that should answer your questions once for all. Is Close involved?'

'Close has gone to Western Australia. He had some sort of dust-up with his people, and he's gone.'

'What happened?'

'There was a meeting of the Githabul Elders Council in Kyogle in April 2009, where Close wanted to raise issues about the handling of public money by the corporation. Apparently the director of the elders' council took exception; according to Close, he and his three sons waylaid Close on his way out of the meeting, forced him back into the hall and knocked him to the ground. Twenty or thirty people then gave him a hiding and he only escaped serious injury because his aunts intervened. This was the bloke who had had the biggest win of any native title claimant ever in New South Wales, on the floor, getting a belting from the people he'd been working for for sixteen years.'

'That's a terrible story,' said Ann.

'That's not all. The elders made a complaint to the police and Close found himself up on a charge of assault. He had the bad luck to come up in March 2010 in front of a magistrate who disbelieved his testimony which was disputed by the community. Close's aunts denied that he had been forced to the ground, or that they had had to protect him. Close ended up with a criminal conviction and was released on bond.'

'You need to talk to him, don't you?' said Ann.

'I'm not sure. I haven't been able to track him down. Now that he's said to be working in the resources industry I'm not sure that I want to.'

'There's one big stone still unturned. You ought to drop in to IATSIS on your way home.'

So I did.

The Institute of Aboriginal and Torres Strait Islander Studies is part of the Australian Museum complex, a range of handsome black buildings on the bank of Lake Burley Griffin. When I rang about the deposit made by the Ngarakwal people about the caldera, I found out that it had been placed on closed access. The issue had become so heated and the language so inflammatory that I would have to ask permission of the authors before I could see it. There were other things I could see, and the librarians, who could not have been more helpful, made sure that I did.

I was struggling to decipher an old microfilm of 'Bundjalung Social Organisation', the 1959 Sydney University Ph.D. thesis of anthropologist Malcolm Calley, when I read:

The McPherson Ranges seem to have restricted intercourse between New South Wales and Queensland clans: besides being rugged and inhospitable they were infested with <u>boiun</u> (<u>ogres</u>) and <u>derangan</u> (<u>ogresses</u>) whom only the accomplished magician would dare face. Most <u>boiun</u> were <u>brothers</u> of the clansmen in whose country they lived and would not harm them, but at least some of the McPherson <u>boiun</u> had no such affiliation and so were doubly dangerous. Of one of these, <u>Ililarng</u>, it was said that 'he had no friends'. It seems that no clan occupied the mountains themselves and that parties travelling to Queensland bunya feasts avoided them and followed the beaches.

If no clan occupied the mountains themselves, then no clan claimed CCRRS. This had to be my answer, unsatisfactory though it was.

I ferreted through all Calley's boxes of papers hunting for one more scrap of information. At the bottom of the last one I came across the penny notebook where he jotted down the notes of his original conversation with his Aboriginal informant. On one page he had scribbled:

Ililarng = vampire – a spirit that removed corpses from graves by magic and fed on them – found in very rugged country – head of Albert R. Lamington. Informant Tom Close.

The name 'Ililarng' was written in phonetics. I sat still, holding the small slip of paper as if it were a sacred relic, overhearing in imagination Trevor Close's kinsman speaking seventy years ago of the lonely ghoul that is the tutelary spirit, the *genius loci* of Cave Creek. My grove is sacred to a single friendless ogre. I poked around for more information and sure enough Sharpe recognised 'boiun', though she spelt the word 'buyuny'. They are 'fairymen' who infest parts of the mountains and the clanspeople leave them to it.

Ann rang from Melbourne.

'So, who owns CCRRS?'

'I do.'

'You've only got a whitefella title bought from another whitefella. I thought you didn't believe in Australian freeholds.'

'I don't.'

Australian freehold is not a historic title testifying to generations of occupation and use of the land but created by a stroke of the pen. I held freehold title to my land for what it was worth, but I didn't think it was worth much.

'What I found out at IATSIS is that Numinbah Johnny told the truth. Numinbah is a place of demons. CCRRS is in no-man's-land.' (Holmer, 1971)

'So how does that fit with your idea that the Natural Bridge is a sacred site?'

'The buyuny are ghouls, so they'd be right at home in a killing zone. When I find a human with a better claim I'll hand it over.'

Whenever I look at the forest, and the creek, and the animals and birds who live here, it seems utterly barmy that anyone could imagine that she owned all this. Do I own the great python sliding through the forest as slowly as a glacier, or the Red-necked Pademelon that is hopping into range of those implacable jaws or the unnamed orchid that nods from the rock-ledge above them? According to Australian law I don't own any mineral wealth that lies under the soil, but apparently I can lay claim to the rare creatures that live above it. I can certainly prosecute anyone removing materials animal or vegetable from the property without my permission. The only way I can make sense of my anomalous situation is to tell myself that I don't own the forest; the forest owns me.

THE PIONEER

The person who is credited with opening up the valley of the upper Nerang is a man called Frank Nixon. Legend has it that when his property in the Tweed Valley was flooded out at the end of 1873 he went over the McPherson Range in search of pastures new, helped by Aboriginal people who showed him the way through the Numinbah Gap. This version of events may yet turn out to be historic truth, but the documentation of the Nixons and their in-laws the Brays, alongside whom Frank Nixon was living at the time, makes no mention of any flood, let alone a huge one, while Nixon's own account suggests that he found his way to the Queensland half of Numinbah by a different route altogether. Local historians tell us that he had 'the assistance of his employee Tune, a South Sea Islander or Kanaka as they were known at the time' (Hall *et al.*, 51), so Numinbah Valley had two pioneers rather than one.

The Islander's name was not 'Tune' but Toon, and he was from Ureparapara, one of the Banks Islands, now part of Vanuatu. We know this because in 1885 Frank Nixon's younger brother Arthur published a series of articles under the heading 'Sketches of the South Sea Islands', in which he sang the praises of Ureparapara:

The inhabitants make splendid servants, being intelligent, faithful, and docile. I had one many years ago, a boy called Toon, and when I found I had no more use for him I gave him to my brother, with whom he has remained ever since – a period of over ten years. No inducement would make him go back to his own country, beautiful

though it is. He reads and writes well, has his banking account – no
mean one either – and a number of cattle and horses, but added to
all he is true as steel and more faithful than a dog. (*SAR*, 18
February)

Arthur's way of praising Toon by comparing him favourably with
a dog must strike us now as repellent. Family historians are anxious
to have us believe that the Nixon family were descended from aboli-
tionists, but Arthur talks about Toon as if he was his property to give
away. As 'Nixon's employee', Toon became a well-known character
in Numinbah, often to be seen 'bringing any needed supplies up
from Nerang by packtrain' (Hall *et al.*, 51). If I am ever to decide
whether the Pioneer was a blackguard or a hero, I need to know just
what became of Toon. He is the more difficult to trace because
Toon would have been a nickname given him by his white bosses;
to trace him I need his true Islander name.

Toon probably came to Numinbah as Nixon did, via the Tweed.
Nixon's brother-in-law Joshua Bray and his brother-in-law Samuel
Gray had begun planting sugarcane on their properties on the Tweed
in 1865. By the mid-1870s they were entirely reliant on Islander
labour (Bray Diaries, 11 March 1874). In 1875, when the sugar
pioneer William Julius was looking for labour to work his sugar
plantation at Cudgen, he had to round up 200 Islanders, described as
having 'completed their contracts in Queensland' (Boileau, 110–11).
Toon is mentioned in the Bray Diaries twice, on 25 and 26 February
1874, his name there spelt Thoon.

The Nixons had not been in Australia long before they were
involved in the 'recruitment' of Pacific Islanders to work in the cane
fields. Nixon's younger brother, George Louis Nixon, was only a
boy when he was taken on as a midshipman on the sailing sloop
Lavinia which regularly visited the South Seas. In 1872 while the
Lavinia, ostensibly collecting bêche de mer, was anchored in the
Mboli Passage off the island of Florida in the Solomons, Islanders
boarded the vessel and massacred the crew, apparently in reprisal for
outrages perpetrated by other recruiting vessels. Louis escaped only
because he and the captain were away in the longboat looking for a
safer anchorage (*BC*, 7 August).

In 1876 Arthur Nixon gave up trying to grow sugar in New South Wales, and accepted an appointment as government agent in ships carrying Polynesian labourers between the South Seas and Queensland (*BC*, 2 October). He then wrote 'A True Account of a Recruiting Voyage' which gave a first-hand account of the widespread abuse of the system, and submitted it to *The Patriot* as by 'a Government Agent'. The article was roundly denounced as 'hysterical' and the hunt was on for its author, who was eventually identified. Arthur then resigned his government post (*BC*, 3 July 1878) and for some time after he worked with Louis, now Captain Nixon of the schooner *Pacific*, based at Ugi in the Solomons (*ISN*, 19 February 1881).

The only difference between indentured labourers and slaves is that indentured labourers may not be bought or sold, and they will eventually be free to return home or to find other employment. History tells us that many Islanders died before they were out of their indentures. From 1906 to 1908 most of the 60,000 Islanders still working in Queensland were repatriated under the provisions of the Pacific Island Labourers Act. It seems that while some South Sea Islanders might have been eager to work in Queensland, many, possibly the majority, were tricked into leaving their homelands, while others were kidnapped with maximum violence. Just where Frank, Arthur and Louis Nixon fit into this spectrum is not clear. When Arthur took up the government post of assistant inspector of Polynesian labourers at Mackay, he was described by the opposition as having 'been in the blackbird trade before' (*WA*, 2 November 1888); when he resigned the post in 1893, he was rewarded with 'a testimonial and a purse of sovereigns by the employers of kanakas' (*CP*, 11 February 1893), so it seems that he was not opposed to the system in principle.

In the Pioneer's own account of how he came to Numinbah, in a letter he wrote to the land agent William Henderson in 1883, he doesn't mention Toon, who was still working for him:

> Eleven years ago the Upper Nerang where I am now living & for several miles below me was unknown country, no white man had ever been here – I found the country through the blacks, explored the whole of it and decided to take up land & make a home here . . . I applied for [the selection] on the 22nd July 1874. I immediately set to

work & cut a bridle track up to this place so as to enable me to get my horses and cattle up. (The country was so rough that the blacks & I had to explore it on foot.)

Local tradition holds that soon after being shown the way into the valley Nixon 'cut a track through the Numinbah Gap' (Hall *et al.*, 51). Nixon's own words tell us that the track he cut led 'up' the Nerang rather than down, and he brought his horses and cattle 'up' rather than down, so he probably did take the usual route from the Tweed over the foothills of the McPherson Range at Tomewin northwards across the Currumbin and Tallebudgera Creeks on to the junction of the Little Nerang and upstream to the river flats, where he marked blazes on the trees that were to serve as the corner posts of his first selection.

Nixon's once ubiquitous presence in the Numinbah Valley is gradually receding. His homestead is gone; Nixon's Gate has vanished and Nixon's Gorge is now called Egg Rock Valley. The creek that ran through his original selection is still known as Nixon's Creek, or would be if the Australian authorities had not decided that apostrophes were too hard and simply dropped them, so Nixon's Creek is signed Nixons Creek. The Committee for Geographic Names of Australasia has gone one further and it is now officially Nixon Creek. A ford across the Nerang River is still known as Nixon's Crossing. Of Nixon's Track there is no sign.

Local historians believe that Nixon's Track was a 'pack track' that 'became well-known as settlement increased in the Natural Bridge area' (Hall *et al.*, 112). When three teenaged children of Nixon's sister set off on horseback from Kynnumboon to spend the holidays in Numinbah in the winter of 1884 they became hopelessly lost soon after entering the 'dark scrub track'. As daylight began to fail, knowing that before them lay 'the Big Hill and after that the dreaded Four Mile Scrub which lay across the top of the Range with a narrow track sometimes skirting a hundred foot precipice and always winding through great rocks and boulders and overhung with huge trees so draped with vines and ferns and orchids as almost to obscure the path', the children had no choice but to make camp and spend the night in the open (Florence Bray, 56–7). Tracks in rainforest have to be regularly slashed if they are not to disappear within weeks, and a bridle or pack track is narrow to start with. No path through the Numinbah Gap would have skirted 'a hundred foot precipice'. It would be many years before travel from Queensland into New South Wales became at all regular. When the first bullock track was cut it did not lead, as far as can now be ascertained, through the Numinbah Gap but up from Currumbin via Pine Mountain (now Pages Pinnacle).

So who was the Pioneer? His family was distinguished, on his mother's side as planters and traders in the West Indies and Central America, and on his father's side as members of the British cultural and religious establishment. His parents may have hoped to establish a respected dynasty in the Great South Land and, on the face of it, they appear well qualified to have done so, until history decided otherwise.

Frank Nixon's paternal grandfather, Robert Nixon, was an Anglican clergyman and graduate of Christ Church, Oxford, who served as curate of Foot's Cray in Kent from 1784 to 1804. Both Robert and his brother John were noted amateur artists, who exhibited regularly at the Royal Academy. It was at Rev. Nixon's house that his friend and protégé J. M. W. Turner completed his first oil painting in 1793 (Cust). By his wife Anne Russell, Robert Nixon had two sons, Frank's father, George Russell Nixon, born on 20 March 1802, and Francis Russell Nixon, born sixteen months later. In 1810 both boys were sent to Merchant Taylors' School in London. George was taken out of the school within a year, while Francis stayed eleven years, and went on to graduate from St John's College Oxford in 1827. In 1842 he was made a Doctor of Divinity and consecrated bishop of Tasmania. His distinguished career is the subject of one of the longer entries in the *Australian Dictionary of National Biography*. Frank was obviously named for his uncle, but it is notable that he never answered to Francis but always, no matter how formal the occasion, identified himself as plain Frank. If he had a middle name, as all his siblings did, he never used it.

Frank's father George was twenty-eight years old when he entered Trinity College Cambridge as a pensioner in 1830. After he graduated in 1834 he led a peripatetic existence as tutor to the children of the rich in finishing schools in Italy and Switzerland. What this odd sequence of events suggests is that George Russell's health was always fragile, or thought to be so.

Frank Nixon's mother was Rosalie Adelaide Dougan. At least three generations of Dougans had been traders and planters in the West Indies, first in St Kitts, then Tortola and finally Guiana. Of the three sons of Thomas Dougan one, Robert, took up land near Stabroek (today's Georgetown) in what is now Guiana. His 'rich sugar plantation bordered with coffee and fruits' was uncompromisingly named 'Profit'. George Pinckard, who visited it when he came to Guiana with General Abercromby in 1796, rhapsodised that 'having every advantage of culture, it exhibits, in high perfection, all the luxuriancy of a rich tropical estate . . . A private canal leads through the middle of the grounds, and serves, at once, for ornament and pleasure, as well as for bringing home the copious harvests of coffee and sugar.' What was more, 'to the slaves it affords a happy home!' (Pinckard, ii, 203–4)

Robert Dougan's brother John Dougan, Rosalie Adelaide's father, is described variously as a merchant and a navy agent. In 1798 he married Clarissa Squire, daughter of a Plymouth merchant. Their first three children were christened in England. In 1803 the family travelled back to Tortola, where a fourth child was born in 1804. In August 1805 the family returned to England, and in May 1806 Dougan returned to the West Indies once more, this time without his family. He was then acting as agent for prizes, that is to say, ships thought to be bound for French colonies in the Caribbean, the cargoes of which were forfeit according to the British interpretation of the rules governing the maritime war with France. As such his activities came under bitter criticism from the American sea-captain Richard J. Cleveland, whose two ships, the *Cerberus* and the *Telemaco*, called in at Tortola on 22 April 1807.

The agent for prizes, a Mr. Dougan, came on board, and to him were delivered the ship's papers. He then very civilly accompanied me on shore to aid me in procuring lodgings. This being accomplished, I returned on board, at the expiration of about two hours, to take my baggage on shore; and to my surprise found, that during that short interval, Dougan had been on board, had broken open my writing-desk, and had abstracted from it all my private letters and papers. This wanton outrage was entirely unnecessary, as he might have had the key by asking for it . . . (Cleveland, ii, 21)

The seizing of the vessel, which was not bound directly or indirectly for a French port, was illegal; according to Cleveland the trial that followed 'was neither more nor less than a shield to cover an act of villainy'. Cleveland may have been under a wrong impression about the legal case, but he can hardly have been wrong about what followed.

> The *Telemaco* and cargo being condemned, it was no easy matter for the prize agent [i. e. Dougan] to dispose of them, excepting at a very great sacrifice. The ship possessed an intrinsic value at Tortola, which the cargo did not . . . The prize agent was extremely embarrassed with the peculiarity of this case, aware that, without the intervention of a neutral, nothing could be made of it. In this extremity, he made a proposal to me to take it at about half its original cost, and, as an inducement, would engage to provide protection against detention by British cruisers on its way to Havana. What effrontery! What impudence! What villainy! To rob me of my property on pretext of inadmissibility of voyage, and then propose a passport for the more safe prosecution of the same voyage, for pursuing which the property was confiscated! (Cleveland, ii, 24)

Cleveland, who had no way of raising the money to purchase his own vessel and cargo, took ship for New York, leaving Dougan in possession. By such shifts Dougan became a very wealthy man. In May 1808 he returned to England, where he stayed until 1812. In 1808 Dougan's brother Robert died in London. In his will, written on 6 January 1806, he makes no mention of children and appoints his 'beloved brother John late of the island of Tortola and now residing in Great Britain' his sole legatee and executor. A codicil dated 26 March 1807 left to his nephew Thomas Dougan of Demerara (son of another brother) 'a certain plantation in Demerara aforesaid called the Profit plantation with the Negroes Cattle and Stock thereof or of any Sum or Sums of Money to arise from the sale thereof' (NA, PRO, 11/1492).

The Dougans' sixth child was christened at East Teignmouth, Devon, in 1810, and a seventh at St George's Hanover Square in 1811. In 1812 Dougan left England again, but this time with his wife, bound for Halifax, Nova Scotia, where a ninth child was born. The family returned to England, landing at East Teignmouth on 15 November 1815. In January 1816 he was obliged to be in London, to give witness against a former employee who had forged a bill of exchange for £800 in his name. In a begging letter in which he demanded £1,000 from Dougan, the prisoner excused the amount as small in comparison with Dougan's great wealth. Rosalie Adelaide was the second-last of the Dougans' twelve children, born according to Dougan family historians in Bedford Square on 4 June 1817; a younger brother was baptised at East Teignmouth on 13 September 1818. Not long after that Dougan's fortunes changed drastically.

On 14 July 1821, we find him writing a desperate letter to Lord Bathurst:

> I feel it incumbent on me now to mention, what your lordship is already apprized of, that lately Failures of Mercantile Persons and other Disastrous events, the Pressure of Calamity has borne heavily upon me, and left me with a family of 14 persons to provide for, and commence life anew after having conveyed to the Treasurer of Greenwich Hospital all my Effects and Debts, amounting to £18,000 to meet a Demand of £26,000 of Late Naval Prize Creditors. (NA, CO 323/195)

He was appointed one of two commissioners charged to investigate the situation of 'certain Africans' who had been found aboard French vessels captured during the Napoleonic wars and 'condemned to the Crown' by the Vice Admiralty Court in Tortola under the provisions of the Act for the Abolition of the Slave Trade. The freed slaves were then apprenticed, that is, indentured, to various planters in the West Indies for fourteen years apiece (NA, PP 1825, vol. xxv, 5). The substitution of indentured labour for outright slavery was a typical British compromise, designed to keep everyone happy, everyone except the labouring people themselves, who had as little chance of defending themselves against exploitation and abuse as ever they had.

Dougan's fellow commissioner, Major Thomas Moody, was married to a daughter of one of Dougan's two sisters. The two men took very different views of the treatment of the indentured servants; Dougan objected that Moody favoured the colonists, taking their part even in cases where there was clear evidence of ill-treatment. The two were required to submit independent reports, but Dougan's health was failing and he was not able to see the matter to a conclusion. In September 1826 he died intestate, leaving his brother's estate unadministered. His eight daughters were all unmarried; of his four sons, two had joined the British army in India.

Thirteen years later, on 21 September 1839, in London, twenty-two-year-old Rosalie Adelaide Dougan married thirty-seven-year-old George Russell Nixon. Their first child, George Dougan Nixon, was born in Switzerland in 1840 and died there the same year. Frank was born in Rome in 1842. A sister Angela was born in Bagni di Lucca in 1843, a brother Edward (1845) and sister Gertrude (1846) in Tenby in Wales, where their father was running a small private school, another brother, Frederick Dougan, in Verlungo (1848), another, George Louis, in Bristol (1851). Three more siblings were born in Switzerland, Arthur in Vevey (1852), and Anna (1853) and Clara (1855) in Veytaux. Clara died in infancy.

Frank was eighteen when his parents decided to send him and his brother Edward to Australia, where Rosalie Adelaide's elder sister Mary, who had virtually brought her up, had emigrated with her husband Richard Walkden and her children and stepchildren. The Nixon boys arrived on the *Owen Glendower* in January 1860. Rather than staying and working on the Walkden farm at Pakenham in Victoria, they travelled to another Walkden property at Brungle in New South Wales where three of Mary's sons, Frederick, Frank and George Walkden, were breeding horses for the East India Company and the British army in India.

Brungle, nestling in the lee of the Snowy Mountains, twenty kilometres north-east of Tumut, is a special place, with rolling hills, deep valleys and rushing mountain streams. The winters are bright and cold, the summers bright and hot. There Frank bought a property in the name of his family and hired a carpenter to build a split-slab house with bark roof, apparently without assistance from their father, who had come out to Australia in October 1860 to visit his brother in Hobart. By the time Mrs Nixon and the other six children arrived aboard the *Albion* in January 1862 and travelled to Brungle by bullock dray, the house was all but ready. They called it 'Avenex' after one of the places where they had lived in Switzerland, a hamlet on the Balcon de la petite Côte, overlooking Lake Geneva.

On the voyage out nineteen-year-old Angela Nixon, who was usually called Nina, had caught the eye of Percy Spasshat, the ship's doctor. After a wedding at Brungle the couple went to live in Armidale, taking Frank's ten-year-old sister Anna with them. Seventeen-year-old Gertrude Nixon soon attracted the attentions of twenty-five-year-old Joshua Bray, who with his brother James was working for his father on the neighbouring Brungle Run. Bray's sister Mary was married to Samuel William Gray, who at a government auction in 1862 bought the lease of 16,000 acres in the Mount Warning caldera, and offered his brother-in-law a partnership. In 1865 Bray proposed to Gertrude and was accepted. He then travelled up to the Tweed, where he set about building a house on the north arm (now the Rous River), and gave it the Aboriginal name for the place, 'Kynnumboon'.

Raising horses in Brungle may have suited Frank and his brother Fred, but their parents and siblings could not settle. In December 1864, George Nixon travelled to Sydney to visit an old friend who was rector of Christ Church St Laurence, to find that he was on the point of returning to England on sabbatical leave. Bishop Nixon was already in England on sabbatical so George decided to accompany his friend and visit his brother. When the bishop realised that his failing health did not permit a return to Tasmania and retired to Stresa on the Lago Maggiore, George went with him. He would not return to Australia until 1868.

On 19 July 1865 Gertrude wrote to Joshua from Avenex:

Frank came home on Monday and we have been having long consul-tations as to the future Ect. If Fred went up [to the Tweed] he might see to a little house being put up for Mama and Anna. Mama supposes you will let her build it on a small portion of your land . . . We are very glad to have dear old Frank back again – he likes your song 'To the West' so much we tried it over together last night. (Bray Papers)

When sixteen-year-old Fred turned up at Kynnumboon, Bray found him a good worker but 'low-spirited', and permitted himself to observe that 'his Mama scolded him too much'. In fact Fred was

in love with a Brungle girl called Charlie Rankin. She had promised
to wait for him and the boy considered himself engaged. Meanwhile
Frank, who was enjoying life in the Tumut, and the cross-country
trips driving cattle and horses to market, showed no sign of joining
in the rush to the north. On 14 October Gertrude wrote to her
betrothed:

> Nothing has been decided [about Avenex] as yet. I want them to let
> it or sell it – which wd be for the best, for it would be absurd for
> Frank to stay on. (Bray Papers)

After Gertrude's wedding, which took place in Armidale in June
the next year, her mother did not return to Avenex, but stayed in
Armidale with the Spasshats. In August Bray wrote from the Tweed
to assure her that a house was being built for her there. By the end of
1867 though the house was still unfinished Mrs Nixon and Anna
were living in it; it was called the House on the Hill, or simply the
Hill. Frank, Edward, Arthur and Louis were still at Avenex, while
Frederick was working on a property outside Armidale. By 17 April
Frank, Louis and Arthur had joined their mother at the Hill, because
it was then that they climbed sacred Mount Warning, something that
only the most senior Aboriginal elders were allowed to do.

Selections had been taken up in the names of various members of the
Nixon family: George Russell Nixon had 160 acres and Arthur twenty-
two, on the east bank of the North Arm. Only forty acres upstream
from Kynnumboon had been taken up in Frank's name, probably
because he was hoping against hope to be able to keep Avenex.

In his diary for 29 April 1868, James Bray noted that 'Frank Nixon
came over to say goodbye' on his way back to Brungle (Bray Papers).
He stopped in Armidale and there, on 13 May, he married Catherine
Elizabeth Cameron (New South Wales marriage certificate no.
1868/001527). Kate, as she was known, eldest of the seven children of
Hugh and Anne Cameron, was born in the tiny fishing village of
Garmony on the isle of Mull off the west coast of Scotland. The family
arrived at Botany Bay on the *Walmer Castle* on 30 December 1848 and
settled in Armidale. By the time Kate was wed to Frank Nixon, she
had seen all five of her surviving siblings married to members of the

Armidale Scottish community. She herself had been married in 1859 to a Donald Cameron, who died in 1862, leaving her childless. When she married Frank she was thirty-eight years old, twelve years older than he. They were to have no children that we know of and Kate remains a shadowy figure in Nixon's story, to the point of being confused with his mother. They were married according to the rites of the Presbyterian Church, with Catherine's father and her brother John as witnesses. No member of the staunchly Anglican Nixon family appears to have been present. Frank gave his occupation as grazier and his residence as Tumut. He took his wife back to Avenex where he and Fred continued to make their living as farmers and graziers. Frank was still in the Snowy in February 1870 when he stood witness for Fred, who had attained his majority and was at last free to marry Charlie Rankin (New South Wales State Records, 3504/1870).

When Avenex was finally sold, Fred stayed in the district. Frank had no choice but to take Kate north where his younger brothers had formed a company to produce sugar. More land had been taken up, and machinery for the purpose had been imported from Britain. The Tweed correspondent of *The Queenslander* reported on 11 October 1873:

Mr Gray will have over thirty acres of cane planted this season and that with last year's planting will make a total of some sixty acres or more, almost enough to start a mill. Mr A Nixon (for Nixon Brothers) is also forming a plantation this season as fast as he is able, with the intention I have heard of erecting machinery as soon as he has cane sufficient to keep a mill going for the season. Theirs is the only plantation on the North Arm and from what I have seen it is likely to be the most successful on the river.

These sanguine expectations were not borne out. Gray and Bray knew little of sugar chemistry and never succeeded in getting their machinery to work properly. Before they could get their problems sorted out, a more efficient mill at Tumbulgum began producing the first marketable sugar.

On Saturday 13 February 1874 Gertrude noted in her diary that 'Frank and Kate moved up to their own place', which they had called

Jijiga. Six weeks later she 'went up to Frank's with Mama, Anna and children'. On April Fool's Day, 'Frank came down to get some tea'. From the Bray diary we can see that Frank and Kate continued to live close enough to Kynnumboon to be able to walk over for Sunday prayers, long after Frank is supposed to have been living on the land he had selected on the Nerang River. The diary entries refer to the Queensland properties as 'Numinbah', 'Numinbar' and even 'Nummingbar'; on 13 September 1874 Gertrude records 'Frank started to Numinbar. Kate down in the evening.' On 28 December 'Kate and Anna went out to Numinbah', so it seems that the Nixons made their marital home in New South Wales at least until the end of 1875. A list of Kynnumboon residents dated 1875–7 includes Frank, along with the gang of Brays, Grays and assorted Nixons. He was listed as a magistrate in New South Wales as late as 1879. Numinbah local historians do not explain why they believe that, when he settled in Numinbah, Frank brought both his wife and his mother with him (Hall *et al.*, 51). Rosalie Adelaide was certainly not one for roughing it. If there was an older lady with the couple it was not Kate's mother either, for she died in 1868. It looks very much as if the older lady must have been Kate herself, and the younger her attendant.

When the country reporter of *The Queenslander* visited the township of Nerang in 1873 it consisted of 'two public-houses and nothing else'. He could not find anyone in the district who could identify the source of the Nerang River: 'the government maps afford no information on the subject and it seems to be a mystery to all except some of the old timber-getters.' (Q, 20 September) Joshua Bray noted in the Diary for 8 June 1874: 'Frank Nixon returned from looking at the head of Nerang Ck – he does not like it.' Notwithstanding, five weeks later, on 22 July 1874, Nixon rode over to Beenleigh where he applied at the Lands Court for selections on the Nerang River (*BC*, 15 August).

The land had to be surveyed, measured and given an identifying number. When the government surveyor George Pratten came up to survey Nixon's selections, he brought with him two speculators from Coomera who had already selected land closer to Nerang. When they saw the land Nixon had selected they announced that this adjoined the very land that they had already selected, even though they could not

show the marked trees that were usually taken as evidence. As Nixon
told Henderson, 'They said they were on horseback when they found
it, but no horse could have got up the creek before I cut the bridle
track.' (Again we find Nixon travelling up the river rather than down.)

Nixon was convinced that the speculators who came up with
Pratten 'only took up the land in the hope of making capital' out of
him, which suggests that he was perceived to be a gentleman farmer
with more money than sense. He may very well have given that
impression. Though he seems to have had no formal education, he
could speak both French and German, and his manners may well
have been more polished than those of his fellow selectors. To hear
Nixon tell it he was not afraid of hard work.

> As you know I have been here some eleven years, & during the
> whole of that time, the whole of my rations, goods & chattels have
> been packed up here on horseback at a considerable expense to
> myself. I have now made a dray road from my homestead to the Pine
> Mountain, about 9 miles from here . . . as the Pioneer of the Upper
> Nerang I think I deserve some consideration. It was I who opened up
> the upper part of this creek. When I first came I made the track from
> the junction of Little Nerang to here. I cut through the scrubs around
> & I found all the crossing places in the river between here and there,
> & between here and the Tweed River I made 15 miles of a track over
> the Mac Pherson Range, on to the Casino road.

We may be sure, I think, that Nixon did none of the hard labour
of opening the tracks himself, but directed his gang of Aboriginal
workers from horseback. Many of the difficulties he was later to
encounter could be explained by the rapid attrition of his Aboriginal
workforce.

The first of Nixon's selections in Queensland was Portion 1, a
homestead plot of 120 acres at the confluence of Nixon Creek and
the Nerang River; the second, of 384 acres, adjoined it on the south,
along the west bank of the Nerang River. A third portion of 200
acres, which was known after his wife as Catherine's Flat, on the
other side of the Nerang River was acquired at the same time (QSA,
LAN/AG17).

On the 5th September 1874 Mr Pratten came up to survey my land
– John [a mistake for Jesse, or 'Jessie' in Nixon's spelling] Bird &
Stephen Hall followed my track & came up too – & liking the country
here better than the land near the Aboriginal Reserve, said at once
that my land was the land they had selected. By the act of 1868 they
were supposed to have marked a tree as their starting point, but they
had done nothing of the kind. Mr Pratten however considered their
claim prior to mine.

The records confirm that Jesse Bird and Stephen Hall had indeed
made prior selections further downstream, that these were cancelled
and they were allowed to select two lots of 120 acres immediately
downstream from Nixon's homestead. Worse, Pratten surveyed 160
acres for a William Hall who had never made application. In the
latter case Nixon moved at once; on 6 March 1875 before Joshua
Bray at Kynnumboon he made application for the selection, which
he claimed William Hall had never seen, but it was not until Hall had
defaulted on payment that the selection was declared forfeit and
selection reopened on 26 March 1878. Nixon, who had probably
been forewarned, selected it on that very day. On 10 April he
followed through by selecting Portion 14, the sixty acres that lay
between the 160 acres he had just secured and Jesse Bird's 120 acres.
Dispossessing Bird and Stephen Hall was to take a little longer.

Nixon had already profited from Pratten's survey by adding two
more selections of his own. On 25 September 1874 he secured a
fourth parcel which extended his run by ninety acres to the east bank
of Nixon's Creek, and a fifth on 2 October gave him eighty acres on
the east bank of the Nerang, 874 acres in all. To this were added selections made in the name of two of Nixon's brothers. In 1875 Portion
10 of eighty acres, five kilometres upstream from the homestead, was
selected for Louis, whose occupation was given as timber-getter
(QSA, LAN/AG19). He was in fact a trader based in the Solomons
(Corris, 99). According to Bray family historian Mary Kinsman:

Soon after [the massacre] he settled on an island which he bought
from a chieftain in the Solomon Group of Islands . . . He bought
another island for Joshua [Bray] for £50.0.0 . . . He wrote of the

customs of the Solomon natives in a journal which makes quite fascinating reading, which perhaps one day might appear in print.
(Kinsman, 80)

When Dr Henry Brougham Guppy visited the Solomons in 1881
with the survey vessel *Lark* he found Nixon to be a helpful and
reliable informant, 'one of those traders whose name should not be
forgotten amongst the pioneers, who, in working for themselves,
have worked directly for the good of their successors in the Solomon
Group' (Guppy, 1887a, 35). According to Guppy, Nixon resided on
the island of Savo 'at various times between 1874 and 1882'. Nixon
told Guppy of his exploration of the island:

> From Mr Nixon's description there would appear to be in the central
> elevated portion of the island a large crater-ring, in the middle of
> which there is a small cone, composed of *lapilli* and ashes, and traversed
> by deep fissures, from which at the time of his visit to this locality
> sulphureous vapours were escaping. A white cloud displaying
> lightning (*ferilli*) in its midst used to form over the mountaintop in the
> evening ... The inhabitants do not visit the high parts of the
> mountain, alleging that men who have been there have always fallen
> sick shortly afterwards and some have died. (Guppy, 1887b, 56)

Anyone who knows Wollumbin, with its cone within a crater and
its head in the clouds, will be struck by the resemblance between it
and the core of Savo. Louis Nixon had dared to defy augury by
climbing that too, with the inevitable result: 'a few days after Mr
Nixon's visit to the summit, he was attacked by a low fever that
confined him to his couch for three months.' (Guppy, 1887b, 57)

In 1876, at the Crown Land Sales in Beenleigh, we find Fred
Nixon, giving his occupation as mailman, buying Portion 11,
upstream from Nixon's holdings. He was not long from Tumut,
where the birth of his fourth child was registered in 1875. The fifth
birth was registered in Queensland in 1879, but in 1880 he transferred his Numinbah lease to an Anne Stephens and moved over the
border to the Tweed, where he apparently took over as the proprietor of the Tumbulgum Hotel a few kilometres downstream from

Kynnumboon. In 1883, giving his address as Gudgen (Cudgen), Tweed River, he went out of business and claimed bankruptcy, which was granted the next year. He would go on to operate rather more successfully as a publican elsewhere in New South Wales, much to the disgust of his family.

These were happy times for the Squire of Numinbah, who had leisure for gentlemanly pursuits. On Boxing Day 1877 the new Nerang Racecourse was inaugurated with a racing carnival at which Nixon and Nixon bloodstock were represented. Nixon was thereafter regularly involved in organising and adjudicating at the regular meetings of the racing confraternity and was a foundation committee member of the Nerang Turf Club (*LW*, 11 October 1880; *BC*, 30 October 1880). He was also a prominent member of the Nerang cricket team. In the Tweed–Nerang match of 23 March 1878 he was caught for five, run out for a duck, bowled out the last man in the batting order and made a catch. After a dinner that evening the players 'adjourned to Mr Nixon's residence (who had kindly given a room for the occasion) and dancing was kept up till the small hours' (*LW*, 30 March).

The Numinbah homestead was twenty-five kilometres away and accessible only by a rough bush track; no room in it can have been big enough to accommodate two cricket teams and their womenfolk. Local historians describe the house as having '4 rooms and a wide front verandah. The 2 front rooms consisted of a living room and bedroom with the kitchen joined to the main building by a short landing.' Frank must have been living in a house closer to Nerang, leaving Toon in residence in Numinbah, but if he was to fulfil the conditions for acquiring the freehold he had to convince the inspectors that he was a full-time resident of his homestead selection.

The system by which unsurveyed land was made available to settlers in 1874 assessed its value at £1 per acre, of which five shillings had to be paid as a deposit, the rest to be paid within three years. After 1876 Nixon paid nothing on Portion 3, and the selection was eventually declared forfeit. As it was not reopened for selection until after Nixon died, it looks as if his friends at the Beenleigh Lands Court assumed that he would one day pay the arrears and the forfeiture would be reversed. The parcel lay across the river from Nixon's main run and Nixon may have wished to concentrate on consolidating his holdings west of the river. Contrariwise, the Nerang flooded eight times between January and August 1877, and Nixon may have decided that Portion 3 was a bad proposition.

After the death of Nixon's father in 1878 Numinbah historians have it that he built another house, connected to his own by a verandah, for his widowed mother (Hall *et al.*, 51). If he did Rosalie Adelaide seems never to have lived in it. Instead she moved to Carlon Street in St Leonards, as the north shore of Sydney was then known. In 1880, her youngest child, Anna, now married to Joshua Bray's half-brother James Rowland, went to stay with her mother in preparation for the birth of her first baby, which was registered in St Leonards.

In June 1879, Frank was asked to serve in the Nerang Police Court as one of the two magistrates to hear the case of the wounding of an Islander known as Billy Tully by the Chief Magistrate and leading sugar grower Robert Muir. Billy Tully's deranged behaviour, dancing naked, yelling and banging a tin with a stick, had terrified Muir's small children and their nurse. Muir had let off a shotgun blast to frighten the Islander off and wounded him in the thigh. The magistrates decided that the wounding was not intentional and that the shotgun was used in the legitimate defence of Muir's wife and family (*LW*, 21 June). Muir was absolved of blame and Billy was taken under guard to the Brisbane madhouse. Apparently Nixon did not warm to the job of magistrate, for he did not appear on the bench again until 14 February 1883 (*LW*, 23 February).

Nixon usually described himself as a grazier; local historians are doubtless correct in saying that 'he was grazing cattle and horses over the entire valley, wherever the open country provided natural pasture', but not in saying that his 'registered cattle brand was F. N. G.' (Hall *et al.*, 51) – it was actually FN6. His string of freehold portions gave Nixon toeholds in what he was actually running as a ranch, said to have had a carrying capacity of between 600 and 750 head. His most important colleagues and allies were the bullockies who bought his animals for their teams, in particular Ernest Belliss and Hector Burns. Nixon didn't bother to fence his individual portions but contented himself with building 'a two-rail split mortised

post fence on the North end' of his land along the boundary of Jesse
Bird's Portion 6, about where the Numinbah Valley School of Arts
stands today. Everyone travelling south had to pass through Nixon's
Gate; 'this gave him the grazing rights of all the crown land in
between and practically all Numinbah Valley' (Cowderoy).

It was not until 1880 that Nixon's homestead selection was
inspected to ensure that he was complying with the conditions of his
lease. The inspectors reported that 'he had resided on the selection
since July 1874 and had constructed a slab house with shingle roof of
five rooms, a slab kitchen of three rooms, a stable, stockyards and pig
styes, had some nineteen acres cultivated, mostly under maize, and
had a garden planted with oranges, lemon trees, vines etc.' (QSA
LAN/AG 17) Local historians tell us that 'the main part of the
dwelling was built of pit–sawn Red Cedar and had a high–pitched
roof for coolness'. According to their account (for which no authority
is cited), 'The house had 4 rooms and a wide front verandah. The 2
front rooms consisted of a living room and bedroom with the kitchen
joined to the main building by a short landing. It was built of split
slabs and, like the main structure, had a shingle roof.' The inconsist-
encies might be a consequence of the descriptions having been made
at different times. A photograph of the house – if indeed it is the right
house – shows that it is raised on massive stumps that appear to be of
White Beech (Hall *et al.*, 50). Numinbah Homestead, as the house
was known, has disappeared; even its site cannot now be securely
identified.

In March 1881 Louis Nixon made landfall in Sydney; on 14 March
at his mother's house in St Leonards, he made his will, which was
witnessed by his brother Arthur (QSA 3564/741905). On 17
November 1882, on the tiny islet of Santa Ana (now Owaraha) in the
Solomons, he died, aged thirty-one. As his executor, Frank, who had
occupied Portion 10 as his bailiff, assumed his lease. He was still
struggling to secure the missing pieces in his jigsaw of freeholds. As
he wrote to Henderson in 1883:

No. 578 is Jessie Birds forfeited selection 120 acres, one of the portions
that I am now applying for. The other selection 577 was Stephen Hall
120 acres. Jessie Bird could never have even seen No. 578 . . . Neither

Jessie Bird nor Stephen Hall have ever been near these selections. Stephen Hall saw the land once, & that was all. In fact, as you know, they only took up the land in the hope of making capital out of me. They have certainly done me injury enough for if they had not dummied the land it would have been part of my freehold before now. The 200 acres I have now applied for adjoining our homestead includes the 120 acres formerly selected by Stephen Hall.

Nixon was eventually successful; the missing portions became part of his estate in 1883. In the same year he was elected a member of the Nerang Divisional Board. In mid-1885 Louis Nixon's will was proved and Nixon set about adding Portion 10 to his freehold (BC, 14 May 1885). On 11 May J. G. Appel swore an affidavit saying that he 'knew and was acquainted with George Louis Nixon late of Numinbah Nerang Creek ... the permanent domicile of the said George Louis Nixon was at Numinbah Nerang Creek aforesaid where the said deceased resided on his selection ... the absence of the deceased was caused by his ill health.'

Appel, who was to hold several important positions in the Queensland government, was then working as a solicitor in Brisbane. He would eventually buy Nixon's Portion 3; he and his brother would eventually become the largest landowners in the Numinbah Valley. The report of the inspection of Louis Nixon's selection prior to the Deed of Grant seems to describe a fairly typical dummy run:

There are about 16 acres of scrub and forest land, full and partly cleared and planted with artificial grass value £1

House 16 x 10, one room, hardwood slab walls, shingle roof, not floored, in good condition, unoccupied, value £14.00

No fencing – Grazing land, unstocked

The application for the Deed of Grant was successful, and in 1886 Nixon added Portion 10 to his freehold property.

On 25 September 1885 the Nerang Divisional Board heard a proposal from the surveyor Roessler for an improved road from Nerang to Upper Nerang. 'It was recommended that a small sum be expended in cutting a bridle track Mr Nixon agreeing to act as pilot.'

Nixon moved the motion and 'the sum of £5 was voted for the
work.' (QSA, aNER/D1) At the next meeting 'Mr Nixon reported
that he with the overseer had gone over the route proposed by Mr
Roessler . . . but could not procure labour to cut the bridle track.' At
the next meeting of the Board on 19 September, Mr Nixon's letter
of resignation was acknowledged and accepted with regret (BC, 6
October). Nixon must have offered some explanation of his sudden
resignation but history has not recorded it. Its suddenness suggests
some unexpected calamity. This may have been the juncture at
which Nixon lost the services of Toon. As a consequence of years of
revelations about the realities of the 'recruitment' system, the
Queensland government was repatriating Islanders who ran away
from their employers. Certainly when new settlers arrived in 1903
the homestead had been standing empty for some time (Hall *et al.*,
63).

By mid-1885 Nixon was experiencing serious cash-flow problems.
Payments on Portions 6, 8 and 14 had fallen into arrears and the
selections were declared forfeit; in 1887 Nixon managed to pay the
arrears and the forfeitures were reversed. By this time the boom of
the early 1880s, when Premier Thomas McIlwraith borrowed money
to finance infrastructure development and solicited migrants to come
north, was well and truly over. McIlwraith's Queensland Land
Mortgage and Investment Company had lent far too much money
on flimsy security and on dummied properties. As the sugar and
arrowroot mills and the sawmills that had opened in south-east
Queensland ran out of operating capital, one by one they were forced
to close. *The Bulletin* reported in 1888: 'Large numbers of travellers
pass through here daily seeking employment. Even many of the old
residents on the creek here cannot find work' (Hall *et al.*, 85).

In January 1889, after leasing most of his land to a family of dairy
farmers, Nixon left Numinbah. He probably expected to come back,
for he left behind his dogs, a black dog called Rough, a black and tan
bitch called Vic, and their offspring, Tiger (Hall *et al.*, 55). He took
up positions as registrar of the Central District Court in Isisford and
district receiver in insolvency and high bailiff of the Barcaldine
district (BC, 10 January). He and Kate went to live in Isisford. In
February he was appointed to the Barcaldine Hospital Committee

(*BC*, 4 February 1890). A year later the *Brisbane Courier* reported his first 'tour down the line' and a sitting of the Barcaldine Police Court in which he had to deal with a case of attempted murder, another of horse-stealing and another of giving wine to a 'prohibited person' (*BC*, 9 September 1891). A year after that he chaired a public meeting in support of setting up a cottage hospital at Isisford.

In 1891 Kate returned to the south-east, to Beenleigh for the Crown Land Sales of 13 February, when she bid for Portion 5V which consisted of eighty acres on the east bank of the river, connecting Nixon's Portion 1 with his Portion 6. Her purchase was ratified on 25 October 1893. Nixon had been after the land for years, even though, as he said in his letter to Henderson in 1883:

> With the exception of some 4 or 5 acres the whole of the 80 acres piece is useless, bad, worthless land. It is bastard scrub, rocky, stoney, and cut up by small blind rocky creeks & water courses. In fact it is not worth 1/- per acre. My reason for taking it up is, that I shall save the price of the land in the fencing . . .

On 1 October 1894, eleven years later, he secured title to it. His country estate was complete.

Later in 1891 Nixon was obliged to return to the coast, to Southport, where his mother was living. His father's will was still unproved, mainly because the other executors, Rev. George Watson Smyth of Cheltenham College, and Frank's brother-in-law Francis Robert Bedwell, both appointed in 1860 on the eve of the elder Nixon's departure for Australia, lived outside the jurisdiction. Nixon had therefore to obtain Ancillary Letters of Probate before the matter could be finalised. The business was long, slow and complicated. In his depositions and affidavits Nixon described himself as late 'of the Tweed', and presently of Isisford, as if he had no connection past or present with Numinbah (QSA 7000/742029). In an affidavit dated 19 April 1892, Nixon stated that his mother was living at a property called Dunmore, on the Esplanade at Southport. Nevertheless Numinbah historians believe that 'Nixon's mother, when over eighty years old, frequently rode through the bush with her maid, to meet the coach going to Brisbane.' (Hall *et al.*, 51)

According to the inscription of her tombstone in Murwillumbah Rosalie Adelaide was only seventy-five when she was buried there on 28 January 1894. She had been living in Southport for some years before her death. The Mrs Nixon who rode through the bush, supposing there ever was one, could only have been Kate. In his affidavit Nixon listed his surviving siblings but he could not name all his nieces and nephews.

On 15 June 1893 Nixon's younger brother Edward died suddenly and without making a will, on a station west of Townsville where he had been working as a bookkeeper. The records suggest some disarray in proceedings thereafter. Nixon was eventually granted Letters of Administration after producing evidence that Edward's mother and other surviving siblings agreed. By then, Fred was running a hotel at Brunswick Heads; Nina and Anna were both widowed and Arthur, who had resigned from a government job as assistant inspector of Polynesian labourers at Mackay, was working as a journalist in the gold-rush town of Croydon in far northern Queensland. Their agreement to Frank Nixon's administration of their brother's will was signed before Joshua Bray. Nixon gave his address as Southport and his occupation as 'gentleman'; his sureties were a storekeeper and a publican, both of whom had to swear that they were good for half of Edward's estate of £418 (QSA 1894/19 935785).

In August 1894 Nixon resigned his post in Barcaldine and was appointed clerk of petty sessions and police magistrate to the new boom town of Thargomindah, where his niece, Fred's daughter, twenty-four-year-old Rosalie Jessie Nixon, kept house for him at 351 Dowling Street, probably because Kate was still in Isisford. The summer of 1895–6 was 'the severest that has been experienced for years'; so many people fell victim to typhoid fever that the Wesleyan Chapel was fitted out as a hospital ward. On 26 January 1896, Nixon fell ill of the 'heat fever'; the doctor was called but there was little he could do. Eight hours later Rosalie came to inform the doctor that her uncle was dead. By Frank's will (QSA 9007/742107) dated 4 August 1883 Kate Nixon inherited everything Frank owned in Queensland, Portions 1, 2, 4, 5, 6, 8, 10 and 14 in Numinbah, subdivisions 2 and 5 of suburban allotment 1 of section 14 of the town of Nerang, allotment 8 of Section 1 in the town of Longreach and Subdivision 14 of an allotment of section 3 in Southport (*BC*, 4 May 1896, 22 June 1896, 14 November 1898). Frank's widowed sisters and his nieces and nephews got nothing. The selections made in Frank's name on the Tweed were left to Joshua Bray and Samuel William Gray. The only executor was Kate's sixty-year-old brother, John Cameron, because the other, Edward Nixon, was dead. Besides his land, Nixon died possessed of £48.18.3 in the Commercial Bank at Thargomindah, and £412.19.11 on fixed deposit in the Bank of New South Wales.

Kate never went back to Numinbah. Two years after her husband's death, she can be found living in the mining town of Kilkivan, west of Gympie. The electoral rolls of 1903 and 1905 show her living with her sister Flora and her son William Grant Fraser, butcher, in Fraser Street, Kilkivan. At some point Kate and Flora decamped to Southport. When Flora died in 1909, she was described as 'late of Southport'.

Within months of securing probate of Nixon's will in 1902, Kate began to sell off his properties in Numinbah. In 1903 she sold Portions 7 and 14 to James Holden, and in 1904 Portions 2, 4, 5V, 6 and 10 to the timber-getters and bullock drivers George and Arthur Warples. No one connected with Frank Nixon would play any further role in the development of the Numinbah Valley. Kate eventually moved back to Armidale where she died in 1914. Her first husband and others of her kin were buried in Armidale, but Kate's body was taken on the long and difficult road north to be laid beside Frank's in Thargomindah General Cemetery. It is this that gives one to suspect that what may have seemed like a marriage of convenience was no such thing. Perhaps Nixon was not the callous adventurer he is usually made to seem.

There are some who would say that the story of Frank Nixon's failed experiment in the Numinbah Valley set a precedent. Every year brings new settlers into the valley, with all kinds of plans and schemes for making money, but the land refuses to cooperate. Pedigree beasts fall sick and die; plans to build tourist villages are thwarted or run out of time and money; bush tucker withers on the twig; campsites remain empty; vineyards moulder; rough scrub invades the pastures; eroded slopes slide and fall; termites eat away the old houses and the new. The forest waits to resume its own.

TIMBER

Frank Nixon certainly bred horses and bullocks on his ranch in the valley of the Upper Nerang, but what really brought him there was what lured practically everyone who settled in south-east Queensland in the second half of the nineteenth century – timber. To many it seemed like easy pickings. According to one mildly facetious account of a visit to the Tweed River in 1876: 'Much money has been made at cedar-getting, and several stick to it in preference to farming. You are your own master; go to work when and where you like, live a life of satisfied solitude amongst the Samsons of the forest, rejoice in the sound of the mohawk [?] or the cockatoo, the red-breasted parrots and the native woods . . .' (*BC*, 5 August)

Samuel Gray's reason for buying a four-year lease of the Upper Walumban Run, just over the border in the Mount Warning caldera, in 1862 was that Red Cedar was still to be found there. Gray had grown up in the Illawarra where nine-tenths of the cedar had been felled and shipped to Sydney by the end of the 1820s. As soon as he had secured the lease Gray signed up two sawyers to provide him with 20,000 super feet of Red Cedar and Cudgerie to be felled by Aboriginal workers. When Gray's partner, his and Nixon's brother-in-law Joshua Bray, got to the Tweed he found that they had competition. About twenty cedar-getters were living in huts at Terranora, at the mouth of the river, where the *Francis George* regularly called to collect the cedar that they rafted down the river. Bray lost no time. He wrote to his fiancée Gertrude Nixon on 27 September 1864, about a trip he was making round the base of Mount

Warning to Tyalgum: 'I had the blacks felling a lot of cedar up there . . . I found a great deal of cedar there, I intend to get it out if I can.' (Bray Papers)

Bray was already having trouble keeping his Aboriginal workers; when he visited their encampment one night he 'found two of the cedar choppers (white people) with rum making the blacks drunk, doubtless with the intention of coaxing some of them away, or taking them away after they were drunk'. The cedar-getters had travelled from forty kilometres away (Bray Papers). Bray succeeded in getting rid of the interlopers, but from then on finding the manpower to exploit the timber would become more and more difficult. Of the thirty-eight settlers who collected mail at Bray's Post Office in 1867, nine were timber-getters or timber-cutters and fourteen were sawyers. Nearly all of the male population of the Tweed was already involved in the timber industry in one way or another when the Bray–Gray partnership arrived. Bray hooked his own chain across the Tweed to catch the logs that came down with each fresh. While he struggled to grow arrowroot and sugar and lost money on both, it was the timber that supported him and Gertrude, and their brood of children. By the time Frank and Kate Nixon came north after the sale of Avenex to join the other members of the Nixon family on the Tweed, the cedar was almost exhausted. According to the *Brisbane Courier*, 'much fine cedar has been sent away; but cedar getting has become now a restricted trade, as it is difficult to get.' (5 January 1872)

Nixon, whose maternal grandfather had made fortunes out of shipping cabinet timbers out of virgin forest in the West Indies and Central America, must have been well aware of the value of the timber he saw still standing in Numinbah; when he told his sister that he didn't like what he saw there, he was probably referring to the extreme ruggedness of the terrain. There was red gold in them thar hills, but getting it out was going to be difficult and costly.

In 1846 two boys, Edmund Harper and his fourteen-year-old friend William Duncan, who were working with an earlier generation of cedar-getters in the caldera, made their way through the Numinbah Gap and down the valley to the point where Cave Creek enters the Nerang River, where they stumbled upon the biggest Red

Cedar they had ever seen. The boys, with no way of exploiting their find, had no option but to return to cutting among the gangs on the Tweed, but Duncan never forgot what he had seen. Forty years later he found the magnificent tree again; it was eventually felled and reduced to a column of timber 127 feet long, with a girth of 17 feet, yielding a total of 13,763 super feet.

It is probably useful to explain at this point that the Australian Red Cedar, *Toona ciliata* var. *australis*, is not a cedar, but a mahogany, a member of one of the seven genera in the Meliaceae family. George Bentham's belief that the Australian tree was identical to the Indian Toona (*Flora Australiensis*, 1:387), also called Suren or Indian mahogany, has now been vindicated, but not without a good deal of intellectual ferment. In 1843 Leichhardt lamented he didn't know the scientific name of the 'noble red cedar' (Bailey, J., 102). Many had been proposed. In 1840 Austrian botanist Stephan Endlicher included Toona as a section of *Cedrela* (2:1055); in 1846 Swiss botanist J. J. Roemer realised that there were sound grounds for elevating Toona to the rank of a genus (139). Victorian state botanist Ferdinand Mueller disagreed, and for years he prevailed (*Fragmenta*, 1:4). Even J. H. Maiden accepted the Muellerian name *Cedrela australis* in preference to Bentham's *Cedrela toona*. It was after a revision by David Smith in 1960 that the Australasian and Asian *Cedrela* species were finally placed in the genus *Toona*, it being understood that the genus *Cedrela* was confined to central and tropical South America. The Australian cedar was then thought by botanists of the same mind as H. A. T. Harms (270) to be a separate species, *Toona australis*, until Bentham was proved right once again. The genus was revised again in 1995 by Dr Jenny Edmonds of Kew. The Australian Red Cedar is now to be called *Toona ciliata* var. *australis*. There are still botanists who believe that *Toona* and *Cedrela* together form a single genus, so anyone studying our cedars has to remember all the names. The matter cannot be allowed to end there, because there are botanists who would place both in the order Cedrelae, and those who would place the order Cedrelae in the Cedreloideae and those who would put it in the Swietenioideae.

The ships' carpenters of the First Fleet no sooner clapped eyes on the Australian cedars than the race was on.

Cedar quality was well known in the naval timber trade, for India had over many years supplied both cedars – the coniferous Indian cedar (*Cedrus deodara*) and the deciduous toon – to European navies and civilian merchants. It would seem that most British naval personnel and officers of marines at that time could easily identify cedar by sight and smell. At least one would have thought so. Yet it did take a while for Phillip, Hunter, Collins, White, Tench, Dawes and others who were bright enough to be excited at the discovery of a marvellous timber to drop the 'walnut' and 'perhaps mahogany' and state the obvious – those huge trees, with their beautiful rich canopy of leaves in summer, growing on the banks of the Nepean/Hawkesbury were cedars. (Vader, 21)

To the simple-minded among us, among whom I am proud to count myself, there is nothing obvious about the cedar-ness of *Toona australis*. If the Cedar of Lebanon and the other members of the genus *Cedrus* are cedars, then the Australian Red Cedar is not one. No one has ever argued that the White Cedar (*Melia azedarach*) is a cedar, obviously or otherwise. The White Cedar and the Red, and the Incense Cedar (*Anthocarapa nitidula*) are in the Meliaceae, as is the Onion Cedar (*Owenia cepiodora*), whose wood, when the genuine article was exhausted, was soaked in running water to remove the characteristic onion smell, sawn and sold as Red Cedar, to such an extent that mature Onion Cedars are now almost as rare as old-growth Red Cedars. There are no fewer than three species called Pencil Cedar. One of them, *Dysoxylum mollissimum*, is in the same family, as is its relative *D. rufum*, sometimes called Bastard Pencil Cedar. The other two Pencil Cedars, *Polyscias murrayi* and *Glochidion ferdinandi*, are not even distant relatives, nor is the Black Pencil Cedar, *Polyscias elegans*. *Euroschinus falcata* is not a cedar either, though it is called by some Chinaman's Cedar because its wood is another cheap substitute for Red Cedar. It is a member of the Anacardiaceae, along with Yellow Cedar, *Rhodosphaera rhodanthema*. Every one of these pseudo-cedars grows in the Cave Creek rainforest. Catch me calling anything an 'obvious' cedar.

In 1791 Governor Phillip sent samples of Red Cedar collected from the Hawkesbury district back to England, together with potted sample plants for Sir Joseph Banks (Vader, 21). Within a few months Hawkesbury cedar was being felled wholesale and delivered to Port Jackson for use in the new colonial buildings. What made the process easier was that Red Cedar floats high in the water. For the early timber-getters, who were working along the coastal forests and lower reaches of the rivers, it was a relatively easy matter to fell the trees, and snig the logs to the nearest watercourse, where they were lashed together and floated to coastal ports to be shipped overseas. The work was dangerous: 'There is much bullock-punching and rafting up to your middle in water. A timber-getter has much of the aquatic animal about him, and does not care much for sharks, fiddlers or stingarees, in the muddy waters. He is a caution to snakes at any time . . .' (BC, 5 August 1876)

The first attempt at regulating the industry was made in 1795 but, with no way of policing the area or of exercising legislative control, the activity of the timber-getters continued unchecked. Ships making landfall anywhere along the coast were only too ready to load up with cedar as ballast. Within months of the discovery of the Hunter River in 1797, the timber-getters had felled most of the cedar that grew along its banks. By 1798 Red Cedar was the colony's third-largest export. In 1802 the colonial administration issued a more rigorous order, which simply proved that earlier attempts to stop the rush for 'red gold' had been ineffectual. The timber-getters, way ahead of the game, had already pressed northwards into uncharted territory. By 1829 they had opened up the Manning River, by 1832 the Macleay, by 1838 the Clarence, and in every case the result was the same. Once the forests were torn apart, the increased run-off brought more topsoil to the rivers. The once deep and fast-flowing streams became shallow and sluggish.

The cedar-getters forged onwards, into the vast rainforest known as the Big Scrub in the valley of the Richmond River and swiftly on to the Tweed. Others were also moving southward from the new convict settlement of Moreton Bay, now Brisbane. Here they encountered resistance from the local Aboriginal peoples but, even so, 'valuable rafts of cedar, beech, pine &c' were a common sight on the southern reaches of Moreton Bay (BC, 5 August 1876). By 1870 the valuable timber was gone from all the accessible parts of south-east Queensland. One of the few places where it could still be found was Numinbah.

Timber-getting was a tough way to make a living anywhere. Bernard O'Reilly gives a wonderfully vivid account of how his brothers and cousins dealt with forest on the other side of the Nerang Valley, on the Lamington Plateau, forest very similar to CCRRS. 'First hooks were used to slash the thorny, stinging entanglements that defied entry to the great forest . . .' (O'Reilly, 101–2) The hooks were what Australians call brush hooks, which are the same as the British hedging tools called slashers. To keep its operator out of range of lashing spines and stinging leaves, not to mention the odd affronted snake, the brush hook has a long straight handle and a heavy slightly curved blade. It is used as much to bash down the brush as to slice through it, but the blade is kept razor-sharp, to fell at a stroke any of the many saplings that crowd the forest floor. The understorey for several yards all around the target tree would be slashed with the hook to allow room for the axe swing, leaving serried ranks of pointed stakes.

The thorny entanglements are many, most commonly Cockspur Thorn, Lawyer Vine and Prickly Supplejack. Cockspur Thorn (*Maclura cochinchinensis*) will grow right through forest trees, to emerge in the canopy as branching sprays of long sharp spines. Lawyer Vine (*Calamus muelleri*), also known as Hairy Mary and Wait-a-while, is actually a palm, that grows in long canes that loop and snake through the undergrowth. Every part is armed with thousands of spines, all sharp and capable of drawing blood, but worst of all are the almost invisible developing flower spikes whose tiny hooks catch in flesh or cloth and hold on. To struggle is to give the springing fronds another opportunity to take hold. To pick the toothed fronds off is to end up bloody. Prickly Supplejack (*Ripogonum* spp.) is easier to deal with, but not much.

The stinging guardians of the forest are first and foremost what the old botanists called *Urtica gigas*, the tree nettle, now called *Dendrocnide excelsa*, but still in the Urticaceae. O'Reilly, who tells a harrowing tale of how his brother Tom ended up wrapped in the branches of a giant stinger, called it Gympie Gympie. (Gympie is a version of a Yugambeh word meaning 'stinging tree'.) The true Gympie Stinger is *D. moroides*, common further north. Our Giant Stinger has bigger leaves that are truly heart-shaped, whereas the Gympie Stinger leaves are ovate and often peltate, which means that the leafstalk instead of attaching to the edge of the leaf blade is attached within it. Both trees sting like fire, delivering formic acid through fine stellate hairs that cover every part of the plant. From the beginning of our work in the forest I have loved this species and worked hard to propagate it. (No professional grower will offer it, for obvious reasons.) Not only are the young trees very beautiful with their foot-long heart-shaped leaves of apple-green silk-velvet, each accurately pinked around the margin, they are exceptionally willing, springing up wherever there is disturbance, holding up their huge leaves like shields to screen the wounded forest from draughts and other noxious influences. They offer a salient reminder that trees are not for hugging. There is no room for touchy-feeliness in the forest.

You'd reckon that such offensiveness in a plant would be principally a protection against being eaten, but in fact *Dendrocnide excelsa* is the worst victim of herbivory in the whole forest community. Every mature stinger has leaves reduced to lace by a chrysomelid beetle, *Hoplostines viridipennis*, whose mouth parts are not such that it is troubled by stinging hairs.

It is strange, but becoming less strange to me as I begin to understand the forest, to think that the role of the Giant Stinger is not to protect itself from herbivory but to defend the forest. The leaves of mature trees up in the canopy sting far less than the leaves that their juvenile offspring present at the level of face or neck. *D. excelsa* is helped by a sneaky relative, *D. photinophylla*, the Shiny-leaved Stinger, which is far less distinctive, having leaves of regulation Hookers Green that resemble the leaves of lots of other understorey plants. The native herbaceous nettle, *Urtica incisa*, stings with almost as much vim as its tree relatives. In all three cases, to wet the skin is to reactivate the delivery system in the hairs, renewing the painful burning, sometimes for weeks.

In the Cave Creek rainforest the huge trees clutch at the rocks with wandering flanges rather than sending down a single anchoring root. As O'Reilly says, the trees 'are supported mainly by high buttresses which in many cases extend more than twelve feet from the tree proper and which make tree-felling from the ground level an impossibility. This calls for the use of a springboard; made of light wood, four feet long and a foot wide, it has at one end a steel tip, which is inserted into a horizontal slot cut into the tree.' (102) The tip of just such a springboard has been found by the workers at CCRRS. The timber has rotted away; all that is left is the massive forged iron V and four stout nuts and bolts still hanging in their sockets. There is a downturned tooth at the apex of the V so that as the axeman bounced on the board he drove the tip further into the trunk.

Some fellers cut toe-holes in the tree so they could climb up and fix the springboard, others knocked up a makeshift platform-cum-ladder. Before chopping or sawing could begin, the cutters had to study the tree, assess any twist or hollow in the trunk, decide which way it would fall, and cut out a shallow wedge or 'scarf' on that side. They would tap the tree with the back of the axe, listening to hear if it was 'piped', that is, if there was a hollow running up inside it. The scarf was offset slightly to leave a heel, in the hope of preventing the tree's suddenly snapping off as the saw teeth or axe blade cut further into it. The bark was then peeled away so that it wouldn't clog the teeth of the saws. If the scarf was wrongly placed, and the weight of the tree pulled it in the wrong direction, the saw would be trapped, so wedges were driven into the cut to keep it open.

> on this narrow rocking perch the settler swings his razor-edged axe, sometimes twenty and even thirty feet from the ground, which bristles with the sharp stumps of slashed undergrowth. Then, when the tree begins to go, he must descend swiftly, bringing not only his axe but his springboard. All good fellers bring their boards to the ground to obviate the possibility of fouling by the falling tree. (O'Reilly, 102–3)

There is no knowing now how our springboard came to be abandoned in the forest. The forged iron tip would not have been jettisoned even if the springboard had broken; it would have been unscrewed from the broken board and fitted to the new one. If it was left behind, it was because retrieving it was impossible. For a springboard to be abandoned, there must have been an accident, one of many in the forest. I keep the iron tip as a sacred relic, sacred to the memory of the human beings – and the trees – that lost their lives.

The O'Reilly boys all at one time or another sustained terrible injuries from their own axes. Ped and Herb both severed leg tendons; Pat buried his axe in his abdomen; Norb stitched a cut on his leg with needle and cotton. By way of variation on the self-injury theme, Mick fell from his springboard and was impaled on a spike. The most dangerous things in the forest were not however the men's axes but the enormous trees, with their long clear boles and heavy canopy. The largest living Red Cedar recorded was 54.5 metres tall; dropping it must have been like dropping Nelson's Column.

> The swaying of the heavy tops may form wind cracks right up through the heart of the tree. Suppose – and here I quote a case that is not infrequent – a man on a springboard fifteen feet from the ground has just chopped into the heart of a tree: a puff of wind bends the heavy top outwards. Then with the sound of a bursting bomb, the trunk splits up through the heart as far as the branches; the riven half lashes out and upwards, perhaps sixty feet, with a fearful sweep, as the head drops forward; for a split second the tree may balance horizontally by the middle on the shattered, upright trunk sixty feet above, then, pivoting wildly, it drops full length beside the stump. From first to last the calamity may have taken three seconds or less; even had there been time for action, no one could predict the ultimate position of that one hundred and fifty feet of tree as it struck the ground . . .
> (O'Reilly, 103)

Once the trees began to fall, the cutters had to leap for their lives, hoping to avoid not only the sharp stakes beneath them, but the torn-off branches that came crashing down from above. They called those branches 'widowmakers'. Each tree was knitted to its neighbours by tough vines that played their own role in strengthening the underpinnings of the canopy.

> A big tree in falling, may, through the medium of these vines, tear off large portions of a tree-top fifty yards behind it, in the direction an

axeman is most likely to run for cover; again, a big vine, well anchored behind, may by its pull, deflect the falling tree into a high fork from which it will slide back off its own greasy stump and bury its butt in the earth a chain away. (O'Reilly, 104)

In attacking the bases of trees more than a hundred feet tall the fellers were invoking chaos. Each time a forest giant measured its length they were at the mercy of unforeseeable consequences. Nobody knows how many of the men and boys who tried their luck at timber-getting lost their lives or were permanently maimed. For an injured man there was nothing for it but to attempt to control bleeding and infection by any means to hand. If it was decided that he had to seek medical attention, he ran a significant risk of dying before he got to it. The only available painkiller was also the only available disinfectant, rum.

The men who went after red gold in the Australian rainforests had little hope of getting rich. The money would be made by the middlemen, the sawmillers and timber merchants, who could buy cheap from the timber-getters who had nowhere else to go.

These sawyers and their mates are a strange wild set, comprising in general a good proportion of desperate ruffians, and sometimes a few runaways, they themselves being commonly ticket-of-leave men or emancipists. Two or three pair, accompanied by one or two men for falling, squaring small timber, and digging pits, shoulder their axes and saws, and with a sledge and a dray-load of provisions, proceed to some solitary brush where they make a little 'gunya', or hut, with a few sheets of bark, and commence operations. (Henderson, 88–9)

Because cedar-getters were prevented by law from actually settling on crown land, they had no way of investing their money and no incentive to save it. When supplies ran out, they would head back to the nearest township to sell the cut.

The cedar dealers furnish them from time to time with salt provisions, flour, tea and sugar; and every three or four months the sawyers travel down to the cedar dealers, who live at the mouths of the rivers, for a settlement of their accounts . . . [The dealers] take care to have a good assortment of clothing, tobacco, &c in their huts, with which they furnish the sawyers at an advance of about three hundred per cent on the Sydney prices: this with a cask or so of rum and wine, to enable the sawyers to have a fortnight's drinking bout, generally balances their accounts. (Hodgkinson, 28)

The timber-cutters, it seems, were vulnerable to their own version of the 'lambing down' that kept shearers poor. Clement Hodgkinson is here describing the cedar-getters he observed on the Macleay in 1847; much the same situation was observed further north on the Clarence.

The old cedar-getters usually worked about three months in the year, taking a load of cedar to Grafton or Bellingen, and with the proceeds buying enough food and grog to do them three or four months. When this was gone, they would then go in to the scrub for another load, and so on until the timber cut out.

In 1869, when New South Wales premier John Robertson visited the Tweed, the reporter who accompanied him waxed hyperbolic about cedar-getters.

They are the roughest of rough fellows – muscular as a working bullock, hairy as a chimpanzee, obstinate as a mule, simple as a child, generous as the slave of Aladdin's lamp. A fondness for rum, and a capacity for absorbing vast quantities of that liquid, are among their prominent characteristics. They are also in the habit of 'bruising' each other upon the smallest provocation; and it is a noticeable fact that one of the surest ways of securing the friendship of a cedar-cutter is to knock him down. (*SMH*, 26 August)

Edmund Harper, one of the two boys who found the huge cedar in 1846, tells us in an article written nearly fifty years later for *The Queenslander*:

Times were pretty rough . . . We generally went in little bands of 4 to 8 and made our huts close to the sawpits. We had to carry our water for over a mile on some of the mountains; we used to carry a five-gallon keg each . . . There was no scarcity of kegs on the Tweed in those days or of raw rum either I am sorry to say . . . (Q, 1 September 1894, 410)

Harper, thought to be the son of a man transported for house-breaking, was educated at Sydney College. How he ended up cedar-getting on the Tweed with William Duncan has yet to be explained. For a time Harper and Duncan were based in Brisbane, working as pit-sawyers. In 1863 Duncan sold up, bought a bullock team and travelled south through virgin bush to Nerang, where a cotton manufactury was to be set up, and cut and hauled timber for the construction of the factory. When that job was finished, he went timber-getting again. By 1869 when Duncan applied for a homestead grant of forty acres on the Nerang River at Gilston, he had been felling timber in the area at least since 1866, when he first applied for a licence, and possibly much longer. The Post Office directory gave his occupation as sawyer. Both Harper and Duncan could speak a number of Aboriginal languages, so it seems likely that in the beginning at least their workforce was Aboriginal. Duncan's six sons all became pit-sawyers and bullockies. Harper set up a wharf on Little Tallebudgera Creek where cedar logs from the upper Nerang River were 'dogged' (chained together) for rafting.

At first Nixon exploited the timber he found on his own selections. In August 1878, in return for a payment of £3.15s, he secured three General Timber Licences that would permit him to log in the 40,000 acres of Timber Reserve. In November 1879 he took out two more, in May 1880 two more, and in October 1880 three more, and so on until December 1888. Rather than expose himself to the hardships and privations of cedar-getting, Nixon probably followed Bray's example and recruited an Aboriginal workforce. As soon as they were felled the cylindrical carcasses of the trees were stripped of their bark, then of their sapwood, and then squared for transport or for 'slabbing up'; the work was done in the Queensland brushes by eye, without the benefit of any sort of marking or measuring. When

'G. C. C.' visited the Tweed in 1876 he was impressed by the contribution of Aboriginal workers. 'I found them engaged the same as the white men – viz. squaring cedar logs, and I was told that they had a truer eye in squaring the side of a log straight than the best timber-getters.' (*BC*, 5 August)

Aborigines were employed also to find the cedar, cut the tracks to the trees, cut them down, snig the logs to a watercourse and ride them down to Nerang, where other Aboriginal workers would tie the logs together to be rafted to Brisbane. This they did often for no other reward than a weekly plug of tobacco. According to Carl Lentz, 'They mostly got their own food, game, yams, etc., were in abundance' (Lentz, 25). 'G. C. C.' corroborates this: 'For a little tea and tobacco, [the blackfellows] find out where the cedar is on the mountains or pocket scrub.' Clearly they would not allow themselves to be so callously exploited indefinitely.

There is no way of removing canopy trees that will not cause utter devastation. The trees are knitted together by lianes; what surrounding trees are not themselves knocked down by the fall of the heavy crown will be dragged down by the vines that knit them to it. Whether the sawn logs are dragged to a shoot to slide down to a collection point, or snigged, that is, dragged through the jungle, even if roads are cut to them, the forest is utterly devastated. Somehow, Nixon acquired a reputation for being unusually destructive. According to Numinbah historian Donna Yaun:

> the later trade (forestry) he abused to a great degree, having the idea of getting the logs into the stream with the medium of the aboriginal inhabitants, payment being made in those unbecoming habits of white men and the promise of better things to come, which was in all the death knell for the children of the Australian bushland. (undated newspaper clipping, Gold Coast City Library)

Mrs Yaun did not come to the valley until 1984, nearly a hundred years after Nixon left it, but her husband's ancestors actually knew Nixon. When Gresty, who was for many years Senior Park Ranger for the National Parks Division of the Department of Forestry, singles out Nixon for condemnation in 1946, he cites a persisting oral tradition.

His methods were ruthless and his indiscriminate despoliation of the red cedar is still an unpleasant memory among the descendants of the pioneer timber getters. (59)

Some notion of the devastation can be gleaned from an account given by Nixon's niece Florence Bray of her attempt to travel from the Tweed to her uncle's homestead in 1884:

we set out to spend the winter holidays at Numinbah. It was about twenty miles away . . . there seemed to be a perfect maze of paths and track after track that we tried ended up in a large felled cedar tree, or the patch where one had lain before being cut up and drawn away by the bullock teams . . . (Bray, Florence, 56)

What the children encountered in the devastated forest was the evidence of the mismanagement of a mission that had always been impossible.

The cutters felled the trees and walked out over the rough miles to explain to the bullockies if possible, just where the big logs lay. Many cut logs could not be reached, they were too deep in the forest and too far away from the bullocks' feeding grounds . . . Nixon tried to slide them into the Nerang River, where, he reasoned, the next flood racing down from the mountain heights would sweep them into the backwater estuary at Southport. (Groom, 90)

There was nothing unusual in Nixon's attempt to use the freshes to shift his timber; it was what everyone did. For years correspondents of *The Queenslander* had been complaining of logs left to decay in the forest and of creeks jammed with half-rotten timber. For months on end the rain was not enough and the creeks were too low to move anything. Then, when the skies opened, roaring torrents would leap down the gulleys, rolling massive boulders as they went, bouncing even the biggest logs end over end until they were splintered.

> The scheme was a big failure, a huge waste of timber. Many logs were left in the jungle, some found this century half rotten, others washed out to sea or smashed against boulders . . . (Groom, 90)

One condition of timber licences was that the felled logs had to be removed from the forest within twelve months. Any that were left lying longer would be forfeit to the state. In 1880 a duty of two shillings per 100 super feet was imposed on fallen cedar, in the hope of slowing down the rate of deforestation.

It was already far too late. An observer noticed in 1876:

> The devastating axe of the timber-getter has made dire havoc among the cedar brushes, and where a few years ago immense quantities of the wood were to be found, there is not now a single tree worth the cutting. The sawyers are a most wasteful set of men. They spoil more timber than they use. They cut and square only the very best parts of a tree, leaving great masses of cedar, which would fetch a great price in the market, to rot unheeded in the brushes. They destroy young trees, too, with most culpable carelessness, and wishing only to seize present advantages, care not a button how many young trees they destroy in cutting down an old one. In about twenty years such a thing as a cedar tree will not be found in the country. (BC, 5 August)

This dismal prediction was only too true. For years too many people had been getting too much cedar too fast. In Queensland a thousand men were said to be 'engaged in this one industry'. Cedar was being stockpiled; sawmillers and shippers alike were refusing to take new rafts at any price. It was in this situation of crisis that the Queensland government decided that the state should gain more from the wholesale exploitation of its most valuable commodity, and announced the imminent increase of the duty on cedar from two shillings per 100 super feet to twelve shillings.

The tax on felled timber not did apply to sawn timber. Canny operators, some of whom were timber-getters themselves, were already acquiring sawmilling equipment. The felled timber was considered the property of the feller, who had no way of earning income from it until it was sold. The proposed tax of twelve shillings per super foot on unsold timber was more than its value, once the costs of transport had been paid.

All over Queensland, timber-getters organised to defeat the government's intention. On 9 September 1882 a meeting was convened at Tobin's Music Hall in Nerang, in the presence of the local member of the state parliament. Nixon seconded the first resolution, to get up a petition against the proposed tax; and proposed the third:

> 'That the timber-getters, being the pioneers, and having gone to considerable expense in making roads etc., and as they form a considerable proportion of the population of the district, claim consideration at the hands of the government.'
>
> He stated that the roads had been formed by the timber-getters in places where the Government could never have gone and that the roads being made opened up the country and induced settlement. The timber-getter was already heavily taxed, with license fee, divisional board rates, &c. (*BC*, 12 September)

Another motion provided for a committee charged with preparing and presenting the petition to the state parliament, on which Nixon was slated to serve. This motion was seconded by a 'Mr Ginnay', probably Timothy Guinea, who had selected one half of what is now CCRRS for timber, or perhaps his son John, who selected the other half.

Selectors were of course entitled to fell and/or sell the timber off their own land either as standing timber or logs.

> Quite a raid is now set in upon all useful timber, whether pine, beech, or hardwood, and the number of saw mills south of Beenleigh has, during the past year, quite doubled the power of reducing logs into quartering and boards, so that every settler who has trees is courted by two or three parties till he sells all the trees on his selection . . . Further south, settlers without means to obtain bullocks and trucks for drawing

logs are casting about for someone to find the money, so that their sons may go to work in stripping the farms of the timber. But settlers and millowners both in the bush and in the town should recollect that while cabbages may give a crop every year, it will be widely otherwise with crops of timber trees. (*BC*, 25 April 1884)

It was already too late to protect the forests, even if a timber royalty, as the cedar duty came to be called, had been the way to do it. On 20 May a meeting of timber-getters was convened at Nerang.

There were about 60 persons present representing about 60 teams engaged in the timber trade. Frank Nixon Esq. J.P. of Numinba, Upper Nerang, occupied the chair.

Eight resolutions were passed *nem con*, including:

1. That the proposed new timber regulations would materially cripple the interests of the district
2. That the proposed royalty will be (a) unjust, (b) excessive, (c) vexatious, and (d) almost impossible to collect
3. That the Ranger could not distinguish on a wharf the timber taken from Crown lands from that taken from free-holds
4. That it was an utter impossibility for a ranger's measurement to be anything like a buyer's measurement
5. That New Zealand timber could be sold in Brisbane at less price than the Queensland timber getter could produce it for . . .

Nixon made his own contribution, which was reported thus:

From the Coomera River to the border there were six rivers, viz., Coomera, Nerang, Little Nerang, Mudgeraba, Tallebudgera, and the Currumbin. All the timber on those rivers that is get-at-able with horse or bullock teams has been removed years ago. The timber now left was in small patches, and very little in a patch, at the heads of these rivers, in difficult places near the main range. Cedar was not even found there in more than 2 or 3 in a group, and sometimes were from half a mile to a mile apart . . . The only payable method of working these cases was to put the timber into the river and wait for a flood, and sometimes 3 or 4 years are lost before anything can be realised.

Charles Batten, Ranger of Crown Lands, was already busy seeking out and confiscating felled timber that had not been removed from the forest. On 2 June 1885, 99,000 super feet of cedar, marked with a broad arrow, were sold in four lots at the Nerang police office (Q, 23 May). A smaller lot was marked and sold in August to be followed by an astonishing 115,229 super feet in October (Q, 8 August).

Government inspectors kept pointing out that certain clauses associated with the timber contracts had lapsed. In one inspector's count Nixon had 62 logs of cedar, totalling 54,000 super feet, left in the forest. The timber was seized on paper and put up for sale in the hope that some other person might risk the transport difficulties. Nixon bid unsuccessfully, three pence per 100 feet for his own timber, which was passed in without a sale being made. He gave up the cedar business as a costly failure. (Groom, 90–1)

In 1888 the timber taxes were abolished, but for Nixon as for many another timber-getter, it was already too late. The recession in the rural economy had bitten deep; bullock teams had had to be sold; sawmills had been closed down, and their equipment sold off. Nobody could afford to move the fallen timber.

All over the mountain slopes at the head of the Nerang River huge logs of Rosewood and Red Cedar are lying rotting, so slowly that after rather more than a century some are still solid. Dozens lie jammed in the creeks or thrown up on the banks, festooned with mat rush and climbing ferns, starred with elaborate fungi that shine out like lamps in the arboreal gloom. The CCRRS workforce knows better than to suggest moving them, even when a flood banked behind two of them wiped out the better part of a creekside planting. We could sell them even now, but to me they are monuments, not simply to the lost grandeur of the virgin forest, but to the many nameless men and boys who struggled to make a decent living the only way they could. Above all they commemorate Frank Nixon's unfortunate Aboriginal workers, who could expect no medical attention for the terrible injuries that were the timberworkers' lot and could well have paid for their weekly plugs of tobacco with their lives. Carl Lenz recalled a meeting with an Aboriginal forestry worker who he hoped would tell him the truth about the Bunyip:

> I met a Richmond River native – his two mates arrived to take him away. They had a job scrub falling. The poor chap got a cut on the leg with an axe, they had no doctor, and he died . . . (Lentz, 26)

When the most inaccessible recesses of the Numinbah Valley were finally surveyed, and opened for selection, they were selected for their timber. The first owner of CCRRS, Timothy James Guinea, arrived in Australia from Ireland in 1836. The two parcels that make up CCRRS were among six selected by Guinea and two of his sons. The whole Guinea family, who made their home at Advancetown, the hub of the timber traffic, was involved in logging and hauling of timber with bullock teams. As they gradually exploited their craggy holdings, hunting out the remaining Red Cedar deep in the gorges, and scanning the steep hillsides for signs of the deciduous trees in winter, or the flushed pink new growth of spring, they would carve out tracks to get to it. Once they had felled the target tree they often had to build roads with picks and shovels to haul out the carcass.

In 1893 Timothy's youngest son Din Guinea, working in the forest at Cave Creek along with his mate Sandy Duncan (who found the Natural Bridge), came across the biggest cedar they had ever seen. Confronted with this botanical marvel with its unusually bottle-shaped trunk, deep in the trackless forest, the only thing they could think to do was to cut it down. This proved something of a challenge, because they couldn't find anyone who had a cross-cut saw that was long enough. Eventually, having joined forces with Hector Burns, a famous bullocky and an erstwhile confederate of Nixon, Guinea found a Canadian who did.

> The splitting of the big cedar log was done by an American named Henry Fritch, who had at one time in his adventurous career been a

trader among the Red Indians. He had his special saw which he brought from America, with what he called the 'Lumberman' tooth. With great skill he bored a row of holes along opposite sides of the log, using a six foot long auger. These holes were only two or three inches apart, and he used blasting powder in them to start the splitting process which was finished with huge wedges and a screw-jack. (Burns narrowly escaped death with a mistimed blast.) The edges were then squared with a broad-axe to reduce the width to what would fit on the bullock waggon beds. After all this wastage Messrs Guinea and Burns were paid for more than 4,100 super in the two pieces of one ten foot long log. The tree was believed to contain a total of 11,000 super feet in five logs. (Hall *et al.*, 82)

The butt log of the great tree was full 34 feet round.

The second log was the best and was sent to the first World Fair to be shown in Paris, 1900 A. D. It was then sent to the Crystal Palace in London, put in a glassed-in room for show with bright metal plates of the names of the getters, also where it grew, to be left for perpetuity.

Perpetuity is not what it used to be. The Crystal Palace burnt down in 1936 and the great log went with it.

That amazing tree was not the only candidate for the biggest Red Cedar ever; every district had its own and the Numinbah Valley had several. A cedar removed at about the same time from CCRRS is said to have yielded a record 18,000 super feet of marketable timber. It is odd to think now of the Guineas felling and carting hundreds of trees off Cave Creek properties, yet leaving the valuable timber felled by Nixon to lie where it fell, but there was an honour among timber-getters which required them never to saw or ship another man's wood. Duncan and Guinea were probably not informed when Nixon died in Thargomindah in 1896. Perhaps they were afraid of Mrs Nixon, who until 1904 was the most powerful landowner in the valley.

The land that is now CCRRS changed hands regularly. At one point part of it became the property of one Albert P. Abraham, who lived there with his family until one rainy night in January 1910 tragedy struck:

> Albert F. Abraham was ... last seen alive at Upper Nerang on Saturday evening, and left about 9.30 to ride to his home. Rain was falling heavily, and the creeks and gullies which he had to cross were flooded. About 5 p.m. yesterday a search party discovered the dead body of the unfortunate man in the creek, about three chains from the crossing. His horse was found alive near by, having been caught in the vines growing on the bank. Abraham was a native of the district, 30 years of age, unmarried, and resided with his parents. (*BC*, 19 January)

There was no other way for young Abraham to get from 'Upper Nerang', since 1939 called Numinbah Valley, to his parents' property than to follow the track that crisscrossed the river, in those days still known as Nerang Creek. When rain falls along the McPherson Range, the headwaters of the Nerang can become raging torrents shifting millions of tons of turbid water, rolling rocks as big as houses, only to subside within a few hours, leaving the streambeds entirely reconfigured. These were the 'freshes' that the timber-getters hoped would shift their timber. Travelling along these mountain streams was always dangerous; drownings of men and beasts were common. Soon after the loss of their son, the Abraham family sold up and left Numinbah.

The devastation of Numinbah did not stop when the Red Cedar and White Beech were exhausted. There was still demand for cabinet timbers like Black Bean (*Castanospermum australe*), 'used for veneers, radio cabinets, turnery and furniture' (Floyd, 2008, 159). The Tulip Oaks or Booyongs (*Heritiera trifoliolata* and *H. actinophylla*) were also sought for their fine grain, as was the sweet-smelling fine-figured Rosewood (*Dysoxylum fraserianum*), one of the biggest but also one of the slowest-growing trees in the forest. Next to be cut out was the Hoop Pine that grew on the upper reaches of the valley floor under the scarps. It was used for 'plywood veneer, butter boxes, all indoor work, flooring, lining, and all joinery' (Floyd, 2008, 59). After Hoop

Pine disappeared from the wild an attempt was made by the Queensland Department of Forestry to grow it in plantations. The remainder of a plantation still survives within the confines of the neighbouring national park, a mass of close-planted dark trees that cannot now be felled. Instead they are gradually falling, as the rainforest rises slowly, inexorably around them.

The Numinbah Valley was the preserve of timber-getters and bullockies for a hundred years. For most of the 1920s twenty-six bullock teams were occupied full-time in removing its timber. Some was shipped whole; more was sawn into slabs in sawpits where the tree trunk was laid over a trench, so that the two-handed cross-saw could be used to cut it longways into slabs, with one man working from above and another below. The earliest dwellings in the district were built of pit-sawn slabs. For twenty years the only sawmill was at Nerang; in 1881 another was built down the valley at 'Pine Mountain' (now called Pages Pinnacle) for a Brisbane firm specifically to mill Hoop Pine.

From the beginning Cudgerie (*Flindersia schottiana*) had been harvested along with Red Cedar. Crow's Ash (*Flindersia australis*), sometimes called teak, which was greasy like teak, with a hard inter-locking grain, was the timber of choice for ballroom floors, as well as railway sleepers, decking, and carriage and coach building. Next came Bolly Gum (*Litsea reticulata*), Red Carabeen (*Geissois benthamii*) and Yellow Carabeen (*Sloanea woollsii*), which took over some of the uses of White Beech, as well as serving for plywood and boxes. Brush Box too was sought for heavier duty in wharves and bridges.

The coming of the Second World War simply accelerated the despoliation of the forests. After the war the devastation accelerated because the loggers now had bulldozers to cut the snigging tracks and trucks with caterpillar treads to carry the logs out. 'Homes for heroes' was the watchword: Forest, Spotted, Red and Flooded Gums, Grey Ironbark, Carabeen, White Mahogany, Brown Tulip Oak, Blackbutt, Tallowwood, Red, White and Yellow Stringybark, and Brush Box, all were felled to answer the demand for hardwood timber. The timbers were needed too for electricity and telephone poles and for railway sleepers. Sawmills sprang up everywhere, including in the forest above CCRRS (Portion 182). A sawmill operated there from the mid-Fifties until 1972, when it was moved to a more convenient location (Portion 190). (It has since been burnt down.)

To walk in the old-growth forest now is to walk in the deep scars left by this relentless exploitation, along tracks that have been gouged out of the mountainside, in a mess of tangled vegetation and torn roots. The decapitated boles rear up alongside, sometimes surrounded by a ring of young trees sprung from their spreading buttress roots. Often the bole bears a headdress of some precious epiphyte, *Vittaria elongata* maybe or *Asplenium polyodon*. The gaps in the forest have been colonised by myrtaceous Brush Box, which outgrew the rainforest saplings that still stand in their dappled shade waiting for their opportunity. With us Brush Box is a handsome tree, with stout rose-pink limbs, thick, glossy leaves and fringed white flowers. A ridge a kilometre or two north of CCRRS supports what appears to be a monoculture of opportunist Brush Box. Occasionally I see the tall column of a Flooded Gum, *Eucalyptus grandis*, a sign that the beloved forest had to cope with fire, as well as with axes and cross-cut saws, chainsaws and backhoes, bullock teams and bulldozers.

One day, high up in the forest on an old snigging track, I found steel cable nearly as thick as my wrist with a lading hook at one end. I followed its snaking length into the undergrowth till I found the other end, its steel strands splayed and frayed. Sixty years ago or so, as a tractor snigged a tree carcass, the cable hooked around it must have twisted, overheated and suddenly, terribly, burst apart. The cable would have sprung and lashed wildly before it came to rest here on the track. Whenever I pass that way, I stop amid the ferns to pay my respects.

CREAM

When Nixon left Numinbah in 1889, the valley was much as he had found it. He had almost certainly found it as it had been cleared by its Aboriginal inhabitants. If he noticed the earthen ring on the eastern bank of the river, there is no record of his having done so. He almost certainly assumed that the grassland he found was natural, not suspecting that it had been kept clear by regular burning to provide a wallaby and pademelon trap. He ran the 1,264 acres to which he had secured title as ranchland, simply grazing his six or seven hundred head of cattle and horses up and down the valley on the native grasses. Every now and then the steers would be rounded up, branded and castrated; these formed the early bullock teams that dragged the timber out of the rainforests. When Nixon's property was sublet to a Southport dairy farmer called Tom Lather in 1889, most of the land was still forest and scrub. Only the horse paddock, which ran along the river bank from the homestead, had been fenced. Hoop Pines still grew at the foot of the scarps.

To run the property at Numinbah, Lather, who was already dairying near Southport, installed his brother-in-law, Tom Cowderoy. Now that government subsidies have been withdrawn, dairying in south-east Queensland is over. We can only wonder now why so many of the early settlers could think of no better way to use the land. Perhaps the green of the subtropical vegetation reminded them of home; the grass was certainly lush but the climate was largely unsuitable. Because of dingoes roaming the scrub, all calves and even young heifers had to be penned up at night. As well as the animals he brought with him, Cowderoy caught as many as he could of Nixon's wild cows, lassoing them and dragging them into the bails to be milked. The milk was poured into large flat bowls and left in a cool house to separate, then the cream was skimmed off by hand, churned by hand, salted and put up in boxes. Once a week the boxed butter was taken to market in Southport by packhorse. The journey up and down the pinches of the rough track along the Nerang took many hours; if it had been raining, as it often had, the horses slipped and slid. If it kept raining, the river would rise and the farmer and his horses would have to swim for their lives. Cowderoy's son Tom remembered:

> One pack day my father had to take the pack down to Southport. He rode Torrelilla and led the packhorse Morra. He arrived safely and delivered the butter and farm produce but coming up the Valley the following afternoon, a sudden storm at the head of the Valley caused the river to rise suddenly. At one crossing he had to swim the horses across, but Torrelilla would not swim properly – he would do nothing but rear up in the water, so my father had to let Morra the packhorse go. He managed to reach the bank but poor Morra was swept downstream by the swift current, and finally stopped by hanging his head over a log. Fortunately Mr Din Guinea whom my father knew well happened to be there with his bullock team. He crept along the log and managed to rescue Morra, who was none the worse for his ordeal. (Cowderoy, 13)

It rained for most of 1890.

> With the constant rain the stockyards got from bad to worse. The poor calves used to get bogged, and had to be dragged out of the mud and brought shivering to the great open fireplace to get warm again.

In 1890 in the depth of the recession Nixon's agent W. Castles sold Tom Lather bullocks to the value of £125. Lather immediately sold them on to a W. Ferguson and accepted his promissory note as payment, simply endorsing it to Nixon. The note was dishonoured and Castles took a mortgage over Ferguson's property. Meanwhile, like many other farmers in the district, Tom Lather was going broke. In June 1891 he attempted to sell a hundred head of bullocks and fifty

head of 'quiet female cattle' at the Beaudesert auctions. 'Terms –
Cash. No Reserve'. (*Q*, 13 June)

On 8 February 1894 a civil action for recovery of Lather's debt was
heard in the District Court (*BC*, 9 February). Nixon had instructed
his solicitor to accept the security in lieu of payment, realise on it,
and claim the rest from the defendant, but the defendant demanded
an immediate release. The judge found for Nixon with costs. On 19
July, at a meeting of Lather's creditors, 'the causes of his insolvency
were put down as inability to carry out a contract with Mr F. Nixon
for the sale and purchase of cattle Etc.' (*BC*, 20 July) In September
Lather was declared bankrupt, owing Nixon, his chief creditor,
£415.14*s*.9*d*. (*BC*, 4 September) Among Nixon's assets at his death
were bills of mortgage Nos 219529 and 219530, of securities to the
estimated value of £184 (QSA 9007/742107).

The Cowderoys did not struggle in the Numinbah Valley for long.
Even so, when they left more land had been cleared, to grow potatoes
and pumpkins as well as maize. The lease was taken over by Nixon's
old racing buddy, Tom Gaven, licensee of the Royal Mail and
Commercial Hotels in Nerang, who owned a string of butcher's
shops. We may conclude that, after this first attempt, dairying on the
Upper Nerang was given up as a bad job, and the milch cows used
for beef production. Gaven also took up Nixon's old portion 3,
Catherine's Flat (*BC*, 5 February 1897 and 11 September 1915).

Another of the early settlers who tried his hand at dairying was a
William McLaren who took it up on his own account after the
Cowderoys had left. As he told Charlie Lentz:

'We ran in heifers with calves, from the bush. We tied the calves up
but most of the heifers cleared out and left the calves to starve, so
the dairying was not much of a success. The heifers were rather
wild. They did not return. Now those people summonsed me for
wages, and I will have to pay them. I don't know much about
dairying, and I don't think they knew much about it either. I dare
say if you come up you would still see a few horns lying about in
the yard yet.' I said, 'You must have had some fun to get them
bailed up.' 'Aye that we did while it lasted, but it did not pay
though,' he replied. (Lentz, 36)

In 1895 a new set of settlers began to move into the valley, taking up smaller selections of about 160 acres. Many of them took up dairying in a small way, producing skim milk to feed their pigs and a can of cream to send each week to the butter factory at Southport.

> Land for selection was purchased at the rate of 2/6 per acre on poorer soil, to higher rates on better country in proportion to its timber species. Land with standing Hoop Pine was widely sought as this was by now the next in demand to Red Cedar which was nigh exhausted. Generous terms allowed selectors upwards of 20 years to pay for land. (Hall *et al.*, 56)

Such favourable terms had to be earned; land that was not 'improved' would be forfeit to the crown. A dwelling had to be built, and the land had to be fenced and cleared. The settlers' way of improving the native grass pasture was to do as the Aboriginal people had done, burn it off regularly. The cattle would willingly eat the soft new grass, keeping it down until gradually the tussocks aged and it was time to burn them again. As late as 1903 the valley could be described as 'still in its natural state, the only thing missing was the red cedar . . . there was no land cleared, only the open grassed forest was used.' (Holden, 14) The 'open grassed forest' was itself an artefact, made and managed for eons by Aboriginal hunters. (Gammage, *passim*)

As more and more land was surveyed and offered for selection, the available grassy sclerophyll forest was all occupied, and only the rainforest was left. The same conditions applied; the selectors had to clear the land. Clear-felling trees a hundred feet tall, chained to each other by massive vines and interlaced with canes, was the most gruelling and terrible work, as well as horribly destructive. Yet it never occurred to any of the settlers that there was any alternative to dairy farming in Queensland the way they had in Ireland or Germany. European dairy cattle that were offloaded in Queensland had no defences against an array of pests and plagues the like of which had never been seen in Europe. The dairy farmers worked all the hours God sent, and all the while they had to watch their animals suffer.

The koalas, bandicoots and Mountain Brushtail Possums of Numinbah had grown up with the paralysis tick, *Ixodes holocyclus*, but imported animals had no resistance to it. A two- or three-week-old calf with ten ticks on it would become paralysed and almost certainly die. In 1843 James Backhouse gave an account of the 'Wattle Tick' as destroying 'not only sheep, but sometimes foals and calves'. (Backhouse, 430) Even today the only treatment is injection with an anti-tick serum developed for dogs, which is far too expensive to use for regularly dosing cattle. The paralysis tick also carries the bacteria *Rickettsia australis*, which causes Spotted Fever, and Borrelia, which causes Lyme Disease in humans. In the warm dampness of the Upper Nerang the so-called New Zealand tick *Haemaphysalis longicornis* also flourished.

Worse was on the way, in the shape of the introduced cattle tick *Rhipicephalus microplus*. In August 1872 twelve Brahman cattle from Indonesia were landed in Darwin. They were destined for slaughter but somehow ended up at Adelaide River, where they mixed with station cattle. Within a generation the cattle tick had crossed into Queensland and was rapidly spreading south and east. An outbreak in Brisbane in April 1898 resulted in the declaration that no cattle or horses would be permitted to cross into New South Wales 'from any portion of the Queensland coast country east of the 148th meridian'. The experience of northern farmers had proved that dairy cattle were least able to withstand the consequences of tick infestation, in particular red water fever, which killed infected animals in a matter of hours. Carl Lentz recalled:

> I had just got started [dairying] when cattle ticks got there from the north, and red water fever broke out everywhere. I lost most of my cows. Some people lost almost all of theirs. (Lentz, 35)

Dairy farmers also had to battle lice, tuberculosis, brucellosis, bloat and anthrax, which turned up in the 1880s under various labels, as 'Cumberland Disease', or splenic apoplexy or pleuro-pneumonia or blackleg. In 1901 the Warples brothers got Henry Stephens to build them stock-dipping yards on Nixon's old Portion 2. Passing teamsters were welcome to use the dip at a cost of 'tuppence' or 'thrippence' a head. The legacy of such dips, which poisoned the land around them, is still a problem today.

The dairy industry lurched from crisis to crisis, and yet year on year more and more settlers destroyed more and more native vegetation so that they could embark on a life of hopeless struggle. In 1911, when the Queensland government opened land on Lamington Plateau for selection, eight members of the O'Reilly family, brothers Tom, Norb, Herb, Mick and Paul, and their cousins, Pat, Luke and Joe, acquired a hundred acres each at a price of 35/- an acre, to be paid off over thirty years at 5 per cent. Three months later the government closed the area to selection, leaving the O'Reilly boys the sole white settlers on the plateau. Their possession of the land was contingent on their clearing it, fencing it, planting pasture grass, and running dairy cattle on it. It was part of the terms of their selection that a certain acreage of rainforest had to be cleared within a year of their taking it up.

> In the felling of rainforest, much chopping may be saved, especially in hilly country, by the use of the 'drive' system. This, roughly, is the cutting of say half an acre of trees only two thirds of the way through and then 'sending them off', with a big drive tree dropped from the uphill side; the pressure goes on slowly at first and then gains momentum, as each tree is pushed from behind and in turn pushes the one in front; the big water-vines too play an important part. The trees do not break off level at the cut; they rip and burst under the pressure, and it is a terrifying sight to see a large strip of lofty forest tearing itself to pieces to the accompaniment of sounds which cannot be described. (O'Reilly, 104–5)

If a single tree refused to give way and held up the drive, the most foolhardy member of the gang might venture in to help it on its way by sawing or chopping a little further into it. Otherwise it was a matter of waiting, for the pressure to increase, for a wind, or, some said, for the next ebb tide.

If everything went as planned each falling tree struck others until all the trees in the drive came crashing down. This was quite a spectacle, and if a really big drive was ready to go, favoured friends might be invited to watch . . . if those invited were girls, they could be counted on to bring a cake or batch of scones and boil the billy, so all present could have a picnic during the lunch hour. (Lentz, 68)

Destruction of the forest was the best entertainment going; sometimes it was done simply for the hell of it. In about 1897 Carl Lentz and his sister were invited by friends who lived at Pine Mountain (now Pages Pinnacle) to explore Connell's Creek (now called Waterfall Creek) and view the spectacular falls (now called Horseshoe Falls). They scrambled up a high spur to the top of the falls.

The spur we were on was very narrow along the top, and open forest, very steep down both sides with dense scrub. One place along the top was full of boulders, some bigger than thousand gallon tanks. One, a very big one, was just on balance. We had an axe, cut a strong sapling, stuck one end to a glut, levered, canted it over. It rolled down against a big bloodwood tree, pushed it over, rolled along it. Near the tree head was a low sharp rock ledge. As the enormous weighty boulder rolled over that, it cut the tree clean off, catapulted the great stem, roots and all, clean over itself and speared it ahead, away down into the scrub below. The boulder gained more momentum, took everything before it and started more rocks going. It was an avalanche, the rumbling noise was terrific, and lasted a good while too. (Lentz, 70)

The entertainment value was not exhausted with the smashing of the trees. The next step in clearing land is the burning off:

The burning of felled jungle is a splendid spectacle. You have perhaps a hundred or more acres covered to a depth of twenty feet with smashed timber and dry leaves . . . The torch is applied along the foot of the clearing, and flames, advancing in a wall, rush up the slopes with a roar which may be heard for many miles. Black smoke, boiling fiercely, shoots up to one thousand feet, and there the terrible heat, contacting the icy upper air, generates a giant thunder cloud which rides majestically above the inferno . . . the steady boom of exploding

rock ... goes on for many hours after the fiercest of the blaze has
subsided. (O'Reilly, 112)

In the course of such a burn millions of creatures lose their lives,
from the possums and gliders in their houses in the tree hollows, the
snakes and lizards that are roasted in their hidey-holes between the
rocks, the tree frogs, and the giant snails, to the whole host of invertebrates. By the time the O'Reillys were clearing rainforest in
Queensland in the nineteen-teens, most of the accessible rainforest
areas on the east coast of Australia had already been felled, burned
and turned to cropland or pasture. The process had been breath-
takingly rapid; within a decade thousands upon thousands of hectares
of forest that had stood for millennia had gone up in smoke.

The distinguished English scientist Sydney Skertchly, who retired
from his post as assistant government geologist in 1897 and settled at
Molendinar, was in no doubt about the folly of clearing and burning
the rainforest.

> Any sap-thirsty ignoramus with an axe can destroy it in an hour; and
> the biggest fool burn it in a day. What does he get? – a light, feathery,
> white powder charged with all the potash and other salts laboriously
> stored in the tree, and he knows this is the plant-food par excellence,
> and thinks he is going to get it. But he won't. Half of it is scattered by
> the wind, most of the residue washed out by the rain and sent into
> Moreton Bay, and his remaining soil is due at the same depot, for
> there is nothing left to hold up the water, and a few hours after a
> heavy downpour the vaunted scrub soil comes floating past my house.
> (Q, 13 May 1922)

On 18 December 1923, Skertchly delivered a lecture on 'The
Nerang River, its past, present and future' to the Institute of Surveyors
in Brisbane.

> The scrubs, Professor Skertchly pointed out, were the greatest holders
> of water we could possibly have. Before they were cut down rain that
> fell at the source of the Nerang River took five days to reach the spot
> at which he lived, but when it fell now the water reached him in five

hours. Not only were the waters not held up in what he described as a sponge – masses of moss and other vegetation – but they were wasted.

To-day's forests had taken thousands of years to grow. They had been there before the arrival of the mammals, but a tree that had been growing for 2800 years could be destroyed by any dairy farmer in 20 minutes. (*BC*, 20 December)

In Skertchly's grim vision the ultimate result of the clearing of the forests would be desertification. He reckoned without the energy with which the farmers set about replacing the destroyed forest with exotic vegetation. Superbly orchestrated forest systems are now cacophonies of weeds.

Kangaroo Grass may be good for growing kangaroos but not for European cattle bred to produce excess milk. The next great 'advance' in Australian husbandry came with the introduction of pasture grasses from other parts of the world. The obvious choice was Paspalum, from the humid subtropical areas of South America. The first species to be introduced in the 1870s, probably at the instance of our old friend Ferdinand Mueller, was *P. dilatatum*, which was well adapted to our high rainfall and fertile soil. Paspalum made its way to Numinbah in 1901, when Henry Stephens seeded it on his property in the Pocket. (Henry Stephens's son Ted became the owner of what is now CCRRS in 1968.) By 1907 Paspalum, Rhodes Grass (*Chloris gayana*) and Prairie Grass (*Bromus cathartica*) were all established in the Numinbah Valley (*BC*, 18 June).

Paspalum dilatatum still grows at Cave Creek as a weed. In deep shade it has been replaced by another member of the genus, called by the locals 'wet styanide', actually *P. wettsteinii*, an indistinct species that seems to include two others, *P. mandiocanum* and *P. plicatulum*. Whatever name this wretched invader actually ends up with, it is shade-tolerant, which means that it can survive under the rainforest canopy. We expect to have to keep removing it for ever. Nothing eats it, the native herbivores finding it just as unpalatable as intro-duced farm animals do. Unchecked, it spreads by seed and by stolons, up and down the steepest slopes, across rocks, smothering all the mosses and ferns and the rainforest grasses.

In the 1920s a new pest threatened to cross the border between the Northern Territory and Queensland. The Buffalo Fly, *Haematobia irritans exigua*, had been accidentally introduced to northern Australia with the water buffalo, which was intended to provide transport and food to remote settlements, first to Melville Island, then to Port Essington on the mainland in 1838. The settlements were abandoned, the buffaloes went feral, and the Buffalo Fly population exploded. The Buffalo Fly breeds in cattle dung; in its native habitat its breeding was controlled by the activities of dung beetles that removed and buried the dung. Australia had its own dung beetles but they had evolved with marsupials and could not process the sloppier cattle dung. Moreover, when scrub was cleared for dairying the ground-dwelling beetle population was usually exterminated. The build-up of cattle dung in the pastures became a problem in itself, because it fouled the pasture grass and encouraged rank growth which was unpalatable to the cattle. Native flies bred exponentially in the decaying cow pats, along with various species of biting midges. The mature Buffalo Fly lives on its host, feeding continually on its blood, the female only descending to lay eggs in fresh dung. Some animals cannot tolerate the flies and rub up against rough surfaces until they have made huge sores in their withers and flanks. The Buffalo Fly also introduces a parasitic worm (*Stephanofilaria* spp.) that burrows under the animals' skin.

The first act of the authorities was to attempt to set up a quarantine: Buffalo Fly infestation was declared a disease and stock crossings were closed. At the annual meeting of the Queensland Co-operative Dairy Companies Association in December 1929, the opinion was voiced that 'its introduction to the coastal districts of the state would be followed by severe losses in dairying produce; the fly would cause more harm to the dairying industry than ever it caused to the beef industry' (*BC*, 14 December). By the mid-1940s the fly had reached our corner of south-east Queensland. Its arrival coincided with the beginning of a campaign to convert people from butter to margarine.

Farmers faced the decision to: 1. increase in size and try to live on butter and pig production, 2. change to beef production, 3. change to whole milk production, 4, sell the farm. The result was a combination of all four, leading to a decline in the number of farms which stabilised in the seventies to a total of sixteen farms in the valley . . . (Hall *et al.*, 92–3)

One of the sixteen farms was what is now CCRRS.

In the meantime dozens of exotic grasses had been introduced to the valley. Vast amounts of energy and enterprise had been expended on finding pasture species that would grow cattle faster. Ultimately no fewer than fourteen species of Paspalum have been naturalised in the Numinbah Valley. To these may be added the improved strains that are produced by plant breeders every year. Paspalum was followed by other grasses. Cocksfoot, sometimes called Orchard Grass (*Dactylis glomerata*), has now colonised all the states of Australia except the Northern Territory. Japanese millet (*Echinochloa esculenta*) was grown for forage, as was a European fescue (*Festuca arundinacea*). European bents (*Agrostis* spp.) were introduced as lawn grasses and are now weeds of pasture.

Paspalum was eventually displaced in our neck of the woods by *Pennisetum clandestinum*, Kikuyu Grass, as more palatable and nutritious. In temperate conditions with an average rainfall of two metres a year, Kikuyu is appallingly rampant. If it is not kept short by continuous grazing, it will grow into massive, matted sward in a few months. Along roadsides all over Australia you will see other Pennisetums, descendants of those imported by the nursery industry. There is a native Pennisetum, *P. alopecuroides*, which could be selectively bred into a useful ornamental, but as two introduced species are easier to grow, being less choosy, they are what you will find in your garden centre, and in council plantings, and on road verges in remote Australia. Another Pennisetum, *P. macrourum* or *P. purpureum* or some hybrid of the two, Elephant or Bana Grass, was imported to serve as windbreaks for crops like bananas and sugarcane. This has found its niche in creeks and watercourses, where it grows in dense eight-foot-high tussocks, completely smothering the complex and delicate riparian ecosystem.

Other grasses were introduced by accident. Meadow Foxtail and Bulbous Oatgrass (*Arrhenatherum elatius*) from Europe were introduced as hay grasses. Sweet Vernal Grass (*Anthoxanthum odoratum*) was introduced to give a pleasant smell to hay. Marram Grass comes from western Europe, where it grows on sand dunes. As far as we can now tell, Wild Oat (*Avena fatua*) was an accidental contaminant of seed. Imported cereals came in with Quaking Grass (*Briza maxima*), which is now all over temperate Australia. How did we end up with *Cenchrus incertus* from tropical America – a vicious pest, injuring the mouths of grazing animals and making wool dangerous to handle, or the barley grasses (*Critesion* spp.) that pierce the skin and damage the eyes of grazing beasts, or Twitch or thirteen introduced species of *Eragrostis* as well as sixty or so of our own? What reason can there have been to introduce *Digitaria sanguinalis*, now a troublesome weed of lawns, gardens and irrigation areas, when we had Digitarias of our own? European Barnyardgrass (*Echinochloa crus-galli*) can mature several generations in a year and outgrows irrigated rice. Attempts to introduce South American Prairie Grass (*Bromus catharticus*) as an out-of-season forage crop in cooler areas failed but the plant now persists as a weed; we did a little better with veldt grasses (*Ehrharta* spp.) and Rhodes Grass, from tropical and subtropical Africa, introduced *c.*1900, but neither proved as drought-tolerant as Buffel grass or Green Panic. The process of acclimatisation never stops. Indeed it gathers momentum year on year.

> Between 1947 and 1985 463 exotic grass and legume species were introduced to northern Australia. (Lonsdale) Of these, only four species were subsequently found to be useful, 43 became listed weeds, while another 17 were found useful but weedy. (Fox, 230)

The worst grasses to be introduced to the Numinbah Valley may eventually prove to be bamboos. Lately a new craze has been spreading, this time for the planting of long lines of bamboo, in this case *Bambusa arnhemica*. These may be simply windbreaks, themselves made necessary because of the clearing of forest. Though *B. arnhemica* is a clumping rather than a running bamboo, it does spread outward in rings around a dead centre and will gradually become bulky and difficult to remove. The rush to bamboo could also be a response to the increase in noise and nuisance, as our remote area has become a favoured site for boy racers and bikies and parties of howling schoolies.

This human infestation is an understandable cause of fear and loathing on the part of the locals, but if bamboo barricades are to be their response the result will be catastrophe. A bamboo with any degree of tolerance for shade would be an utter disaster for regenerating rainforest.

The grasses were just the beginning; as O'Reilly says, 'swift in the wake of a new grass came the dreaded fire-weeds, tobacco, inkweed and lantana.' (118) CCRRS has to deal with all of these. Fireweed is the name given in Australia to a South African ragwort, *Senecio madagascariensis*, which was first reported from the Hunter Valley in 1918. It is now ubiquitous in south-east Queensland. As it is poisonous to horses and cattle enormous amounts of energy have been expended in efforts to control it, to no avail. 'Wild tobacco' is *Solanum mauritanicum*, which grows into a small tree with purple potato flowers and large grey leaves. Brown Cuckoo Doves love its heavy clusters of berries and sow them throughout the plantings in their droppings. Inkweed is *Phytolacca octandra*. Nobody knows how any of these exotics made their way to Australia. Lantana on the other hand was deliberately imported, propagated and planted for forty years. It now covers 4 million hectares in eastern Australia.

The amount of energy and ingenuity invested by the first settlers on introducing Lantana is truly amazing. They had hardly pushed a trowel into Australian soil before they were sending orders to nurserymen in London for cultivars of Lantana, the new wonder-shrub from the American tropics. William Macarthur, youngest son of pioneer settler John Macarthur, began making a garden at the family property in Camden in 1820, when he was just twenty years old. The Hackney nurserymen who supplied Macarthur began listing *Lantana camara*, one of the seven species originally named by Linnaeus, among their wares in 1825 (*Loddiges Botanical Cabinet*, 1825, No. 1171). *L. camara* appears in all the printed catalogues of Macarthur's garden, from 1843. His 1850 catalogue lists two more, another *L. camara*, var. *crocea grandiflora*, and *L. montevidensis*, otherwise known as *L. sellowiana*, after the Prussian botanist who originally collected the seed in Montevideo in 1822. This species with purple flowers was much desired as a summer bedding plant for English planting schemes in the 1850s. At some point Macarthur acquired the West Indian

species *L. trifolia* (formerly known as *Camara trifolia*) under the name
of *Lantana annua*.

The passion for Lantana did not slacken; more and more cultivars
were introduced, adding to the weed potential of the eventual hybrid.
In 1847 Messrs Dickenson and Co., Florists of Hobart, offered *L.
nivea mutabilis*, as described in Hooker's *Botanical Magazine* (5:3110)
in 1831 (*The Courier*, 4 September). In 1848 the Rev. R. R. Davies
of Longford in Tasmania imported two varieties of Lantana under
the names *L. drummondii* and *L. sellowii* (*The Courier*, 13 September).
In November 1850 a Mr Woolley showed his version of the *L. camara*
var. *crocea grandiflora* at the Australasian Botanic and Horticultural
Society Summer Exhibition in Sydney (*SMH*, 30 November) and
the next year saw it being regularly advertised by Sydney
nurserymen. In 1851 a Surry Hills nurseryman was offering three
varieties of Lantana (*SMH*, 29 April 1851). Within weeks two more
Lantanas, *L. aurantica* and *L. aculeata*, were being offered at auction.
By 1852 *L. camara* was on show in the Sydney Botanic Garden. In
1860 Sir Daniel Cooper won the silver medal at the Autumn
Exhibition of the Horticultural and Agricultural Society for a 'new
and rare' plant reported as *L. grandiflora alba* (*SMH*, 9 February).
Brisbane nurserymen began offering Lantana in June 1862; in July
1867 the garden correspondent of the *Brisbane Courier* was telling his
readers that among plants that 'are adapted to this climate and very
desirable for the beauty of fragrance of their flowers' 'various lantanas'
were some of the best (25 July).

The invasiveness of Lantana had already been noticed. In 1864 a
visitor to a property at Lake Innes, near Port Macquarie, reported
that 'The trees are getting destroyed by a shrub imported by the
original proprietor for hedging, namely, the lantana; it has now
grown everywhere, and covers hundreds of acres, "thick as black
night".' (*SMH*, 1 July) Even so, still more Lantana cultivars were
being imported into the colony. In 1868 Mr R. Stephen, Florist,
showed 'four varieties of lantana', described as 'new to the colony
and worthy of cultivation' (*SMH*, 5 November). The *Brisbane Courier*
was still describing Lantana as one of 'our best hedge plants' in 1877
(15 October), although *L. camara*, 'A tall rambling shrub from tropical
America, used in some places for hedge making', had been listed in a

series on weeds in the same newspaper on 19 April 1873. By 1880, when Lantana was finally being described as 'a wretched pest', it was far too late to arrest its onward progress.

Lantana affords valuable cover not only to birds and one vulnerable species of native bee but also to small macropods and large lizards, and to possums when they are feeding on the ground. Birds, especially the tinier fairy wrens and finches, love it. The pademelons are never safer than when they are within their tunnels in the Lantana. Nevertheless, it has to go.

At CCRRS every year we remove tons of Lantana with chainsaws and brush hooks. Sometimes we use our minidigger to drag it down from steep slopes and sometimes we simply roll it over and over and leave it to rot down in a gully. The soil where it grew is always clean, friable and cool, immediately ready to plant into, once we have painted any remaining rooted canes with neat herbicide. Lantana needs sun; once our little trees are high enough to cast shade, Lantana is no threat at all. What is more, if the canopy is restored, none of the other weed species associated with Lantana will take over the space that it has vacated. The message is simple: if you want to eliminate Lantana, restore the forest. Nothing else will work.

Eliminating Lantana by shading it out is not an option for many of the managers of the 4 million hectares that it now covers in Australia, which is why it was the first plant species ever selected for biological control. The scientists could hardly have selected a more challenging candidate.

The aggregate species known as *L. camara* is a 'variable polyploid complex of interbreeding taxa.' It contains a wide diversity of varieties arising from horticultural and natural hybridisation, selection and somatic mutation. (Johnson, S., 9)

There are by now many biotypes of weed Lantana in Australia. What this means is that Lantana is incredibly adaptable and can cope with a vast range of cultural conditions; the dozens of insect species that were chosen as biological controls had to be specialists. Out of the twenty-six insect species released in Australia to prey on Lantana, only four are said to be reducing its vigour: the sap-sucking bug

Teleonemia scrupulosa; the leaf-mining beetles *Uroplata girardi*, released in 1966 and 1972, and *Octotoma scabripennis*; and the seed-eating fly, *Ophiomyia lantanae* (Day *et al.*).

Attention then turned to fungus infections as a means of control. In 1999 *Prospodium tuberculatum*, a fungal leaf-rust collected from Lantana in Mexico, was released in Mount Warning National Park. Most people think that biological controls are greatly to be preferred over chemical controls, but chemical controls can be targeted in a way that biological controls cannot. Though it might seem that an insect or a fungus is a specialist and will attack only the target plant, the matter cannot be proved until the agent is released in a new environment, and that might well be too late. *Teleonemia scrupulosa* attacked Lantana in its native Mexico, but in Uganda it developed a taste for sesame (Greathead). In the US it attacked plants in the genus Diospyros as well as Lantana (Pemberton, 492). Since the rust was released at Mount Warning in 2000, it has been released in more than a hundred locations in New South Wales. So far it has not been detected on any but the target species. Unfortunately none of the Cave Creek Lantana has shown any sign of a rust infection, possibly because the winters are just too cold for the rust spores to survive.

Tree weeds and Lantana are troublesome enough, but the soft weeds that infest the Numinbah Valley are in some ways worse. Stinking Roger (*Tagetes minuta*) comes originally from the southern half of South America, but has been spreading around the world since the Spanish Conquest. The species name '*minuta*' refers to the flower; in our conditions the plant itself grows to shoulder height. It is usually accompanied by Cobblers' Pegs, also called Farmers' Friends (*Bidens subalternans*), now cosmopolitan, originally from tropical central America. Both weeds have allelopathic properties, which enable them to suppress competition (Lopez *et al.*). Then there is Paddy's Lucerne (*Sida rhombifolia*), which is almost impossible to uproot. When it turned up in pasture in southern Queensland, the first observers were bemused:

> It is not a foreigner, however, being indigenous to northern Australia. We know nothing of the history of its spread, which is unaccountably rapid and formidable. Why it should have existed all the years it did

in north Australia, without spreading, and then to come trooping all over the land, must remain an unsolved problem. (*BC*, 4 March 1879)

The common name is an old corruption of 'Paddy Lucerne'. It was early realised that this tough plant was a source of strong vegetable fibre, as useful potentially as jute, and specimens were sent to Europe. The plant needed to be improved and sown thick, so that it grew without branching, and then retted (soaked in soft water) like flax, to extract crude fibre for processing, but the industry never took off, partly because of a chronic shortage of labour. (Maiden, 1891)

Then there is Blue Top, 'identified by the Government Botanist in 1924 as a South American species of heliotrope that has been naturalised in Queensland for some years past . . . A few years ago it appeared about Warwick and has established itself as a very bad weed, most difficult of eradication.' (*Q*, 15 March) 'Blue Top' is not a heliotrope, but *Ageratum conyzoides*, known to English gardeners as 'Bachelor's Buttons', which is so rampant in subtropical conditions as to be virtually unrecognisable. It is usually accompanied by its relatives, Mist Weed (*Ageratina riparia*) from Central America and Crofton Weed (*Ageratina adenophora*) from Mexico. These are all handsome plants with considerable horticultural potential, but in subtropical rainforest they spring up where there is the least spill of sunlight. Creek banks are particularly vulnerable. In 1951 it was reported that Crofton Weed invasion had caused some farmers in the upper Numinbah Valley to abandon their land (*The Courier-Mail*, 22 February 1951). Even harder to eradicate is another garden escape, *Tradescantia fluminensis*, which was smothering our native ground-covers until we found a truly nasty and extremely expensive herbicide that knocks it. Amid the mess of Blue Top and Stinking Roger you will find Purple Top, *Verbena bonariensis* from Brazil, and Red Milkweed (*Asclepias curassavica*), recognised as invasive weeds as long ago as 1879. Nowadays the Red Milkweed has been eclipsed by the Balloon Milkweed (*Gomphocarpus fruticosus*). This made its initial appearance in Australia as a garden plant. As a little girl I used to pick the inflated seed capsules when they were still green, and float them in a dish of water, because with their curved stems they looked like green swans. Now I yank them out by the hundreds.

The lack of awareness about the weed potential of garden escapes even on the part of self-styled experts is bad enough now, but sixty or seventy years ago it was truly shocking. This is 'Chloris', garden correspondent for *The Queenslander*, writing in 1931:

> Speaking of indigenous plants, in the Mount Coot-tha reserve recently I saw some lovely specimens of Baccharis halimifolia, the Groundsel Bush, and thought how pretty they would be in the garden. I see no reason why they should not cultivate well. The shrub is graceful and decorative and the flower is produced in white masses developing into white feathery seed which is long persistent and very pretty. (30 April)

In fact Groundsel is not native to Australia, but to the southern United States, and it was already well known as a weed. A year earlier a better-informed correspondent of the same newspaper had noted: 'This native of tropical North America has become a naturalised weed in Queensland, and has increased considerably of late years. It is capable of becoming a considerable pest if not checked.' (Q, 15 May 1930) Groundsel was officially declared a noxious weed a few days after this article appeared, but 'Chloris' writing a year later was unaware of the fact.

The condition which made the unbalancing of vegetation communities inevitable was clearing. Clearing opened the land to drying winds and burning frosts, as well as to burgeoning annual weeds that set billions of seeds. As the forest canopy grows up, and the weeds die out, we see the return of the forest groundcovers. These may not be spectacular, but they are precious. They are also the first to be destroyed by the introduction of hard-hoofed animals. Most vulnerable are the mosses. There was a time, in the eighteenth century, when British people were enthusiastic about mosses, when they grew moss gardens and made moss houses, but that time is long gone. Moss is now best known as an enemy of that great British garden fetish, the lawn. At Cave Creek we have a whole panoply of mosses. Most spectacular is our Giant Moss, a species of *Dawsonia*, of which each frond looks like an inch-high palm-tree. Last year we grew some in the shade house and planted it out on the kind of steep bare bank it likes, and it has grown apace. Mosses will grow on just about everything in a rainforest, including man-made structures.

The forest has its grasses too. There are the three species of Oplismenus, basket or beard grass, *O. aemulus*, *O. imbecillus* and *O. undulatifolius*. The genus name is a version of the Greek word meaning 'armed', referring to the spikelets on the awns. The plant is so small and low-growing that its complicated inflorescence appears to the naked eye as a pale fur hovering over the neat patterning of the woven stolons and their short leaves, which are often so undulate as to appear almost corrugated. A closer inspection using a glass reveals a wealth of elaborate detail. All three species are in flower most of the year. The awns are sometimes sticky, so that passing animals help with dispersal of the seed to new sites. The appearance of these rainforest grasses on the forest floor is one of the first signs that order has been restored and the forest has taken charge. Alongside the Oplismenus grows another dainty grass, *Panicum pygmaeum*, Pygmy or Dwarf Panic. All these are self-limiting, never getting higher than a foot, and usually much smaller, as native ruminants tend to graze on them. They don't mind being mowed either, and will make something like a lawn, but much prettier, if given a chance. They are accompanied by four kinds of pennywort (*Hydrocotyle* spp.).

Commelina cyanea, which gallops over our mulchings, rather as the introduced weed *Tradescantia fluminensis* does, is sometimes mistakenly called *C. diffusa*. It looks rather like a delicate Tradescantia, but with a flower of the purest cobalt blue. In deeper shade you are likely to find one or other or both of our Aneilemas, both members of the Commelinaceae. The alternate leaves of all three present similar patterning which in the case of the Aneilemas is enlivened for three months a year by the appearance of sparkling white flowers like tiny three-petalled stars, floating over the dark foliage, which is sometimes tinged with purple. In the suburbs Whiteroot (*Pratia purpurascens*) is despised as a weed of lawns, but in the forest its flat stems make dark mats of purple-tinged leaves spangled with purplish-white flowers. Our Geranium (*Geranium solanderi*) is fluffier and more rampant than most of our groundcovers, and looks a bit weedier, and we're not sure whether our tiny yellow wood sorrel (*Oxalis chnoodes*) is a weed or not. For years we thought our violet was *Viola banksii* but the fashion now is to include it as one of the forms of *V. hederacea*. Every forest herbivore from the pademelon to the Brush-turkey adores the native violets. It is one of the special satisfactions of the forest to look on as a Red-necked Pademelon teaches her joey to eat violets. Pademelons will overgraze choice plants, so we grow the violets by the square metre, to plant out wherever there is shade and bare soil. One surprise has been the appearance of a crop of terrestrial orchids, *Zeuxine oblonga*, alongside our busiest track.

Our sedges and rushes could all be used in gardening if they were planted in drifts and swards, and our pademelons seem to prefer grazing on them to eating grass. Most promising for the rainforest garden is our Lomandra or mat rush. All over the Gold Coast, wherever you see native planting, you will see *Lomandra hystrix*, named for the European porcupine. Not a golf course, not a public park but is fenced off by vast clumps of *Lomandra hystrix*. All Lomandras have strap-like leaves; the species is usually identified by the patterning of the leaf ends, which are pointed or toothed, sometimes asymmetrically, and by the arrangement of the flower spike. The Cave Creek dark green, rather gracile Lomandra is usually identified as *Lomandra longifolia*, though it has its own patterning on the leaf points and the wrong inflorescence. Contrariwise what was sold to us by a nurseryman as *L. longifolia* is way too big, so it has been back to the drawing board and propagation from our own seed.

The workforce have little patience with me and my groundcovers because so many of them are nuisances in the propagation unit and the shade house. They particularly dislike one of my favourites, *Juncus usitatus*, the Common Rush. When this is young and happy, it is a very beautiful plant indeed, that throws up a waist-high spout of fine, dark, cylindrical green fronds, usually garlanded with flower or seed. Elsewhere in Australia it can be a pest, but in the rainforest it is a true beauty. The rainforest sedge is *Cyperus tetraphyllus*. Like the rush it is quite common, but in the forest it is more elegant than elsewhere. Less common is another sedge, probably the one Robert Brown called *Cyperus enervis*, which has since been renamed *C. gracilis* var. *enervis*. I say probably because the one at CCRRS doesn't quite correspond to the type, being longer and finer, like pale green hair. It is exceptionally willing; wherever I put it it grows. The forest harbours another exceptional plant, but this one will not grow for me. *Gymnostachys anceps* or Settler's Flax is usually classed as an aroid, *faute de mieux*. It is a monotypic genus and the one species grows only in Australia. It too was found by Robert Brown, who called it after itself, the ambiguous (*anceps*) plant with the twining (*gymno-*) inflorescence (*stachys*). It forms a spout of flat strap-like leaves anything up to two metres long, that could make wonderful accent plants in a rainforest garden if they could be persuaded to clump up. If anyone could be persuaded to try to grow a rainforest garden, that is.

The workforce has its collective eye on the large-scale restoration, and finds fussing about with tiny things just a bit girly. They think all these small natives will return as the forest builds itself, in their own time. I'm not so sure, because there are so many exotic creeping plants that will compete with them, the worst being *Tradescantia fluminensis* which in a single season can drive out Aneilemas that have been established for years. So you may find me on my knees weeding the rainforest, like Canute trying to hold back the tide, while Golden Whistlers do their best to sing me away.

BLOODY BOTANISTS

Every day, as we write labels for the boxes where we sow our freshly gathered seed, we do homage to dead white men, from Johann Georg Gmelin and Sir Hans Sloane, to Joseph Banks, George Bentham, Robert Brown, Alan Cunningham, so on and so forth. In the case of generic names existing before Australia was opened up, there was little choice to be exercised in the matter. Gmelina and Sloanea were both named by Linnaeus, but many newer names, Macadamia, Hicksbeachia, Baloghia, Davidsonia, for example, besides being cacophonous, commemorate otherwise totally forgettable individuals while telling you nothing whatsoever about the plants themselves.

Botanical names old and new are certainly hard on the ear. What is worse, they are also disputed. Under the Linnaean system plants with certain attributes in common, principally those of the plants' reproductive processes, were grouped as belonging to the same genus and then distinguished within the genus by specific characters, which supplied the species name or 'specific epithet'. With plant hunters working all over the world there was bound to be some duplication. In September 2010 the Royal Botanic Gardens at Kew and the Missouri Botanical Garden announced their collaboration in compiling 'The Plant List', a single worldwide inventory for all plant species, including ferns and their allies and algae. In the course of drawing up their inventory they had junked 477,601 names as synonyms, listed another 263,925 names as unresolved, and accepted only 298,900 names. Ironically this work has been undertaken at a time when the number of plant taxonomists is declining even faster than the number of species.

Botanists, like other academic scientists, cannot be got to agree. The Plant List itself is disputed, because it deals solely with recorded data, simply combining multiple data sets and assessing the degree of duplication and overlap. The procedure to be followed by naturalists recording new species is first to find, observe and collect a specimen, which in the case of a plant species should include leaves, flowers and fruit if possible. The specimen must then be keyed out using first of all a field guide, and then one of several authoritative indexes of plant names. The first specimen of a new genus will be called the 'type' of that genus; as it cannot be a member of a genus unless it is also a species, it will also be the type of the species. Such specimens must then be preserved in a collection or collections where subsequent discoveries and identifications can be compared with them. The objection to the Plant List is that it has been compiled without examination of the specimens to see if they are distinct or not. The result is a list that has to hedge its bets by giving each plant identification a confidence rating. As techniques of genetic identification are being perfected, it is only a matter of time before the Linnaean binomials are supported by barcodes, and then perhaps the disagreements will cease. Until then we workers in the forest have to remember all the names, disputed and accepted.

Botanists haven't been on earth very long – the word 'botany' crept into English rather self-consciously at the end of the seventeenth century – and it seems that they mightn't be around much longer. These days people who study plants are more likely to call themselves plant geneticists or plant biologists or phytochemists. The individual specialties are among those grouped under the slightly disparaging name 'life sciences', an inferior replacement for the older umbrella name 'natural history'. The life sciences are the girly version of the hard sciences, and their inferior status is reflected in their career structure. A double first in a life science at Oxbridge is good enough to get you a badly paid dead-end job as a laboratory assistant. These days you are more likely to find that people who are interested in vegetation will seek a qualification in ecology or environmental studies or phytobiology. Among the courses they will take as undergraduates there won't be a single one labelled botany, alone or in combination. Chairs of botany are beginning to disappear from our universities. The schools of botany at Oxford and Cambridge now call themselves departments of plant sciences and divide their discipline into specific areas of research, biochemistry, including cell and molecular biology, plant metabolism, comparative developmental genetics and evolution, ecology and systematics, epidemiology, virology, and so forth. The era of the plant-hunter is well and truly over.

Historically, botany has been the preserve of enthusiasts and amateurs, too many of them keen to make a name for themselves by finding something new and wonderful. As the Enlightenment spread through continental Europe, ladies and gentlemen busied themselves collecting and describing plant specimens that they dried in presses between sheets of thick blotting paper. Some filled sketchbooks with plant portraits in watercolour. As they were likely to be butterfly collectors, birdwatchers and anglers as well, they were more likely to call themselves naturalists than botanists. In Britain the process was accelerated by the enforced retirement of the Jacobite gentry to the country after the Bloodless Revolution of 1688; excluded from court and parliament, they devoted their energies to annotating the countryside. Such people accumulated collections of all kinds of natural curiosities, and fitted out rooms in their country houses with display cabinets to keep them in, as well as recording their ramblings in diaries and notebooks. Humbler countryfolk knew the local vegetation, and gave names to most of the common species of plants they saw growing around them, but there was no consistency in their practice. Things were called roses or daisies or lilies that weren't roses or daisies or lilies at all. The same species had different names in different districts, and often names of distinct species were interchangeable.

Early scientific nomenclature was hardly more reliable and much more unwieldy. Caspar Bauhin, professor of anatomy and botany at Basel, had arrived at a version of a binomial system in *Pinax Theatri Botanici* (1596), but it was diagnostic simply; Bauhin had no thought of an underlying system. His book would be one of the many sources used by Linnaeus. As was *Eléments de Botanique ou Méthode pour reconnaître les Plantes* by Joseph Pitton de Tournefort, first published in

1694, with a Latin version in 1700, and a further revised Latin version in 1719. Many of the genera now credited to Linnaeus were actually named earlier by Bauhin and Tournefort. Linnaeus outlined his system of scientific nomenclature in his *Systema Naturae* in 1735, and developed it further in *Genera Plantarum* in 1737, but not all European naturalists were persuaded of its rightness.

It was Tournefort who began the practice of naming new genera and new species after his colleagues, as an expression of his gratitude for their supplying him with specimens and detailed descriptions. All subsequent botanists including Linnaeus have followed suit. As a consequence the Cave Creek rainforest is haunted by the ghosts of a vanished tribe of European naturalists. The White Beech that gives this book its name belongs to a genus Linnaeus called Gmelina, in honour of Johann Georg Gmelin, professor of chemistry and natural history at the University of St Petersburg, principal author of *Flora Sibirica* (1747–69). The type of the genus Gmelina was a night-flowering Asian shrub, given the species name *asiatica*. It was better known to the Ayurvedic practitioners, who used a decoction of the root bark as an anti-inflammatory, as 'biddari' or 'badhara'. It is as 'Badhara Bush' that *Gmelina asiatica* has become known as a weed in Central Queensland; otherwise it and its near relatives are commonly known as 'Bushbeech', for no reason that I can intuit.

Linnaeus and his academic colleagues came by their botanical training in university faculties of medicine. Plant recognition was an essential prerequisite for a career that was then understood to consist principally in the administration of remedies derived from plants. Linnaeus held the chair of medicine and botany originally established at the University of Uppsala in 1693. In France the post of Botaniste du Roi grew out of the directorship of the Jardin Royal des Plantes Médicinales. At the University of Glasgow botany was combined with anatomy from 1718 to 1818, when a separate chair of botany was founded. When the first chairs of pharmacology were established in Europe, the study of botany formed part of the course of study. Pharmacognosy required a close and accurate observation and classification of the plant species that provided most of the materials of the pharmacopoeia, so we are not surprised to find that many of the first professional botanists originally qualified in pharmacology.

The first person to collect any Australian plant species was an amateur, the freebooter William Dampier. In 1688 when his ship *Cygnet* was beached on the north-west coast of Australia near King Sound, Dampier passed the time while it was being repaired making notes on the native flora and fauna. On a second voyage, in the *Roebuck*, he came ashore at Shark Bay and travelled north-east as far as La Grange Bay, all the while collecting specimens and making records, which were illustrated with sketches by his clerk James Brand. Back in England in 1701, though in serious trouble for the loss of the *Roebuck*, Dampier remembered to send his materials to Thomas Woodward of the Royal Society. Woodward sent them on to John Ray, pioneer naturalist and author of the *Historia Generalis Plantarum* (1686–1704), and his collaborator Leonard Plukenet, Royal Professor of Botany. The meticulously pressed specimens of the plants Dampier collected on the north-west coast of Australia in August–September 1699 may still be seen today in the Sherardian Herbarium in Oxford, with William Sherard's speculative Latin labels attached.

It was only when Robert Brown was working his way through Dampier's specimens in 1810 that they were given systematic names. When Brown recognised one specimen as being from a new, unnamed genus he had no hesitation in naming it after its original collector, Dampiera. Dampier's specimen, being the first to be collected, is therefore to be considered the type for the whole genus, which turned out to consist of more than fifty species distributed all over Australia. The Dampiera Dampier collected was one of the more spectacular, with violet-blue flowers borne on silver-white foliage, in Latin *incana*, 'hoary'. The genus is at present undergoing revision, but it will never acquire a more readily accepted common or scientific name. There could be no vaster, more durable or more engaging memorial available to anyone than to have a whole tribe of beautiful living things named after him.

The most important figure in Australian botany is another highly endowed amateur, Joseph Banks. Banks became interested in botany when he was a small boy. As a student in 1764, when he found that there was no teaching of botany at Oxford, he paid for a series of lectures to be delivered by Cambridge botanist Israel Lyons. He then continued his studies in botany at the Chelsea Physic Garden and the British Museum, where he met Daniel Solander who put him in touch with his own teacher, Linnaeus. In 1766 Banks travelled to Newfoundland and Labrador, and published an account of the plants and animals he found there. When he heard of the planning of an expedition to the South Seas to observe the transit of Venus, desperate to be appointed naturalist on the voyage, he stepped in with a donation of £10,000 towards the cost of the expedition. When the *Endeavour* set out from England in 1768 Banks was aboard, along with a retinue of illustrators and scientists, including Solander. Banks's purpose was to collect specimens of the flora of the remotest parts of the earth, for his own collection and for the royal collection at Kew. He succeeded admirably, bringing back specimens of about 110 new genera and 1,300 new species.

Some of the Cave Creek flora were first collected by Banks's cohort in 1770, some at Botany Bay and some on the Endeavour River, but the specimens were not studied in time to provide the types. The Black Bean, for example, was originally collected on the Endeavour River in 1770, but not identified until 1830, when Hooker described the specimens collected later by Cunningham and Frazer, by which time the name had already been used by Robert Mudie in two books, *The Picture of Australia* and *Vegetable Substances*, both of 1828 (Mabberley, 1992).

Every naturalist botanising in the New World had to send all his specimens back to the big European collections for identification; of these by far the most important was, and is, Kew. The introduction to the 'Australian Virtual Herbarium' on the Royal Botanic Gardens, Kew website gives a pretty fair assessment:

Australia has a vascular flora of about 20,000 species. Of these, 8,125 had been described by the completion of Bentham's *Flora Australiensis* (1863–1878), written at Kew, and of this group, comprising more than a third of the current total taxa, most have Type material of some kind at Kew. These include collections by R. Brown, J. Banks & D. Solander, J. D. Hooker, A. & R. Cunningham, R. C. Gunn, J. Milligan, C. Stuart, G. Caley, F. Mueller, J. Drummond, J. McGillivray, T. Mitchell, A. F. Oldfield, G. Maxwell, L. Leichhardt,

B. Bynoe, C. Fraser, H. Beckler, H. H. Behr, W. Baxter, J. Dallachy and many more. Taxa described later are also represented to a lesser extent in Kew. For many taxa there are multiple Type specimens in Kew (holotypes, isotypes, syntypes and lectotypes), and many associated historical collections (e.g. non-type specimens cited by Bentham, 1863–1878), vital for interpretation of early botanical works.

Thus the old world, in the name of scientific method, extended and intensified its control over the new. After his first foray Banks concentrated on building up a network of scientific contacts all over Europe, and employed troops of botanists whom he sent hither and yon to every part of the known world, to continue amassing specimens for his own herbarium and the royal collections at Kew, and any other establishments that might have materials to offer in exchange. In 1778 he was elected President of the Royal Society, a position he would hold till his death; he would eventually take over the botanic garden at Kew, set up the herbarium there, and organise, finance and direct the scientific exploration of Australia from the other side of the world. Banks is commemorated at Cave Creek by the specific name of our violet, *Viola banksii*, and Solander by our crowsfoot, *Geranium solanderi*. In 1782 in the *Supplementum Plantarum* (15:26) the younger Linnaeus named an important genus (seventy-seven species at the present count) *Banksia* for Banks, who had been created baronet in 1781. Australia was by then so much Banks's domain that when a name for the continent was being sought Linnaeus suggested 'Banksia' for that too. Happily the suggestion was not heeded.

After the arrival of the First Fleet in 1788 the amateurs John White, surgeon-general (*ADB*), and Richard Johnson, colonial chaplain (*ADB*), took up the work of sending Australian plant material to Banks. In 1791 Banks arranged to pay the Superintendent of Convicts David Burton an annual stipend for collecting seeds and plant material. Unfortunately Burton accidentally shot himself the next year (*ADB*). In 1798 Banks sent out George Caley (*ADB*). As Caley had no formal qualifications Banks himself paid his salary of fifteen shillings a week; Caley collected for both Banks and Kew, and was allowed to sell extra specimens to nurserymen.

Banks was also responsible for the presence in Australia of one of my heroes, Robert Brown (*ADB*). Brown had come to botany through the school of medicine at Edinburgh University where he enrolled in 1791 only to drop out in 1793, possibly for lack of money, and maybe for lack of attention to his studies as well. He had perhaps spent too much time botanising in the Highlands, sometimes with the nurseryman George Don. In 1794 he joined the army, serving in Ireland as a surgeon's mate, which took up so little time that he was able to concentrate on his botanical researches. At this stage he was fascinated by cryptogams and pioneered the use of the microscope in examining minute plant parts. The genera of many of our rainforest mosses and ferns were first identified by Brown, who contributed (unacknowledged) to James Dickson's *Fasciculi plantarum cryptogamicarum britanniae* in 1796. In 1800 Banks offered to appoint the twenty-seven-year-old Brown naturalist to Matthew Flinders's circumnavigation of Australia, and provided him with the services of the botanical artist Ferdinand Bauer. Brown prepared for the trip by studying the collections already made by Banks and Solander. HMS *Investigator* sailed in July 1801; when it called at Port Jackson for the second time in June 1803, signalling the completion of the circum-navigation of the continent, Brown and Bauer decided to stay and continue collecting in New South Wales. In three and a half years in Australia Brown collected 3,400 species, more than half of them previously unknown. Though many of his specimens were lost aboard a ship that was wrecked on the return journey, he was able in 1810 to publish a preparatory Australian flora, *Prodromus Florae Novae Hollandiae et Insulae Van Diemen*. When Leichhardt set off on his first botanising rambles he carried a copy in his saddlebag. Allan Cunningham too carried a copy.

Brown's was not the first attempt at a provisional Australian flora. The naturalist on the expedition of d'Entrecastaux to Oceania (1791–3), Jacques de Labillardière, who collected specimens in south-west Australia and Tasmania, had brought out his *Novae Hollandiae Plantarum Specimen* in instalments between 1804 and 1807. Sir Joseph Banks, whom he had met on a visit to England in 1783, intervened when the British confiscated Labillardière's scientific collections as spoils of war and arranged for their restitution, unmindful that the royal collection would be poorer for lack of them. Labillardière got his reward in 1793 when Sir James Edward Smith named a genus of Australian plants Billardiera (Smith, 1:1).

Labillardière has been criticised for making unacknowledged use of specimens from the collection of the amateur naturalist Charles Louis l'Héritier de Brutelle, who is principally famous, at least among Australians, for naming the genus Eucalyptus. L'Héritier published the name in his *Sertum Anglicum*, an account of his botanising among the British collections in the 1780s. The species on which he founded the genus Eucalyptus was *Eucalyptus obliqua*, originally collected by William Anderson, physician on board HMS *Resolution*, on Cook's second expedition when it visited Tasmania in 1774. Anderson had called his sample 'Aromadendron', the smelly tree. L'Héritier renamed it after the pretty (*eu*) cap (*calyptera*) made of fused petals that encloses the anthers of the gum-blossom in bud. Anderson was assisted by David Nelson, a gardener from Kew, who was employed, paid, equipped and trained by Banks. Other species of eucalypt had been collected earlier by Banks and Solander, but when L'Héritier was working at the British Museum in 1786–7 they had not yet been named. And so it was that a man who never glimpsed the great south land, never saw a eucalypt in the wild, succeeded in naming the genus of the 'most important and dominant trees of the Australian flora'. He also named the Kangaroo Paw Anigozanthos and a species of tree fern Dicksonia after James Dickson.

Though he was not the first botanist to describe Australian flora, Brown has a pretty good claim to being the best. His grasp of plant anatomy was unparalleled, partly because of his innovative use of microscopic examination. He was also unusually self-effacing. When a rival botanist supplied a good name for a new genus Brown made no bones about accepting it. To study the whole list of plant names authorised by Brown is to realise that for the most part he bucked the trend of using plant names to oblige his colleagues and superiors. He preferred to name his plants for themselves; he gave the Bolwarra the scientific name Eupomatia, 'eu' meaning 'pleasing' and 'pomatia' referring to the pixie cap of the flowerbud. The type he called *E. laurina*, meaning like a laurel, referring to its leaves. Forty years later, when Victorian government botanist Ferdinand Mueller was sent the

Small Bolwarra collected by Charles Moore, he typically named it for George Bennett, *E. bennettii*. Bennett, an Englishman who travelled extensively before settling in Australia in 1836, when he went into medical practice in Sydney, was a founding member of the Australian Museum, the Acclimatisation Society and the Zoological Society (*ADB*).

Brown was obliged to name another large proteaceous genus *Grevillea* in memory of the algologist Charles Francis Greville, one of the founders of the Royal Horticultural Society, because the name had already been published by Joseph Knight. How this came about is a tale of the kind of skulduggery that is not expected of scholars and gentlemen. Knight worked as head gardener for a gentleman botanist called George Hibberd, who had fallen for the new fad of growing proteaceous plants. In 1809 Knight published *On the Cultivation of the Plants belonging to the natural order of Protëeae* which, as well as providing ten pages or so of instructions for the successful growing of Proteaceae, included a revised taxonomy for the group. This taxonomy had been copied down by Robert Salisbury from a lecture given by Robert Brown to the Linnaean Society, and published by Knight before the text of Brown's lecture could be published in the *Transactions of the Linnaean Society*. For this piece of piracy Salisbury was ostracised by the botanical fraternity, but nothing could alter the fact that Knight had published before Brown, and so we read that the genus Grevillea is 'R. Br. ex Knight', even though Knight had been unable to name or describe the type specimen which was in fact Brown's *Grevillea gibbosa*, the Bushman's Clothes-peg (Brown, 1810b, 375). Within the genus Grevillea Brown remembered Banks, Bauer, Baxter, Caley, Cunningham and Dryander. He also named a monotypic genus Bellendena after Sir John Bellenden Ker.

As a man without liberal education who had no Latin, Brown's colleague George Caley, who was otherwise an expert botanist, was never permitted to publish under his own name. Though he was a rather morose individual who often made life difficult for Brown, Brown made sure he was not forgotten by naming a small genus of flying duck orchids after him, Caleana. Brown named four more species for Caley as well, a Grevillea, a Banksia, a Persoonia and an Anadenia. To another Grevillea and another Banksia Brown gave the specific epithet *goodii*, in honour of the gardener on the *Investigator*, Peter Good, whose job it was to tend any live plants being taken back to England, and make sure that the collected seed remained viable. Good had died of dysentery shortly after the *Investigator* docked in Port Jackson in 1803; the plants to which Brown gave his name are his only memorial (Brown, 1810b, 1:174)

Brown collected the plant we now call Brunonia, but he did not name it after himself. Sir James Edward Smith, lecturer in botany at Guy's Hospital, who had acquired all Linnaeus's collections after his death in 1778, chose the name but, because Brown published it in his *Prodromus* in 1810, before Smith's paper was published in the *Transactions of the Linnaean Society*, he is credited as the author (Smith, 1811, 366). The name Brownia has never been used so there was no need to latinise it as Brunonia. In 1863 Ferdinand Mueller attempted to confer Brown's name on the Australian Flintwood, which Brown had originally collected on the Hunter River (*Fragmenta*, 3:17, 11). Mueller had originally identified his specimen as a Phoberos as described by Loureiro, and named it *Phoberos brownii*; by 1863 he reclassified it as a Scolopia, but he was not able to retain his original species name *brownii* because of an odd circumstance. In June 1854 German botanist Johann Friedrich Klotzsch had come upon a specimen of the same species in the herbarium of the Berlin Botanical Garden marked 'patria ignota'. Klotzsch described it, named it *Adenogyrus braunii* for his friend and colleague Alexander Carl Friedrich Braun, and the name was published the same year (Fischer and Meyer). The genus name was not good but there was no way of removing the specific epithet, so *Scolopia braunii* it is and ever will be. Botanists who treat *braunii* as if it were a variant spelling of *brownii* (and they include the great Floyd) are simply wrong. *Scolopia braunii* is a wonderful slow-growing tree with glossy lozenge-shaped leaves and scented flowers; it is a real shame that it was not named for the best botanist of them all. At one stage the Queensland Kauri was being referred to as '*Agathis brownii*', but that name too was without authority (Mabberley, 2002). That still leaves more than 150 plant species with the specific name *brownii*, nearly all of them named by younger generations of botanists who are all aware of how much we owe to Robert Brown. One of the earliest plants named for Brown is *Banksia brownii*, which was collected by William Baxter at King George's Sound in 1829; it is now facing imminent extinction in its native habitat in south-west Western Australia.

Brown is the original collector of many Cave Creek natives. Some he was able to name with purely descriptive names in the peculiar mixture of Latin and Greek that is called botanical Latin: the genera Asplenium and Cryptocarya, *Aneilema biflorum*, *A. acuminatum*, *Adiantum formosum*, *Alpinia caerulea*, *Alyxia ruscifolia*, *Gymnostachys anceps*. There was nothing Brown could do to stop the Cave Creek *Commelina* commemorating Jan and Caspar Commelijn, because Linnaeus had already named the genus in 1753, but typically he chose a descriptive epithet, *cyanea* – blue. Our Koda belongs to a genus named in 1756 Ehretia for the great botanical artist Georg Dionysius Ehret, and again Brown applied a descriptive epithet, *acuminata*. Brown listed *Olea paniculata*, an important member of our plant community, which had been tentatively named '*Ligustrum arboreum*' by the botanists on the *Endeavour*. He also named *Clerodendrum floribundum* and *Callicarpa pedunculata*. Brown also identified *Pseuderanthemum variabile*, tentatively labelled '*Iusticia umbratilis*'. And so on, to the end of the alphabet.

Though Alan Cunningham and Charles Frazer accomplished much less than Brown, at Cave Creek their names crop up every day, Frazer's being usually and apparently incorrectly spelt as 'Fraser' (*ADB*). Cunningham was a gardener's son, who found work in 1810 as a cataloguer of Banks's collections at Kew. When the post of travelling plant collector was advertised in 1814, Banks encouraged Cunningham to apply and he was duly appointed. After travelling in South America, he arrived in Port Jackson in 1816, the same year that Frazer arrived in New South Wales as a soldier. Within a year Frazer had been appointed Superintendent of the Botanic Gardens and first Colonial Botanist. Both men joined John Oxley's expeditions to north-eastern New South Wales in 1818, and in 1828 they accompanied Captain Patrick Logan's expedition from Brisbane south to Mount Barney in the McPherson Range, which was named by Cunningham after Major Duncan McPherson, an officer in the 39th regiment. Bentham credits Frazer as the original collector of more than 230 New South Wales species. Our most spectacular rosewood is *Dysoxylum fraserianum* and the sandpaper fig, *Ficus fraseri*, is one of the most important trees for our fruit-eating birds.

Cunningham's memory haunts the treescape; the Hoop Pine, *Araucaria cunninghamii*, the Bangalow Palm, *Archontophoenix cunning-hamiana*, the local Casuarina, *Allocasuarina cunninghamiana*, the Native Tamarind, *Diploglottis cunninghamii*, the Brown Beech, *Pennantia cunninghamii*, are all named for him. Lately Cunningham has been losing some of his titles; *Diploglottis cunninghamii* is now to be called *D. australis*, *Clerodendron cunninghamii* *C. longiflorum* var. *glabrum*, *Cryptocarya cunninghamii* *C. macdonaldii*, but then *Kreysigia multiflora* was renamed *Tripladenia cunninghamii*, so what Cunningham lost on the roundabouts he made up on a swing. In 1831 Cunningham went back to England, to join the other botanists working on the 200 boxes of Australian specimens he had sent to the Kew herbarium. He published little, and it would probably be unfair to suggest that it was he who called some of the most frequently encountered species in the McPherson Range after himself. One thing he did do was to ensure that a 'majestic bluff' encountered on Oxley's earlier expedition was named after George Caley.

Even more important than Robert Brown in arriving at an authoritative account of the Australian flora is another gentleman amateur, George Bentham (*DNB*). Bentham was virtually self-educated; he became interested in botany when his father moved his household to France in 1816, eventually settling near Montpellier. He diverted himself by applying the logical principles developed by his uncle Jeremy Bentham to anything that interested him. He was impressed by the analytical tables for plant identification that he found in Augustin Pyramus de Candolle's *Flore française* and began to apply them to his own botanising. On a visit to London in 1823 he made his first contact with British botanists. In 1831 his father died, and in 1832 his uncle; Bentham inherited from both. As a gentleman of independent means he could now spend all his time botanising. In 1836 he published his first work of systematic botany, *Labiatarum genera et species*, for which he had visited every European herbarium at least once. He then travelled to Vienna to study legumes, and produced *De leguminosarum generibus commentationes*, which was published in the annals of the Vienna Museum. He went on to collaborate with De Candolle on the *Prodromus systematis naturalis regni vegetabilis*, producing descriptions of 4,730 species.

In 1855 Bentham had all but decided to retire from botanical work when the elder Hooker and other members of the botanical establishment persuaded him to move to London and work on the preparation of the floras of the British colonies using the collections at Kew. In 1862 or so he began work on the *Flora Australiensis*; it was to take him fifteen years. Bentham is honoured in the naming of the Red Carabeen, *Geissois benthamii* and a native gardenia, *Atractocarpus benthamianus*. (The genus Atractocarpus has been through an extraordinary succession of names: Sukunia, Trukia, Porterandia, Sulitia, Neofranciella, Franciella and Randia; as it has been Atractocarpus only since 1999, the name might not have jelled yet.)

Though they had established a formidable presence elsewhere, German naturalists were late arrivals in Australia. In 1842 the naturalist Ludwig Leichhardt arrived in Sydney from Germany and began collecting botanical specimens in north-eastern New South Wales. In November 1843 'in silvis ad amnem Myall Creek Australiae orientalis subtropicae', Leichhardt collected, amongst much else, the first recorded specimen of White Beech. In October 1844 he led an expedition from Jimbour on the Darling Downs to Port Essington near Darwin, and got there fifteen months later. On this trip he collected thousands of specimens but, as his horses and oxen perished one by one, he had no way of transporting the material back to civilisation and had to dump it. In December 1846 he set out to travel from Dalby on the Darling Downs across to the west coast, but was driven back by heavy rain, malaria and shortage of food (Bailey, J., 267–323).

Ferdinand Mueller first heard of Leichhardt when he was a pharmacology student at the University of Rostock. When he arrived in Adelaide in 1847 to take up a position as a pharmacist for the German firm of Büttner and Heuzenroeder, his real intention was to make of himself the same kind of heroic naturalist explorer as Leichhardt, who was about to set out on a second attempt to cross the continent from east to west. This time, after leaving McPherson's sheep station at Coogoon, Leichhardt and his party vanished. Mueller, who could hardly believe that his hero would never return, was by then botanising around Adelaide, moving ever further afield, until he penetrated as far as the Flinders Ranges and Lake Torrens. From every excursion he brought back masses of specimens to be sent to every learned society in Europe. He was not content to allow European experts to identify and describe the materials he brought back from these forays, but struggled to do it himself, without the necessary resources of a large herbarium and the full phytological record. Just how foolhardy this was had been illustrated by the humiliation of the natural scientist William Swainson, who tried to sort out the genus Eucalyptus, and ended up in a morass of 'reckless species-making' (Maiden). Mueller knew the risks he was running, but his arrogance and recklessness were even greater than Swainson's; fortunately for him so was his expertise. Governor La Trobe of Victoria was so impressed with the indefatigable Mueller that in 1853 he appointed him government botanist. Mueller was then at leisure to organise his herbarium; within five years it contained 45,000 specimens representing 15,000 species; ultimately Mueller would claim to have amassed between 750,000 and a million specimens. He cultivated a close relationship with Kew in the hope that he would be allowed to write the official flora of Australia, but the job fell to George Bentham, which in my view was just as well.

My sister Jane, as a good alumna of the University of Melbourne Botany Department, is an admirer of Mueller.

'You have to appreciate his incredible achievement in penetrating so far into the inland with no support whatsoever. This is the man who explored alpine Victoria on his own, and made his way back to Melbourne with nothing but a pocketful of Bogong Moths to eat.'

'Ambition, girl. Blind ambition.'

'Hooker and Bentham white-anted him. They wouldn't support him.'

'That really isn't fair. Bentham acknowledged Mueller as a co-author of the Flora Australiensis which, considering what a nuisance the man was, was incredibly gracious. Mueller drove them both crazy. He drives me crazy.'

'Mueller wanted Australians to name Australian plant species, and he wanted the types to be held in Australian herbaria. He was resisting imperial control. Bentham was on the other side of the world and had never even visited Australia.'

'Yes, but he had access to the huge collections of Kew, Paris, and elsewhere in Europe, as Mueller did not. You and I both know that Gondwanan genera are distributed all round the southern hemisphere. Mueller was like a blind man with only one foot of the elephant.'

Jane's jaw was set. I shut up.

In his private correspondence Joseph Hooker described Mueller as 'devoured of vanity and jealousy of Colonial notoriety'. For years Mueller had bombarded Kew with specimens, together with his own descriptions, many of which were wrong. At length, on 10 October 1857, Hooker wrote to him from Kew:

> The verifying of your new genera is a work of much greater labor than you suppose; & you must not be surprized to hear that some of them are common & well-known Indian genera & even species. Thus [it is] not I assure you from want of will on my Father's & my parts, that we do not publish more of your MSS; but from want of time &[,] on my own part at any rate who am engaged on the Tasmanian Flora & the Indian[,] much averseness to committing both yourself & myself by publishing old plants as new. (Home *et al.*, 1, 329)

Mueller didn't heed the advice. In December 1858 Hooker wrote again:

> I have studiously abstained from publishing any of your Victorian plants, though I have a great majority of them from Cunningham, Robertson & others, because I knew you were at work on that Flora & like to have the credit of naming your plants. You again go on naming & describing Tasmanian plants though you know I am engaged on that Flora! . . . pray describe the Chatham & Tasmanian & Indian plants too if you wish – you must not expect however that when I have occasion to work at unpublished plants to which you have given mss names I am to take your names wherever the species are good only!

(In other words, Hooker worked on all Mueller's descriptions, including those he did not credit because they were wrong.)

Hitherto I have done so & have not quoted your MSS names when I have considered them as synonymous, both because I thought that it would be unfair to point out your mistakes when there was no occasion to do so, & it would only encumber Botany with MSS synonyms to no purpose. (Home *et al.*, 1, 434)

Despite Hooker's common sense, Australian botany is heavily encumbered with synonyms, and not a few of them are attributed to 'F. v. M.' or 'F. Muell.'.

It was only at the end of his life that George Bentham permitted himself to write as sharply to Mueller as the occasion warranted. Cockily, Mueller had sent Bentham in April 1883 a copy of his rival publication, *Systematic Census of Australian Plants*. Bentham replied heavily:

I have to thank you for your Systematic Census of Australian Plants received yesterday. The work is beautifully printed and shows a great deal of laborious philological research into the dates of plant names (rather than of genera) which will be appreciated by those who occupy themselves in that subject . . . but all that is not botany. With regard to that science, it grieves me to think that you should have devoted so much of your valuable time to a work which, botanically speaking, is not only absolutely useless but worse than useless.

. . . let me entreat you to give up the vain endeavour to attach the intials 'F. v. M.' to so many specific names, good or bad, as possible . . . (Home *et al.*, 111, 311–12)

Mueller obtained rather more gratifying responses from the continental institutions to which he sent all kinds of Australiana. He sent Aboriginal cadavers to museums in France, Germany and Russia, live thylacines, already on the verge of extinction, to Stuttgart and Paris, and black swans anywhere and everywhere. He sent away thousands of tree ferns for the conservatories of Europe, including specimens of the King Fern, *Todea barbara*, weighing more than a ton apiece (Daley). In 1867 he was appointed Companion of the Order of St Michael and St George, and from Württemberg, in exchange for scientific materials plus £600 in cash for the establishment of a

Ferdinand von Mueller Stiftung, he received the title of Freiherr or Baron. Such toadying was not likely to appease British chauvinism. The most bizarre of the tributes paid to Mueller must be the attempt by the maverick German botanist Otto Kuntze to rename the genus Banksia after him, Sirmuellera.

Even though he was doing so well out of exploiting the unique-ness of Australian species, Mueller had no interest in maintaining the integrity of Australian flora and fauna. As fast as he was sending Australian creatures to the other side of the world, he was importing exotics. In his report of 1858, among trees of practical value imported for the Botanic Garden, he mentions 'the Camphor Tree' *Cinnamomum camphora*, now the most serious tree weed in the rainforest. He imported quantities of European songbirds with the aim of naturalising them, including the now ubiquitous blackbird. Each year the Botanic Garden grew thousands of plants for public distribution, nearly all of them exotics. If you want to know why the sidewalks of most Australian country towns and the leafier suburbs are being torn apart by the proliferating roots of avenues of gigantic poplars, planes and beeches, why every cemetery is overhung with cypresses and pines, Mueller is your man. So enthusiastic was he in his dissemination of exotics that horticulturists accused him of ruining their trade.

'Have you got Heritiera here?' Jane was changing the subject.

'I don't think so. Why?'

'I was reading this article about complex notophyll vine forest and it talked about *Heritiera trifoliolata* as a key species.'

The species name gave the game away. 'Argyrodendron must've had a name change. Damn.'

The name Argyrodendron is thoroughly Greek and sweetly descriptive: '*argyro*' – silver, '*dendron*' – tree. The distinguishing characteristic of the Argyrodendron is that the underside of the leaf is clad in microscopic scales that are visible to the naked eye as a silver sheen. One of the Cave Creek Argyrodendrons is surnamed *trifoliol-atum*, which is Latin for 'three-leafleted' and typical of the way Latin gets yoked onto the Greek. The other is surnamed *actinophyllum*, which is an adaptation of the Greek '*aktis*', meaning ray, and '*phyllon*', meaning leaf, because its leaflets radiate from the tip of the leafstalk.

The revered Queensland dendrologist Bill McDonald had dubbed our subtropical rainforest type the 'Argyrodendron Alliance'.

' "Heritiera Alliance" won't sound the same,' I moaned. ' "Heritiera" is no language at all, and carries no information about the thing it refers to. It makes more sense to call the damn' things Booyongs; at least the Aboriginal name doesn't change every five minutes.' (Gresty records the name 'booyong' in his Numinbah word list (71); it is not recorded by Sharpe or any of the Yugambeh word-collectors.)

After L'Héritier de Brutelle was assassinated in 1800, his herbarium of 8,000 species was acquired by Bentham's friend and colleague De Candolle, but it was not he who named the principally Asian genus in L'Héritier's honour but William Aiton, director of the Royal Botanic Garden, in 1789 (Aiton, 3:546). In 1858 Mueller did not recognise his specimen as a member of an older genus but created the new name Argyrodendron for it; the type for the new name was a specimen of *A. trifoliolatum* collected by Walter Hill on the Brisbane and Pine Rivers (*Fragmenta*, 1 (1):2). In the first volume of his *Flora Australiensis*, published in 1863, Bentham preferred C. L. von Blume's older (1825) name for the genus, and called it *Tarrietia argyrodendron* (1:230), but Mueller's name clung on until 1959, when A. J. G. H. Kostermans included the Booyongs in the genus Heritiera. The Australian Plant Name Index still includes both names, so we shall have to treat them as synonyms after all, which is what usually happens in practice.

Amid all this botanical brouhaha the common name of the Booyongs remained the same. Mueller had no time for common names. In a lecture at the Melbourne Industrial and Technological Museum on 3 November 1870 he demanded how botanical knowledge could be:

> fixed without exact phytological information, or how is the knowledge to be applied, if we are to trust to vernacular names, perplexing even within the area of a small colony, and useless as a rule, beyond it? Colonial Box trees by dozens, yet all distinct, and utterly unlike Turkey Box; colonial Myrtle without the slightest resemblance to the poet's myrtle; colonial Oaks, analogous to those Indian trees, which

as Casuarinae were distinguished so graphically by Rumpf already 200 years ago, but without any trace of similarity to real oak— afford instances of our confused and ludicrous vernacular appellations.

He demanded a total change:

> resting on the rational observations and deductions which science already has gained for us. Assuredly, with any claims to ordinary intelligence, we ought to banish such designations, not only from museum collections, but also from the dictionary of the artisan. How are these thousands of species of Ficus, all distinct in appearance, in character, and in uses— how are they to be recognised, unless a diagnosis of each becomes carefully elaborated and recorded, headed by a specific name? (Mueller, 1872, 81)

How indeed? The genus Ficus was a bad example to have chosen, because its taxonomy is fluid to say the least. And Mueller was the wrong person to have mounted the attack on common names, given his own propensity for generating synonyms.

The Bible tells us that God created the world, and then Adam, and then bade Adam name his creation, before he created Eve. Feminists have argued persuasively that naming and classification are mechanisms of male control. Nowhere is this more evident ·than in the practice of botany. Once Linnaeus had published his binomial system the animal and vegetable kingdoms were up for grabs. European plants and animals were protected because the genera already had Latin names in the scientific literature. Australia lay helpless under the onslaught of scientists determined to inscribe their own names and the names of their forerunners, patrons, collaborators and friends across its length and breadth. The naturalists who came haring to Australia from all over the world knew that by collecting samples of flora and fauna, and either contriving their preservation by drying them or bottling them in spirits, or keeping them alive for dispatch to European museums, herbariums, zoological and botanical gardens, and to private collectors, they would secure for themselves both reputation and reward. Even more seductive than a title for oneself was the opportunity to name animals and plants after oneself, or the people with whom one was currying favour. No other continent has as bizarre a collection of botanical names as Australia, and no Australian vegetation is worse served when it comes to nomenclature than the rainforest.

Nobody was less likely to give up the pernicious habit of calling plants after colleagues and friends than the egregious Mueller. Mueller surnamed one of our Sloaneas '*woollsii*' after William Woolls (1814–93), an Anglican minister and schoolmaster who collected for him. No one would jib at calling a genus Flindersia after Matthew Flinders, especially when the first example of the genus was collected by Robert Brown on his expedition, but our dominant species was named by Mueller *F. schottiana* for Heinrich Schott of the Austrian Botanic Gardens. An important tree for us is the unspellable Guioa, named for J. Guio, a botanical illustrator of the eighteenth century. Mueller got himself into a fearful tangle with this, identifying our Guioa, which is *G. semiglauca*, so-called because the underside of the leaf is bluish-white, as an Arytera and then as a Nephelium; even Bentham got it wrong, and decided it was a Cupania, and it was not until 1879 that L. A. T. Radlkofer correctly understood our tree to be a member of the genus Guioa. Our Foambarks are named Jagera, for Dr Herbert de Jager, who collected for the Dutch botanist Rumphius in Indonesia in the mid-nineteenth century.

For years we have been referring to one of our best performers as *Caldcluvia paniculata*. The genus is named for Scottish botanist Alexander Caldcleugh who collected the first specimens in South America in the early nineteenth century. Interestingly, Cunningham, who had botanised in New Zealand, correctly recognised the Australian tree as a member of the genus Ackama, of which the type was first collected in New Zealand, hence the version of the Maori name 'makamaka', but he was overruled by Mueller, who first misidentified it as a member of the genus Weinmannia (named for eighteenth-century German pharmacist J. W. Weinmann), to which inadvertently he gave two species names *paniculosa* and *paniculata*, before deciding that it was a Caldcluvia after all. Bentham accepted Cunningham and called the species, with admirable forbearance, '*Ackama muelleri*', but Mueller's name prevailed. Justice has finally been done, and we must get used to calling our trees *Ackama paniculata*.

A similar tree, the Rose Marara, like Ackama in the Cunoniaceae, has the appalling systematic name of *Pseudoweinmannia lachnocarpa*. The specific name is useful, for it means 'woolly fruit', but the generic name identifies it as a pretend Weinmannia, as if it deliberately misled people (Engler, 249). As the genus Pseudoweinmannia consists of this species only, it seems likely that it will one day be revised. Our Bosistoas have no accepted common name, so whenever we refer to them we have no choice but to do homage to the Melbourne chemist J. Bosisto, who collaborated with Mueller in the preparation of eucalyptus oil. Another of our genera carries the hideous name Baloghia, after Dr Joseph Balogh, author of a book on Transylvanian plants; this is the more galling because the Baloghia blossom has perhaps the loveliest scent of any in the forest. It's bad enough to have to call a beautiful big tree a Grey Walnut, when it is neither grey nor a walnut, but when its scientific name is Beilschmiedia, in honour of C. T. Beilschmied, a botanist and chemist from Ohlau, it is ill-served indeed. As annoying is the name Mueller gave to the Queensland Nut, which eternises John Macadam, Secretary of the Philosophical Institute of Victoria; not content with this, Mueller named another genus Wilkiea for the vice-president of the society, Dr D. E. Wilkie. Worst of all is the ridiculously clumsy name Mueller gave the adorable Bopple Nut, which he named after the Secretary of State for New South Wales, Hicksbeachia. Such mad coinages can have no uniform pronunciation; what has grown up instead is a culture of sanctioned mispronunciation. Botanists demonstrate their membership of the inner circle by using agreed or 'correct' mispro-nunciations. 'Sloanea' was named by Linnaeus for Sir Hans Sloane, founder of the British Museum; people who know who he was tend to call the trees 'Slow-nia'; people who don't render it 'Slow-aynia'. I pronounce the genus 'Olearia' 'Oll-ee-arr-ee-ah', my sister 'O'Leary-ah'. Actually, the genus is not called after O'Leary but after the olive tree or Olea. People like me who have not mastered the sanctioned mispronunciations can be instantly identified as outsiders and their expertise ignored, which is fine with me.

If you look up White Beech in a botanical textbook, you will find it listed as '*Gmelina leichhardtii* (F. Muell.)'. What that means is that the plant or 'taxon' was first described and recognised as a separate species by Mueller, who published his description in 1862 (*Fragmenta*, 3:19, 58). What it doesn't tell you is whether he got it right. He didn't. He mistook the genus and identified the specimen, which had been collected by Leichhardt at Myall Creek in New South Wales on 20 November, 1843, as a Vitex. He sent Leichhardt's specimen with another collected by Hermann Beckler on the Clarence River in 1859 plus his own description to Bentham. In 1870 in Volume 5 of his *Flora* Bentham published Mueller's Vitex as *Gmelina leichhardtii* (66).

Altogether Bentham identified three Australian species of Gmelina, a genus which 'extends over tropical Asia and the Indian Archipelago. The Australian species, though with the aspect of some Asiatic ones, appear to be all endemic.' Bentham described the fruit of G. *macro-phylla* as 'closely resembling that of G. *arborea*', a valuable timber tree native to wet forests from Sri Lanka through India and Burma to Southern China, and well known to European botanists. He also noted that Robert Brown had misidentified G. *macrophylla* as a Vitex in the *Prodromus*. Mueller had not only made the same mistake, he had also changed the descriptive species name, which means 'large-leaved', for 'Dalrympleana', honouring the explorer George Augustus Frederick Elphinstone Dalrymple. The next Gmelina Bentham described was G. *fasciculiflora*; in this case Mueller had not understood that he was looking at a distinct species and described it as a variety of his *Vitex leichhardtii*.

'Why wouldn't Mueller have known a Gmelina when he saw one?'

Jane stopped drying her hair and looked at me sternly.

'For the same reason that Robert Brown didn't know what he was looking at was a Gmelina. And anyway, his name is von Mueller.'

'Von Mueller is a ridiculous name. His family name is the German for Miller, *tout court*, a good artisan class name, not to be cluttered up with particles of imaginary nobility.'

'He was awarded that barony. It's not up to you to strip him of it.'

'I thought you said he was resisting imperial hegemony. Accepting foreign honours was against British law. He didn't just have the barony – he had twenty knighthoods as well. I think he wore his medals in bed.'

Mueller was my *bête* and I was determined to paint him *noire*. I banged on.

'The man was a menace. Surely he should have known better than to introduce and aggressively propagate tamarisks?'

Jane's eyes widened. 'Did he?'

'He actually boasted about it.' (In a lecture Mueller claimed that his nursery had propagated 'from a solitary Tamarix plant, 20,000 bushes, now scattered through our colonial shrubberies . . .')

Jane protested. 'He thought his introductions would be useful. He hadn't any experience of how introduced plants could behave in a place like Australia.'

'That simply isn't true. He knew what invasive weeds were, and how rapidly they spread.' Mueller protested that he was not responsible for the introduction of Capeweed, 'as it had already impressively invaded some parts of Australia as early as 1833'. (Mueller, 1872, 179; Ewart, 38) Clearly he knew how problematic plant introductions could be, but the knowledge did nothing to abate his enthusiasm for acclimatisation. Though willows, first brought to the colony in 1800 (Bladen, iv, 277), were already choking whole river systems, he thought nothing of importing more, apparently for basketmaking.

> It should be ascertained how many of the 160 true species of Willows and of their numerous hybrids are available for wickerwork; and we should learn, whether any of the American, the Himalayan or the Japanese Osiers are in some respect superior to those in general use.

No one had put more energy into mapping the biodiversity of Australia, yet Mueller had no qualms about eliminating it.

> Test experiments initiated from a botanic garden might teach us whether the Silk Mulberry Tree can be successfully reared in the Murray desert, to supplant the Mallee-scrub . . .

Supplant the Mallee-scrub! Such reckless arrogance is breathtaking. I don't know what the Red Kangaroos would have to say about supplanting the Mallee-scrub, or the Paucident Planigales – if there are any left. Or the poor old Mallee Fowl.

It must not be thought that after Mueller's orgy the fashion for naming plants after botanists slowed down. If anything it has got worse. When Wayne Goss, premier of Queensland from 1989 to 1996, gave substantial funds to the Queensland Herbarium, a part of the genus Austromyrtus was renamed Gossia in his honour; the other part was given the grotesque name Lenwebbia, in memory of pioneering rainforest ecologist Len Webb, who died in 2008.

'They're a blokey lot these botanists, don't you think?'

Jane looked up from her book.

'Not any more. Some of the most influential botanists in Australia are women – Gwen Harden, Pauline Ladiges . . .'

'I'm thinking more then. Linnaeus preferred to send unmarried men on plant-hunting expeditions because they so often lost their lives, and he didn't want any more widows hassling him. Solander never married. Dryander never married. Banks was supposed to have been extra keen to accompany the *Endeavour* expedition because he needed to get away from a woman he was expected to marry. When he got back to England he had to pay compensation for messing her about. He married later in life but the marriage was childless. Brown never married. Neither of the Cunninghams married. Frazer didn't marry. Caley brought his black tracker Moowat'tin back to England with him only to have Banks send him straight back again.' (Currey, xi, 140, 173–4, 191, 194)

'Perennial bachelors,' said Jane. 'So?'

'You have to wonder whether plant-hunting was a way for gay men to escape from societal pressure. I can't help thinking of my darling Leichhardt.'

'You think Nicholson and Leichhardt were lovers.'

'I don't know whether they had sex together, but it's clear that they were as close as people can be, with or without sex. But when Nicholson decided not to go to Australia Leichhardt didn't act like a man who was broken-hearted, so you do wonder if he was just a leech and a chancer. The thing that strikes you about Leichhardt is his optimism, his trustingness. He is incredibly lovable.'

'Not to the men who accompanied him on his expeditions, he wasn't. Men lost their lives because of his poor management.'

There was no denying this, so I changed the subject.

'Mueller's an even more interesting case. He was engaged to be married twice, in 1863 to Euphemia Henderson who painted flowers for him, and in 1865 to Rebecca Nordt, but he couldn't bring himself to marry either of them. He waits till he's nearly forty, and then funks it, tries again and funks it again. He kept Rebecca waiting around so long he ruined her chances of finding a man, and that at a time when women were in distinctly short supply. He ended up like Banks, having to pay her compensation. His reason for not marrying her was that she was no longer of child-bearing age! Whose fault was that? The man was a wretch.'

Part of the blokiness of botany stems from its needing to be done in Latin; girls' schools were more likely to teach modern languages than Latin. Many women botanised, and bred and grafted horticultural varieties, but the intellectual conquest and ordering of the vegetable world cannot have held the same appeal for them as it did for men. The number of women who authored plant names is pathetically small; not only did very few women do it, they only did it once or twice, whereas men like Hooker, Bentham and Mueller authored literally hundreds of names.

When Jane asked me if any of the plant species at Cave Creek was named by a woman, all I could say was that I didn't think so. 'We've got one named for a woman but none named by a woman, as far as I know.'

The one named for a woman is *Syzygium hodgkinsoniae*. The Hodgkinson in question is supposed to be Miss M. Hodgkinson, a collector of plants in the Richmond River area.

'What does the M. stand for?' Jane asked.

'No idea. She isn't even on the Australian National Botanic Garden Biography database. No dates. No nothing. One of the most beautiful trees at Cave Creek to remember her by and we've got no idea who she was.'

Syzygium is a myrtaceous genus, with shimmering paired leaves of forest green, and flowers in terminal cymes. Though *S. hodgkinsoniae* is supposed to need rich alluvial soil it seems happy enough at Natural Bridge on the montane basalt. It's rare and listed as threatened, but at CCRRS there are hundreds of them. The ghost of Miss Hodgkinson is always with us, especially when the tree is in flower and the glades are full of its seductive scent. The man who named the plant for Miss H. was none other than Ferdinand Mueller. Needless to say he got the genus wrong: he thought it was a Eugenia, as did everyone else until Lawrie Johnson sorted out the Syzygiums by phylogenetic analysis in 1962. Till then the Syzygiums were called Acicalyptus, Acmena, Acmenosperma, Anetholea, Caryophyllus, Cleistocalyx, Jambosa, Lomastelma, Pillocalyx, Waterhousea, Xenodendron – and Eugenia. Not everyone has accepted Johnson's revision, which has resulted in an enormous and rather too various genus. So the old synonyms are usually listed along with the Johnsonian name. Mueller published his *Eugenia hodgkinsoniae* in the *Victorian Naturalist* No. 8, in July 1891, but it seems that F. M. Bailey had already published the plant in the *Botany Bulletin* of the Queensland Department of Agriculture, as *Eugenia fitzgeraldii*, citing two isotypes, one collected on the summit of the Blackall Range in March 1891, the other at the Richmond River by R. D. Fitzgerald, and in the possession of 'F. v. M.' (APNI). Miss Hodgkinson could have lost her tiny claim to fame there and then but, incomprehensibly, she didn't.

Mueller named another species after a Hodgkinson. *Hodgkinsonia ovatiflora* is named for his boss, Clement Hodgkinson, Deputy Surveyor General and later Assistant Commissioner and Secretary of the Board of Crown Lands and Survey. Although it may look very likely that the Hodgkinson who received the honour of having a Syzygium species named after her is one of Clement's connections, it seems rather that it is not a Miss Hodgkinson whom we seek, but Mary, wife of James Hodgkinson, the first settler at Lennox Head, near the mouth of the Richmond River. Mary lived at North Creek from 1866 until her death in 1889 at the age of sixty-five. Contrariwise it may have been one of her five daughters, none of whom however has the initial M. The holotype of a lichenised fungus *Pseudocyphellaria glaucescens* (Lobariaceae) was collected by a 'Miss Hodgkinson' on the Richmond River in 1880 (*Flora of Australia*, 58:1, 62).

Louisa Atkinson collected for both William Woolls and Ferdinand Mueller. Mueller named a genus of mistletoe Atkinsonia after her, as well as two Asteraceous species and a species of fern. In 1869 at the age of thirty-five she married James Snowden Calvert, a survivor of

Leichhardt's expedition of 1844–5. Mueller then named two species for her, *Epacris calvertiana* and *Helichrysum calvertiana*. Sadly, she died not long after the birth of her first child in 1872.

With Mary Strong Clemens (*ADB*) we find ourselves once again in the company of an amateur botanist. She was married to a chaplain in the US army; from 1905 to 1907, when her husband was serving in the Philippines, Mary made field trips to Luzon and Mindanao, collecting plants, apparently for Elmer Drew Merrill, USDA botanist in the Philippines. After her husband's retirement from the ministry he assisted her. Between the wars the couple made collecting trips to China, Indo-China, North Borneo, Sarawak, Java and Singapore. In August 1935 they transferred their operations to New Guinea. When Mary's husband died, five months after their arrival, she stayed on collecting in the New Guinea highlands until the Japanese invasion, when she was compulsorily repatriated to Queensland.

When Mrs Clemens arrived in Australia in December 1941 she was sixty-nine. She recommenced work at once, in a shed behind the Queensland Herbarium. At first she slept in the shed, but she was eventually persuaded to accept accommodation in a hostel. All day and as much of the night as she could, she spent pressing and labelling the plants she collected on her walk to work or on excursions by train, tram or bus. Her labels were based on identifications made by her colleagues at the Herbarium. These were not always correct but, with no formal training, she was in no position to question them. Some new species have been identified from specimens she collected, while information gained on her wanderings has increased the range of many known plants. The botanists she helped have generously remembered her in the naming of their species: the specific epithet 'clemensiae' is to be found on more than seventy species. However botany wouldn't be botany if her biographer, R. F. N. Langdon of the Department of Botany at the University of Queensland, hadn't decided to reduce her to size. His verdict is that 'Mrs. Clemens probably lacked the capacity to determine plants. As years passed botanists became very wary of Mrs. Clemens and her plants.' (380)

BANANAS

The Australian writer Rosa Praed, who was born in 1851, spent her early childhood not far from Numinbah, at Bromelton on the Logan. She hardly noticed that her family was poor, because she had the riches of the rainforest.

> . . . a huge Moreton Bay fig tree . . . gave us more delicious fruit than any we could get in the garden. Then there were mulgams – native raspberries peculiar to the Logan; and there was the chucky-chucky, a most pleasant tasting wild plum, which had a way of hanging tantalisingly over the water, so that if the pool were deep, there was a little difficulty in gathering it. The geebong was not so nice – its fruit was slimy and rather sickly, though not unpalatable . . . There is no end to the delights of a scrub.

Little Rosa was more easily pleased than today's children, who would never dream of putting a mulgam or a chucky-chucky into their mouths. 'Mulgam' or, in his spelling, 'malgum', is listed by Gresty as the local Aboriginal name for the wild raspberry of the Numinbah Valley (Gresty, 62, 72). According to the Macquarie Dictionary the chucky-chucky is usually the fruit of the American snowberry, or the Tasmanian Gaultheria. Praed's 'geebong' is nowdays better known as 'geebung', a name given to various Persoonia species. In Western Australia and South Australia geebungs are known also as 'Snottygobbles'.

In the Cave Creek rainforest at all times of the year there is fruit. Sometimes there is so much squishy fruit underfoot that you find yourself walking in jam. Most prodigal are the figs, being in fruit all the year round. The botany of figs is still in its infancy, which is the kindest way of saying that the botanists have signally failed to answer any of the big questions about figs. What we think of as the fruit of a fig is actually a hollow structure called a synconium, like an inside-out umbel, containing hundreds of male pollen-bearing and/or female seed-forming flowers. In about half the 800–1,000 fig species in the world the fig contains flowers of both sexes; in the other half the synconia are unisexual. All fig species breed their own pollinators, tiny symbiotic wasps, inside the synconia; the adult wasps travel from fig to fig through the tiny hole at the bottom, carrying pollen from the male synconia to the female, or from one bisexual synconium to another. Some synconia will be visited by more than one species of fig wasp, and some of the wasps are cuckoo-wasps that live on the flesh of the synconium, or the seeds or the wasp larvae in it.

The entomologists have performed marvels in studying the complex interaction between fruit and insect. Unfortunately the botanists are still in total disarray when it comes to the systematics of fig species. None of the botanists who have visited Cave Creek can establish how many species of figs grow there, or just which species they are. Dearest to my heart, and the easiest to identify, are our sandpaper figs, called that because their leaves, abrasive as glass paper, were used by the Aborigines for smoothing off spears. There are supposed to be two species of these: *Ficus fraseri* which grows on the drier slopes, and *F. coronata* which grows on the creeks, in rainforest and in open country from far eastern Victoria as far north as Mackay. In our rainforest some *F. coronata* produce swarming clusters of fruit on the trunk (cauliflory) and branches (ramiflory) as well as in the leaf axils. The species name *coronata* refers to the crown of rather stiff silvery bristles at the tip of the fruit, which ripens to a rich purple if the birds will let it. Though usually these trees are smallish and fairly shapeless, a few put out beautifully regular branches with fruit in every leaf axil. Breeding from these could result in a very handsome garden cultivar. *F. fraseri*, which has a much more restricted range, grows into a full-sized forest tree which bears copious hairless fruits that ripen from orange to red. Both trees are favourites of the Figbirds, who wear natty suits of olive green and big red sunglasses.

Neither of our sandpaper figs is a strangler; all our other figs are. The existence of strangler figs is one of the first phenomena that suggest to the amateur dendrologist that the much-vaunted equilibrium of the rainforest is actually a state of constant war, in which no side can be allowed to win. Of the billions of seeds produced by each of our huge fig trees, only those will germinate that have been dropped in a fork of another tree, usually by a defecating bird or bat. The seedling lives at first as an epiphyte, but soon sends long slender roots in search of the ground. Once it has tapped into the available nutrients, the root grows stouter, and sends out side roots that link all around the host tree. These grow thicker, and contract, till they gradually strangle the host tree, which is already suffering because the stiff, dark foliage of the fig topping out over its own canopy is shading it out. The host tree dies, and rots away inside, leaving a massive crown of fig leaves atop a tall hollow tower pierced by many gothic windows, where the Boobook likes to sit and watch for prey.

All up and down the east coast of New South Wales and southern Queensland you may see huge strangler figs standing all alone in otherwise cleared paddocks, the only survivors of the vanished rainforest population. Just why the figs should survive is not immediately clear. It helps that no particular use has ever been found for fig timber, which is soft, light and perishable. In the memoir of Numinbah Valley compiled by public-minded denizens to mark the bicentenary of the arrival of the First Fleet in 1788 may be seen a reproduction of a charcoal drawing by Tom McGeown of the trunk and spreading buttresses of a giant fig tree. The caption reads:

The Memorial Fig Tree – a tribute to Marion Yaun from her sons . . .
It stands like an island of vegetation in the cleared paddock, the long sinuous roots snaking up the hill as if holding it together. It is dark and cool beneath its massive branches – a sanctuary for animal life, bird life and humans alike. Often did Marion stand on her verandah and remark at the beauty of that tree, and when her grown sons came to clear the vegetation round it for their growing dairy herds, they remembered their mother's words and could not destroy it. For us today it is a reminder of the height of the forest canopy that once

covered the river flats and no doubt Marion would be pleased to know that the fig is still growing and giving pleasure so many years into the future. (Hall *et al.*, 23)

Given the extraordinary number of lone survivor fig trees in Australian pastureland thousands of other farmers' wives must have had the same idea as Marion Yaun. The giant dome of fig foliage can provide a haven for plants as well as animals and birds. If there are no cattle in the surrounding paddock, the area shaded by a fig tree will become an oasis of amazingly varied regrowth, because fruit-eating birds have nowhere else to perch, and, wherever they perch, they defecate. A lot of what germinates will be exotic fruit species, guavas, persimmons, loquats, mulberries, grenadillas, passionfruit and goodness knows what next.

The names suggested for our strangler fig trees begin with *Ficus macrophylla*, the Moreton Bay Fig, *F. obliqua*, the Small-leaved Fig, *F. superba*, *F. superba* var. *henneana*, *F. rubiginosa*, *F. watkinsiana* and even *F. virens*. The chief candidate for the *macrophylla* ID is a huge fig growing in what was pasture. It seems near enough to the commonly accepted type, although its leaves are hardly big enough. The dusting of rust on the underside may indicate kinship with *F. rubiginosa*. All of our figs seem to be intermediate species, which makes nonsense of the taxonomy, you would think.

F. superba, found at the Endeavour River in 1770, is the first Australian fig to be collected, although not identified until 1866 by Friedrich Anton Wilhelm Miquel; the finished painting based on the drawing made by Sydney Parkinson at the time of collection clearly shows fruit with whitish polka dots. We have a fig that produces similar dark purple fruit with yellowish spots, but it isn't deciduous, as *F. superba* is supposed to be. None of the common names of this fig, 'cedar fig' or 'white fig' or 'sour fig' or 'mountain fig', seems to fit ours. *Ficus superba* is not only extremely variable but widely distributed around the Pacific; one lot of botanists, led by O. K. Berg and E. J. H. Corner, have now excluded the Australian *superba*-type figs from the Asian species and elevated the *henneana* variety or subspecies to full speciesdom as Maiden did before them but, as the type comes from islands in the Torres Strait, it seems unlikely that our figs could be identical. Bailey had tried to establish the Australian species as *F. gracilipes*, Hiern as *F. parkinsonii*, and Warburg as *F. pritzelli*, and at one point Corner suggested *F. superba* var. *muelleri*, all of which is as nothing compared with the nomenclatural uproar surrounding other fig species. There has even been an attempt to split the Linnaean genus and add a subgenus Urostigma, to which the Australian figs would belong.

To *Ficus watkinsiana* are sometimes attributed the spots clearly visible on the fig species collected by Banks and Solander, but this species is also called the 'Nipple Fig', as if the nipple at the base of the fruit was diagnostic; in our experience spots and nipple do not always occur together. Watkins's fig is also known as the 'Grey-leaved Moreton Bay Fig' and the 'Green-leaved Moreton Bay Fig', as well as *F. bellingeri* and *F. simmondsii*. How it could be all these at once is nowhere explained.

So much for our large-leaved figs. Some of our figs are distinctly small-leaved and you would think that they had to be *Ficus obliqua*. Aha no. They have fruits of different colours; some mature to red, some to gold, some to orange. Even the revered Bill McDonald has hesitated to give these figs of ours a name. There are plenty to choose from – *F. tryonii, virginea, backhousei, eugenioides*, or *Urostigma obliquum*, which is the name Georg Forster supplied in 1786, or *Urostigma backhousei*, or *eugenioides*. One of our visiting botanists suggested that our small-leaved figs were *F. obliqua* var. *obliqua*. Some of our fig twigs have bright red stipules, so might be *F. triradiata*.

Margaret Lowman, aka 'Canopy Meg', who single-handedly invented canopy science, has written that in the rainforest struggle, the strangler figs will eventually win.

> The figs . . . germinate in the crowns of trees, extending their roots downward to the ground, rather than conventionally of [*sic*] sending shoots up to the canopy. This habit is termed hemiepiphytic, because the plants begin life as an epiphyte (air plant) but eventually extend down to root on the forest floor. The top-down pattern of fig growth is not only unique among rain-forest trees, but I privately believe it is destined to be the most successful pattern over evolutionary time . . .

My prediction is that figs, with their innovative mode of securing a spot in full sunlight and then growing top downward, will dominate the forests. (Lowman, 100)

If the strangler figs win the eternal battle that is the rainforest, they must also eventually lose, because there has to be a forest for them to climb onto and into. When the birds perch in the forest trees and defecate, the crotches where the seeds end up are sometimes only a few metres off the ground, way below the canopy. What is more, if there is nothing to provide a rooting medium in the tree crotch – decaying leaves, fungal matter, frass – the fig seedling will be slow to develop and may die. All the fig species produce huge amounts of fruit, some of them all the year round, yet the proportion of rainforest trees coping with fig invasion is actually quite low. In terms of invest-ment of reproductive energy therefore, figs would appear to do very badly. Some tree species may even be able to repel stranglers by secreting inhibiting chemicals, for the stranglers certainly don't seem to be having things all their own way.

It is not usually a good strategy on the part of a parasite to kill its host. The fig canopy is thick-leaved and dense, therefore very vulner-able to high winds, while the lacework trunk is too vulnerable to decay for a fig tree ever to live for a thousand years as many rainforest trees can. With a weak trunk and a huge head of spreading branches weighing many tons, the triumphant strangler fig may overreach itself. At Cave Creek several huge figs that topped out above the rest of the forest have recently fallen. One of them, with a canopy that spread over a third of an acre, fell into the national park and scored a king hit on the footbridge, reducing it to matchwood. By some blessed chance, though tourists come in their droves by day and by night, no one was on the bridge when the fig came down. For two days chainsaws roared as the fallen canopy that crammed the gorge was reduced to lumber. Some crafty person collected all the orchids off the tree and hid them, intending to come back later and collect them. (Rainforest orchids, especially the rarer ones, fetch high prices in neighbourhood street markets.) By good hap I found the stolen hoard before it could be collected and took the orchids back into the rainforest.

Lowman is certainly right to see the rainforest symbiosis as an eternal war, but it will be won by no single species. If the rainforest is a lottery (another of Lowman's parallels) the house will always win.

At Cave Creek rainforest species flower and fruit according to a timetable all their own. Trees on north-facing slopes will flower profusely when trees of the same species on slopes facing east or west don't even look like flowering. Sometimes it's available water that seems to make the difference. Most plants will be forced into flower by stress; in the rainforest this seems not to be the case. In a dry season, our trees are less likely to flower; if we get 400 millimetres of rain out of season, as sometimes happens, we will have a burst of flowering afterwards. It pays us to look for fruit in every season but, though we find tons of it, often we find that the fruit contains no seed. The worst offender in this regard is one of the lilly pillies, *Syzygium corynanthum*, which produces sour cherries in stupendous quantities, so that the ground underneath the trees is blazing coral red. I have sat for day after day, gently opening the fruit with a scalpel, hunting for something like an endosperm in thousands of fruits and finding nothing.

'Stands to reason,' said Jane. 'If you expected to live for five hundred years or more, would you bother ovulating every year? You wouldn't need offspring for every year of your life, would you?'

'Plenty of trees, most trees in the rainforest, set hundreds of times more seeds than could ever germinate.'

'And *Syzygium corynanthum* doesn't. It's an option, is all I'm saying.'

I considered this for a bit. 'So you produce the fruit without the seed because you will eventually need the birds to distribute your seed, and you have to keep them interested?'

'It's probably not that simple, but, something like that, yes.'

In 1866 pioneer sugar grower John Ewen Davidson (*ADB*), exploring 'the scrubs round Rockingham Bay' between Townsville and Cairns, came across a fruiting tree which the Tully River Aboriginal people called 'Ooray'; he showed it to John Dallachy, ex-curator of the Melbourne Botanical Garden, who had retired to a property near Rockingham Bay. Dallachy was still collecting for the Melbourne Herbarium, where Ferdinand Mueller named the genus for its discoverer, Davidsonia, with the specific name *pruriens*

(*Fragmenta*, 6:41, 4). At first prospects for its commercial exploitation seemed good: 'the fruit is dark purple in colour; the flesh a rich crimson, very juicy and of a sharp, acid flavour.' (*BC*, 23 June 1881)

To ordinary mortals *Davidsonia pruriens* was simply Davidson's Plum. It is not in fact a plum, not a member of the genus Prunus or even of the family of Rosaceae. It was thought to have not only a genus, Davidsonia, but a family all to itself, the Davidsoniaceae (Bange, 294) but in 2000 Gwen Harden and John Williams restored it to the family of Cunoniaceae (Harden and Williams, 414). For a while it looked as if the Davidson's Plum was going to be one native fruit with a future. The Intercolonial Exhibition of 1877 was one of several where potted Davidsonias were among the exhibits (*SMH*, 12 April). This 'blue-black plum about the size of a duck-egg' had obvious potential for improvement, and for some time it seems to have been a popular inclusion in Queensland gardens. A reviewer of J. H. Maiden's *Useful Native Plants of Australia* in 1889 was surprised to find that he had left out such a well-known and common fruit (*Q*, 9 March, 452).

In 1900 F. M. Bailey split the species into two subspecies; the second, which he found on the Tweed, he called *D. pruriens* var. *jerseyana* (*The Queensland Flora*, ii:538). This was eventually understood to be a species in its own right. In 1949, plant taxonomist Lawrie Johnson, examining collections of Davidsonia made in north-east New South Wales in 1926, 1939 and 1944, segregated some and labelled them 'clearly a new species'. There the matter rested until 1958, when Alex Floyd and H. C. Hayes collected specimens of the same plant at The Pocket, north of Mullumbimby, and noticed that unlike the type it was hairless; their samples were placed in the Coffs Harbour Forestry Herbarium and forgotten. In 1977 Graham Watson sent a specimen he had collected on his property at Huonbrook west of Mullumbimby to Gwen Harden and J. B. Williams. More collections were then made, some as far north as Currumbin, but still the species languished without a name until Harden and Williams named it *Davidsonia johnsonii*, in memory of Lawrie Johnson (Harden and Williams, 416). It is fitting that the rarest plant at CCRRS should carry this distinguished name. Mind you, if I should find a new species, I should like to call it *briggsae*, for Barbara Briggs, who was for many years Johnson's faithful co-worker. Johnson is remembered all over the place, including a whole genus of proteaceous nut trees saddled with the name Lasjia (for his initials) and the largest of the Macrozamias, which is *M. johnsonii*, but you will search in vain for a memorial to Dr Briggs.

From the day I became responsible for CCRRS I knew that the survival of *Davidsonia johnsonii* was up to me. On every visit I made sure to see how it was getting on. I directed the workforce to remove competing weed vegetation, including a coral tree that grew amongst its suckers. Imagine my horror when, on the way to visit it one day, I found the top half of the biggest Davidsonia lugged out of the forest and dying beside the track. At first I didn't believe my eyes, but the elegant compound leaves with their winged stalks and flared stipules were unmistakeable. The workforce was duly hauled over the coals. How could we have been so careless? The answer came that as the coral tree slowly succumbed to repeated doses of poison, its head had snapped off and taken out the head of the Davidsonia as it fell. Simon had removed damaged growths and now the Davidsonia would just have to get on with it. I preached a bit about how much vegetative material had been wasted because we didn't take the broken bit to a propagator, but the workforce was unmoved. The damaged tree, they thought, would grab its opportunity, which in fact it did.

In December 2004 the New South Wales Department of Environment and Conservation joined forces with the Queensland Environmental Protection Agency and the Queensland Parks and Wildlife Service to produce a 34-page recovery plan for *Davidsonia johnsonii*, which is classed under every system as endangered. On page i the plan says that 'populations in Queensland have been recorded from freehold land only', which rather makes you think that before spending scarce resources on helping to generate this expensive 34-page statement, QPWS should have tried to find out where their *D. johnsonii* population actually was and how big it was. Two years ago CCRRS worker Luke came across a clump of more than a dozen plants just over our boundary in the National Park. He showed the new find to an official from the Queensland Environmental Protection Agency, who verified it and left. One way conservation bureaucrats might encourage the owners of private land to do the right thing for their threatened plants might be to say hello when they come to visit, and maybe utter a few encouraging words. So far they would appear to be as inept at people management as they are at environmental management.

The recovery plan gave itself the task of determining the long–term survival potential of our smooth Davidsonias, but the current state of their understanding seems unlikely to serve them well.

> In some specimens . . . the female flowers are rudimentary, almost vestigial. At other sites, female parts were normally developed, comprising two fused carpels with four or five ovules (up to seven at one site) per carpel. Those sites with the best development of female parts in the flowers are also the heaviest fruit-bearing stands . . .
>
> The method of pollination of Smooth Davidsonia flowers is not understood. The size and form of the flower suggests that the vectors are likely to be small insects. Bees (including native bees), beetles and ants have been observed visiting the flowers. (*Recovery Plan*, 6)

Seed production was an even greater mystery.

> There have only been two instances of seed being found within the fruit of this species.
>
> Possible explanations for the low incidence of seed production by this species may include isolation from compatible plants, lack of production of pollen, no transfer of pollen from anther to stigma, non–viable pollen, self-incompatibility mechanisms, and early abortion of developing embryo. (*Recovery Plan*, 6)

All of which are good guesses, but they are guesses. What this sterility has to mean is that *D. johnsonii* can propagate itself only vegetatively, in other words, that our plants are clonal. This could be a sign that the species has run to the end of its evolutionary tether, having lost all genetic variability. It may survive like that for millennia, but not if it is required to adapt to changed climatic conditions. What does seem odd is that the plant tends to turn up in the ecotone between cleared land and the forest rather than in the undisturbed forest. Its suckers, which are its sole way of propagating itself, tend to proliferate where the ground has been disturbed. We have propagated it successfully from those suckers, and planted them, not where they were originally found on the steep dark slope where tenants of the past threw their tin cans, beer bottles and car tyres, but on the edges of our forest tracks where they can see the light. Meanwhile, since the coral tree rotted away, the original Davidsonia stool has suckered all over the creek bank. The next move will be to encourage the Davidsonia's tendency to form a monoculture by removing all competing vegetation within the circumference of the stool.

None of the three species of Davidson's Plum is being produced commercially on a large scale. In 1999 botanist Kris Kupsch set up Ooray Orchards at Burringbar south of Murwillumbah; he is now growing upwards of 2,000 Davidsonias, including eighteen *D. johnsonii* types from eighteen different sites. It is Kupsch's intention to collect and propagate Davidsonias from as many genetic populations as possible, in a bid to increase their chances of survival.

Most of the seed developed by any rainforest fruiting species is first and foremost a life-support for the invertebrate members of the forest community and for its birds. Ripe fruit hits the ground carrying a larval load that can be anything from microscopic to gross. All the seeds we collect for planting must first be soaked to drown the larvae that would otherwise eat the seed before it germinated. For the fruit-eating birds, the worms that infest the fruit they eat are an important, often their sole, source of protein. Every single rainforest tree has at least one dedicated insect species that pollinates its flowers and lays its eggs in either flower or fruit. Drosophila, the genus that includes the fruit-fly species that helped us to understand genetic mutation, is well represented in the rainforest. No sooner had the settlers cleared the rainforests and planted their fruit groves than the dispossessed fruit flies mounted their counter-attack on behalf of the nurturing forest.

In the rainforest a single tree species is likely to host up to three fruit-fly species in densities of up to seventeen fruit flies per 100 fruits. What this signifies is that populations of endemic fruit flies exist in balance with their host trees and do not threaten their survival. The great majority of fruit flies in their natural habitat are limited to a single plant genus, and most to a single species within the genus (Novotny *et al.*). Pest fruit flies, whether from the Mediterranean or islands in the Pacific, tend to infest a wide variety of fruits, from stoned fruit to citrus, guava and papaya. Attempts to keep pest fruit flies out of Australia have been both expensive and largely ineffective. Our best bet is to nurture the native fruit-fly populations in the hope that they can hold their own.

For years Australians have been planting olive trees, some as a tax dodge, others because lifestyle magazines recommended them for hedging, and some because they hoped to make money from olive oil. Unfortunately the select European types were deemed unsuitable for Australian conditions, and vigorous new varieties were grafted onto African rootstocks (Spenneman and Allen). Because the cost of the manpower needed to collect the fruit and prune the trees was prohibitive, many commercial olive groves were found to be uneconomic and subsequently abandoned. Birds ate the fruit left on decorative olive trees, foxes ate the fruit that fell in the abandoned orchards, and both excreted the seed kernels up hill and down dale, where they sprouted, grew into more trees, produced more olives that fed more birds and foxes and so on exponentially ad infinitum. Since 1992 the olive has been listed as a noxious weed in South Australia, Victoria, New South Wales and Queensland. I would have grown the native olive, *Olea paniculata*, even if it hadn't been eaten by eight rainforest bird species and even if it hadn't been impossibly elegant, with its glossy dark leaves and pale branchlets, because its dedicated fruit-fly species are our only defence against weed olives.

It is probably important to point out at this juncture that the Queensland Fruit Fly that is a major pest of Australian horticulture is not a Drosophila but a tephritid fly called *Bactrocera tryoni*. This fly too is endemic to northern New South Wales but, unlike the dedicated Drosophila species, it attacks more than a hundred different fruit crops; its hosts in its native forests are thought to be Syzygium species.

The forest fruit harvest is deeply unpredictable. One year we will have cartloads of native tamarinds and another year none. Some years the forest will be carpeted with black apples, variously called *Planchonella* or *Pouteria australis*. As I crawl around the forest floor, picking up black apples and ticks in almost equal quantities, I am very aware that I am in competition with other animals. One (or more) species eats the apple flesh, leaving the big seeds in little heaps, and the other (or others) leaves the flesh and eats the seed. I needn't have begrudged them. Pouterias were amongst the first tree species we propagated, and we propagated far too many. We would have had to turn our rainforest into a black apple orchard if I hadn't taught the workforce their first bitter lesson and made them throw half the precious seedlings away. I stewed the black apple flesh, which was woody enough to make your teeth squeak, and then strained it, to see if there was any pectin in it. There wasn't. The syrup didn't set, so I added water and froze it in moulds to make popsicles.

The exploring botanists of the nineteenth century were supposedly looking for 'useful' plants that might be suitable for cultivation. Any botanist must know that even the most delicious European apples are descended from small sour crabs, and all the plums from bitter sloes, but wild Australian fruits were expected to be of the same order of toothsomeness as highly bred European ones. It was not until 1851 or so that Australians were informed that they had a native version of the famed Tamarind: 'The Australian Tamarind is a tall tree, growing in nearly all the scrubs and jungles near the coast, and bears a fruit resembling in appearance and taste the tamarind of the West Indies.' (*SMH*, 28 August) The Australian tamarinds belong to the sapinda- ceous genus Diploglottis, whereas the historic Tamarind, originally endemic to the Sudan, and now grown from West Africa to China, is fabaceous. The fruits of the Australian tamarinds are held in brown, furry capsules, which split to release brown seeds encased in orange- yellow arils. The sharp tang of the fruit of *Tamarindus indicus* is a valued element in cooking across half the world, but rather than develop the Australian fruit to rival it, Australian horticulturists imported seedlings of *T. indicus* from anywhere and everywhere. The Australian version remained unexploited until 'Bush Tucker' became the fashion in the 1980s. Even now nobody seems to want to do anything with Australian tamarinds but make them into jam or a drink.

The settlers in the Numinbah Valley were not horticulturists but farmers with families to feed. One of their motives for choosing the

Numinbah Valley was that it gave them the opportunity to grow a
wide range of tasty and nourishing fruit. The trend was set by the
very first settler. From childhood Frank Nixon would have been
regaled with his mother's praises of the paradisaical fruit gardens
made by her forebears in the West Indies. Thomas Dougan's Profit
plantation boasted an astonishing array of fruiting trees.

> At its sides are smooth walks of grass; and between these and the
> sugar-canes are borders planted with all the choice tropical fruits,
> rendering a promenade upon the water, or its banks, most fragrant
> and inviting, and offering to the eye and the palate all the variety of
> oranges, shaddocks, limes, lemons, cherries, custard apples, cashew
> apples, avagata pears, grenadilloes, water-lemons, mangoes and pines.
> (Pinckard, 203–4)

Shaddocks are the citrus we now call grapefruit; cashew apples are
Linnaeus's *Anacardium occidentale*, which is called 'marañon' in most
Spanish-speaking countries, and 'caju' or 'cajueiro' in Portuguese;
'avagata pears' are avocadoes, 'pines' pineapples. When William
Guilfoyle visited the Tweed in 1870 he was impressed by the fruit
garden Rosalie Adelaide Nixon had planted at the Hill.

> Mr [George] Nixon's house stands upon a very charming site and one
> day, not far distant, it will be surrounded by an orchard of the choicest
> fruits. (*BC*, 7 January)

Around his Numinbah homestead Frank Nixon had 'a garden
planted with oranges, lemon trees, vines etc.'. The settlers who
moved into the valley after him followed his example. Queensland
government agents tried to lure settlers by portraying the colony as
offering extraordinary opportunities for horticulture, with 'super-
natural yields of fruit . . . oranges and grapes growing by the
wayside . . .' ([Carrington], 8–9)
The very first exotic fruit to be grown in Australia was probably
an apple. In 1788, when his ship the *Bounty*, then charting the south-
east coast of Tasmania, called in at Adventure Bay on Bruny Island,
William Bligh planted 'three fine young Apple-Trees in a growing

state'. When he returned in 1792 he found that one had survived. In the 1820s Tasmanian settlers began to sell the surplus production of their private orchards on the open market and by 1860 apples were an important export. In 1966 6 million boxes of apples were shipped from Port Huon, but the industry was already in decline. Australia now produces only 0.1 per cent of the world's apples, while China produces 40 per cent. The variety most often chosen for Tasmanian cider is the Sturmer Pippin, born and bred only fifteen kilometres from my house in England. In England it has never been favoured for cider production, which is centred not on Essex in the rain-poor south-east of the country where I live, but on Somerset and points south-west.

In 1797 when George Suttor decided that, with twenty pounds to his name, he would emigrate to the infant colony of New South Wales, he turned to Sir Joseph Banks for assistance. He and the other settlers who arrived on HMS *Porpoise* in 1800 were each given a grant of 200 acres of land, a house, tools and two or three indentured labourers. Suttor had no sooner secured his land in the Baulkham Hills than he set about growing oranges; by 1807 he was selling them at the market in Charlotte Square for the considerable sum of two shillings and sixpence a dozen. In 1839 Richard Hill acquired land on the Lane Cove River, where he established a successful citrus orchard to which he often travelled in a boat rowed by ten Aboriginal oarsmen. When George Bennett visited The Orangery, as it was called, in 1858, he found Seville, Navel and Mandarin oranges as well as lemons growing in profusion; Hill, who was shipping oranges to the goldfields, had already sold nearly half a million that year, and was making £50 profit per day (*ADB*).

Nobody stopped to consider whether or not such introductions might disrupt the native vegetation. The native vegetation, on which the indigenous inhabitants had thrived for forty thousand years or more, was thought to be mere scrub, valueless. Nobody sought to quarrel with the conviction that 'There are few wild fruits in Capricornia, and such as there are, are poor and tasteless.' (Bennett, 131)

Even as they headed out to collect specimens of an astonishing variety of native plants, the first explorers took with them cherry pips and peach stones to plant as they went along. Allan Cunningham, travelling with John Oxley along the Lachlan River in 1817, planted acorns, quince seeds and peach stones wherever the soil seemed particularly good. As the son of the head gardener at Wimbledon House, Cunningham must have known not only that his peaches were most unlikely to survive without cosseting, but also that if they did, they would almost certainly revert to a wild form. The many cultivars of the peach are assumed to belong to a single species which, although it is originally Chinese, was named by Linnaeus *Prunus persica*. What the type may be nobody knows, because Chinese horti- culturalists had been selectively breeding peaches for at least two thousand years before the fruit came to the knowledge of Europeans. Self-seeded peaches have turned feral in thirteen of the United States; they are listed as significant weeds in the Adelaide Hills and on the Galapagos Islands.

Ludwig Leichhardt too was given peach stones to take with him on his journey overland from the Darling Downs to Port Essington. On 26 January 1845 he reached a creek north of the Mackenzie River which he named Newman's Creek after the horticulturist Francis William Newman: 'Here I planted the last peach-stones, with which Mr. Newman the present superintendent of the Botanic Garden in Hobart Town kindly provided me. It is however to be feared that the fires, which annually overrun the whole country, and particularly here, where the grass is rich and deep even to the water's edge, will not allow them to grow.' (Leichhardt, 122) When Leichhardt passed that way again two years later he found no vestige of a peach tree (Bailey, J., 304). We should be grateful that Leichhardt's peaches didn't grow. Thanks possibly to that same Mr Newman, feral peach trees are now serious weeds in the bushland around Hobart.

Leichhardt never gave up hope that he might find on his travels some delicious new something. He tasted every single fruit he encountered.

In the gully which I descended, a shrub with dark green leaves was tolerably frequent; its red berries, containing one or two seeds, were about the size of a cherry and good eating when ripe. (Leichhardt, 71)

He ate many of the native fruits in quantity, defying gripes and diarrhoea:

> Yesterday in coming through the scrub, we had collected a large quantity of ripe native lemons, of which, it being Sunday, we intended to make a tart; but, as my companions were absent, the treat was deferred until their return, which was on Monday morning, when we made them into a dish very like gooseberry fool; they had a pleasant acid taste and were very refreshing. They are of a light yellow colour, nearly round, and about half an inch in diameter; the volatile oil of the rind was not at all disagreeable. (Leichhardt, 77)

Like most of his contemporaries Leichhardt was attracted by the idea of 'acclimatisation', which prompted the founding of 'acclimatisation societies' in all the Australian states. Their primary aim, as defined in the First Annual Report of the Acclimatisation Society of Victoria, founded in 1861 with the Government Botanist, Ferdinand Mueller, as its guiding light, was the 'introduction, acclimatisation and domestication of all innoxious animals, birds, fish, insects, and vegetables whether useful or ornamental'. Nobody knows whether any species is truly 'innoxious', that is, harmless, until years after it has been introduced into a new ecosystem.

Acclimatisation had been one of the pet projects of Sir Joseph Banks, who in 1788 sent Bligh in the *Bounty* to collect breadfruit seedlings from Tahiti and transport them to Jamaica to be grown to provide food for the slaves in the sugarcane plantations. (Sugarcane, indigenous to south-east Asia, is the earliest example of spectacularly successful acclimatisation.) Bligh's crew mutinied, setting him adrift in a small boat, and threw the breadfruit seedlings into the sea, but a second attempt in 1792 resulted in breadfruit's becoming a staple food of the West Indies. It was also established in South India and Sri Lanka. Even more famous feats of nineteenth-century acclimatisation were the establishment in India in the 1860s of plantations of *Cinchona succirubra*, indigenous to Peru, for the industrial production of quinine, and the collection of 70,000 seeds of the Amazonian rubber tree by Sir Henry Wickham at the behest of Sir Joseph Hooker, who distributed them to Colombo, Singapore and Bogor in

Indonesia. In both cases the plant material was removed surrepti-
tiously, in an act of botanical piracy, for both the Peruvian and the
Brazilian authorities were aware of its commercial value. Australia
seemed to have no indigenous plants worth acclimatising elsewhere
– at least not before an unsuspecting world acclimatised the eucalypt.
Now Spain, Portugal, California and Brazil are amongst the many
countries learning the hard way that eucalypts cohabit with fire.

The first colonists were reminded every year that the south-east
coast of Australia was very much warmer than northern Europe, and
that was thought to mean that the mouth-watering fruits that were
raised at home in greenhouses could be grown much more cheaply
and easily than in the old country. Mueller exhorted his listeners to
be mindful:

> how we can have under the open sky around us the plants of all the
> mediterranean countries, Arabia, Persia, the warmer Himalyan
> regions, China and Japan; how we can rear here without protection
> the marvellously rich and varied vegetation of South Africa; how in
> our isothermal zone we can bring together all the plants of California,
> New Mexico and other southern states of the American union; and
> how we need no conservatories for most of the plants of Chili, the
> Argentine state and South Brazil. (Mueller, 1872, 157)

The die was cast. Since that time the fabulous biodiversity of the
island continent has been reduced year on year as weed after introduced weed rampages through one finely balanced ecosystem after
another.

The genus Rubus, from which hundreds of European fruit cultivars
have been grown, is represented by several Australian species. In his
'Account of some New Australian Plants' published in the *Transactions
of the Philosophical Insititute of Victoria* in 1857 Mueller described *Rubus
moluccanus*, which he called *R. hillii*, because the specimen he had
before him was collected 'on the Brisbane River' by Walter Hill.
The plant collected by Hill was the same as that identified by Linnaeus
in *Species Plantarum* (1753) as *R. moluccanus*, originally collected in
Amboina. Mueller's mistake was, as usual, silently corrected by
Bentham in his *Flora Australiensis* of 1864 – at least, I think it was. As

usual in such matters there are dissenting voices. Eric Lassak, in *Australian Medicinal Plants*, states quite confidently that *Rubus moluccanus* is not an Australian species and prefers to follow Mueller in calling what appears to be an identical species *R. hillii*. In the same article Mueller identified another *Rubus* which he dubbed *R. moorei*, after Charles Moore who collected it on the Clarence River. Our commonest wild raspberry, *R. rosifolius*, was named by Sir James Edward Smith in 1791, from a specimen collected in Mauritius by Commerson.

Any one of these native brambles could have been improved by selective breeding to produce desirable fruit. Instead, as Mueller botanised all over Victoria in 1861, he carried in his saddlebags seeds of the European blackberry, *R. fruticosus*, and sowed them everywhere he went. For this crime every Australian landowner would consign him to the lower depths of hell. Mueller did not limit his nefarious activities to Victoria. In 1868 a visitor was delighted to see four varieties of blackberries growing well in the garden of the Queensland Acclimatisation Socety at Bowen Park, from cuttings kindly given to the president of the society by 'Dr Mueller' (*BC*, 29 December). The European blackberry is now the most intractable weed in Australia, infesting more than 9 million hectares in five of the six states. The Animal and Plant Control Act of 1986 requires land managers to spend time, money and energy in futile attempts to eradicate it. At Cave Creek can be found two of the Australian Rubus species. *R. rosifolius* is so vigorous as to be a nuisance but the fruits are too insipid to eat, unless you're a wren or a mouse and covet the seeds. *R. moluccanus* on the other hand is not rampant, very handsome and rather tastier.

European brambles cannot survive in subtropical rainforest, thank goodness. In their stead, we have to struggle with descendants of Suttor's oranges. We call them 'bush lemons'. They are probably versions of the 'rough lemon' or *Citrus jambhiri* that was used extensively for more than a hundred years as the rootstock for Australian citrus, especially in Queensland. *Citrus jambhiri* was thought to have originated as a distinct species in the foothills of the Himalayas, but biotechnological data now suggest that it is a hybrid of *Citrus limon* and an unknown co-parent. Because they are highly sensitive to citrus root rot (*Phytophthora citrophora*) and to citrus nematodes, rough lemons do best in land where citrus has never been planted before, which means that they do especially well in rainforest.

Given copious rain and rich basalt soil a bush lemon grows into a stout suckering thicket, so well equipped with long sharp spines that the only way to get rid of it is to thread a chain around it, hook it up to a tractor and drag it bodily out of the ground. Every fragment of root left behind will send up an aggressively spiny new shoot. The fruits, often huge and knobby, are jammed with seeds. Cockatoos, corellas and other fruit-eating birds besiege the bush lemon trees when they are in fruit, so that the seeds are scattered far and wide. Often as I tramp in the most inaccessible parts of the forest, a citrus twig will catch at my leg and my eyes will suddenly water as the bruised leaves emit their piercingly acrid smell, vaguely recognisable as an intensification of the bridal scent of the cultivated varieties. Then I open my scrip, take out my bright yellow plague tape and brave the stout spines to tie a fluttering length around a branch. Next time the workforce comes by with the herbicide and the brush hooks it will be put to death. Except for one tree, that I have marked three times and still it survives. It bears a thin-skinned fruit rather like a clementine, brim-full of sweet juice much appreciated by the workers. So far the young'uns have refused to kill it, and simply assure me that no fruit is ever left for the birds and that all the seeds end up in the garbage.

There are native citrus species that could have been developed to provide the infant colony with its necessary Vitamin C, but nobody was looking for them. The first was not discovered until Walter Hill came across it 'in nemoribus circum sinum Moreton Bay' in 1857 and called it '*Citrus cataphracta*'. Because its fruits were small, when Mueller came to revise Hill's work in 1858 he called it *Microcitrus australiasica* (*sic*), and published the new name in his *Fragmenta* (2:26). He should have known better; a citrus is a citrus whether it is small or large. He made a similar mistake in dubbing the desert citrus '*Eremocitrus*'. Both fake genera have finally bitten the dust. *Eremocitrus glauca* is now *Citrus glauca*, while the rainforest Finger Lime is *Citrus australasica* (Mabberley, 1998, 4). The native citrus that grows along Cave Creek produces an abundance of fruit of an irregular fusiform shape that might suggest a swollen finger, on some trees dark green, on others almost black and on others red or translucent yellow. A red form found at nearby Tamborine Mountain in 1892 was identified by F. M. Bailey as *Microcitrus australasica* var. *sanguinea*, but the variability demonstrated by those at Cave Creek suggests that the varieties are anything but distinct. The flesh, whether palest green-white, blush-pink or red, is formed of tiny faceted vesicles much more solid than the vesicles in oranges or lemons. It takes a strenuous tongue to pop one against the roof of the mouth, but the taste is worth it.

I use Finger Limes to make an Australian version of the Brazilian caipirinha. After the seeds have been removed for propagation, I pound the whole fruit, skin and all, in a mortar, then add cane syrup and a measure of white rum, leave it to steep for five minutes, and then pour the lot over cracked ice. In the wild *Citrus australasica* grows leggy and straggling in deep shade. It responds well to shaping at first, growing into a handsome buffle-headed tree, but the tighter vegetation soon develops fungal diseases, the overcrowded head dies back and the tree reverts to its old habit. Like many citrus the Finger Lime has fruit and flowers all the year round, and a clean and pleasant scent. There should be one in every frost-free garden in Australia, but you are much more likely to find nurserymen offering any of literally thousands of exotic citrus cultivars – bergamots, calamondins, clementines, mandarins, orangelos, satsumas, tangerines, tangors, tangelos, Buddha's hands.

Part of the job description of a nineteenth-century government botanist was to search for new cash crops; appointed Queensland Colonial Botanist in 1881, F. M. Bailey played his part by sending examples of Australian citrus to Kew for the Economic Botany Collection in 1895. Then the species of native citrus were thought to be three: the finger lime, *Citrus australasica*, the round lime, *Citrus australis*, and *Citrus inodora*, the Russell River lime, discovered by Bailey in 1889 and described by him as 'resembling a small Lisbon lemon with a flavour like that of West Indian Lime'. Besides examples of all three preserved in spirits, now kept in the Joseph Banks Building at Kew, there is a small wooden box of dried Finger Limes. Alas for Bailey, another botanist has horned in on his *Citrus inodora*; a subspecies has been reclassified as a species of its own, *Citrus maidenii*, in honour of J. H. Maiden. It's enough to make Bailey regret he didn't call his lime 'Citrus baileyii' when he had the chance. Another rainforest lime has now turned up on the Cape York peninsula, *Citrus garrowayae*, Mount White Lime. Those who, like Queensland government botanist C. T. White, cannot believe that Bailey named the species for Mrs Garroway rather than her husband, often render the name incorrectly as *Citrus garrowayi*.

For a hundred years nothing was done about exploiting the Australian citrus species, although early settlers did use them for marmalades. In the 1960s there was some investigation of their possible usefulness as rootstocks for exotic species and possibly breeding desirable characteristics into new cultivars, but no one attempted selective breeding within the species themselves. In the 1990s, with a new awareness of native food sources, exploration of the potential of the Australian citrus species suddenly took off. By 2005 six cultivars had been registered with the Australian Cultivar Registration authority: 'Alstonville', 'Jali Red', 'Judy's Everbearing', 'Mia Rose', 'Purple Viola' and 'Rainforest Pearl'. At CCRRS we concentrate on propagating our wild stock, so that it will still be there when the cultivars conk out. Meanwhile both the Mount White Lime and the Russell River Lime have been brought to the verge of extinction.

Most of the early settlers in the Numinbah Valley had a go at growing exotic citrus; Carl Lentz's experience was fairly typical:

> The citrus fruit trees grew splendidly in those times, but a disease got into them just as they came into bearing. I wrote to Mr Benson the government fruit expert and he came and prescribed a remedy. I had to spray the trees with boiled Stockholm tar, rosin and caustic soda. It killed scale disease alright but then they got fungus growing on the roots and there was no hope for them.

When apples, pears, peaches, cherries, mulberries, apricots and plums failed to naturalise and quickly succumbed to pests and infestations of all kinds, the settlers tried avocados, passionfruit, guavas, pomelos, loquats, mangoes, papayas, tamarillos, kiwi fruit, custard apples, durians, persimmons, sapodillas, grenadillas, breadfruit, jakfruit, abius, rambutans, Panama cherries, lychees, mangosteens, carambolas, nashi pears, longans, acerolas, jaboticabas, grumichamas, Malabar chestnuts, pecans, pomegranates, casimiroas, okra, feijoa, and so forth. Nobody knows or apparently cares which of these fruits might colonise the wilderness. Every day we come across self-seeded mulberries, guavas, loquats and tamarillos growing under the canopy. For years an acre of pasture has been covered by the spread limbs of a single vast passionfruit vine. None of these has had as devastating an impact as a fruit that cannot seed itself at all, the banana.

Commercial bananas are sterile hybrids that were first bred millennia ago by crossing *Musa acuminata* with *M. balbisiana*. They therefore cannot naturalise and cannot become weeds. It was the clearing of tracts of montane subtropical rainforest that had previously been spared because they were too steep for cattle, to make space for bananas, that scarred the highest forest slopes for ever. All around the Mount Warning caldera and the Numinbah Valley, what were once luxuriantly forested mountainsides are now great tracts of Lantana, the only memorial to the heroic effort put in by struggling farmers who thought that the new cash crop would finally free them from the tyranny of the banks.

The banana was brought to Australia with the First Fleet in 1787; the *Sydney Gazette* assured its readers in 1809 'that the banana can be reared in the Colony, there being now two trees, each bearing a bunch whereon are two to three dozen nearly ripe, in the garden of a Gentleman a few miles from Sydney . . .' (The banana is, of course, not a tree, but a herb.) Commercial banana growing was established as early as 1858 when George Bennett could say:

> The Banana-tree grows luxuriantly in New South Wales, more partic-
> ularly at Broken Bay, extending to the north as far as Moreton Bay;
> from the latter district large supplies are sent, together with Pine-apples,
> to the markets of Sydney and Melbourne . . . Many persons in New
> South Wales acquire a good income by growing Bananas and
> Pine-apples as a commercial speculation . . .' (Bennett, 331)

We can only wonder which bananas were being grown on a commercial scale in the 1850s. The usual account of commercial banana growing in New South Wales credits 'Herman Reich' with bringing Dwarf Cavendish cultivars to Coffs Harbour in 1891. Within a few years banana growing had spread north to Woolgoolga and ultimately to the Tweed. As nothing beyond the name is known about Herman Reich, and bananas were grown in the colony long before he got into the act, I have begun to wonder whether he ever existed.

It was not until the 1920s that the Western world woke up to the food potential of the banana which had long been a staple of the diet of poorer people elsewhere in the world. Huge tracts of land in the tropics were taken up for commercial banana production. Eventually Australia too climbed onto the banana bandwagon, but it was already too late.

The pioneer of bananas in the Numinbah Valley was Jack Morgan, who in the late Twenties acquired two properties above CCRRS and cleared them for planting. In December 1928 Morgan, with Fred Lentz, another of the succession of owners of CCRRS, and Alex Ferndale, travelled to Goomboorian near Gympie to fetch banana suckers. Morgan planted 2,000 of them on his portions before cunningly selling out. All over Numinbah, on both sides of the border, people were clearing, buying, selling and renting land to grow bananas. In 1931 Fred Lentz, who may have learnt a thing or two from Jack Morgan, leased his land to Harold Smith, Bert Harrison and Tom Stephens who, with almost unimaginable effort, cleared and burnt off fifteen steeply sloping west-facing hectares of the CCRRS forest and planted bananas. That winter the plants were badly frosted (Hall *et al.*, 97). One can only wonder why, before crippling themselves with such backbreaking toil, the planters did not consider the chances of such an outcome. At Cave Creek we calculate about ten nights of frost a year; perhaps the west-facing slopes of the property were chosen because it was thought that frost would drain down them, but if frost meets a thirty-metre wall of rainforest it will pool and stay. On a clear winter's day the banana plants on such a west-facing slope would remain frozen until the sun came over the scarp late in the morning and hit them like an acetylene torch.

The Great Depression had bitten deep when, in 1932, a plan was launched to subdivide the properties in the Upper Nerang and lease them to unemployed men for banana growing. For years arguments for and against the scheme raged in the correspondence columns of the local newspapers. Meanwhile the Australian banana-growing industry was collapsing because the frenzy for producing the new cash crop had produced the inevitable glut. The price of bananas tumbled even before the government entered into a deal with the Fijian government allowing cheaper Fijian bananas onto the Australian market. By 1935 most of the Numinbah banana plantations were abandoned and many of the people who had arrived during the banana boom had left the valley. That year Fred Lentz sent off a consignment of sixty cases – and got back a postal note for one shilling and sixpence, which was nowhere near enough to cover the cost of cases and cartage (Hall *et al.*, 97).

Nevertheless banana growing continued off and on in the Numinbah Valley until the Seventies. Elsewhere in south-east Queensland and north-eastern New South Wales people who still grow bananas are reduced to selling their crop on roadside stalls, which are among the few places where one can find delicious Lady Finger bananas; the supermarkets are interested only in the much larger and starchier Cavendish varieties. Even when a cyclone wiped out the entire north Queensland banana crop, the supermarkets could not turn around and give the southern growers their first profitable year in a generation. All that remains of the short disastrous career of CCRRS as a banana plantation is fifteen hectares of steep Lantana scrub and, somewhere in the middle of it, the footings of the flying fox by which the banana boxes were sent on a cable suspended above Cave Creek towards the Nerang–Murwillumbah Road. A few weeks after one of our periodic summer deluges, we found that a banana plant had washed up on the creek bank, hoisted itself upright, spread its roots and set fruit. It was more than we could do to put such a valiant survivor through the mulcher but, now that it has become a stout thicket of ragged fronds twenty feet high, its days are numbered.

NUTS

'Are these Macadamia trees?' asked Jenny. We were standing beneath a knoll in rolling country at Umawera, north of Hokianga Harbour on the west coast of the North Island of New Zealand, on a chunk of her native land that Jenny had just acquired. I had come to see her in her green domain, away from the pressures of her busy life as a professor in Cambridge.

I was also keen to take a look at a different kind of Gondwanan rainforest, only to realise as we drove the length of the North Island that virtually all of the New Zealand rainforest was gone. Jenny took me to Waipoua in Northland, and there I met the greatest of all Gondwanan survivors, the huge Kauri called by the Maori, and therefore by all New Zealanders, Tane Mahuta. This fabulous tree is nearly as big as the Leaning Tower of Pisa, being 51.5 metres high, 13.8 metres round. Waipoua was bought from the Maori in 1876 for £2,000; in 1895 it was dubbed a State Forest Reserve; in 1913 part of it was set aside as a national Kauri forest. In 1952 after decades of popular agitation led by zoologist William Roy McGregor the area was proclaimed a forest sanctuary. Even so the New Zealand government began clear-felling there in the 1960s; by the time this was stopped in 1972, by an incoming Labour government in response to public outcry, a fifth of the forest had been cleared.

Neither Jenny nor I knew when we came to pay homage to Tane Mahuta that a new Kauri-specific fungus infection called *Phytophthora* taxon *Agathis* had made its way to Waipoua. PTA was first recognised on an offshore island in 1972; in 2006 it was found on the mainland.

The symptoms, yellowing of the foliage, thinning of the canopy, stem girdling of lower branches and gummosis, bleeding of resin from lesions near the foot of the tree, are slow to appear. The only precautions that can be taken are the ones that have not worked in controlling the spread of *Phytophthora cinnamomi* in Australia. Tane Mahuta was alive when Christ was born; it may not survive for much longer, because in 2006 an advanced case of PTA was found on another Kauri in Waipoua, less than half a kilometre away. A proposal for a 14,000-hectare Kauri National Park is at present under discussion; if it should go through it looks very much as if a substantial part of the park will have to be closed to the public if the Kauri is to survive.

Most of the Kauri in the Northland was felled and replaced by Monterey Pine, which New Zealanders know by its botanical binomial as *Pinus radiata*. At 2,900 square kilometres the Kaingaroa Forest on the North Island is the largest planted forest in the world. Most of the trees on Jenny's property were seedlings of *P. radiata*, often called wilding conifers.

The trees Jenny and I were looking at were buffle-headed with stiff leathery leaves, more or less opposite and mostly stalkless.

'They are Macadamias, aren't they?'

'They look proteaceous but if they're Macadamias they're a bit different from mine.'

'They're not natives,' said Jenny. 'There are only two proteaceous species in New Zealand, Rewarewa and Toru, and they're not either of them.'

Rewarewa, *Knightia excelsa*, is a lovely thing, especially when it is young, with stiff, narrow, bright green, saw-toothed leaves sometimes edged with red, growing in whorls. Its wine-red flowers with projecting styles are typical of the Proteaceae, and they turn into a cluster of cigar-shaped nuts that still carry a long whisker of withered style. The species, which was collected by members of the *Endeavour* expedition, is supposed to grow all over the North Island, but I didn't see a single specimen of it in the wild or anywhere else. If I were Jenny I'd be propagating it like mad. Toru, *Toronia toru*, is a columnar shrub with an open tetramerous flower that smells strongly of honey, rather like our Persoonia. It too should be growing on Jenny's property, but we didn't see it. Instead we were looking at fourteen Macadamia lookalikes.

I wasn't enjoying being at a loss. 'I'd have said these were cultivars of some kind, but I thought all the cultivars were selected from *Macadamia integrifolia*, which has leafstalks and entire leaves and cream flowers. The ones at Cave Creek are *Macadamia tetraphylla*, and these look a bit like them.'

'How old would you say they are?'

'They grow slowly. Twenty years, mebbe?'

'That would figure,' said Jen. 'About twenty years ago there was a push to get New Zealanders growing Macadamias. A lot of people got burned, because there was no infrastructure or marketing strategy. I think the trees produced all right but there was no way to sell the crop.' I found out later that the cultivar of choice was and still is 'Beaumont', costly to acquire and to farm because it is a 'sticker' and doesn't release its fruit, which means that it is a variety of *M. tetraphylla*. Because all NZ cultivars are grafted, none of them looks quite like its ancestor in the understorey of the CCRRS rainforest.

Macadamias were one of the first trees I could identify at Cave Creek. I was excited at first, not because Macadamias are now the world's favourite and most expensive nuts, but because Macadamia trees were becoming rare in the wild. Since then they have become even rarer. The latest (2010) research by the World Wildlife Fund Australia and the Spatial Ecology Laboratory at the University of Queensland found only 3,000 wild trees surviving in their native habitat.

So first I was thrilled and then I got worried. Maybe the people who had tried to make a living at Cave Creek had imported some of the new improved cultivars and maybe it was their progeny I could see growing along the creek and up in the high forest. If that had been the case I would have had to think of removing them. I love everything about the Cave Creek Macadamias, their stiff geometric habit, the ruby glow of the young foliage, the long pink helical flower tassels that hang vertically, the clusters of fruit dangling on strings, the spherical nuts straining against their pointed follicles until they split, the piles of empty nutshells hidden in the forest, each with an immaculately machined hole through which the littlest rodents have been able to feast on carbs and fat and protein.

Macadamias look like many of their Gondwanan relatives. If you have ever had the great pleasure of seeing *Hakea victoria* in her full flaming glory in Western Australia, you would recognise a family trait in the structure and leaf colouring of the juvenile Macadamias at Cave Creek. I really didn't want to have to destroy them. Hoping against hope, I kept them in the planting lists, and the workforce propagated them, not particularly willingly, because they'd much rather grow the forest emergents that put on three metres of height in a year. The Macadamias were slow, and prickly to boot. But I loved them, we had millions of easily collected seeds, and so we kept propagating and planting them.

Generally speaking, Australian common names are specific, but the names Queensland Nut and Bush Nut have been muddled ever since Allan Cunningham collected 'a Queensland Bush Nut' (which he identified as *M. ternifolia*) in 1828. In his report to Governor Darling Cunningham remarked, 'independent of its highly ornamental habit and refreshing shade afforded by its densely leaved branches, its nuts are produced . . . in such abundance as to be ere long worthy the attention of the farmer.' (McMinn, 93) It would be more than a hundred years before any Australian farmer would avail himself of the opportunity, even though a correspondent calling herself Pomona wrote to *The Queenslander* in 1876 to point out that 'The Queensland nut is already in our gardens, and bearing fruits under conditions favourable to its permanent improvement.' (Q, 16 December, 22)

The specimen of the Queensland Nut Cunningham sent back to Kew in 1828 probably sank to the bottom of the vast mass of plant material arriving from all over the world, because it cannot now be traced. The species, or something like it, was collected again by Leichhardt in 1843, according to his note, in the 'Bunya Bunya brush' and sent to the Melbourne Herbarium. The area where he found it is now known to have been the Conondale Range. Mueller later wrote on the label 'Dawson and Burnett Rivers', which is simply wrong. Mueller collected the plant again himself in 1857, with Walter Hill, along 'the Pine River of Moreton Bay'. The next year Mueller published his description in the *Transactions of the Philosophical Institute of Victoria*, placing it in a new genus which he called *Macadamia*, after Dr John Macadam, Honorary Secretary of the Institute. The type species name was *ternifolia*, three-leaved, and all the specimens preserved in the Economic Botany Collection at Kew still bear this name. Dr Macadam must have done something to annoy Mueller; two years later he described the Queensland Nut again and decided that it was a member of the south-east Asian proteaceous genus *Helicia*. Though Mueller was using the same material as he had for the earlier description he seems not to have recognised it and made no reference to his own earlier identification. It was Bentham, toiling away in England at his *Flora*, who saw that Mueller had been right the first time and resuscitated the genus *Macadamia*, using the grounds alleged by Mueller in his earlier publication.

Nobody seems to have realised that the plants they were discussing produced palatable nuts of high nutritional value. Dutch botanist Maurits Greshoff, who examined the specimens at Kew, was convinced that *Macadamia ternifolia* was 'among the most strongly cyanogenetic plants; in the fresh leaf the hydrocyanic content was more than 0.1 per cent' (*Kew Bulletin* No. 10, 1909, 413). Perhaps what happened at Kew is that Greshoff was given immature kernels to study, possibly in a fermented state. This curious chain of accidents has given rise to the erroneous belief, cherished by American Macadamia growers, that there is a poisonous wild Macadamia species that has never been culti-vated. This may have been the Gympie Nut, proteaceous, small-fruited and extremely bitter. It was not until 1897 that Maiden and Ernst Betche collected smooth-shelled Macadamias from Camden Haven, and suggested a new species, *Macadamia integrifolia*, so called because the leaves were less serrate than those of the type. Two years later they decided that they were wrong and reduced their separate species to a subspecies. 'We found all degrees of transition between the two extreme forms and have been forced to the conclusion that it is merely another instance of the great variability of the Proteaceous trees . . .' they explained (Maiden and Betche, 1897). Attempts to separate the entire-leaved Macadamias from the serrate-leaved Macadamias failed because single trees were capable of displaying both leaf forms at different stages in their development. There was one point of distinc-tion between them which was not debated: the entire-leaved Macadamias grew only in Queensland (hence Queensland Nut), the serrate-leaved grew on both sides of the border (hence Bush Nut).

In 1954, Lawrie Johnson came to the rescue: the confusion 'has been due to several causes; firstly semi-juvenile stages of one species resemble the mature stage of the other species in the possession of toothed leaves; secondly two states of the first species have been described under two different names; and, thirdly, the second species has not been named at all' (Johnson, 1954, 15). In fact Bentham had worked on specimens of both species, but Johnson was on the money. The name he suggested for the second species was *Macadamia tetra-phylla*, and those are the Macadamias of the upper Nerang Valley. At least, I think they are. The CCRRS Macadamias are not reliably tetraphyllous; the first stem to appear above ground usually carries whorls of three leaves each, and continues to do so until the first fork; the growths above the fork will show whorls of four leaves – mostly. The leaves however are always serrate, but the flowers are not always pink but occasionally white or cream.

By 1954 the phylogeny of the Macadamia was being obscured by the breeding and cross-breeding of selected strains by American horti-culturists who recognised the nut's commercial potential. The first Macadamia trees in Hawaii were planted as ornamentals in 1882 by William H. Purvis, manager of a cane plantation at Kapulena, who was an enthusiastic plant collector. Forty years later another American, Ernest Shelton van Tassell, tried to grow the nuts commercially, but the trees performed inconsistently, producing nuts of varying quality at varying intervals. The Agricultural Research Station of the University of Hawaii then stepped in. They recognised *M. ternifolia* as having almost sessile leaves in whorls of three or four with serrate and sometimes prickly margins; *M. integrifolia* was described as having spatulate leaves with a distinct petiole and entire margins. As cultivars were developed the two kinds resolved themselves into the rough-shelled type and the smooth-shelled type, with only the smooth-shelled type considered suitable for cultivation. As late as 1957 William B. Storey of the University of California, who described the genus as 'possibly half a dozen species', was still having difficulty separating them. In his version *M. integrifolia* was a subspecies of *M. ternifolia*. His account is remarkable because of its geographical detail.

> *M. ternifolia* occurs naturally only in south-eastern Queensland. Its range extends a distance of about 175 miles, from Beechmont on the south to Maryborough on 25°30' S. *M. tetraphylla* occurs naturally

only at the south-eastern extremity of Queensland and the north-eastern corner of New South Wales. Its range extends a distance of about 75 miles, from Mt. Tamborine on the north to Lismore on the south between the latitudinal limits of 28°S and 29°S. The ranges of the two species overlap for a distance of about 15 miles in the Guanabah and Tamborine Creek regions of southern Queensland. Types of trees intermediate in characteristics between the two species have been seen in the regions of overlapping ranges. These are thought to be interspecific hybrids. (334)

This doesn't quite make geographic sense but it does predict the variability that we have observed in the Cave Creek species. By 1970 Storey had accepted Maiden and Betche, and recognised *M. integrifolia*, but he thought it could be found in the Numinbah Valley. Maybe it can, but not at CCRRS. Perhaps botanists have had so much trouble distinguishing these species because in fact they are not distinct.

Commercial production of improved cultivars in Hawaii got under way in the 1950s. The first country to import and grow Hawaiian cultivars was Guatemala, followed by Australia (Cheel and Morrison, 23). Australia now produces 37 per cent of the world's Macadamia nuts, Hawaii 22 per cent. New varieties are produced every year, not only in Hawaii but in South Africa, New Zealand and Australia as well. The breeders' aims are to produce strains that will crop heavily and drop their nuts easily, so that they can be harvested mechanically off the ground, and with thinner and more brittle shells so that the kernels are not damaged when the shells are removed. Nowadays the cultivars have numbers instead of names. No more than 2–3 per cent of the Macadamia nuts produced round the world end up being eaten as nuts; three-quarters of them are processed to go into cakes and biscuits, the rest into chocolates, ice cream – and cosmetics.

We were back in Cambridge when the subject came up again. Jenny listened to me bumbling for as long as she could stand it and then grabbed the laptop.

'Let's get some answers here. How big's the Macadamia gene pool? How many species in the genus?'

'Two,' I said confidently. Jenny did a spot of googling.

'Wikipedia says there are nine species in the genus Macadamia.'

'According to whom?'

'It doesn't say.'

'Does he, she or it name them?'

'Hm. Seven from eastern Australia, one from New Caledonia and one from Sulawesi.'

'That's easy. There was a group of proteaceous plants growing in north Queensland that got lumped in with the Macadamias but they've been lumped out again. The one from Sulawesi was *Macadamia hildebrandii*. They've all been relocated in the genus Lasjia.' I pronounced it to rhyme with 'mass jeer'.

'Never heard of it.'

'Me either. I'm not even sure how to say it. It's a made-up name to honour the Australian expert on the Proteaceae, L. A. S. Johnson. Have a look at APNI.'

APNI is the on-line Australian Plant Name Index. As Queensland has yet to publish a state Flora, and the 3-volume 1986 *Flora of South-Eastern Queensland* by T. E. Stanley and E. M. Ross is both out of date and out of print, we tend to consult APNI in the first instance.

Jenny's fingers skated over the mouse-pad.

'Sure enough, five one-time Macadamias are now in the genus Lasjia: *Macadamia claudiensis*, *M. whelanii*, *M. grandis*, *M. erecta*, and *M. hildebrandii*.' (She might have added four more: *M. praealta* is now *Floydia praealta*, *M. youngiana Triunia youngiana*, *M. angustifolia Virotia angustifolia*, *M. heyana Catalepidia heyana*.)

'Cross-check with Tropicos.'

'What's that?'

'The data base of the Missouri Botanical Garden.'

Jenny did. I could hear her growling in her throat.

'What a mess. Thirteen species listed and no sign that the taxonomy has been revised.'

'That may be because they don't accept the revision.'

As a proper scientist who works on the pharmacology of brain function, Jenny was distinctly unimpressed with the mare's nest that is botany.

'The sooner they find an objective way of identifying plants the better. This is hopeless.'

I couldn't disagree, even though I would miss the barminess of the binomials once barcodes had taken their place. Given the bossiness of the Australian academic establishment, use of the binomials will probably be banned once a barcode system is adopted.

The Tropicos list included four species that have now been classified as belonging to another new genus called Virotia, plus two of the five that are now Lasjia, and two mysteries, *M. francii* and *M. alticola*. '*Macadamia alticola*' was first called that by René Paul Capuron, who found it 1,600 metres up in the forest of Ambohitantely on the island of Madagascar, where he had spent a good deal of his life studying the tree flora (Capuron, 370). When Lawrie Johnson and Barbara Briggs examined the type specimen, they soon realised that it was not a Macadamia but a new genus that they called Malagasia, after the island itself (Johnson and Briggs, 1975, 175).

The more we foraged, the more Macadamias we found. All but four had been reidentified as something else.

After some more rambling round the net, Jenny stood up and stretched.

'I get it. Austin Mast at Florida State University got an award in 2005 to run a research programme with Peter Weston and Greg Jordan in Oz and David Cantrill in Sweden where they work on a phylogeny for the Grevilloideae section of the Proteaceae using nuclear and chloroplast gene sequencing. The idea was to track the breaking up of Gondwana by tracking the genetic relationships between members of the group. They published their results in December 2007. Apparently it went a bit pear-shaped.'

She sat down again. 'Listen to this:

Ever since continental drift and plate tectonics displaced the stable earth model in geological theory, the Proteaceae have been generally regarded as a classic 'Gondwanic Group' – one that originated well before the fragmentation of the ancient supercontinent Gondwana, and which achieved its widespread distribution in the southern hemisphere as a result of vicariance.

'Vicariance?'

Jenny explained. 'It's the word they use for what happens when the range of a species is split and two different species evolve from a common ancestor. It's only a theory. If it's correct the distribution of taxonomic groups has been determined by ruptures in the range of ancestral species, by continental drift or an eruption or a flood. What our colleagues were trying to do was trace the splitting process by a phylogenetic examination of a group of Proteaceae. However' – Jenny paused for dramatic effect –

> However, molecular dating analyses recently conducted by Dr Weston's research group are suggesting that the first of these ideas is false and the second only partly true.

'Then, what . . .?' I stared at her. I'd just got my head round the Gondwana hypothesis and here it was disappearing like the Cheshire Cat, leaving only Jenny's delighted grin behind.

'Wait,' she said. 'There's more.'

> Mast et al. (2008) published the results of a phylogenetic analysis and molecular dating of the most biogeographically interesting clade in the Proteaceae, the tribe Macadamieae—

Jenny turned to me. 'Which would be?'

I had to ferret in my files for the answer. 'The tribe is made up of four subtribes, the Macadamiinae, the Malagasiinae, the Virotiinae and the Gevuiinae.' The Macadamiinae are three genera, Macadamia, Panopsis (from tropical America) and Brabejum (from the south-west Cape); the Malagasiinae two, Malagasia (from Madagascar) and Catalepidia (from Queensland); the Virotiinae three, Virotia (from New Caledonia), Athertonia (Queensland) and Heliciopsis (Burma to central Malesia); and the Gevuinae seven or eight, depending, Cardwellia (Queensland), Sleumerodendron (New Caledonia), Euplassa (tropical America), Gevuina (Chile and Argentina), Bleasdalea (western Pacific to eastern Australia), Hicksbeachia (up the road from Cave Creek), Kermadecia from New Caledonia and Turrillia (probably synonymous with Bleasdalea). OK?'

Jenny turned back to the computer screen. 'The analysis was based on DNA sequence data for seven nuclear and chloroplast genes plus morphology. Are you with me?'

I thought so. 'Hang on tight,' said Jen.

Their results strongly suggest that at least 8 of the 9 clades in this tribe showing continental disjunctions are too young to have dispersed between the continents over land.

'What?' I was dumbfounded.
'Hold on,' said Jen.

It suggests—

'What suggests? That "it" has no antecedent.'
'He's a botanist. You can't expect grammar.'

It suggests instead that what is now the Australian craton is the centre of origin for this tribe and that the clades now found in tropical and temperate South America, New Caledonia, Fiji, Vanuatu, south-east Asia, Madagascar and southern Africa got there by long distance dispersal across significant ocean gaps. Moreover, the reconstructed dispersal events all post-date the onset of the circum-polar current and are significantly correlated with multiple evolutionary origins of indehiscent fruits, suggesting that the intact fruit wall has played a key role in protecting the seed from immersion in salt water.

The suspicion that the commonly accepted version of the evolution of the Proteaceae was wrong had been around for years. Nigel Barker, who began working on the Proteaceae as a graduate student in South Africa, was granted a fellowship to work at the Royal Botanical Gardens in Sydney with Peter Weston in 1996 and formed his hypothesis then, but it was not until he met Frank Rutschmann, who was completing a Ph.D. at the Institute for Systematic Botany in Zurich, that he was able to avail himself of the newest computational expertise in molecular dating. Hervé Sauquet's revision and reassessment of the fossil evidence completed the array of skills needed to calibrate the molecular clock as the mutation rate of the various DNA sequences they had assembled was established by comparison with that of the fossils. The genus

Protea turned out to be genuinely Gondwanan but other of the fynbos genera were much younger and had closer Australian relatives (Barker, N., *et al.*).

In 2005 botanist Robert Price introduced me to Christopher Spain, a student from Southern Cross University who was studying the genetics of *Macadamia tetraphylla* and needed a sample to analyse. I showed them trees high up in the forest, and on the edge of the cleared land and down on the creekside. Eventually Rob and Chris marked out a quadrat and Chris went to work. The upshot was that the selected trees were genetically identical. It was back to the drawing board for the proponents of accidental hybridisation.

I took a chance on another proteaceous species as well. I hadn't seen a Floydia at Cave Creek, but I knew it had to be there. It was the tree that Ferdy Mueller had originally called *Helicia praealta*; Bailey then decided that, like another of Mueller's Helicias, it was a Macadamia (*The Queensland Flora*, 4:1330); in 1975 Lawrie Johnson and Barbara Briggs finally determined that it was a distinct genus, and called it after our guru, Alex Floyd (APNI). The name didn't appear on Jinks's survey, but every now and then as I rambled around the forest I would pick up a perfectly round and perfectly rotten nut, about the size of a squash ball, that seemed as if it had to be the Ball Nut that gives the Floydia one of its common names. It is also known as Big Nut and Possum Nut. Floyd remarks that the woody outer shell of the Ball Nut encloses one or two seeds 'which are somewhat bitter'. Another popular reference book updated as recently as 2009 declares that the fruit of *F. praealta* is downright poisonous (Leiper *et al.*, 334).

Floydia is listed as endangered, which made it even harder to resist the impulse to plant it, but we couldn't find it on the property. I weakened and, breaking all my own rules, bought in twenty from a nursery. One day I was botanising on the old snigging track with Rob, when he stopped to look at some fallen blossoms among the leaf litter. He held one up, so I could see that it was a short helical raceme of tiny tubular flowers that split into fours, with a style projecting from each.

'Floydia,' he said.

'Where?' I squinted up into the canopy forty metres above our heads.

'Here.' Rob slapped his palm against a solid column that soared into the foliage far above us. I swung the binoculars over my shoulder and peered through them. I was looking for the lanceolate leaves with the wavy margins that I knew from the baby trees.

'I can't see it,' I moaned.

'That's because the canopy leaves are smaller, and don't have wavy margins. This is it all right.'

'Good Lord! Everyone says Floydia's a middle-sized tree. This is huge. This must be the biggest ever recorded.'

Someone has revised the data on *Floydia praealta*, because the new edition of Floyd says it grows up to thirty-five metres and sixty centimetres in diameter. Cave Creek isn't listed among the places where it does that, which is fine with me. The giant Floydia is beyond price, more than we could ever have hoped for. The best way of keeping it safe is to create a haven for it, and keep it well away from people and barbecues and four-wheel drives. That's what they haven't been able to do for another recently identified proteaceous species, the Nightcap Oak, one of only two species in a sole genus in its own subfamily, with the scientific name *Eidothea hardeniana*. The binomial is cooler than usual: Eidothea, for whom the genus was named in 1995, is one of the daughters of the god Proteus; the name given to the second species found in 2006 honours a woman, one of very, very few. She is Gwen Harden, distinguished editor of *The Flora of New South Wales* and one of the authors of the field guide *Rainforest Trees and Shrubs*, otherwise known as the Red Book, that we use every day. The entire population of *Eidothea hardeniana* numbers only sixteen trees living somewhere in the Nightcap National Park. The whereabouts of the Wollemi Pine was kept a secret too, but walkers found it, brought pathogens into the gorge with them, and *Wollemia nobilis* is now said to be extinct in the wild. The only place for the vulnerable Floydia is in the wild, the unvisited wild, nowhere near the beaten track.

It's easy to become obsessed by the Proteaceae. The family numbers about eighty genera – I say about because they're always changing. About half of them are Australian, a quarter South African, the rest are endemic to South America, New Caledonia, New Guinea, Malesia, South and East Asia, tropical Africa, Central America, Madagascar,

New Zealand, Fiji, southern India, Sri Lanka, Vanuatu and Micronesia. They are a quintessential Gondwanan family.

'Funny isn't it?' said I to Jenny. 'In Enzed you've got two genera of Proteaceae and both are monotypic, making a grand total of two species. Mind you, there are many monotypic genera in the family. Out of forty-two genera in Oz sixteen or seventeen have only one species. Isn't it odd that New Zealand only 2,000 ks or so off the coast of Australia should have only two proteaceous species when Australia has more than 850?'

Said Jenny, 'There used to be many more; they've found a high proportion of different kinds of proteaceous pollen in coal deposits in the South Island. You have to remember that New Zealand suffered a massive extinction event at the end of the Cretaceous and then most of it gradually sank below sea level, so it was just a chain of small islands. These grew into today's New Zealand, as the Australian and Pacific tectonic plates kept on grinding against each other and pushing up new mountains, and the vegetation was regularly incinerated by eruptions. So the biodiversity took a bit of a hit. How many proteaceous species have you got on this property?'

'More than you've got in the whole of Enzed. Let's see. There's my precious *Macadamia tetraphylla*, which grows in isolated patches in the coastal ranges from the Richmond River northwards. *Grevillea robusta*, on the other hand, grows all over the place. It's as common as dirt and we have thousands of them, but I tolerate them because the bowerbirds love them. We've got a Triunia, as well. I assumed it was *Triunia youngiana* when I first collected it, but the flower doesn't seem quite pink enough, and it has a dusting of moss green, almost metallic. *Orites excelsus*, *Stenocarpus sinuatus*. I found a Helicia growing down on the creek, *Helicia glabriflora* I suppose, but the inflorescence is a bit more gracile and greener than the type. It's supposed to have dark purple fruit, but I haven't found any yet. And then there are the Floydias.'

'What – no Banksia?'

'There's one near the old house. *Banksia filicifolia*. It grows on the rhyolite; I don't know how one ended up down here, but we've propagated it because the bats and birds besiege it for the flowers.'

I couldn't stop thinking about Macadamias. It seemed obvious that

Aboriginal people would have been eating the Queensland or Bush Nut for sixty thousand years or so before Allan Cunningham is supposed to have 'discovered' it in 1828. You might ask which of the two it was he found, Queensland or Bush, because though there is a tendency to call *Macadamia integrifolia* the Queensland Nut and *M. tetraphylla* the Bush Nut, the practice is not consistent. For example, Tom Cowderoy recording his childhood in Numinbah in the 1890s says that Aborigines used to turn up in the valley 'when the Queensland nuts were ripe' when the nuts that grow in the Numinbah Valley are *M. tetraphylla*. Jenny Graham, a Kombumerri woman from Beechmont, is said to have told her grandchildren that as a young girl she would carry nuts with her when she travelled and plant them along the way. 'The Macadamia nut trees that can still be seen on the upper reaches of the Nerang River may be the same ones she planted as she strolled as a child around the 1870s.' (O'Connor, 33)

When I read that I yelped so loud that Jenny spilt her tea.

'For goodness' sake. Is there no end to this Kombumerri nonsense? Here they are trying to get me to believe that they planted the Macadamias on the Upper Nerang!'

'They might have,' said Jenny. 'We're only just learning how much of the Australian vegetation was managed by Aboriginal people. But I grant you, it's hard to think of them traipsing up here to stick Macadamias all over the place.'

'Especially when they were already growing around Tamborine and Guanaba, which is a lot closer to Beaudesert where she was actually living.'

Jenny brandished a piece of paper. 'I printed this up for you, from the Springbrook website.' She began to read:

Gumburra (macadamia nut) were grown in this region long before Europeans arrived.

I interrupted. 'Were grown my foot. Grew dammit. Grew.'

The Yugambeh traded them with settlers for tobacco and other goods.

(I have yet to come across a contemporary reference to Aborigines of any clan using Macadamias for barter with white people.)

Jenny kept reading:

It is believed that long before Australia was mapped by European explorers Aboriginal people would congregate on the eastern slopes of Australia's Great Dividing Range to feed on the seed of two evergreen trees. One of these nuts was called gyndl or jindilli, which was later corrupted to kindal kindal by early Europeans, while in the southern range of the tree it was known as boombera—

I interrupted. 'In 1843, when Leichhardt was staying on the Darling Downs and using the Archers' station at Durundur as a base, he got a young Aboriginal stockman called Kippar Charley to guide him around. Charley's supposed to have taken Leichhardt to the summit of Mount Bauple, where he saw a tree that Kippar Charley told him was called "Jindilli". Leichhardt's biographer gets into a muddle with this, saying that this was the first time the Macadamia was described, which is wrong, because Cunningham collected a Macadamia specimen near Tamborine Mountain and sent it to Kew in 1828 [Bailey, J., 111]. He also describes the Macadamia Leichhardt found as "a middle-sized tree with sawtoothed leaves". The species found at Mount Bauple is *Macadamia integrifolia*, which has entire leaves. And it gets worse; Leichhardt himself said he collected his specimen in the "Bunya Bunya brush", which is 140 kilometres or so south of Mount Bauple.'

Jenny simply repeated:

One of these nuts was called gyndl or jindilli, which was later corrupted to kindal kindal by early Europeans, while in the southern range of the tree it was known as boombera – We now know it as the Macadamia. There were at least twelve Aboriginal tribes in the region where the tree grew and they were used as an item of trade with other tribes.

I interrupted again. 'Who were used? The twelve tribes?'

'Oh, shush. You and your grammar. You know what they mean'

With the arrival of white settlers nuts were bartered, often with native honey, for rum and tobacco . . .

I interrupted again. 'It would help if we knew where Kippar Charley originally hailed from. He might have given the New South Wales name for the Queensland Nut. If Kindal kindal is the name from northern New South Wales it does in fact apply to *Macadamia tetraphylla*. The only near-contemporary mention of trading nuts I've been able to find refers to a "King Jacky", possibly Bilin Bilin, Aboriginal elder of the Logan clan and sole patriarch of the Kombumerri, doing so in the 1860s.'
Jenny read on:

. . . some coastal middens contain large quantities of bush nut shells along with sea shells, often 15–20 kms from the nearest trees.

'Surely any nutshells would have rotted away within months. The midden with Macadamia shells in it is supposed to be one at Redlands, south of Brisbane, but I've never seen any documentation.'
Jenny ignored me and read on.

Nuts were eaten raw or roasted on hot coals. Many processing stones have been found in eastern rainforests, consisting of a large stone with a delicate incision for holding the nuts and sometimes a smaller, flat stone sits on top which is then struck by a larger hammer stone.

If it is true that the Yugambeh traded Macadamia nuts with all and sundry, it is strange that there is no word or group of words in Yugambeh which can be securely related to the trees or the nuts. Bullum does not mention them at all. W. E. Hanlon, who grew up in 'the Yugambe language region' and was the first postmaster at Southport, collected words and phrases, largely from the family of the same Jenny Graham as is supposed to have planted the Macadamias in Numinbah. He includes two versions of a name for the Queensland Nut, 'gumburra' and 'bumburra', apparently because he confused it with the 'Honeysuckle', that is, *Banksia latifolia*. The version 'boombera' that Jenny read out seems to be simply a continuation of the same mistake, but the confusion persists (Sharpe, 1998, 45, 78).

The Aboriginal peoples can hardly have traded nuts, be they Queensland or Bush, with clients who believed them to be poisonous. Botanists continued to believe that the Queensland Nut was poisonous until at least 1867, when Walter Hill, Director of the Brisbane Botanic Garden, asked his assistant to crack some Queensland Nuts in a vise, thinking that he needed to free them from their hard shells to assist germination. He forgot to tell his assistant that the nuts were poisonous and was horrified to find him eating them. Seeing that the young man came to no harm, Hill tried one for himself and found it 'tastier than a filbert'. He wrote to the *Brisbane Courier* announcing the discovery of a 'new fruit indigenous to Queensland' and confessed, 'I was not aware until recently that it bore an edible fruit, and, singular to say, the aborigines appear to have been equally ignorant.' (*BC*, 6 March 1867) This was greeted by a chorus of disagreement. As one correspondent to *The Queenslander* (6 April 1867, 11) pointed out: 'The nut is now well-known to the timber-getters, to the natives and others, and quantities are being daily gathered and eaten, this proving its wholesome qualities.' Within days another letter arrived in the offices of the *Brisbane Courier* informing readers that the tree was growing 'in considerable abundance, though circumscribed in locality, on high exposed ground about ten miles nearly due south from Brisbane'. (*BC*, 17 April)

Hill is credited with the establishment of 'the first commercially grown macadamia, which he brought from the Queensland bush to the Botanic Gardens in 1858' (*ADB*) which, seeing as he didn't know that the nut was edible until nine years later, is curious, to say the least. Nuts collected around Lismore had been planted in the Sydney Botanic Garden three years before this (*SMH*, 5 November 1867). Within the year plants were available from commercial nurseries (*SMH*, 3 February 1868). These must all have been *Macadamia tetraphylla*, the rough-shelled nut, which was still confused with at least two other species of Macadamia and with other proteaceous species as well.

Faulty botany continued to befuddle horticulturalists who had still to take advantage of their opportunity to develop a new cash crop. In *Flora Australiensis* (5:406) Bentham, who was obliged to acknowledge the assistance of Mueller, includes *Triunia youngiana* (with extremely poisonous nuts) and *M. verticillata* as two of his three

Macadamias, citing Mueller but including the variant names for which Mueller was also responsible, which placed all three in the genus *Helicia* (*Fragmenta*, 2:91, 4:84, 6:191). Which leaves only one Macadamia species, *M. ternifolia*, with a description quoted from Mueller's original description as given in his talk to the Philosophical Institute of Victoria:

> A small tree with very dense foliage, glabrous or the young branches and inflorescence minutely pubescent. Leaves sessile or nearly so, in whorls of 3 or 4, oblong or lanceolate, acute, serrate with fine or prickly teeth, glabrous and shining, from a few in[ches] to above 1 ft. long. Racemes often as long as the leaves, with numerous small flowers, the pairs often clustered or almost verticillate. Pedicels at first very short . . . (Mueller, 1857, 72)

The illustration to the talk as published shows a section of twig, with four leaves, of which only three are prickly, arranged in a whorl, with four flower spikes springing upward from the four axils (when they actually hang downward), in a peculiar composite of attributes of at least two distinct species. To this day the Economic Botany Collection at Kew acknowledges only one Macadamia species, and has filed all its specimens under the name *Macadamia ternifolia*.

The first Australian to try to grow Macadamia Nuts as a crop was Charles Staff, of Rous Mill near Lismore in north-eastern New South Wales. The species he chose was the despised *M. tetraphylla*, so evidently he was of the opinion that the nuts were palatable.

The total number of species in the genus seems to have settled at four. The name *Macadamia ternifolia* has been resurrected for the small-fruited Macadamia or Maroochy Nut (probably identical with the aforementioned Gympie Nut). Twenty-one individuals of a fourth species have been found in a rainforest gulley off Granite Creek, north of Gin Gin, in the Bulburin Forest in Central Queensland. These multi-stemmed trees springing from a lignotuber were given the specific name *jansenii*, for the original collector, R. C. Jansen, a cane farmer from South Kolan. He was bushwalking with friends in 1983 near Granite Creek, north of Gin Gin, when he came across what he recognised as some kind of Macadamia trees and informed the Macadamia Conservation Trust (Gross and Weston, 725). The trust has enlisted the aid of the traditional owners, the Gidarjil Aboriginal community, in protecting the trees and in finding more. Gidarjil elder Merv Johnson was quoted in the local press as saying: 'It's a big thing for us. We come from a hunter-gatherer background; our people hunted and gathered nuts . . . I went out and saw the nuts. They're only small but they taste beautiful, I reckon – a little bit bitter, but very sweet.' The hope is that genes from *M. jansenii* can be bred into commercial varieties of Macadamia to improve their heat tolerance.

All four Australian species of Macadamia are now listed as endangered, so we don't hesitate to propagate and plant as many of our native Macadamia as we can at CCRRS, mindful that, in our plant community, it is an occasional, slow-growing and rather picky about where it grows and with whom. It fruits erratically, but when it does, and the nuts finally fall, small earthbound mammals have a party, gathering in their hundreds to gnaw round holes in the woody nutshells and feast on the starchy kernels rich with oil.

Across the wide spectrum of rainforest nut nomenclature flits the ghost of the Bopple Nut. According to some, the name refers to Mount Bauple, in which case it should be Bauple Nut, but it is also Poppel Nut and Popple Nut. Just what the name refers to is anybody's guess. Some think it refers to *M. tetraphylla*, others *M. integrifolia*, and others both. The Mount Bauple National Park Management Plan (2011) identifies the local Macadamia species as *M. integrifolia*, which puts the matter beyond doubt. What is baffling about this situation is that an unattributed and apparently unscientific notion persists that 'wild nut trees were first found growing around Mount Bauple', 220 km north of Brisbane, in 1858, when the first wild Macadamias had been collected thirty years earlier. Certainly Macadamia nuts are recorded as a staple food of the Dowarbara and Butchulla peoples of the Mount Bauple area. As for the Cave Creek Macadamias, the Macadamia is not listed among the foods eaten by the Kombumerri, who did eat the fruit of *Hicksbeachia pinnatifolia*, otherwise known as the Red Boppel Nut (or simply the Red Nut, or the Monkey Nut). The Hicksbeachia, so named by Ferdinand Mueller to oblige Sir Michael Hicks-Beach, Secretary of State for New South Wales, is a wonderful tree with fantastically lobed juvenile foliage, purple pendent flower spathes, and vermilion fruit hanging in clusters, but it does not grow north of the border.

The most important nut for the local Aboriginal people was the Moreton Bay Chestnut, which is not a nut at all, but a huge bean. The tree, which is in the subfamily Faboidae of the family Fabaceae, is usually called Black Bean, though its seeds compressed into their fat pods look more like gigantic brown peas. The Black Beans show up on the slopes of our rainforest as faintly bluish smudges on the green, probably because of the reflection of the sky on their glossy leaf surfaces. They flower prodigiously; when racemes crowded with red and gold bean flowers burst from the scars left by fallen leaves every nectar eater in the forest comes crowding in, honeyeaters by day, possums and bats by night.

The Black Bean was first collected at the Endeavour River in 1770. Sydney Parkinson drew the original plant portrait, and in 1779 Frederick Polydore Nodder produced the finished sketch that was engraved by Gerald Sibelius for a Florilegium that cost Sir Joseph Banks £10,000 though it was not actually printed until 1962. No attempt was made to name the plant until it was collected again by Alan Cunningham on his trip to the Brisbane and Logan Rivers in 1828. Cunningham named it then *Castanospermum australe*. When Hooker came to publish the new taxon in his *Botanical Miscellany* in 1830 he attributed it to both Cunningham and his travelling companion, Charles Frazer, evidently by mistake. Cunningham's specimen was forwarded with the rest of Banks's collection to the British Museum, and is now in the Natural History Museum.

A desperate hack called Robert Mudie, who is responsible for ninety volumes on all kinds of subjects, collared the new information for two of the books he churned out in 1829, *The Picture of Australia* and *Vegetable Substances*. He correctly described Castanospermum as a 'pea tree' but slightly mis-rendered its name as 'castanospermum Australis'. He then waxed lyrical.

> The odour, especially when they are undergoing the process of roasting, is agreeable, intermediate between that of good oaten bread and a potato newly dug and roasted. The flavour, though not so sweet, is nearly as grateful as that of the Spanish chestnut. As the tree

produces abundantly, if it be found in sufficient quantity it may be an object of commerce, or may be worthy of cultivation, especially if the wood correspond in value with the seeds. (150)

If you simply roast a Moreton Bay Chestnut and then eat it, you are certain to be very sick and you may possibly die. Floyd tells us: 'The seeds are poisonous to man and beast, although they were reportedly eaten by Aborigines after preparation and prolonged washing in water to remove the saponin.' (159) Cattle agisted at Cave Creek regularly ate the Black Beans whenever they could find them. This may not have done them any good. In 1987 eighteen Brahman bulls grazing in a paddock where there were fallen Black Beans were found on testing to be heterozygotes for Pompe's disease (Reichmann *et al.*).

For Black Beans to be wholesome, they must first be split, then soaked, skinned, sliced and pounded into a meal. The meal is then placed in a woven bag and left in running water for several days, then drained, dried, shaped into cakes and roasted. The active toxin in the seeds, castanospermine, has been shown to have anti-HIV and anti-cancer properties (Roja and Heble). The Black Bean's range extends from Lismore in New South Wales as far north as Vanuatu and New Caledonia. (Dispersion over such vast expanses of ocean is possible because when the Black Bean pod is wet it seals shut.)

Our true nut trees by contrast are genuinely Gondwanan. Most of them are lauraceous; the fossil megafloras of 50 million years ago show the Lauraceae to have been the most numerous family in Gondwana subtropical rainforest; at the present count there are seventeen lauraceous species in the Cave Creek rainforest in six genera, and quite a few of them are called nuts.

The genus Endiandra was named by Robert Brown. The name means 'inner male', referring to the inner series of stamens which are the fertile ones in this genus. All six of the Cave Creek Endiandra species are called walnuts in common parlance. In 1864 Meisner gave two of them scientific names. One is the Endiandra we know best, *E. pubens*, also known as the Hairy Walnut; the other, Mueller's Walnut, he called *E. mulleri*, so perhaps Mueller misspelt Meisner on purpose when he named *Cryptocarya meissneri* two years later. Bentham named the Rose Walnut *Endiandra discolor* (*Flora Australiensis*,

5:301). The Black or Ball-fruited Walnut was named *E. globosa* by Maiden and Betche in 1899 (149). The last to be named, by Kostermans in 1970, was *E. hayesii* after H. C. Hayes who first collected it.

When I learnt from the third edition of *Mabberley's Plant-Book* (2008) that the edible fruit of *Floydia praealta* (*prealta* in Mabberley's spelling) was called a 'coohoy', I pounced on the word and used it in as many ways as I could, until I began to wonder why nobody else did. The *Australian National Dictionary* illustrated the word by a quote from a diary of the trailblazer Christie Palmerston. On 21 January 1885, when he was amid the headwaters of the Johnstone River, he recorded:

> dinner consisted of a few coohoy nuts, so named by the aborigines. The nut is perfectly round and about six inches in circumference, with a thin shell. When in fruit it is green and ribbed with a few converging [lines]. The fruit, which is useless, fastens to the nut like glue. Hit it against some hard substance and the fruit breaks, allowing the nut to roll out clearly. The nut needs no preparation, only roasting till nicely browned. If eaten raw it resembles the uncooked English potato. Some of the trees run to the height of 100 feet before breaking. They are as straight as an arrow and the stems measured four arms' length in circumference. (Savage, 181)

In the diary of a later expedition, in the entry made on 12 July 1886, Palmerston tells us: 'The nut can be gathered all the year round in countless numbers, containing no evil properties. The simple operation of roasting it on coals will prepare it for food; or, if crushed to meal, it assumes a coffee-color, and can be mixed and be cooked into excellent cakes.' (Savage, 190) Though Palmerston was no botanist his description is exact. The species was eventually collected by Bailey on the Russell River during the Bellenden Ker expedition and in 1891 named *Cryptocarya palmerstonii*. Twenty years later when William Guilfoyle gave the name 'coohoy' to the fruit of *Helicia praealta*, as the Floydia used to be known, he was simply wrong (Guilfoyle, 1910, 210), and Mabberley has repeated the error. Eventually it was realised that the Cryptocarya was in fact an

Endiandra (White & Francis, 1920), but nobody remembered that it was also the 'invaluable' Coohoy. Palmerston also describes the preparation by which the fruit of *Endiandra pubens* is divested of its poisonous properties. That does grow at Cave Creek, but *E. palmerstonii* does not grow south of Millaa Millaa.

The most important of the many lauraceous genera at Cave Creek is Cryptocarya. The name Cryptocarya means 'hidden nut', and, again, given the fact that the name is simply descriptive, we are not surprised to find that it too was coined in 1810 by Robert Brown (402). Brown did not name a type. What he seems to have had before him were specimens of two species, *Cryptocarya glaucescens*, and again the specific name is descriptive, referring to the bluish bloom on the underside of the leaves, and *C. obovata*, referring to the shape of the leaves which are upside-down-egg-shaped, broadest at the tip. So the type is one or other of these. CCRRS has both. *C. obovata* is also known as White Walnut. The next to be named was *C. laevigata* by Carl Ludwig von Blume in 1826 (11:556), and then *C. microneura* by Carl Daniel Friedrich Meisner, Professor of Botany at Basel and expert on the Lauraceae, in 1864 (de Candolle, 15(1):73). Mueller intended to name the next one for Meisner but spelt the name wrong (again) and gave it the wrong suffix (*Fragmenta*, 5:38, 170); it was not until 1976 that D. D. Frodin sorted it out, but even he misspelt the species name as 'meisnerana' when it should have been 'meisneriana'.

The next to be named was Stinking Cryptocarya, *C. foetida*, by R. T. Baker, economic botanist at the Technological Museum in Sydney, in 1907 (517, *ADB*). Why he called it that nobody knows. The flowers are actually sweet-scented and beloved of bees. (The species had in fact been collected much earlier, by Cunningham in 1828.) The tree is now so rare as a consequence of the clearing of its coastal habitat for development, that the Cave Creek specimens are amongst very few surviving. In the same year Maiden named *Cryptocarya erythroxylon* in his *Forest Flora of New South Wales* (3:26, 111). In 1924 C. T. White and W. D. Francis named one of the biggest Cryptocaryas *C. foveolata*, known to some as Mountain Walnut (APNI).

One afternoon as I mooched about the forest I found myself

standing ankle deep in shiny black berries. I took some to the
workforce who knew it at once as the fruit of *Cryptocarya erythrox-*
ylon, the Pigeon-berry Ash. Who wouldn't grow pigeon berries,
especially when our pigeons are killing themselves by eating immature
Camphor Laurel fruit? In the caldera, known to me as Laurel Canyon,
multiple death events of Topknot and Wonga Wonga Pigeons have
been reported, and in each case the birds' crops and stomachs
contained nothing but Camphor Laurel berries.

One of the first revelations of what regrowing the forest might
bring was the arrival in numbers of pigeon species that are known to
be in serious decline. These days we often see Topknot Pigeons who
wear a toupee of swept-back ginger plumes and fly in battalions.
Wompoo Fruit Doves, papally magnificent in their white, green,
gold and purple vestments, can be heard making their obscenely
gobbling call. I sit on the verandah with my binoculars following
Rose-crowned Fruit Doves, Cicadabirds and Green Catbirds as they
work through the canopy. Every now and then a Wonga Pigeon
comes waddling through the leaves. And now we have Emerald
Doves breeding somewhere just off the main track. We collected a
bucketful of pigeon berries; it won't be our fault if *Cryptocarya*
erythroxylon is not soon growing once more all over these mountains.
If you'd like a seedling, let us know.

THE INHABITANTS: NON-FURRY

The most important creatures in the rainforest are the smallest, the microbes and the invertebrates. The survival of the forest ecosystem depends on them. A rainforest, being a closed ecosystem, survives by recycling itself, and for that it needs the help of the living beings that break down dead material. A leaf falls; bacteria help it to decay; worms pull the dead matter back into the soil. A tree falls; wood-chewing beetles transmute its timber into dung which is quickly mineralised and becomes soil. If the process should slow down, the survival of the forest is threatened. So no matter how serious an insect infestation of young trees at CCRRS may turn out to be, we leave it to run its course. Our young Red Cedars, for example, can be severely damaged by the larvae of a moth, *Hypsipyla robusta*, but we make no effort to control any infestation. Generally the affected trees recover but, the leader being irrevocably damaged, they are thenceforward multi-stemmed and will never fulfil their optimum role as rainforest emergents. The continued presence of the moth is necessary if the resistant Red Cedars are not to lose the genetic trait that protects them.

The Cave Creek invertebrates deserve a book of their own, with photographs, and perhaps one day they will have one. I've photographed magenta katydid nymphs, black and white striped worms, green-winged butterflies, huge hawkmoth caterpillars, much bigger millipedes, stick insects as long as an arm, iridescent blue flies with sizzling gold eyes, male and female longhorn beetles in each other's arms, bladder cicadas like green balloons, fireflies, glow-worms, turquoise dragonflies with transparent black wings, and giant land snails. I can put names to no more than half of them; the others may not have been described and may have no names yet, for all I know. (Of the 98 per cent of terrestrial species that are invertebrates only a fraction has ever been described; an estimated five and a half million species await description.) The creek is thronged with water-mites, water-fleas and shrimps as well as the nymphs of stone flies, mayflies, dragonflies, not to mention caddis-flies, flatworms, snails and leeches, more and more of them since we began to remove the weeds that infested the waterway. The most famous inhabitant of the creek is another invertebrate, a blue crayfish, probably but not necessarily *Euastacus sulcatus*. After torrential rain we can come across blue crayfishes washed out of their creeks and wandering about on land. When they see us coming they rear up and wave their red, white and blue claws in a vain attempt to strike fear into our hearts. Our creek is too rocky for platypuses or long-neck turtles to make homes on, or so I think. Besides, when the freshes come, which they do regularly but unpredictably, the creek is so violently reconfigured that the nests of such burrowmakers would be destroyed.

The creek is one place the sun can always get to, and so the weeds come back year on year, and year on year we remove them. As a result even our threatened frog species have been able to build up their numbers. These days, when the rains come, the frog chorus is deafening.

One wet night the frog noise was so very loud that I went out to see what was afoot. I followed the unholy din towards the old muster yard, and the cattle drinker in the middle of it. The drinker, which held a couple of feet of warm rainwater, was full of Southern Orange-eyed Treefrogs (*Litoria chloris*) all yelling fit to bust, their throat membranes inflated to transparency. As I watched other tree frogs climbed in, or hung from the rim of the tank, and joined in the yelling. In the water I could see frogs grabbing other frogs, and other frogs grabbing them, in a mad group grope. When frogs mate the male does not penetrate the female, who simply ejects her eggs into the water while the male frog ejaculates in the same water, so all this embracing was hardly necessary, but the frogs were hugging anyway. Altogether it was the wildest party that could ever be imagined. It went on till dawn. (My rather inept video of this event can be seen on the Friends of Gondwana Rainforest website.)

The next day the drinker was full of spawn, but the sun was up and the water level in the drinker was falling. The tadpoles that hatched ate the tadpoles that hatched after them, till there were only a few dozen metamorphs left to climb out of the drinker on the branchlets I had positioned to take them safely over the rim. A few days after rain we will find tadpoles in most of the puddles, but I have never been able to figure out how many of them ever make it to being frogs.

Frogs are stupendous creatures because, even when they are metamorphs no bigger than a fly, they can hear and see, and catch prey, and leap forty times their own length. It is tempting to think they are smart. An old Green Treefrog who turned up on the bedroom windowsill one evening sat there through the night and the whole of the following day, apparently dozing, but every time I turned to look at him, I'd find his horizontal pupil trained on me. He was as big as a half-kilo bag of sugar and much the same shape. To get to such a size he must have outwitted a long line of predators, for frogs are food for most rainforest creatures, including other frogs. I didn't try to pat him for fear that my hand on his silky green skin would have felt scalding hot. He was still there when I fell asleep the next night; in the morning he was gone as quietly as he came. His scientific name is *Litoria caerulea*; the species name, which means 'blue', came about because the spirit in which the specimen sent to Banks had been preserved had dissolved the yellow glaze over its blue underskin. The genus name has changed several times, but the misleading epithet hangs on.

Tree frogs are the insignia of rainforests the world over. Of the dozen or more species that make their home at Cave Creek my favourite is the Cascade Treefrog (*Litoria pearsoniana*). The scientific name given to the species by Stephen J. Copland in 1960 commemorates Oliver Pearson, Professor of Zoology at Berkeley. Copland had two gos at the name, which he rendered first as *Hyla pearsoni* (1960) and then *Hyla pearsoniana*; in 1970, after the Litoria genus had been separated from the genus Hyla, Michael Tyler renamed the frog *Litoria pearsoni*; that name was corrected to *Litoria pearsoniana* by John

Barker and Gordon Grigg in 1977. The confusion has not quite dissipated; the genus Litoria is once more under revision. There is considerable variation in the colouring of Cascade Treefrogs. The ones at Cave Creek are pale green with pearl-white bellies, and their skin is shagreened, so that it looks like frosted glass. To my eye they are the most beautiful tree frogs of all.

Under the Queensland Nature Conservation Act of 1992 the species is listed as endangered, but you can hear Cascade Treefrogs calling any warm evening along Cave Creek. There is nevertheless a good deal that we don't understand about these little creatures. Immature frogs are very seldom found, so the current thinking is that this is one tree frog that ascends to the canopy as a juvenile and doesn't come down again for two or three years, until it is mature and ready to mate. Until we have ways of observing canopy life without disrupting it, this hypothesis cannot be verified. In the winter Cascade Treefrogs are supposed to group together in large mixed-sex aggregations, squeezed tightly into narrow rock crevices, in lethargy, with their eyes closed.

Even smaller although less vulnerable is the Dainty Treefrog (*Litoria gracilenta*), which overwinters in the canopy. We often find this frog, with its limbs drawn under it and its eyes closed, at the base of the spadix of the Cunjevoi Flower, sleeping off a meal of pollen weevils. I was once scanning the forest edge for birds when the glasses picked up a fringed flower of *Trichosanthes subvelutina*. Inside it, glowing in the early morning sunlight like a chip of polished jade, I could clearly see a Dainty Treefrog. We have many more frogs, tusked frogs, pouched frogs, rocket frogs, froglets, toadlets, thousands of frogs. We also have the odd cane toad. The workforce kill them outright, by cutting them up the middle and turning them inside out, which means the birds can make a meal of them, a technique we learnt from the birds in question. I, being more squeamish, euthanase any toad I find by putting it in the refrigerator and then in the freezer.

The rainforest has fewer lizard species than you will find in other types of habitat, but that's not to say that we don't have at least as many lizards as we have frogs. I have never found our most famous lizard, the Leaf-tailed Gecko (*Saltuarius swaini*), though everyone else seems to have. Herpetologists appear to have decided that the 'ii' ending for the honorific epithet was otiose, and removed the second 'i', otherwise the skink named for Tasmanian herpetologist Roy Swain would be called *Saltuarius swainii*. Some authorities insist on the correct Latin; others don't. If I think botany is a mare's nest, herpetology is worse.

At Cave Creek there are lots of tiny skinks; one, *Calyptotis scutirostrum*, five centimetres from snout to vent, which rejoices in the common name of 'Scute-snouted Skink', referring to the bony plate between its eyes, lays eggs. All our other lizard species, except the monitors, are live-bearing. *Eulamprus martini* grows to 7.5 centimetres or so, if it's lucky; *E. tenuis* grows bigger still, *E. murrayi* bigger than that and *E. quoyii* and *E. tryoni* about the same. I am sorry to have to admit that I can't always tell them apart, all of them being spangled and speckled in similar ways. Moreover they are nearly always running away, and I don't like to grab at them in case they shed their tails. One skink I can tell from the others because it is bigger and less patterned is the Eastern Crevice Skink, *Egernia mcpheei*. Another is the shiny black Land Mullet, largest of our skinks, thirty centimetres from snout to vent when full-grown. Most people know it as *Egernia major*; it recently underwent a long overdue name change to *Bellatorias major*. That name was first published in 1984 by Wells and Wellington, but it was not used until it was 'resurrected' in 2008. Thereby hangs an astonishing tale.

In the mid-1980s Richard Wells, who had been working as a collector for several Australian museums, decided 'that many of the specimens he had provided had simply been ignored by qualified professionals who were comfortably polishing their chairs while producing little if anything of scientific value' (Williams, D., *et al.*, 926). It seemed to Wells that the Australian herpetological establishment was dragging its heels when it came to rationalising reptile and amphibian taxa. He joined forces with Cliff Ross Wellington and together they analysed all the available data and came to their own conclusions, which involved renaming scores of species. To publish the new names they set up a journal which they called *The Australian Journal of Herpetology*, in the first and only number of which they published 'A Synopsis of the Class Reptilia', and its Supplement, 'A Classification of the Amphibia and Reptilia of Australia'. The result was uproar. Wells and Wellington were accused of having broken the rules; their descriptions were too brief, and there was no way they could have examined the type material for so many species. A serious attempt – recorded as Case 2531 in the *Bulletin of Zoological Nomenclature* for 1987 – was made to ban their articles and jettison their names.

Not all the species named by Wells and Wellington were good, but even those that were were not adopted. For years there was resistance; herpetologists frequently referred to species named by Wells and Wellington as undescribed, and continued to use names which they knew were invalid rather than recognise the authority of Wells and Wellington. Eventually, and patchily, common sense has begun to prevail (e.g., Hoser). Wells is still around, still working with reptiles, and profoundly uninterested in public – or academic – recognition. As he is apt to say: 'Universities are not really places where you learn about animals.' Wellington now works for the Central Directorate Threatened Species Unit of the New South Wales Parks and Wildlife Service.

My favourites among the Cave Creek lizardry are the Eastern Water Dragons (*Physignathus lesueuri lesueuri*) that have come into their own since we reforested the headland above the creek. In warmer weather they can be found basking on the causeway and all the way up the steep track to the gate. As the car creeps by they lift their heads and look directly into my eyes, holding my gaze for a second or two before leaping down the rocks. They are the more remarkable because a fossil dragon from the Miocene recently found at Riversleigh is almost identical. The dragons are another reason for keeping the CCRRS gate locked. If deliveries are on the way we have to scare the dragons off before the truck comes in, because not everybody drives as slowly as I do. (Every day, on the main road, you will see dead and dying dragons.) Another dragon, the Angle-headed Dragon (*Hypsilurus spinipes*) forages in the canopy, where it feeds on the invertebrates that defoliate the big stingers.

Most people would be more impressed by the CCRRS Lace Monitors (*Varanus varius*) of which there are many. These are largely diurnal, so we see them quite often but they almost always run off, except when they are in courtship mode, when nothing seems to faze them. One warm afternoon in an otherwise very wet spring I was weeding a patch of Aneilema when I realised that I was not alone. A full-grown Lace Monitor, a good seven feet long, had moved up close beside me. At first I thought he was just basking in the sun, and then I saw the head of the female, less than half his size, emerging under his foreleg. By inserting his tail under hers, the male was manoeuvring one of his hemipenes into her vagina. He would thrust rhythmically for five minutes or so, and then she would slip out from under him. I expected her to run away but she stayed still as he rested, waiting for him to move towards her again. As he slid his body over hers, he would touch her gently all over the head and neck with his forked tongue, almost as if kissing her, before beginning to slide his tail under hers. I removed myself discreetly and ran to set up the video camera, not knowing how often this behaviour had been observed in the wild. (The video can be seen on the Friends of Gondwana Rainforest website.) The lizards continued to perform for a very long time, until the sun slipped behind the trees and the ground began to cool. The truly disturbing thing about the video is that the female is so very much smaller than the male that the whole process looks unnatural, but every time I have seen these big goannas in mating mode, when they usually open their mouths, which are upholstered in knicker-pink satin, and roar hoarsely at me to make me go away, the female has been very, very much smaller. This extreme sexual dimorphism has not been described, let alone explained, as far as I know. (My own attempt can be found in the Prologue, above.)

A few days later I was walking in a five-year-old planting, marvel-ling at how soon equilibrium had been established in it, when I heard a large Lace Monitor moving close by and then another, and another. Altogether I counted five. They could not have been less concerned at my presence. They appeared to be following each other's phero-monal trails, tasting the air with their tongues. I walked at a slow but steady pace, as they circled round me. I was hoping I might see their ritual fighting, for they seemed to be all males, but dusk threw its blanket over us, and I had to make my way back to the house too soon to witness the outcome. As usual I was left marvelling at how little we know of the behaviour of our rainforest species. Those same Lace Monitors eat the corpses of all the animals that meet their death in the forest, bones, hair, eyes, teeth and all. Because they are egg eaters they are the great enemies of the Brush-turkeys, and many carry scars where the turkeys have defended their mounds with beak and claw.

The snakes we see most often, that is to say almost every day, are pythons, commonly called Carpet Snakes. I can still remember the first time I met one. I was walking the forest edge track with Garry, when he gently touched my arm. In front of me a big beautiful bronze and gold serpent was moving almost imperceptibly up the bank and out of our way. I had the distinct feeling that Garry expected me to shriek and flee. I was more likely to fall on my knees before such a beautiful creature. Since then I have seen hundreds of pythons at Cave Creek, greeny-goldy ones, black and grey ones, mahogany and ivory ones, some patterned with black and blood red, a dozen different colourways at least, fat ones, thin ones, torpid ones, wounded ones, dead ones. I was prowling another part of the forest track one afternoon when I became aware that in the forest ahead of me a python had reared up six feet or so off the ground, propping itself on its huge body as it felt for a branch. A stout branch found, it wrapped its neck around it and then hauled the supporting body up loop by loop, from one branch to another and then another, until it had disappeared into the canopy.

Pythons are ambush feeders; they coil themselves up at the side of a track used by warm-blooded creatures and lie there for days at a time, only moving to have a bit of a stretch or to soak up the odd ray if sunlight touches the forest floor. I have had four at a time within feet of the house for weeks on end. One very wet day I was squelching through a planting when I almost trod on the head of a big python that was hiding in a flooded tractor wheel-rut with just its nostrils above the surface of the water. Charlie Booth, who used to grow plants for us, told me he had never seen so many pythons anywhere. Python skins hang like pennants all around the house. I have had a python sliding through the louvres of the bedroom, feeling towards the warmth of my body, his neck concertinaed for the strike. I have seen another python hunting for a way of getting into the house, sliding along the windowsills, following the heat of the marsupial mice snoring in the wall cavity.

I love the Cave Creek pythons at least as much as I have ever loved a cat or dog. I am ashamed that so many of my countrymen think that it is fine to kill Carpet Snakes because they eat domestic fowls. They eat many more rats than fowls, but still people think it appropriate to chop at them with rakes and spades or blow their heads off with shotguns.

Pythons are almost deaf and almost blind, and yet they are our top predators. They detect warm-blooded prey through heat-sensitive pits along their lips. How they detect cold-blooded prey like frogs is less obvious, though it has been suggested they can sense sound and movement through the bones of their skulls. The Cave Creek pythons are supposed to be *Morelia spilota mcdowelli*, the Coastal Carpet Python, identified as a species (*M. mcdowelli*) by Wells and Wellington and then relegated to a subspecies in 1994 by Dave and Tracy Barker, all of which suggests that our most intimate animal associate is not very well understood by even herpetologists and python breeders. Pythons described as separate species are capable of breeding with each other, which is a pretty good indicator that the species are not distinct. *Morelia spilota mcdowelli* is supposed to be 'irascible', which reared in captivity it may well be. I don't find the wild ones irascible in the least. I have all but tripped over them, and they have simply flowed quietly away. I can sit by them reading and they go on dozing, occasionally stretching themselves and rearranging their coils. They happily coexist with dozens of other pythons, their home ranges not so much overlapping as coinciding.

The key to python personality is energy conservation. Because they are cold-blooded, they can shut down their energy require-ments to near zero, by keeping still. They take small prey like frogs and large prey like pademelons that may weigh up to 60 per cent of their body weight; in both cases they do it with minimal exertion. By following each other's scent trails male pythons form 'breeding aggregations with several males attending a single female'. In the late winter of 2011 I had the opportunity to watch this process, as three male pythons waited patiently for a sign of recognition from the huge dark pythoness I call Jessye. One afternoon two of them began mock fighting to impress her, winding their tails together, rearing up, each trying to push the other to the ground. Then Jessye disappeared and they were left grieving.

Jessye may not have been ready to breed in 2011. The generation and laying of up to thirty eggs greatly depletes a python's stores of fat and energy; during the ten- to fifteen-week incubation period she has to keep the eggs at a constant temperature, which she does by shivering, which uses up more of her calories. When the young hatch they go their separate ways, leaving the weakened mother python to recover as best she can. During this period she is extremely vulnerable to a variety of predators and diseases. In 2012 Jessye was courted again by an assortment of younger males; she also attracted a massive grey and gold male python and this time she capitulated. They were together for ten days or more as other snakes came and went, often coiling on top of them and occasionally mating with Jessye. This highly social period persisted for many weeks. The usual notion, that pythons are solitary animals by nature with little or no social interaction, seems completely wrong.

Years ago, Jane and I and a CCRRS worker were clambering through the steep forest, following the boundary which, on the principle of good fences making good neighbours, I had just had very expensively surveyed. I was, as usual, bringing up the rear, so I got the best view of the very large snake that was doing its best to get out of our way. As it slid past at eye-level its tail touched my sister's shoulder. 'Oh, a python,' she said. But it wasn't. When it came towards me I could see clearly that there were no heat pits along its underlip. I would have said that it was a tiger snake, but I'd never seen one anywhere near that big. The snake that flowed past me was nearly two metres long, and the colour of wet sand, with shadow bands of darker brown. It looked as if it might try constriction to immobilise its prey, but it wasn't a constrictor. Its scales were too big, and the wrong pattern and there weren't enough of them. I hunted for it on line and in reptile books, but it was nowhere to be seen.

Nobody had described a tiger snake of such a size – until I read, in Gresty's account of the Numinbah Valley in the early twentieth century, about 'an uncommon member of the reptilian fauna . . . the giant Tiger Snake or Banded Broadhead, said to attain a length of ten feet. The valley Aborigines had an exaggerated fear of the admittedly

venomous reptile, known to them as "Boggul" ... full grown
specimens are now seen on extremely rare occasions.'(58) So lucky
me. And lucky the three of us. If any of us had had the bad luck to step
on the snake the outcome could have been very different. As it is my
sister continues to insist that the snake whose tail brushed her shoulder
was a python. The confusion is inspissated by the fact that until well
into the twentieth century there was a snake known to naturalists as
Hoplocephalus curtus, and to the common folk as the Brown-banded
Snake. The genus Hoplocephalus includes all the Australian broad-
heads, to which many people assumed the tiger snakes belonged. The
Tiger Snake genus was variously called Naja, then Alecto, and in 1867
Hoplocephalus; it seems to have become Notechis in 1948 (Glauert).
As far as I can tell the possibility that the early herpetologists were
talking about two different snake species has not been dispelled.

Earlier observers had great difficulty distinguishing the Brown-
banded Snake from a Carpet Snake. In 1873, the tiger snake is
described in *The Queenslander* as the one 'which resembles in appearance the carpet snake of Queensland' (19 July); in 1874 another tells
us that it is to be 'known by its unmistakable stripes' (Q, 26 December,
273). In May 1879 another observer refers to the tiger snake as 'our
brown banded snake' (Q, 10 May, 588), and 'The Naturalist' writing
in *The Queenslander* in 1879 tells a cautionary tale of this 'the most
vicious and venomous of the serpent tribe':

> Not long ago I came across a young man who had deliberately picked
> up a snake; and on my asking him what he was doing he said, 'Oh this
> wouldn't hurt a baby; why it's the prettiest carpet snake that ever I
> saw.' And yet the foolish fellow was dangling a tiger snake, holding it
> tightly round the neck ... and no sooner did he drop it than it seized
> him by the calf of the leg. (Q, 19 April, 500)

Seizing the young man by the calf of the leg is a reaction more
typical of a carpet snake than any venomous snake. A tiger snake
would have either struck or sprung away. The Englishman who
wrote under the pseudonym 'George Carrington' remarked in 1871:
'There is a great variety and number of poisonous and deadly snakes
in Queensland, yet cases of snakebite are rare, for the reptiles

invariably try to escape, and do not bite, except in self-defence.' Nevertheless TV naturalists who persecute animals for the entertainment of couch-potatoes insist that tiger snakes are aggressive, and not simply towards each other, but towards humans. Certainly the terrified snakes that wildlife warriors manhandle do try very hard to bite them, but this behaviour can hardly be said to amount to aggression. Snakes don't come hunting us. Give them a chance to get out of the way and they will.

The next most commonly seen snake at Cave Creek is the good old Red-bellied Black, *Pseudechis porphyriacus*, possibly the commonest snake in Australia, though few places could harbour as many as we do. According to Rhianna Blackthorn of WIRES Northern Rivers, in every square kilometre of this region there are around three hundred Red-bellied Black Snakes. According to John Drake, writing in *The Argus* in 1952, the Red-bellied Black 'has a sunny, placid nature which causes it to bite only when it is cornered or attacked'. Sunny-natured they may be, but our Red-bellied Blacks have a habit of getting themselves into tight corners, where we are likely to come into contact with them by accident, between empty tubes stacked in the nursery perhaps, or hidden in plant trays or asleep in mulch piles. So far no one has been bitten, but it has been a near thing once or twice.

More numerous possibly are our Yellow-faced Whipsnakes (*Demansia psammophis*) which the locals call copperheads, perhaps because their coppery-pink backs are dusted with pale greeny-blue rather like the colour of verdigris. These small snakes have an odd propensity for hanging out with other much bigger snakes; one used to turn up regularly to bask alongside one of the pythons by the back door. When I appeared it would fling itself over the python to get out of the way, no matter how far away I was, its large black eyes, huge in proportion to its tiny head, being clearly able to focus on distant objects. My theory about this behaviour is that the Yellow-faced Whipsnake, being heavily predated by a variety of raptors, chooses to bask with much bigger snakes for its own protection. One day the workforce came upon two Yellow-faced Whipsnakes that were coiling themselves around each other and spinning in a hoop. This I take to be ritual combat of two males but I have never found any such phenomenon described. We managed to grab a few seconds of video before our tame Butcherbird turned up, whereupon the snakes vanished. To live with snakes and observe them daily is to be disgusted with field guides that give no account of their behaviour and devote far too much space to discussions of the dangerousness of their bite. Descriptions of the habitat of the Yellow-faced Whipsnake do not mention rainforest; the Cave Creek rainforest seems to be full of them, as well as Banded Snakes, Bandy Bandies, various Ramphotyphlops, Brown and Green Tree Snakes, Keelbacks, Rough-scaled Snakes, Eastern Small-eyed Snakes, Eastern Brown Snakes and Marsh Snakes.

The most visible and the most spectacular of the Cave Creek fauna are the birds. The more I see of birds the more I wonder why it is that snakes are considered nasty and birds considered sweet. Bernard O'Reilly tells us in *Green Mountains* that wild birds are 'the most beautiful of living things; the most sweet-voiced and the gentlest of creatures'. (83) I hope I was tough-minded enough even as a nipper to have raised my head when I read this, sniffed the air and thought 'Seagulls? Hawks? Magpies?' Most birds are not sweet-voiced; none, not even the dove itself, is all that gentle. O'Reilly prattles on:

> There is one other great lesson which human neighbours could learn from bird neighbours, and this is why they are gentler and nicer than humans – they never say a cruel word about anyone. You may say that this is just because they cannot speak, but I know birds well enough to know that if they could talk, they would only say the nicest things. So next time you see a gentle feathered creature in a tree, just pause to think how inferior you are.

There is hardly a bird, however cute, that will not steal eggs or nestlings. And practically all of them, bar the ones we least like, the carrion birds, prefer their food alive and vociferating. Even honey-eaters and seed-eating birds need to feed their fledglings on protein, and that means live invertebrates. Lewin's Honeyeaters are amongst the most efficient predators in the Cave Creek rainforest. They are as adroit and acrobatic as any fly-catcher, and when the larvae of the leafrolling moths are at their biggest and juiciest, they will spend whole days unpacking every leaf, cleaning the infested trees completely. Nectar, fruit and seed are not available in all seasons, but invertebrates are.

It is probably inevitable that human beings will play favourites among the lower orders, and that they will express an irrational preference in moral terms. Fluffy means sweet; scaly means nasty. Settlers in Queensland made war on any species that incommoded them, and justified the onslaught on all kinds of moral and aesthetic grounds. A report from Coomera in 1880 exulted:

> morning, noon and night, the sharp report of the gun is heard; . . . For the destruction of flying-fox, whose ghastly flappings and flittings from tree to tree disturb our rest, or cockatoo either, there need be little compunction, but parents and guardians might well forbid the massacre of insectivorous birds, or our fields and gardens will ultimately suffer. (Q, 6 March, 296)

God forbid that our rest should be disturbed, especially by 'ghastly flittings and flappings'. Speciesism dies hard; even at this late stage most people do not understand that if the earth is to survive we have to respect the entire system, not just the bits we consider cute or useful.

Even the fluffiest birds are capable of terrifying ferocity. On spring evenings a Grey Goshawk (*Accipiter novaehollandiae*) will come drifting gently down towards Cave Creek and at once all the other birds will take to the air to drive him away, flying so close to the much bigger bird that they risk serious injury. Most savage in their attacks are the Butcherbirds, that dive on the goshawk, clattering their beaks like machine-gun fire. In fact goshawks feed more readily on small mammals than on birds, but when birds are breeding they will not tolerate a raptor's presence anywhere near a nest site.

The goshawk, which nests in the tallest of the rainforest trees, on a platform of twigs around a central depression lined with green leaves, is one raptor whose life is getting much better as the canopy closes in. For one thing the Butcherbirds have moved to open country elsewhere. For another the possums, bats, reptiles and insects that the goshawk lives on are becoming more numerous. His competitors, the Black-shouldered Kite (*Elanus axillaris*) and the Nankeen Kestrel (*Falco cenchroides*), are now seldom seen, because they exist to hunt small rodents in grassland. Years ago a Collared Sparrowhawk (*Accipiter cirrocephalus*) chased a Noisy Miner onto the verandah and nearly collected me instead, as I put my head out the window to see why all the birds were giving their alarm calls, but I haven't seen one since. It looks very much as if the goshawks are finally coming into their own.

The biggest of the Cave Creek raptors are the Wedge-tailed Eagles (*Aquila audax*). Every now and then a pair will come sailing over the scarps. We know them immediately, no matter how high they fly, not just because of their unmistakeable silhouette and their nine-foot wingspan but because of the dead silence that falls over the valley. In some parts of Australia the Wedge-tailed Eagle has become common, mainly because of the unending food supply afforded by roadkill. If you take the train across the Nullarbor Plain you will see one perched on nearly every fence-post. Semi-arid is much more their habitat; as the canopy closes over Cave Creek we will see them no more.

Ornithologists like to say that Wedge-tailed Eagles display reverse sexual dimorphism, because the female is larger than the male. 'Sexual dimorphism' is the name given to difference in body shape or appearance between male and female. The term should include differences in which the female is larger than the male. By calling this 'reverse' or even 'reversed' sexual dimorphism the scientists are misunderstanding their own terminology as well as betraying their own prejudice. The female Wedge-tailed Eagle is indeed half as heavy again as her male partner; in all our raptor species the female is larger than the male.

The Wedge-tailed Eagle was first named by an English physician who was never in Australia in his life. John Latham is typical of the gentlemanly amateurs who founded what we are now pleased to call the 'earth sciences'. He trained as a doctor and practised for many years at Dartford in Kent. At the same time he was compiling and illustrating what was to be published in 1781 as *General Synopsis of Birds*, for which he designed, executed and coloured all the illustrations, which were based on specimens that had been sent to him from all over the world, including Australia and the Pacific. Latham did not use the Linnaean system of classification; for example he named the kookaburra, of which he had been sent a specimen from New Guinea, 'the great brown King's Fisher' (Latham, 1781, ii, 603).

In 1788 Latham, one of the founders of the Linnaean Society, was busy renaming bird species for *Index Ornithologicus*, published in 1790. In this he was beaten by the same Johann Georg Gmelin whose name was given by Linnaeus to the genus of the White Beeches, Gmelin having already published his own version of Linnaeus's *Systema Naturae* in which he had given systematic binomials to birds originally described by Latham. Nevertheless Latham's contribution is immortalised in the scientific names of a round half-dozen of our bird species, including our Brush-turkey whose proper name is *Alectura lathami*, and our Glossy Black Cockatoo, *Calyptorhynchus lathami*.

White stains on the rhyolite scarps tell us that the Australian Peregrine (*Falco peregrinus macropus*) has made a home there. One evening as I came down from the shade house I disturbed one perched in a Wild Tobacco tree, tiring on a Brown Cuckoo Dove. He raised his cruel head and fixed me with his large dark eyes in their glowing yellow rims as I fumbled with the camera, trying not to make the kind of sudden movement that would cause him to leave his prey, which was flapping feebly. Until he had torn more living flesh from it, it would remain too heavy for him to carry up to share with his mate on the scarp. If he had abandoned it, I would have had to step in and kill the suffering creature myself.

Peregrines are famous for their aerial acrobatics. As a preliminary to mating they show off by flying in high circles, or zooming in figures of eight or rolling like big pigeons. They fly up higher and higher and then stoop, heading straight for the ground at top speed, before pulling up with a bounce. Eventually they will mate on their home ledge, where the female will lay up to four eggs. The Australian Peregrine was identified as a subspecies of the worldwide species by Swainson in 1837. Nowadays they are becoming rare, and so they are being sexed and banded and badgered in the interests of conservation as well as being disturbed by 'sight-seers, bush-wackers and illegal egg-collectors' (Czechura).

The peregrines' favourite food is pigeon. Feral, common or rare, it's all the same to them. From the moment the falcon took after it, the Brown Cuckoo Dove had no way of evading the outsize talons that grabbed it in mid-air. If the fruit pigeons dive into the closed forest where the peregrines cannot follow, they escape the strike, so the peregrines tend to concentrate on high-flying Flock, Topknot and White-headed Pigeons. They also take kestrels, Lewin's Honeyeaters, Lorikeets and Black-faced Cuckoo Shrikes. We don't see them perched on emergent trees, as they do in other environments. At Cave Creek they launch their strikes by plummeting straight down from the scarp.

Our owls are three, the Powerful Owl, the Greater Sooty Owl and the Boobook. The Powerful Owl (*Ninox strenua*) is now rare, probably as a consequence of declining habitat, because this is one owl that hunts in trees. It looks like a wandjina, with two round staring eyes set in a black mask, which tapers to a sudden sharp point. The Greater Sooty Owl (*Tyto tenebricosa*) has an owlier face, with a heart-shaped mask. The Boobook (*Ninox boobook*) is smaller, between twenty-five and thirty-five centimetres tall, with big greeny-yellow eyes set under frowning golden brows. It likes to sit and watch for prey from the windows made by the interlocking roots of the strangler figs. I would be lying if I said I had seen any of these in the wild, but I have heard them all. The nocturnal hunter I know best, having seen it by night and day, and rescued it from mobbing magpies, is the Tawny Frogmouth (*Podargus strigoides*). It too I hear regularly, sounding its soft deep ooom-ooom. When I have supper on the verandah it often perches at the edge of the field of light, waiting for groggy insects, tame as you like. We try to tell ourselves that it is the rarer version, the Marbled Frogmouth (*Podargus ocellatus*), and it certainly has the necessary tuft of feathers over its bill, but it isn't.

We can't leave our hunting birds without considering the kingfisher family. Everybody knows the kookaburra, though very few are aware that kookaburras come in several species. Our is the Blue-winged Kookaburra, *Dacelo leachii*, which cannot manage to laugh. It starts up a kind of manic gargling which builds for a few seconds and then collapses into a gravelly burble. Then there are our Azure Kingfishers (*Alcedo azurea azurea*), that nest in the creek bank. They feed largely on yabbies, freshwater crayfish, which they catch and take to a designated dining rock where they dissect them, leaving a collection of empty blue claws for me to find. Our Forest Kingfisher, *Todiramphus macleayi*, is apparently a summer visitor. It makes its nest in arboreal termite nests. One fisher-bird I never expected to see at Cave Creek was a cormorant. I was scrambling along the creek, pulling out Impatiens and Mist Weed, when I became aware that something was flapping just out of sight around a bend. I waded into the creek until I could see round the bend, and was astonished to see a single Little Pied Cormorant (*Microcarbo melanoleucos*), apparently fishing in water that was no more than a foot or two deep. I watched as it dived and swam until it eventually popped out of the water onto a sunlit rock where it hung out its wings to dry, as all cormorants do.

Large birds nobody has much time for are our Brush-turkeys (*Alectura lathami*). They tend to hang around the car park scavenging for scraps, and scuttling clumsily out of the way of the traffic. I've seen tourists throw stones at them, apparently under the impression that pelting turkeys is one of the legitimate amusements afforded by the national park. Gardeners hate them because they scrape and scratch to build up a large nest mound of leaf litter, destroying cherished planting schemes and turning neat suburban plots into fowl yards. I love the Cave Creek turkeys, not merely because their tails are attached sideways, but also because the first verification I had of my belief that it was possible to rebuild a rainforest was when the turkeys moved into our very first planting and made a huge mound. In the car park they are abject, greasy-looking creatures, but in the forest, where they are truly wild and very timid, they are glossy and their naked heads bright red. If you hear something scraping and rustling in the forest, it is bound to be a turkey. If something bites the head off the wildflowers you have transplanted to your rainforest garden, it will be a turkey. For a few weeks one winter I was accompanied everywhere I walked by a male Brush-turkey resplendent in full mating rig. If he was foraging in the garden when I set off he would trot along behind me; if he wasn't, he would catch me up. If I stopped, he stopped. He caused me some anxiety when he gobbled up a large slab of soap he found in the outdoor laundry, but it didn't seem to do him any harm.

When he was maundering about how nice birds are, O'Reilly must have quite forgotten about cuckoos, which lay their eggs in the nests of other birds, often damaging any eggs they find already there. When the cuckoo egg hatches, the intruder nestling may throw out the host birds' eggs or nestlings. The phenomenon of kleptoparasitism is not of course confined to birds. There are cuckoo bees, and cuckoo wasps as well. The true rainforest cuckoo is the Shining Bronze Cuckoo (*Chrysococcyx lucidus*); the female lays as many as sixteen eggs, one each in sixteen different nests of smaller species: thornbills, wrens, flycatchers and honeyeaters. We also have the Brush Cuckoo (*Cacomantis variolosus*) and the Fan-tailed Cuckoo (*C. flabelliformis*). The Channel-billed Cuckoo (*Scythrops novaehollandiae*) grows to between fifty-eight and sixty-five centimetres, making it the biggest brood parasite on earth. The male will fly over the nest of a sitting magpie, crow, currawong or butcherbird, until the occupants come out to drive him away, when his mate will slip into the nest and lay her egg. When hatched the chick is altricial, that is, helpless, blind and naked, but within weeks it will be bigger than the host bird whose own nestlings will not have survived. The genus Scythrops, so named by John Latham, is monotypic, and seems to be no kin to cuckoos proper at all. They eat insects; the Channel-billed Cuckoo eats fruit, especially figs and mistletoe berries. It tends to keep company with figbirds and cuckoo-shrikes.

Two birds I see often foraging in the rainforest garden are the Grey Shrike Thrush (*Colluricincla harmonica*) and the Bassian Thrush (*Zoothera lunulata*). A forager I didn't expect to see is the Rufous Scrub-bird (*Atrichornis rufescens*). One evening, when I dawdled too long on my walk and found dusk overtaking me, I startled a bird that flew up and landed a few yards ahead. I kept coming, walking at a slow and even pace, and it continued to forage, poking around under the fallen leaves rather than flicking them away. The low light made it hard to see but, as I turned away, it uttered its loud whip-cracking call. It is one bird that has all but disappeared as its coastal rainforest habitat has been built over. To see a Rufous Scrub-bird thriving at Cave Creek is worth every penny that the rainforest has cost me.

From the beginning of settlement Australians have loved and hated cockatoos. The first Moreton Bay settlers lost no time in catching them, taming them, and teaching them to speak, and not simply because good talkers were worth a considerable amount of money. Every day the Brisbane newspapers carried advertisements begging for the return of lost and stolen cockatoos, offering large rewards, as much sometimes as for a dog or a horse. Within months, though the general attachment to pet cockies kept on growing, a different note began to be heard. Cockatoos en masse had turned out to be a serious pest, capable of destroying an entire crop of grain in a single evening. While caged individuals were loved and fussed over, wild cockatoos were being killed in all kinds of ruthless and inventive ways. In 1867 the *Brisbane Courier* ran a dramatic account of the poisoning of a huge flock of white cockatoos by spreading grain soaked in a solution of vinegar and strychnine: 'As lie the thickly-strewn apples ere they are gathered into the press, so under that tree lay the little snowy mounds, each of which had been a white cockatoo . . . Far and wide wherever they winged their flight, there fell their dead; and the dingoes and the crows feasted on their bodies, and died.' (*BC*, 16 March)

Most farmers contented themselves with shooting as many cockatoos as they could, greatly though they resented the cost of powder and shot. As one farmer complained:

> Cockatoos keep us busy watching the little patch of early corn, which is now ripening. Early in the morning and late in the evening they visit us in clouds, their horrible screeching and cawing being equally as irritating an annoyance to the farmer as was ever a bluebottle fly to an editor. Gun in hand you may follow them from tree to tree, round and round your farm, until, wearied, tired and annoyed, you let fly one barrel after the other right at them. (*BC*, 11 January 1868)

Drought in the inland made a bad situation worse as the birds were driven towards the ranges and the coast in search of food (*BC*, 29 May 1868). All kinds of bird-scaring mechanisms were devised but nothing worked. The cockatoos were simply too intelligent. If a scarecrow was placed in a field, the cockatoos would watch it and bide their time. As soon as they registered the fact that the figure didn't move, they simply returned and resumed feeding. In 1877 the first calls for legislation to deal with the cockatoo 'plague' began to be heard (*BC*, 5 May).

The pest cockatoos were mainly white. Far rarer were the black, which were greatly prized as novelties. The newspapers of 1866 carried reports of 'a handsome black cockatoo from Port Denison', rejoicing that '. . . as this bird is extremely rare, it will form an admirable item for export . . .' (*BC*, 11 October) Black cockatoos were said to be selling in England 'for as much as sixty guineas per pair' (*BC*, 30 October).

At Cave Creek we usually see Yellow-tailed Black Cockatoos (*Calyptorhynchus funereus funereus*). They were first described by George Shaw, head keeper of the British Museum, who was working from a specimen from the collection of Sir Hans Sloane. He named it *Psittacus funereus*; French zoologist Anselme Gaëtan Desmarest renamed the genus in 1826 Calyptorhynchus, meaning 'covered beak' (39:21). John Gould called it the Funereal Cockatoo. Its range extends along the Dividing Range from Wilson's Promontory to Cape York.

In most years Yellow-tailed Black Cockatoos have nested in the eucalypts on the top of the ridge to the west of Cave Creek. We generally see them in winter when they come to dig out the larvae of cossid moths and longhorn beetles from their tunnels under the bark of old trees, bringing their newly fledged offspring with them. You hear these family groups before you see them, chuckling and chattering to each other, all the while cracking and crunching through bark and wood. As you peer up into the branches you will see a bright black or brown eye peering down quizzically. They will let you get quite close, as they keep up what seems to be a commentary on who and what you are, for the benefit of the younger generation. As they live for maybe forty years the littl'uns have time to learn. We most often see them flying high through the mountains in formation, screaming 'Yeee-ow!', usually before rain.

The genus Calyptorhynchus has now been divided into two subgenera, *Calyptorhynchus Calyptorhynchus*, and *C. Zanda*, to which the Yellow-tailed Black Cockatoos belong. Our Sulphur-Crested Cockatoos used to be simply *Cacatua sulphurea*, and are now *Cacatua cacatua sulphurea*. These are all in the family Cacatuidae in the order Psittaciformes, which includes as well the Strigopidae of New Zealand, and the parrots. Parrots have besides the obvious parrot face, two claws facing frontwards and two back, a feature called zygodactyly.

Altogether more than a hundred bird species have been observed at Cave Creek. I would happily write about all of them but this book has to end somewhere. You may be wondering if, now that the canopy is closing, I still see the Regent Bowerbird who persuaded me to buy the land at Cave Creek. During the big rains of December 2010, Regent Bowerbirds came every day to the top of the biggest quandong I can see from the verandah. I have seen an extraordinary variety of birds playing in that tree, but the Regent is the one that, when we have big rain, comes every day to groom himself, combing the rainwater through every dazzling feather, as I eat breakfast on the verandah a hundred yards away. His wives and juveniles come with him, and sometimes other males, till there are five or six in the tree together. What can they be doing? What explanation can there be for this socialising? All I can hope is that I will live long enough to find out.

THE INHABITANTS: FURRY

There is no superstar apex predator roaming Cave Creek, no snow leopard, no panther. We just might have a tiger, a marsupial tiger. The last live specimens of the Australian thylacine, now presumed to be extinct, were found in Tasmania, but its image recurs in Aboriginal cave painting from widely separated parts of mainland Australia. It prefers woodland, makes itself a nest in dense undergrowth, hunts by night and avoids extremes of temperature. If the marsupial tiger survives anywhere, the Border Ranges would be the place. Stories of sightings abound.

In 1894 Carl Lentz was hunting with his brother on Tallai Mountain, when his dogs ran into a thicket. Lentz, expecting some bigger game than usual, loaded his gun with 'swoon drops' and waited.

> All at once a limb bent down with the weight of something heavy on my side of the tree. Then I saw a big strange animal's head appear out of the thick foliage. It was about to jump towards me, so I quickly fired and it fell with a hard bump only two yards off. It had just killed and half devoured a native bear. We tied its legs together with tough vines and stuck a long pole through them, by which we carried it home about half a mile. It was heavy. I intended taking it to Nerang, ten miles away, by pack horse the next day, but owing to heavy rain that night I could not cross the creek. I intended sending it by train to Brisbane for the Museum so we measured and skinned it. From tip of nose to end of tail, it was 6 ft, height of shoulder 25 inches, around chest 23 inches.

It was strongly developed on the front quarters, and it had two extra long and sharp fang teeth, besides the four ordinary incisor teeth, puce coloured eyes with five very short, bright, orange coloured haired rings around them. Its whole forehead was the colour of sulphur, which made its whole dial luminous when it looked towards you in the dark. I saw one close at night since, that's how I know. It had round ears of pale fleshy colour, a long thin coat of dark brown hair, under that he had a short thick coat of light pale blue-grey, and white stripes downwards, also bright yellow spots which all shone through the long thin coat, this made it appear a brindle colour at a distance. It looked very pretty close by. Its tail was covered with long black hair underneath that, [a] white and blue-grey ring, an inch wide. It was a magnificent specimen, a male, the size of an Alsatian dog.

If the animal was some kind of thylacine, it is slightly odd that Lentz while noticing that it was male, didn't notice that it had a pouch drawn up over its genitals. The skin never made it to the museum in Brisbane, possibly because in the humid conditions Lentz was not able to prevent its deterioration.

William Duncan told Lentz that he had had a similar experience when he was timber-getting on the Little Nerang.

One mid-day when he got to the camp to boil up his meat was gone. He had hung it on the ridge pole out of reach of the dingoes. He had two natives along on that occasion . . . [they] searched and found the bag all ripped up. They said it was punchum, a very big cat-like animal.

The word 'punchum' can be found in Gresty's word list for Numinbah as 'punchimgun' interpreted by Gresty to mean 'Dasyurus', that is, the 'Tiger Quoll', nowadays the Spotted-tailed Quoll (*Dasyurus maculatus maculatus*). The Geytenbeeks' Gidabal dictionary (1971) records the same word as 'banjdjim'. Lentz's account continues:

They advised him not to stay there by himself, as that fella would sneak onto him while he was asleep, tear out his throat and suck his blood. A black would never camp by himself, when they were known to be in the vicinity. He went straight home and bought a blood-hound and a double barrel shotgun . . . On arrival back at the camp by moonlight, the dog treed a big animal right away. It sat in the fork of a red oak, out of reach, its eyes glowed like red hot fire coals. He fired both charges into it. It jumped down onto the dog and was worrying it, so he bashed it over the head with the gunstock, killing it . . . He said the animal was the size of a massive dog.

Bushmen specialise in tall stories. It is difficult to imagine a blood-hound treeing anything, let alone a thylacine. It should not be forgotten however that both these accounts pre-date any suggestion that the thylacine was on the verge of extinction. In 1923 the assistant government geologist Sydney Skertchly contributed an article to the *Brisbane Courier* in response to the news of Wilkins's Australia and Islands Expedition.

I am glad somebody is in earnest going to probe the truth of the belief in the existence of a larger tiger cat in Queensland than has yet gladdened scientific eyes . . .

As my contribution, here is an extract from one of my 1913 note-books: 'Near Mt. Nimmel, there is a gorge; just below a precipice in Springbrook, which the blacks would not enter as there was a big "tiger cat", large as a big dog, that would kill man or dog. No living black had seen it; but their fathers had told them of it. Can this be a reminiscence of Thylacoleo, or more probably of the Tasmanian Devil?' (Skertchly)

'Thylacoleo' was the name given by Sir Richard Owen to the marsupial carnivore species of which fossils had been discovered at Lake Colongulac and on the Darling Downs. Skertchly goes on:

It is described as having great teeth. The blacks used to try and kill it by enticing it out, by taking a dog, and making it howl; but it always got away; anyhow, they were never successful. James Ferguson, timber getter, reported this to the late Mr. E. Cooper, who told me.

Here is another extract from the same book: 'About the year 1906 a big "tiger cat" took a lot of fowls from Mrs. Richter's, at Nerang. It was as big as a terrier dog, and her dog would not tackle it. It was shot, and was yellow with black spots. What became of the skin Mr. E. J. Cooper, my informant, does not know.' I have just asked him about it, and he said, 'If these good people like to go to Springbrook, they may get one.' When I was up there two years ago Ben Gillespie (a fine bushman) pointed out to me a log on which he saw one sitting a few days previously. He saw it several times. My wonderful timber-getting friend, Jack Duncan, who pretty well lived with the blacks as a boy, has told me much of the beast, though even he, who has spent all his life in our mountain scrub, never saw one.

Jack Duncan was a son of the aforementioned William Duncan, and a brother of Sandy Duncan, the discoverer of the Natural Bridge. The Spotted-tailed Quoll, largest of the marsupial carnivores known to survive at Cave Creek, might be marked like the mythical 'tiger', but it is very much smaller. In 1965, Elspeth Huxley described the quoll for the English readers of her book, *Their Shining Eldorado*:

Attractive little sharp-nosed brown-and-cream spotted creatures, smaller than an average cat, to which they are no relation, they are among the few real killers in Australia. They are marsupials and will carry as many as eight tiny joeys in the pouch. Now they are becoming very rare, because of the destruction of the forests in which they dwell. (357)

I have not seen a quoll at Cave Creek but I have come across its scats, which are unmistakeable. Quolls use communal latrine sites, usually in rocky country, where they leave twisted turds held together by fur and feathers. Unfortunately I have seen the quoll's principal predator, the introduced fox, quite often. Because of the presence of the quolls, we can't bait the foxes. When the quoll is threatened it opens its mouth and utters a piercing scream. It tends to vocalise as well when it encounters other quolls. At night the Cave Creek Forest resounds with shrieks and howls, of owls, of prey animals and of quolls. Awareness of the quolls and of the threats to their survival is growing.

In July 2009 eighty people responded to an invitation from the Gold Coast City Council to attend a Quoll Discovery Day arranged by Wildlife Queensland at the Numinbah Valley School of Arts.

The Cave Creek version of the Long-Nosed Bandicoot (*Perameles nasuta*) is silver-grey; we find signs of its activities on every square metre of the property, and sometimes we find it, dead, with a three-cornered tear in its side, or with signs of owl or quoll predation at throat or anus. One evening I surprised two juveniles who fled at my approach, revealing hinder parts that were very clearly barred, which is not supposed to be the case with *Perameles nasuta*, which is not supposed to be silver-grey either. We have seen the Northern Brown Bandicoot (*Isoodon macrourus*) alive but never found a corpse, which suggests that it is doing something to outwit the local predators, all except the python, which swallows it whole. We watch every day for other members of old Gondwanan families, without success. The vulnerable Long-nosed Potoroo (*Potorous tridactylus*), which digs down like a bandicoot to find fungi, roots, tubers and larvae, is known from Murwillumbah and the Scenic Rim, as is the equally vulnerable Rufous Rat-kangaroo (*Aepyprymnus rufescens*), but none of us has yet seen either of them at Cave Creek. I live in hope.

The marsupial I know best is the Yellow-footed Antechinus (*Antechinus flavipes*). This little creature has excreted in every drawer, every box, every bag, every pocket, in the house. (I use the word excrete because it pisses and shits in the one wet package.) One excreted particularly copiously in my Sydney University D.Litt. hood even though it was hidden away in a dress bag. As I sit reading in the evening, antechinuses venture into the room to wolf the moths that ricochet off the light battens and skitter round the floor on their backs. Antechinuses are curiously constructed in that they can unhinge their various limbs and make themselves rectangular; when it comes to limbo-dancing under a door they can flatten themselves until they are no thicker than a credit card with a minute paw at each corner. They dance over me as I lie in bed, fight battles in my slippers, all the time vocalising, zzzzt, zzzzt like fizzing electric cables. I've lost count of the number of times I've opened a drawer to have an antechinus leap out and run up my arm. One day I was so put out to find an antechinus in a filing cabinet that I slammed the drawer shut with a deafening clang. When I opened the drawer an hour or two later the tiny creature was lying in it, quite dead. I hope it wasn't felled by a lethal level of noise. It may just have been a male.

When the winter solstice is past, the male antechinus begins to think about sex, and then about nothing but sex. He forgets to eat, prowling the neighbourhood incessantly, desperately seeking a receptive female. Stress hormones drain his body of muscle and fat. His immune system breaks down. When he meets his receptive female he acquits himself of a bout of acrobatic sexual intercourse that may last up to twelve hours, until he rolls off dead. Of all the possible adaptations to a harsh environment this seems one of the harshest. In the laboratory scientists succeeded in keeping male antechinuses alive after mating, only to discover that when the season began the next year they produced no semen. Their testes were shrivelled 'a bit like those of 80- or 90-year-old men', according to zoologist Pat Woolley. Woolley is deservedly famous for her work on the morphology of the dasyurid penis, which resulted in the removal of five of twelve antechinus species and their identification as members of new genera, because of basic structural differences in penis shape.

The male antechinus having fulfilled his reproductive duty is not allowed to hang around while his mate gestates her dozen young, which travel through her fur from vagina to pouch after about a month, stay feeding in the pouch for five weeks, and are then left in the nest while she forages on her own. After three months they will be weaned, unless she eats them first. The female antechinus does not eat her offspring because she is hungry. If she eats any, she will eat either females or males, never both. It is thought that raising males, who grow faster, may be less onerous for her, while raising females who will be around when next she comes into season will diminish her own chances of successful mating. As she will not live for a third season, the issue becomes unimportant in her second. In 1960 *Antechinus flavipes* was bred in the laboratory to see if it could serve as a laboratory animal; it was deemed too difficult to handle and too slow to reproduce, and so escaped that fate (Marlow).

The Common Planigale (*Planigale maculata*) is another, slightly bigger, carnivorous marsupial mouse that lives in the rainforest and never comes into the house. It is not, as is claimed on many a website, the world's smallest marsupial.

Three species of gliders have been found in the Cave Creek Forest, the Sugar Glider (*Petaurus breviceps*), the Squirrel Glider (*P. norfolcensis*) and the Yellow-bellied Glider (*P. australis*). The odd thing about all of these is that people who consider themselves to be animal-lovers are prepared to keep these flying creatures grounded in captivity. The Sugar Glider is the smallest and commonest of the Australian species. By spreading its patagium, the membrane that stretches from its fifth finger to its first toe, as it launches itself, the airborne Sugar Glider can travel up to 150 metres through the air, steering itself by altering the angle of its legs and tail. It is a highly social animal, living in family groups of up to eight adults plus the young of the current season's mating, and very active, foraging for up to 80 per cent of its waking time. This wonderful creature is now being bred in numbers for the American pet trade. A pet glider will never know the joy of flight and nights spent foraging in the scented canopy.

The Squirrel Glider, slightly bigger and slightly less cute than the Sugar Glider, is not so far being bred as a pet, but it is kept in captivity. According to the Mammal Society of Australia 'A group of up to 4 Squirrel Gliders can quite happily live in a suspended cage 4x4x10 with the floor of the cage being three foot off the floor.' How this esteemed organisation, which is dedicated to providing information regarding 'keeping our native Fauna in captivity', measures happiness is nowhere explained. Poor old *P. australis* is considered vulnerable in the wild and is therefore sometimes doomed to be kept in captivity as it is at the David Fleay Wildlife Park on the Gold Coast, where 'dozens of threatened species are kept' 'for research, breeding and education'.

Cave Creek is supposed to be home as well to the tiniest glider of all, the Feathertail Glider (*Acrobates pygmaeus*), no bigger than the smallest mouse. This little creature too, though its conservation status is of least concern, is another being bred in captivity. The first European zoo to be successful in breeding it was at Poznan in Poland; Polish Feathertail Gliders are now being supplied to zoos all over Europe. Though you might dream of travelling from one zoo to another to collect them and bring them home, in Australia it is against the law to release into the wild any animal reared in captivity.

All four glider species live in the Cave Creek canopy, on a diet of gum, nectar, pollen, insects, manna and honeydew, and seldom come to the ground. They are said to prefer eucalypts for their abundant nectar, which they need all year round, but our rainforest trees also flower at all times of the year, and the canopy affords plenty of dry nest sites in even the pouringest rain. I would be a liar if I said that I had ever seen any of these little creatures going about their business at night far above my sleeping head; I see them often as patches of roiled fur on local roads. One of the most powerful motives for rebuilding habitat in Australia is the longing to reverse the persecu- tion, suffering and annihilation that is the lot of so many Australian mammal species, from the tiniest to the biggest. They are all, even the gentlest, resilient and tough. Give them a chance and they will take it.

Among the most cruelly persecuted of Australian mammals were possums, which, from the early years of European settlement, were classed as vermin. A correspondent wrote to *The Argus* on 21 March 1857:

On moonlit nights especially, they pour down in great numbers, when neither corn, wheat, fruit, nor vegetables escape their attacks, and in many instances the amount of damage done is really serious . . . owing to the disappearance of the blacks, with whom the opossum is the principal article of food, they have increased to an astonishing extent. It is no uncommon thing, we are told, to shoot forty or fifty in one night, and the fear is, unless some means of extermination are adopted, they will become almost the sole occupants of certain portions of the bush.

The belief that the extermination of the Aborigine had led to an explosion in the possum population was held by many.

The Mountain Brushtail Possum or, as it is now to be known, the Short-eared Possum (*Trichosaurus caninus*) that makes its home at Cave Creek is black with a rather plain doggy face and a big wet pink nose. Although Queensland possums had a slight advantage in that they were usually smaller and their skins less luxurious than those of animals from the cooler south, awareness of the 'opossum threat' led to more and more clearing of the forests that were known to harbour them. Loggers noticed that possums and gliders leapt from trees as they were being felled, while koalas clung on all the way to the ground. Thousands of animals must have perished in agony when they fired the felled wood, and yet enough survived to demolish the monocrops for which the native vegetation had been destroyed.

Killing native animals was one of the few amusements available in the bush. In 1911 a letter to the *Brisbane Courier* lamented: 'It is the universal and deplorable habit of men and youths to go out with rifles and remorselessly slay every native animal they see – Australians like themselves – simply because it is guilty of the heinous crime of being alive'. (21 June)

Trade in native animal skins had been going on at least since the mid-1870s when Queensland traders began advertising for skins 'kangaroo, wallaby, native bear, pademelon, opossum and squirrel'. When the prices for possum skins were good, farmworkers were only too ready to down tools. In 1902 a correspondent of the *Brisbane Courier* asked: 'Why should I work for a squatter at a pound a week and tucker when I can earn £3 a week and tucker and be my own boss at possum snaring?' (13 June)

Snaring or 'possum-choking' saved the cost of ammunition. The snares were simple affairs of twisted twine and wire. The usual method of setting a snare was to fell a sapling, attach the snare to it with a running noose, and prop it against a tree. The possum almost invariably chose the sapling as the easiest means of getting up the tree, and so ran its head into the snare, to be found hanging by its neck when the hunter made his rounds. He would then finish it off with a sharp blow on the head and free it from the noose. When cyanide became more readily available owing to its routine use in mining operations, possum hunters began to use it to poison water-holes. Cattle, horses and sheep as well as all the native species that used the waterhole would perish, but nobody cared because the profits were large. Hundreds of possums could be taken from a single poisoned waterhole. The practice was outlawed, but it continued nonetheless.

By 1911 the wholesale torture of possums had begun to have a perceptible effect on numbers (*BC*, 6 September). The Queensland government declared closed season on possums from October to June because the fur industry itself was in danger of collapse, if possums were not to be given an opportunity to rebuild their numbers. When times were hard, as they were regularly in the early years of the century, labour unions pressured the government to allow an open season. Supporters of the possum pointed out that young are to be found in the mothers' pouches at all times of the year, and demanded a total ban on possum killing, to no avail. As long as the price was right, the slaughter would go on. 'Opossum skins are worth anything from 25/- to 50/- a dozen in the Sydney market, according to variety and quality, and when it is stated that as many as 100,000 skins are sold in Brisbane at one time, to say nothing of those that are sent to Sydney, the slaughter that is going on may be realised' (*BC*, 24 September 1910). During the drought of 1915 an open season was brought in specifically so that dairy farmers could survive by snaring possums. In 1922 a million possum skins were sold in the Queensland fur market, and in 1923, 1,200,000 (*BC*, 31 March 1924).

Few voices were raised in defence of the possum but the persecution of the koala caused uproar. There could be no pretence that the koala was a pest; everyone knew that 'native bears' though numerous did not damage crops of any kind. In 1884 Carl Lentz saw 'nine bears on one little gum tree . . . the bush was full of koalas in those days'. In those early days Henry Stephens could ride the half-dozen kilometres between Tagabalam and the Pocket and see twenty-nine koalas (Hall *et al.*, 19–20). A Bill to protect the Native Bear introduced by the Hon. W. Villiers Brown in the Queensland Legislative Assembly in November 1904 failed for lack of time (*BC*, 24 November 1904; 4 February 1905). By 1910 'the inoffensive native bear ha[d] almost disappeared from most parts of Queensland'. Even so, in 1915 the Queensland government announced an open season for koalas as well as possums. The justification was that impoverished families could use the skins as currency to buy food. Readers of the *Brisbane Courier*, who did not include struggling bushies, gave instant voice to their disapproval. A correspondent identified simply as 'Sympathy' wrote to the editor on 22 July:

I can't speak for other districts but in this one (Wide Bay) mostly every female bear has a baby on her back. Only this morning I was driving on a bush road and saw a bear with a baby on its back. The harmless creature looked at me so pitifully. I drove on, but not half a mile away I heard a shot, then another, and drove back and saw a scalper had shot the poor brute, but it got into a limb of the tree and stuck there, though dead with the baby clasped in its arms. I lectured the man, but his reply was, 'The season is open'. We know it is, but I am afraid it is the wrong season, and if this goes on the children following us will never see a native bear; they will be wiped out. Though I did not see it I was told by a settler that he had come across a dead mother skinned, and the baby a few yards away crying.

Despite the outcry a second open season was allowed in 1917. A third, in 1919, saw more than a million koalas shot, poisoned or hanged (Evans, 168). For eight years thereafter the koala was protected in Queensland, though skins procured illegally were still being traded, according to the retiring president of the Royal Geographical Society of New South Wales, J. R. Kinghorn, usually as wombat skin (*BC*, 23 July 1928). In 1927, to almost universal disgust, the Queensland government announced an open season on koalas for the month of August. As a character in scores of children's stories, the koala had become the favourite pet of Australian children, bringing gladness 'to many a lonely little heart in the back-blocks where pleasures are very few and far between' (*BC*, 19 July 1927). Bunyip Bluegum, hero of *The Magic Pudding* by Norman Lindsay, published in 1918, is the best-known of a succession of koala heroes. On 28 July 1927 'Con. D' thought fit to impersonate a koala in the *Brisbane Courier*:

> I do not hamper the white man's work
>   or live on his fields of grain;
> But I'm doomed to die the dingo's death,
>   for his greed and gain.
> And the tall gums whisper a sad goodbye –
> Your heritage lost, now doomed to die,
> For Fashion you must be slain.

A catastrophic decline in koala numbers was already common knowledge; as early as February 1927 the first suggestions that a disease might be affecting the stressed koala population begin to appear in the popular press. In August all the scientific societies in Brisbane joined forces in a deputation to the premier begging him to rescind his order, to no avail. On 15 December 1927 'Bushwoman' wrote to the editor of the *Brisbane Courier* that 'an open season for politicians would be more in accord with the feelings of the public'. Attempts to place a federal embargo on export of koala skins came too late. In that single month of August 1927 597,985 koalas were killed in Queensland, providing skins to the value of £130,595, of which the state government got 5 per cent (*BC*, 15 December).

By 1931 most people had understood that the true challenge was to re-establish the koala in its old habitat, but according to the Wildlife Preservation Society (*BC*, 7 December) there were already so few koalas to be found in the wild that this was proving almost impossible. Since then the koalas' predicament has steadily worsened. The collapse of koala numbers has entailed a loss of genetic variability and lowered resistance. As the forest ecology has been affected by dieback, and by logging and clearing and subsequent Lantana infestation, the koalas' nutritional status has fallen, and they have become vulnerable to organisms that thitherto they had been able to live with, including Chlamydia and *Cryptococcus neoformans*. Now a retrovirus has turned up and is integrating with the koala genome; the immune deficiency syndrome that it is thought to cause is transmitted not only from one animal to another but genetically, from parent to offspring. As the virus has been found in 80 per cent of the animals that Queensland researchers could get their hands on, *Phascolarctos cinereus* will probably be extinct there within twenty years.

For a mere $8.50 added to the adult entry fee of $17.10 visitors to the David Fleay Wildlife Park, now managed by the Queensland Environmental Protection Agency 'as an environmental education resource', may enter the Koala Contact Zone and take pictures of each other clutching a koala. At Currumbin Sanctuary too you can inflict an embrace upon a koala, but it will cost more than twice as much. In 2009 researchers at the University of Queensland published their conclusion that acute chlamydiosis in koalas is a manifestation of reduced resistance resulting from the stress associated with loss of habitat and human encroachment. And yet people who call themselves animal lovers consider themselves entitled to force their attentions on helpless captive koalas simply because they have handed over money. In his *Histoire Naturelle* the Comte de Buffon accused the koala of 'Slowness, stupidity, neglect of its own body and habitual sadness'. He went on: 'These sloths are the lowest form of existence in the order of animals with flesh and blood: one more defect and they would not have existed.' Even Gerald Durrell called koalas boring. The mildness of the koala continues to be misunderstood and exploited to this day.

One evening when a clamour of butcherbirds announced that something was afoot, I looked out of the kitchen door to see a young koala striding past on all four legs. When she saw me she shinned up a young Red Bean tree. When the tree began to bow beneath her weight, she stopped climbing and sat there, well within reach, wishing herself invisible. To give her a break, I went inside and shut the door. She had a long way to go before she would reach another koala colony that might accept her, and many a python lay in wait. The next time I saw a koala, it had just been regurgitated by a python, in two parcels, one a cylinder of fur and the other the koala's astonishing alimentary canal which even a python could not digest. In 2011 the Queensland EPA (now the Department of Environment and Heritage Protection) sent me a letter informing me that the property at Cave Creek had been deemed suitable for revegetation with sclerophylls for koala habitat under State Planning Policy 2/10. On the map to be seen on their website, the only area nearby where koalas are known to live was coloured pink as 'unsuitable'. Only one of the eucalypt species they recommended would do well at CCRRS, where it already grows as an occasional on the higher slopes. Not for the first time I wondered if the right hand of the Queensland EHP had the faintest idea what the left hand was doing.

'Did you know,' said Jenny, who had been reading this over my shoulder, 'that baby koalas have to eat a special pap from their mother's gut when they're being weaned? That's how they get the right microbes in their gut to break down eucalyptus leaves. It's amazing really, because eucalyptus leaves contain all sorts of terpenes and phenols and are toxic to most herbivores. We know from the fossil record that koalas were originally rainforest animals, so they must have adapted as the rainforests retreated before the onward march of the eucalypts.'

'They're classed as vulnerable round here,' I said. 'You're not allowed to interfere with them.'

'Unless they're at Dream World,' said Jenny sourly.

'That's something I just don't get. Why is handling marsupials allowed? Handling causes them stress. Stress can kill them.'

'Not just marsupials,' said Jenny. 'Stress can kill virtually any wild animal, but marsupials do seem to be specially sensitive.'

'What actually happens?'

'Suppose the animal is being chased or struggling. The enzymes in the muscles start pumping out lactic acid. This rapidly builds up in the bloodstream, the body pH changes and the heart falters. Muscles die, releasing myoglobin, which damages the renal tubule.'

'Multiple organ failure.'

'Quite. Sometimes the process is slow, a week or more, and sometimes it's sudden and catastrophic.'

'I remember when kids at school brought in joeys they found, they were always strangely hot and floppy and they had a peculiar vinegary smell. No matter how hard we tried we simply couldn't keep them alive.'

'In those days you wouldn't even have had any suitable food for them, so it's no wonder you killed them.'

I winced. 'Remember *Skippy the Bush Kangaroo*? He was actually a female wallaby or rather lots of female wallabies. Sometimes they didn't even last a day on the set.'

'Marsupials can go into shock from events as insignificant as being injected or darted.'

'I knew it! Some woman who was studying pademelons rang up to ask if she could come here and study ours. She told me she was working on establishing the pademelons' optimum range. She wanted to trap them, weigh them and take blood from them. I'm afraid I got rather cross with her. The poor beasts would have the shock of being trapped, and the hours of trying to get out of the trap, and then they'd be taken out of the trap, and put in a sack to be weighed, and then restrained while she took blood. Then she'd let them go, lost to follow-up. I felt rather guilty about refusing her access at the time, but I'm glad now that I acted on my instinct.'

At the time I explained to the student that I wasn't creating habitat so that the animals could be badgered for no good reason. She told me that as well as Red-necked Pademelons (*Thylogale thetis*) there were Red-legged ones (*T. stigmatica*) at CCRRS. These are listed as vulnerable in New South Wales, where they were never numerous, the caldera being the southern limit of their range, so I disbelieved her. That was before I realised that more than one kind of pademelon was taking turns to graze in the rainforest garden. The one that tended to nibble at the vegetation like a sheep with her head down was the Red-necked; the one that used her hands to pick up fallen leaves and fruit and carry them to her mouth as a kangaroo does was the Red-legged. The first pademelons I ever saw were grazing on the lawn at O'Reilly's on Lamington Plateau, which led me to believe that they preferred exotic pasture grass to rainforest vegetation. Now that I see them every day I know that they are more likely to reject exotic grasses for rainforest groundcovers and fallen fruits if they can get them. They also chew their way through tougher material, palm fronds, lomandras and sedges.

Most rainforest animals have evolved to eat a fibrous diet, which is why they should not be given picnic scraps, which can cause a bowel blockage and painful death. The received wisdom is that pademelons live on rainforest verges and venture into cleared areas to graze, never more than 100 metres from cover. They are dependent upon their own tracks, which are like tunnels through the rainforest, through which they bound away from trouble using their back legs, whereas otherwise they tend to move on all fours.

I would see more of the Cave Creek marsupials if I went spotlighting at night, but I hate the way the dazzled animals freeze in terror. I'm most likely to see macropods on the first day or two after I arrive, while the animals still think they have the forest to themselves. I was on a track on the forest edge at sunset, when I rounded a corner and surprised two Swamp Wallabies (*Wallabia bicolor*) who stared at me in astonishment. I kept still and talked to them softly. They craned their big ears to hear what noise I might be making. Big black eyes gazed at me out of pointed faces that were sooty from ear to nose, with cheeks picked out with silvery-white guard hairs. The dainty hands and long feet were sooty too, but the rest of their long fur was dusted with silver. For a long moment we looked at each other as I burbled and then the wallabies took off, plunging down the slope with their heads low and their tails stretched out behind.

People working in bush regeneration may tell you that wallabies and pademelons are pests because they eat the young trees in replantings. In our forest they have eaten one tree in particular, namely *Hymenosporum flavum*, the Native Frangipani, known throughout Australia as a street tree. They strip it of young leaves and it usually recovers. Grazing by macropods is not a problem at CCRRS because of the sheer variety of species in the plantings and the scale of the operation. Native herbivores will destroy all the infant trees they find planted in narrow batters surrounded by suburban gardens full of unpalatable exotics, but in broadscale plantings their impact is negligible. When native groundcovers reappear in the place of soft weeds, the pademelons and wallabies graze on them rather than the young growth on the baby trees, and both animals and plants thrive. Pademelons have been hard on the smaller, rarer shrubs in the rainforest garden, but that is a price we are prepared to pay.

The early settlers were even less kindly disposed to macropods than they were to possums and koalas. In 1877, in response to pressure from the sheep farmers of the interior, who were convinced that kangaroos and wallabies were eating out their pastures, the Queensland government passed the first of fifteen Marsupial Destruction Acts. The first version of the act actually imposed penalties on landholders who did not kill marsupials on their properties, as well as a tax on graziers to finance the payments made to scalpers, who travelled the country, setting traps and shooting the animals. The scalper was a despised individual, 'affected by no sentient emotions, void of all romantic attachments, a pariah, an outcast, excluded among his wattle scrubs or sandalwood patches, from the outer world; practically unknown except to his fellow shooters, or the publican and store-keeper of the backwoods township' (Q, 25 May 1895, 981). As government officials didn't know one scalp from another, the scalpers found it sinfully easy to cheat them. Some got Aborigines to get the scalps for them and paid them in tobacco. And it was not only the scalpers who did their best to annihilate marsupials; by 1878 the kangaroo had become 'the common enemy of every man and boy in the bush capable of carrying and using a gun' (*BC*, 14 October). In Queensland by 1930 27 million kangaroos, wallaroos, wallabies, pademelons, kangaroo rats and bandicoots had been destroyed (Hrdina). Many species survived only in inaccessible regions like the Border Ranges. Unbelievable as it may seem, the Marsupial Destruction Act was not finally repealed until 1994.

In hilly south-east Queensland there were very few sheep farmers. The people trying to grow crops in the coastal areas south of Brisbane were up in arms about a different kind of creature, not a marsupial this time. Marsupials were the original mammals of Australia, from about 45 million years ago; the most hated creatures in Queensland were relative newcomers, placental mammals that flew across from south-east Asia about 15 million years ago, namely, bats.

The first settlers who managed to get their cosseted peach trees to set fruit were astonished and appalled when the evening sky was darkened by armies of bats appearing as if from nowhere and helping themselves. In February 1844 one observer described how they flew over Maitland for nearly half an hour in 'dense masses'. 'There was a good deal of firing at them each night, but they fly high and strong and dusk is not the best time of day for taking aim, so that very few were brought down' (*MM*, 3 February). The next year the bats came in even greater force, as more and more of their habitat was felled and burnt (*MM*, 5 February 1845). Even at night the mere sight of the bats flying overhead was greeted with gunfire from all sides. 'As old colonists will know it is the fruit . . . that attracts the "foxes" or, as some call them, the "vampyre bats"; and we can testify from experience to the havoc they make amongst the peaches,' wrote a correspondent to the *Brisbane Courier* (10 March 1863).

Australian flying foxes are not vampire bats. The commonest of them is or was the Grey-headed Flying Fox, *Pteropus poliocephalus*. The name is more than slightly perverse, because the most obvious attribute of this creature is not its greyish head but its bolero of vivid russet fur. As Joseph Bancroft told the Queensland Philosophical

Society on 25 April 1872, 'The natural food of the animal consists of the native fig and other small fruits found in the scrubs' (*BC*, 14 May). The bats were of course the original inhabitants of the land that was taken up for vineyards and orchards. Most of their forest habitat was demolished in a single generation, and the bats driven further into the inland, away from areas of high rainfall. There was no way they could survive except by returning at night to plunder orchards and gardens.

Grey-headed Flying Foxes are remarkable animals; the span of their wings, as thin and stretchy as cured tobacco leaf, is more than a metre and a half. Because the stigmas of many rainforest trees are only receptive at night, bats are the most important pollinators for at least sixty tree species. And because flying foxes travel up to fifty kilometres to find their preferred food, they are also the most important seed dispersers. They prefer to roost in tall trees on mountain streamsides 200 metres or so above sea level. On most nights they will be feeding somewhere in the forest at Cave Creek. As they hustle among the leaves, you can hear their soft chuckling and chiding. More than twenty different calls have been identified. Carers for baby flying foxes say that they are intelligent and responsive. Not that that would do them much good. Rats are intelligent and responsive too and we still consider ourselves entitled to persecute and torture them in their millions.

The early settlers knew next to nothing about their 'nightly visitors of disagreeable and injurious character' (*SMH*, 22 February 1848), whose 'voracious powers ha[d] increased tenfold over the destruction of former years' (*SMH*, 29 January 1848). They didn't know where they came from or where they went when they had finished gorging. Eventually they learnt that the bats roosted in distant camps in the scrub where by daylight they could be shot in their hundreds from point-blank range. Regular flying-fox shoots or 'battues' were organised. Parties of forty or fifty shooters travelled far into the ranges seeking out flying-fox camps. When they found trees full of sleeping bats they simply blasted them with shotguns. A few wet blankets complained that this was not sport but butchery, but they were not allowed to spoil the fun. This enthusiastic account of 'Flying Fox hunting in the Blue Mountains' appeared in the *Sydney Morning Herald* for 26 April 1860:

What a sight! literally thousands of these great bats on the wing, gyrating round high tree tops, ever and anon settling and suspending themselves by their hind feet. Then fired among and rising into the air in the utmost state of consternation yet not forsaking the accustomed roosts. The chirping, clucking and buffetting of the whole; the cries of the wounded, the report of firearms, and shouts of the men in that dense copsewood combined to make a scene rarely equalled for wildness and interest.

A correspondent wrote to the editor of the *Brisbane Courier* on 15 April 1872:

We have found out the haunts of those pests of flying foxes where they during the daytime are congregated together by many hundreds if not thousands.

About a mile or two from the German Station is a country called the Serpentine. A certain portion of this is called the Never country; here they have their home in the daytime, and as soon as the evening comes you can see them come in droves from that direction, spreading all over the district and plundering wherever they find fruit.

Let the young men from town and country fix a day for the sport . . . and come together at the German Station.

The hunters met at the German Station, which was the name commonly given to the site of the abandoned Moravian Mission of Zion's Hill (now Nundah), at 9 a.m. on the Queen's Birthday and a great time was had by all but the flying foxes. Such battues became regular occasions.

Agitation for a Flying Fox Extermination Bill began even before the Marsupial Destruction Act came into force. Farmers who organised flying-fox shoots complained of the cost of the ammunition and the difficulty of disposing of 'dray-loads' of dead bats. Others had been poisoning fruit with strychnine. Though the agitation intensified the government declined to include flying foxes in any of the revisions of the Marsupial Destruction Act, apparently because the damage done by them to the fruit crop did not affect exports and had no obvious economic consequences. The complaints of the fruitgrowers about the costs of ammunition for the battues and bounties for bat carcasses grew ever louder, and still the government failed to act (*BC*, 22 December 1874).

On 22 October 1880, the Queensland Legislative Assembly went into committee to consider amendments to the Marsupial Destruction Bill.

> Mr [Albert] Norton [member for Port Curtis] proposed an amendment having the effect of including 'all marsupials' in the operation of the bill, but subsequently withdrew the amendment it being pointed out that flying foxes could be shot in such numbers in certain localities that all the funds available under the measure would soon be exhausted . . . (*BC*, 23 October)

Nobody seemed aware that flying foxes are not marsupials. (Foraging mothers carry their small young attached to a nipple close to the wing.) George King MLA, who had sold in Japan the skins of 40,000 wallabies killed on his property at Gowrie when it was invaded by marsupials during the drought of 1877–8, moved a similar amendment, and called for a division, but there was only one other member in favour, and the motion failed. By 1884, state legislators had learned more about flying foxes. In the Legislative Council, on 29 July 1884, 'Mr. May pointed out that the bill under discussion was for the destruction of marsupials and he thought flying foxes did not belong to that order.' The honourable gentlemen made a joke of the matter. 'Mr. [Peter] Macpherson stated that as attorneys were made gentlemen by Act of Parliament, no doubt flying foxes could be converted into marsupials by the same means.'

When John F. Buckland MLA for Bulimba addressed voters at Holmview on 3 June 1886, the chairman of the meeting drew his attention 'to the fact that the farmers down in the Beenleigh district were taxed for the purpose of paying for the destruction of the marsupials for the benefit of the squatter's pocket, while they the farmers were troubled with the flying-fox pest, and he considered this vermin should have been introduced among the things for the destruction of which the government was prepared to pay' (*BC*, 5 June). Buckland had no option but to agree. The result was the empowering of the local divisional boards to raise finance for the organisation of flying-fox extermination programmes, which was in effect simply passing the buck. It was not until May 1889 that a specially convened Conference of Local Authorities in south-east Queensland passed a motion 'That the Government be requested to introduce into parliament a measure to provide for the destruction of flying foxes and noxious birds, and give power to a united local authority for the purpose'. The result was the East Moreton Flying Fox Board, which proved just as ineffectual as its antecedents.

Other remedies were tried. To those who observed the Aboriginal method of smoking flying foxes out of their roosts it was clear that 'the fumes of sulphur, burnt under the trees where the flying foxes camp, will bring them down wholesale . . . as the creatures hang in large masses like bunches of grapes, sulphur on a moderately calm day could be used effectively on them.' Orchardists tried ringing bells, leaving lamps lit all night, using various substances said to be bat-repellent, and running wires around the trees. Nothing worked. Many fruitgrowers gave up, leaving their orchards to go feral. Others invested in costly netting and went broke. Twenty years ago electric grids were introduced. These are ranks of live wires inches apart that will electrocute any bat that comes in contact; in 2001 use of these was banned, but as the ban is barely policed and the farmers were not required actually to dismantle the grids, it is thought to be widely flouted.

Grey-headed Flying Fox numbers are now in serious decline, nobody quite knows why. It has been suggested that the fall in numbers and a demonstrable shift of 300 kilometres southwards in their range are responses to climate change. Nearly 50,000 have been discovered dead on their roosts after periods when daytime temperatures reached 42 degrees Celsius. In November 2008 at nearby Canungra Bat Camp 300 baby bats were found abandoned. They were rescued and rehabilitated by a new generation of bat-carers. Roost sites are now legally protected; a recent biodiversity action plan developed for the Border Ranges suggests that a buffer zone of 200 metres must be left around any bat camp, particularly those where females gather to give birth. Meanwhile thousands of bats are injured every year by barbed wire; others become trapped in fruit-tree netting and still more are electrocuted. Even in the inner city you can see flying foxes hanging dead from power lines.

In February 2010 'an estimated 40,000 flying foxes descend[ed] on Canungra'. A local 'Vietnam veteran and retiree' complained that the bats had made him and his wife sick, that they carried E. *coli* and Giardia in their droppings. He demanded a cull. 'The only method I know of that is 100 per cent foolproof is to blow the damn things out of the sky,' he told reporters, blissfully unaware of the lesson of history.

The case against fruit bats has been recently strengthened by the identification of three bat-borne diseases: Hendra Virus, Australian Bat Lyssa Virus and Menangle Virus.

Hendra Virus (HeV) was the first to turn up, in 1994 in the Brisbane suburb of Hendra, where it killed fourteen horses. A trainer and a stable-hand caring for the affected horses also contracted the disease and the trainer died. Black and Spectacled Flying Foxes have antibodies to the disease and are assumed to be the vectors but, though many tests have been done, the way the disease is transferred is still not understood (*Australian Veterinary Journal*, 76:12). The hosts for HeV are now understood to include pet animals, mice, brush-tailed possums, bandicoots, hares, carpet pythons and a variety of blood-sucking insects including March flies. Horses continue to become infected and there is still no treatment. More than forty horses have died, seven people have contracted the disease through contact with infected horses, and four of them have died. In October 2006 a horse died of Hendra disease just over the range near Murwillumbah.

In November 1996 an animal carer was handling a Yellow-bellied Sheath-tail Bat when she received a scratch; four to five weeks later she began to show signs of a rabies-like illness, and twenty days later she died. Another woman who had been bitten by a flying fox which she was trying to detach from a terrified child four months earlier and had suffered no apparent ill effect refused post-exposure treatment only to fall ill two years on. She was admitted to hospital but died nineteen days later. In this case the virus was a lyssavirus (ABLV), from the same family as rabies.

Flying foxes are thought to be the vectors of the third bat-borne virus, which was first detected in 1997 when animals in a piggery at Menangle became ill and two of the humans looking after them came down with something like flu. Research into the bat-borne viruses goes on, but so far neither state nor federal government has voted to fund the development of a vaccine.

Perhaps the slaughter of the 1880s and 90s did have long-term consequences, for flying foxes breed slowly, with only one offspring per female per year. Their range seems to be sliding southwards, and the cause seems to be global warming. In 1999 the Grey-headed Flying Fox was declared 'vulnerable to extinction'. It is now protected everywhere in Australia. Even in Queensland roost sites are supposed to have been protected since 1994. Nevertheless, and despite the fact that shooting flying foxes is known to be inhumane, in 2012 the Queensland government announced its intention to issue permits to farmers allowing them to shoot specific numbers of four species of flying foxes if other control methods had been tried and failed. The reasons given were inconsistent; some said it was to assist beleaguered Queensland fruit farmers, others that it was to limit the spread of Hendra virus, others that bats are a nuisance. The announcement was made on Threatened Species Day.

In 2010 CCRRS discovered its own flying-fox camp. Flying foxes need dense riparian vegetation, which is what we've got. They like altitude, ditto. And they like fruit, ditto again. In March 2010 the workforce became aware of an unusual level of noise emanating from the creekside. As they walked through the bush towards the noise they became aware of an equally unusual level of smell. On the boundary with the national park they found a 50-square-metre bat camp. The tall roost trees were almost completely defoliated and underneath them, the little walking-stick palms, exposed as they were both to the white-hot sun and a rain of bat excrement, were dying. The workforce reckoned that there were 1,000 to 1,500 Grey-headed Flying Foxes in the camp. There was nothing they could do to save the little trees, not even flap their arms and say 'shoo!' It is now illegal to disturb any bat roost. The Gold Coast City Council solemnly intones that 'Camp locations should be excluded from public access. A buffer zone of 200m is recommended.' Our bat camp was within twenty metres of the walkway down which the 300,000 people who visit the Natural Bridge Section of the Springbrook National Park each year are required to walk. There was not so much as a sign to warn them to keep away from the bat camp. At the end of August the bats were gone, as suddenly as they came.

At CCRRS, where there is no barbed wire and power cables run underground, our eighteen bat species, many of which are listed as vulnerable or threatened, can live and breed in relative safety. Besides the Grey-headed Flying Fox, we have the Black Flying Fox (*Pteropus alecto*), thought by some people to be displacing the Grey-headed than which it is slightly bigger and heavier. In the mating season the male of this species has a mildly unpleasant habit of selecting a length of branch upon which to groom himself repeatedly and display his engorged genitalia. The Little Red Flying Fox (*P. scapulatus*), which is nomadic and roosts alone in a different place after every night's foraging, visits when the Silky Oaks and other proteaceous plants are in flower. The miniature flying fox called the Common Blossom Bat (*Synconycteris australis*) is entirely dependent upon rainforest. It too roosts alone in the canopy and feeds nightly among the flowering and fruiting trees. As it bustles among the flower spathes it collects pollen on its fur. Walking in the forest at dusk I sometimes hear it defending its food plant, vocalising and clapping its wings. The Eastern Tube-nosed Bat (*Nyctimene robinsoni*) is another that can only live in rainforest, but its range is even narrower. Like the Blossom Bat it loves the flowers of quandongs and Black Beans and it special-ises in figs. I have never managed to see it or even to hear its characteristic whistling call, but I know it's about.

Many bat species nest in tree hollows. The Eastern Free-tail Bat or East Coast Free-tailed Bat or Eastern Little Mastiff Bat (*Mormopterus norfolkensis*) is one such. Very little is known about it because it is not often trapped but it, or something very like it, has been found in the caldera. Another is the White-striped Free-tailed Bat (*Tadarida australis*) which can form maternal colonies of several hundred in tree hollows of thirty centimetres diameter. The Eastern Long-eared Bat (*Nyctophilus bifax*) is another rainforest denizen, that is likely to roost among the interlaced roots of strangler figs or in tree ferns. The rare Golden Tipped Bat (*Phoniscus* or *Kerivoula papuensis*) is another rainforest bat so tiny that it chooses to roost in the abandoned nests of scrubwrens and gerygones. Unusually its diet consists almost entirely of orb-weaving spiders. There are half a dozen species of forest bats in the genus Vespadelus, and perhaps more. As these can be told apart only by a comparison of their penes, it is more than I can do to tell you which ones live at Cave Creek and which don't.

Several species of bat have probably taken up residence in the old house. Certainly we find droppings on the floor. One day, in an old tar pot hanging on the house wall, I found the tiny desiccated corpse of an Eastern Horseshoe Bat (*Rhinolophus megaphyllus*) with her baby in her arms. These little bats fly by echolocation, hunting moths, beetles, flies, crickets, bugs, cockroaches and wasps through the dense forest; somehow this mother and child ended up in the tar pot unable to get out. Of all the creatures in the forest, the bats are the ones we know least, and of the bats, the insectivores are the ones we know least about. It is my fervent hope that a bat specialist will come to work with the bats at Cave Creek.

We can only wonder now which bats used to live in the cave from which Cave Creek takes its name. These days it houses no bats, though according to a visitor in 1908 it was then 'filled with bats which when disturbed fly about in hundreds; they were so thick in the air that a person kept involuntarily dodging his head to avoid them'. These may have been Eastern Cave Bats (*Vespadelus troughtoni*) typically found close to escarpments along the scenic rim. They like to hunt the insects feeding on Booyongs, Rosewood, Stingers and Carabeens, all of which are common in the Cave Creek forest. The Large-eared Pied Bat (*Chalinolobus dwyeri*) is another that lives in sandstone caves close to the forest edge. It was not discovered until 1966 at Copeton in northern New South Wales, at a site that is now under the Copeton Dam. It has been found in Lamington National Park, where it is supposed that it was roosting in basalt. The land at CCRRS is traversed by a broad stripe of sandstone that crops out over the forest and the creek, perfect habitat for *Chalinolobus dwyeri*.

Placental rats and mice made their way to Australia five to ten million years after the bats. Viewers of *I'm a Celebrity Get Me Out of Here* will have seen C-list celebrities being buried with rats, having rats tipped into their trousers and so forth, and they will have been told that the creatures in question are fierce 'bush rats'. In fact they are common *Rattus rattus*, from the nearest rat-fancy. To have been genuine local bush rats they would have had to be *Rattus fuscipes* subspecies *assimilis*. This animal is not commensal with human beings and would have left the site of *IACGMOOH* as soon as it was taken over by television crews in 2002. Though bush rats are supposed to be strictly nocturnal, I have seen them by daylight. I have never seen more than one at a time, and always in the same place on a track about fifty yards from the old house. The rat would pop out of the kikuyu on one side of a track, cross it and disappear into a tunnel in the grass on the other side. The tunnel appears to have been in use for generations, because I have been seeing a bush rat near it for seven or eight years, much longer than the life cycle of an individual rat, which lives only a year. *Rattus fuscipes* typically has a snub nose, dark feet (hence its name) and a short tail.

There are two species of native mice as well as imported house mice at Cave Creek, but both are elusive and increasingly rare. One is the Fawn-footed Melomys (*Melomys cervinipes*). I am supposed now to call it a Korril, a word that originates from the language of the Stradbroke Island people, but I've never heard anyone call it anything but a mouse. The other is the Hastings River Mouse (*Pseudomys oralis*), which I'm sorry to say was caught in a deadfall trap by someone seeking to display his credentials as an academic mammalologist.

Our biggest placental mammals are our dingoes. I was walking alone on the edge of the forest only days after I first slept at CCRRS, when a big blond dingo with a plumy tail came trotting down a pademelon track to within a few yards of where I had come to a stop. He had been sniffing amongst the undergrowth and hadn't seen me until that point. He stood and looked. I looked back. I vaguely remembered that you're not supposed to stare dogs in the eye, because it is confrontational, so I broke the gaze once or twice. I didn't dare turn my back to him because it might have triggered his chase reflex, so I stood my ground and talked to him, as is my wont. The path was steep and he was slightly above me, motionless, his golden eyes looking intelligently into my face. Then he wheeled and trotted back up the path. I watched his plumy tail floating above the undergrowth until it disappeared.

I have seen him several times since, and even managed to catch him on video. The last time I saw him it was broad midday. I was sitting on the verandah of the old house, reading, when some small unfamiliar sound made me look up. Plumy Tail was standing a hundred yards away keeping nit for his pack, as they crossed the main track on their way to the creek. I was too late to see the leader of the pack, who would have been a senior bitch, but even so I counted more than a dozen animals, as well as a horde of smaller pups of whom I could see just tail tips and the odd ear. Plumy Tail stood still, head up, ears pricked, gazing down the track towards me as they trotted over the crossing and into our planting, almost as if he was showing them to me. Then he too was gone.

Plumy Tail has at least one rival, a darker ginger dingo whom I've seen once or twice from a distance. Now that the forest is growing up we see dingoes less often, but we hear them more and sometimes from very close quarters. They emerge at night from their refuge in the forest to take prey in the neighbouring cleared areas, usually young lambs. Every now and then we get a circular advising us that 1080 baits are being laid, as long as all the landowners within a five-kilometre radius consent. This has the effect of rendering the baiting impossible, which is just as well. We couldn't agree to the baiting of wild dogs if we wanted to because, in an attempt to protect quolls from ingesting the poison, baits may not be laid within 300 metres of a forest edge. There is now nowhere at CCRRS that is more than 300 metres from a forest edge.

A dingo is a dog, nowadays called *Canis lupus dingo*; domestic dogs are also *Canis lupus*. The two can and do breed with each other. One school of thought holds that dingoes have become more dangerous because of interbreeding with introduced dogs, which has weakened their shyness trait so that they no longer avoid humans. This is probably bunk. From what I see of dingoes at Cave Creek they are quite capable of observing humans and familiarising themselves with them. They certainly know me a lot better than I know them. They are as easy to tame and train as any other dog breed. They were essential members of Aboriginal communities, as hunting companions who found, harassed and sometimes took game, and as guardians who identified hazards before humans became aware of them. Yet, from the beginning of settlement 'wild dogs' have been persecuted. Steel-jaw traps were set for them; they were shot and poisoned with strychnine, with small regard to the degree of suffering involved. In Queensland between 1932 and 1967 doggers collected 685,000 dingo scalps. Since 1968 'wild dogs' are poisoned with 1080, sodium monofluoroacetate, a toxin derived from West Australian pea species. The thinking was that because the dingo was introduced from Asia only 4,000 or so years ago, it had no immunity to 1080, but native species could ingest it without ill effect. There was never any good reason to believe that the immunity acquired by south-western fauna was shared with the fauna of the discontinuous eastern region, but for nearly forty years the idea was accepted, along with an equally ill-founded notion that this method of killing was humane. Anyone who saw a dog die of 1080 poisoning knew that it wasn't. In 2007 a Queensland drover called Bill Little, thirty of whose cattle dogs had been poisoned with 1080 over the years, told ABC TV news programme *PM*: 'You get up in the middle of the night and your dog's screaming in pain and he's climbing the wall of your van, you've got to get out in the middle of the night and shoot your best dog.'

At CCRRS the dingo is not a problem that we need to solve. We have no livestock to protect from predation, or from the diseases thought to be carried by dingoes. The way I see it the dingoes have more right to our mountains than do sheep. One morning the workforce surprised a dingo bitch who had chosen to give birth on one of our warm mulch-heaps. She ran away, leaving four newborn pups. When she didn't come back, Luke took the pups home to his mother who reared them. They were supposed to be going to a dingo sanctuary in Victoria, but when tests were done to find if they were pure bred, it turned out that they were only fifteen-sixteenths, mongrels like the rest of us. They are still living over the hill with Luke's mum.

Every day I meet animals going about their business. I have become used to surprises and still they keep coming. I had finished writing this chapter, and was putting the laptop away when I heard a rustling in the gathering dusk. I leaned over the verandah rail and peered into the heaving vegetation. Whatever was causing the upheaval seemed fairly clumsy. Every now and then I glimpsed a round bottom parting the fern fronds. A bandicoot, I thought. But then it climbed onto a rock and I saw that it had a beak and spines.

An echidna. An *echidna*! *Tachyglossus aculeatus*. A creature more ancient than a marsupial. A monotreme! I felt weak at the knees. I had thought that the rainforest was too wet for echidnas, and here, calm and comfy as you like in the sodden forest, was a wild echidna. It rambled off down the gully we have planted with Bangalow and Walking-stick Palms and my heartfelt blessing went with it.

Whenever a truly wild creature lets me see it behaving naturally, I feel a blessedness, as if I had been allowed to enter a realm far more special than the celebrity A-list. When I look up from a book, and see a few yards away a pademelon grazing with her joey, I feel vindicated, as if I had won acceptance as an animal in my turn. Lots of people are persuaded to spend lots of money on shelter and food for wild creatures, when all they have to do is to stop making lawns and weeding and tidying up, and turning the bush into an outdoor room. While it's not true that all you have to do is to let your garden run to seed, before wild vegetation and wild creatures will return to it, it is true that if you remove weeds and do your best to restore the original vegetation, the endemic animal species will reappear as if by magic. You won't be able to keep a dog or a cat or even hens, because all of them do tremendous damage to wild creatures, but you won't miss them, because all around you the bush will rustle with to-ings and fro-ings of a vast range of creatures great and small. A patch of rescued bush is a sanctuary where the special creatures who evolved with the vegetation can stave off extinction.

This book must end, but the story will continue. As the forest community at Cave Creek rebuilds itself, we will do our best to record the process on the Friends of Gondwana Rainforest website.

EPILOGUE

It is done. The project is now run by Friends of Gondwana Rainforest, UK registered charity No. 1145364, UK charitable company No. 7842375, and we are well on the way to transferring the property to an Australian not-for-profit company. Am I bereft? No. If I have not learnt in my seventy-four years that to love and care for something you don't need to own it, then I have learnt nothing. The day I gave away all the cash I had to the rainforest was one of the happiest days of my life. Giving the forest back to itself is taking a little longer.

The process has not been easy. I and my faithful co-directors were given the wrong advice and set off on the wrong foot. In less than a year of little sleep I realised I had to find expert advice and regroup. Part of the difficulty was that conservation charities are new and their rationale is poorly understood. It is not enough simply to restore a forest as a storehouse of biodiversity from which future generations will benefit much as one might endow a library or a museum; the charity had also to claim an educational function. I pored over other rainforest charities' mission statements, and, after a minor tussle with a Commissioner, the concept was eventually accepted. The most intractable difficulties were those that affected the interface between the UK charity and the Australian administration. We were not helped by expensive lawyers' bigging up their own role by exaggerating the already considerable complexity of the operation.

Why Gondwana Rainforest? Because that's what the Cave Creek

forest is. As such it's a treasure house of species that have survived
almost unchanged from the Cretaceous, when the world was divided
into two supercontinents, Laurasia and Gondwana. When Australia
was part of Gondwana it was covered with subtropical rainforest,
which remains the most ancient vegetation type to be found in the
great south land. Many of our plant families, the Lauraceae, the
Cunoniaceae, the Winteraceae and the Eupomatiaceae, for example,
can trace their descent back to the dawn of the evolution of flowering
plants a hundred million years ago.

Over the millennia the drying of the continent and the firefarming
of the indigenous peoples favoured the dominance of sclerophyll
vegetation that encroached on the fire-sensitive rainforest leaving it
to survive in sites that were isolated and disjunct. You will find it also
growing in gullies surrounded by fire-scarred eucalypts, or by treeless
pasture degraded and eaten out by hard-hoofed animals, or by strip
and open-cut mines.

When I bought the land at Cave Creek the World Heritage site
that extended from its southern boundary along the Dividing
Range almost as far south as Newcastle was known as the Central
Eastern Rainforest Reserve Area. In 2007 it was renamed Gondwana
Rainforests of Australia. This broken chain of isolated sites, in all
fifty separate reserves, covering 3,665 square kilometres, represents
the most extensive area of Gondwanan rainforest to survive
anywhere in the world. Just how little that is can be seen by taking
a look at the map on the website of the Australian Government
Department of Sustainability, Environment, Water, Population and
Communities (*sic*), which makes embarrassingly clear that crown
land is set aside for reserves only when it is unsuitable for any kind
of exploitation. These bits and pieces are now all that remain of the
Gondwanan subtropical rainforest. Many of the individual fragments
are too small to provide the larger animals with a range big enough
for them to maintain their genetic diversity. A significant number
were heavily logged state forests that have simply been dubbed
national parks, with no commitment to removing the weeds and
pioneers that have colonised the damaged forest, let alone to
restoring the original vegetation. Many are now mostly sclerophyll
and fire-prone.

The Australian Dividing Range is the eastern extremity of the Samfrau orogenic belt, which originally ran along the southern edge of the southern supercontinent of Gondwana. As Gondwana gradually broke up during the Mesozoic and the five main fragments separated and rotated to form South America, Africa, the Indian subcontinent, Antarctica and Australia, the Samfrau has been reduced to the Andean range of South America, the Ross range of Antarctica and the heavily eroded Great Dividing Range of Australia. The Tasmanian rainforest is also Gondwanan and a World Heritage Site, but it is to be known as the Tasmanian Wilderness.

Friends of Gondwana Rainforest are concerned for subtropical and temperate rainforest wherever it survives. CCRRS is our flagship, where we learnt how to rebuild a forest and how exciting and grati-fying it is to give it your best shot. What we are doing there can be done elsewhere, and we exist to help it happen, not only among our neighbours in Australia, but in New Caledonia, in New Zealand, in Chile, in Argentina, in southern Africa, in Madagascar, in India and Sri Lanka, wherever fragments of the ancient Gondwanan forest survive.

The received wisdom is that only plant and animal species surviving on public land can be protected. In fact, public nature reserves generally suffer from systemic lack of funding. They are usually poorly staffed, poorly equipped and poorly managed. What little funding they receive has to be justified by providing a public amenity. National parks are obliged to spend their slender means on parking, toilets, picnic tables, barbecues, signage, and may even choose to provide facilities for off-road bicycles and four-wheel-drive vehicles, before investing any energy or resources in protecting and maintaining their plant and animal assemblages. At Natural Bridge fortunes are spent on blowing leaves off the paths, in case tourists should slip and fall. In twelve years, not one penny has been spent on removing weeds.

Once I might have thought of handing CCRRS over to the Queensland Parks and Wildlife Service, in the hope that one day they would begin to take their responsibilities seriously and set about conserving and protecting habitat, but that was before state govern-ments all over Australia decided that, if they were to grow revenue

to run the parks, they would have to allow luxury resort developments in them. Now more than ever it is clear to me that if
conservation is to be done at all, it will have to be done by dedicated
individuals and organisations on privately owned land.

Eco-tourism is not the answer. Animals are not performers and
their behaviour is not a spectacle. Whales are already sick of being
watched. People who come with cameras are as much hunters as
people who come with guns. I was once lucky enough to find myself
off the south-east coast of Sri Lanka on a small fishing boat that
suddenly and unexpectedly ran into a pack of hundreds of sperm
whales, all ploughing northwards through the ocean swells. At first
the whales were curious and playful, but after an hour they became
agitated and began breaching and slapping the water with their flukes
(something these whales don't often do). Try as I might I couldn't
persuade the captain to turn the boat around and let the whales be.
He was excited, the tourists were excited and screaming, and the
boat's diesel engine was driving the whales mad. We didn't give up
chasing the whales until there was barely enough fuel left to get us
back to shore. Eco-tourism means interference and interference
means disturbance. Australian animals are very sensitive to stress; all
they ask is to left alone. The greatest irony is that by the time the
luxury developments are built in wild Australia the animals the
tourists will come to see will have retreated up into the deepest gullies
of the most rugged ridges, beyond the reach of their spotlights and
their four-wheel drives. Our threatened plant and animal life needs
space and quiet if it is to survive.

Inaccessible scrubland comes cheap. You don't have to be rich to
make your own nature reserve, especially if you can join forces with
like-minded people. The more marginal the land, the more 'useless',
the lower its market value, the better adapted it is for restoration and
conservation. If you're the kind of person who feels heartache when
you see on a country road the bright plumage of a native bird mashed
into the bitumen or a skittled koala dead on its back with its claws in
the air, you will find great consolation in your mini-reserve. Once
the plants are there, the animals will come. To see and hear them
going about their business brings a special kind of blessedness. Making
a niche for them means finding a niche for you too.

The private landholder, whether individual or corporate, has a better chance of maintaining conservation values than a public entity that has also to provide a public amenity. Private landholders can defend hotspots of endemism as public bodies cannot. Where such hotspots exist alongside public reserves, maintaining them can improve the viability of the reserve community. The fruit of the CCRRS Pigeon-berry Ash trees, for example, will be carried by the rainforest pigeons across the caldera rim to give the Camphor Laurels a run for their money and provide the fruit-eating birds with a food supply that will not kill them. Holders of quite small parcels of land can join forces in providing corridors between isolated patches of habitat. They cannot be expected to do any of these things if no one takes the trouble to inform them about the treasures that have come into their keeping. Most people if told that their muddy stream harbours platypuses would be only too happy to put energy and resources into protecting the habitat of such special and remarkable animals. Expect nothing from people and you will get nothing.

The process by which the forest is being given back to itself is complicated and drawn-out, but now that it has begun a great wrong is on its way to being righted. The stupendous phenomenon that is the forest will have time and space to come into its own again. The charity has been set up to keep the work of rehabilitation going after I have gone to be recycled. One of the workforce said to me the other day, 'Does that mean that I could still be working here when I'm a grandfather?'

I truly hope so.

WORKS CITED

Adams, R. J. L., 2000, *Noosa and Gubbi Gubbi: The Land, the People, the Conflict*, Trewantin, Ultreya Publications

Aird, Michael, 2001, *Brisbane Blacks*, Southport, Queensland, Keeaira Press

Aiton, William, 1789, *Hortus Kewensis; or, a Catalogue of the Plants cultivated in the Royal Botanic Garden at Kew*, 3 vols, London, George Nicol

Alexander, J. E., 1833, *Transatlantic Sketches, comprising Visits to the most interesting scenes in North and South America and the West Indies*, London, Richard Bentley

Allen, John and Lane, John, 1913, 'Grammar, vocabulary and notes of the Wangerriburra Tribe', Appendix to the *Report of the Protector of Aboriginals*, Brisbane

Auld, B., and Medd, R. W., 1992, *Weeds: An Illustrated Botanical Guide to the Weeds of Australia*, Melbourne, Inkata Press

Aurousseau, Marcel, 1968, *The Letters of F. W. Ludwig Leichhardt*, 3 vols, Cambridge, Cambridge University Press for the Hakluyt Society

Backhouse, James, 1843, *A Narrative of a Visit to the Australian Colonies*, London, Hamilton, Adams & Co.

Bailey, F. M., 1889, 'Botany of the Bellenden-Ker expedition', *Report of the Government Scientific Expedition to the Bellenden-Ker Range upon the Flora and Fauna of that Part of the Colony*, 1

— 1891, *Botany Bulletin*, Queensland Department of Agriculture and Stock, 2: 16

— 1899–1905, *The Queensland Flora*, Brisbane, H. J. Diddams and Co.

Bailey, J., 2011, *Into the Unknown: The Tormented Life and Expeditions of Ludwig Leichhardt*, Sydney, Pan Macmillan Publishers

Baker, Jeannie, 1998, *The Story of Rosy Dock*, Milson's Point, New South Wales, Red Fox

Baker, R. T., 1907, 'On an undescribed Species of Cryptocarya from Eastern Australia', *Proceedings of the Linnean Society of New South Wales*, 31: 4

Bange, G. G. J., 1952, 'A new family of Dicotyledons: Davidsoniaceae', *Blumea*, 7: 1

Barker, D. G. and T. M., 1994, *Pythons of the World: Australia*, California, Advanced Vivarium Systems Inc.

Barker, John and Grigg, Gordon, 1977, *A Field Guide to Australian Frogs*, Adelaide, Rigby

Barker, Nigel P., Weston, Peter H., Rutschmann, Frank and Sauquet, Hervé, 2007, 'Molecular dating of the "Gondwanan" plant family Proteaceae is only partially congruent with the timing of the break-up of Gondwana', *Journal of Biogeography*, 34: 2012–27

Bennett, George, 1860, *Gatherings of a Naturalist in Australasia: being observations principally on the animal and vegetable productions of New South Wales, New Zealand and some of the Austral Islands*, London, John van Voorst

Bentham, George, 1863–1878, *Flora Australiensis: A Description of the Plants of the Australian Territory*, London, Lovell Reed & Co.

Berg, C. C. and Corner, E. J. H., 2005, Moraceae – Ficus, *Flora Malesiana Series*, 17: 2, 241–3, Map 3

Best, Ysola and Barlow, Alex, 1997, *Kombumerri – Saltwater People*, Port Melbourne, Heinemann Library

Bladen, F. M., ed., 1896, *Historical Records of New South Wales*, Sydney, Government Printer

Blume, C. L. von, 1825, *Bijdragen tot de Flora van Nederlandsch Indië*, Batavia, Ter Lands Drukkerij, 11: 556

Bofeldt, Anders, *Plants at risk in the Illawarra Region*, Landcare Illawarra, s. d.

Boileau, Joanna, 2000, *Caldera to the Sea: A History of the Tweed Valley*, Tweed Heads, Tweed Shire Council

Bradley, E. B. and Bradley, J. B., 1967, *Weeds and their Control*, Sydney, Mosman Parklands and Ashton Park Association

Bradley, Joan Burton, 1997, *Bringing back the bush: The Bradley method of bush regeneration*, The Rocks, Sydney, Lansdowne Publishing

Bray Papers, Mitchell Library MS 1929

Bray, Florence M., 1997, *My Mother Told Me: Memories of a Pioneer Family*, Cudgen, Noella Ellworthy

Bray, Joshua, 1901, 'Tribal Districts and Customs', *Science of Man*, 4: 1, 9–10

— 1902, 'Aboriginal Customs – Tweed River District', *Science of Man*, 5: 1

Brockie, P. J., Garnock-Jones, R. E. and FitzJohn, R. G., 2007, 'Gynodioecy, sexual dimorphism, and erratic fruiting in *Corynocarpus* (Corynocarpaceae)', *Australian Journal of Botany*, 55: 8

Brown, Robert, 1810a, *Prodromus Florae Novae Hollandiae et insulae Van Diemen: exhibens characteres plantarum quas annis 1802–1805 per oras utriusque insulae collegit et descripsit Robertus Brown; insertis passim aliis speciebus auctori hucusque incognitis, seu evulgatis, seu ineditis, praesertim Banksianus, in primo itinere navarchi Cook detectis*, London, R. Taylor & Co.

— 1810b, 'On the natural order of plants called Proteaceae', *Transactions of the Linnaean Society*, 10

Bulletin of Zoological Nomenclature 44 (1987) 116–121, 'Case 2531: Three works by Richard W. Wells and C. Ross Wellington: proposed suppression for nomenclatural purposes'.

Byrne, Denis R., 1987, *The Aboriginal and Archaeological Significance of the New South Wales Rainforests: a Report to the Forestry Commission of New South Wales and the Australian Heritage Commission*, Sydney, Forestry Commission of New South Wales

Calley, Malcolm J. C., 'Bundjalung Social Organisation', unpublished Ph.D. Thesis, University of Sydney

Campbell, J., 2002, *Invisible Invaders: Smallpox and other Diseases in Aboriginal Australia*, Melbourne, Melbourne University Press

Capuron, René, 1963, *Adansonia*, n.s., 3

[Carrington, George], 1871, *Colonial Adventures and experiences by a university man*, London, Bell and Daldy

Cheel, Edwin and Morrison, F. R., 1935, 'The Cultivation and exploitation of the Australian Nut', *Technical Museum Bulletin*, 20

Chisholm, Alec H., 1973, *Strange Journey: the adventures of Ludwig Leichhardt and John Gilbert*, Adelaide, Rigby

Cleveland, Richard J., 1842, *A Narrative of Voyages and Commercial Enterprises*, 2 vols, Cambridge MA, John Owen

Corner, E. J. H., 1960, 'Taxonomic Notes on Ficus Linn., Asia and Australasia I. Subgen. Urostigma (Gasp.) Miq.', *The Gardens' Bulletin, Singapore*, 17

Corris, Peter, 1973, *Port, Passage and Plantation: A History of Solomon Islands Labour Migration 1870–1914*, Melbourne, Melbourne University Press

Cowderoy, Tom, 1959, *Numinbah Valley and Springbrook,* Bundall, Bundall Printery

Currey, J. E. B., ed., 1966, *George Caley: Reflections on the Colony of New South Wales*, Melbourne, Lansdowne Press

Cust, Lionel, 1912, 'J. M. W. Turner: An Episode in Early Life', *Burlington Magazine*, May

Czechura, G. V., 1984, 'The Peregrine Falcon (*Falco peregrinus macropus*) Swainson in southeastern Queensland', *Raptor Research*, 18: 89

D, Con., 1927, 'The Koala's Lament', *Brisbane Courier*, 28 July, 13

Daley, Charles, 1927, 'The History of *Flora Australiensis* from the Correspondence of Dr William Hooker, George Bentham, and Sir Jos. D. Hooker with Additional Letters to Baron von Mueller from Sir Jos. D. Hooker', *The Victorian Naturalist*, 44: 3–10

Day, M. D., Wiley, C. J., Playford, J. and Zalucki, M. P., 2003, *Lantana: Current management status and future prospects*, Australian Centre for International Research, Canberra

De Candolle, Augustin Pyramus, ed., 1824–73, *Prodromus Systematis Naturalis Regni Vegetabilis*, 17 vols, Paris, Treutel and Würtz

Desmarest, A. G. and Duméril, A. C., 1816–30, *Dictionnaire des Sciences Naturelles dans lequel on traite méthodiquement des différents êtres de la nature*, 60 vols, Strasbourg, F. G. Levrault

Docker, Edward Wybergh, 1970, *The Blackbirders: The Recruiting of South Seas Labour for Queensland, 1863–1907*, Sydney, Angus and Robertson

Dodds, Bert, 1959, 'History of the Numinbah Valley, its Geography, Aboriginal Association and European Settlement', unpublished MS

Dunrabin, Thomas, 1935, *Slavers of the South Seas*, Sydney, Angus and Robertson

Edmonds, J. M., 1995, 'Toona M. Roem.' in Mabberley, D. J., Pannel, C. M. and Sing, A. M., 'Meliaceae', *Flora Malesiana*, Series I, 12: 358–71

Eisler, Ronald, 1986, *Dioxin hazards to fish, wildlife, and invertebrates: a synoptic review*, Washington DC, Patuxent Wildlife Research Center, Fish and Wildlife Service, U.S. Dept. of Interior

Endlicher, S. F. L., 1836–1840, *Genera Plantarum Secundum Ordines Naturales Disposita,* Vienna, F. Beck, 14

Engler, H.G.A. in Engler, H. G. A. and Prantl, K. A. E., 1930, *Die Natürlichen Pflanzenfamilien*, 2: 18

Evans, R., 2007, *A History of Queensland*, Port Melbourne, Cambridge University Press

Ewart, A. J. assisted by J. R. Tovey, 1909, *The Weeds, Poison Plants and Naturalized Aliens of Victoria*, Melbourne, Government Printer

Fanelli, R., Castelli, M.G., Martelli, G.P., Noseda, A. and Garattini, S., 1980, 'Presence of 2,3,7,8-tetrachlorodibenzo-p-dioxin in wildlife living near Seveso, Italy: a preliminary study', *Bulletin of Environmental Contaminant Toxicology*, 24: 460-2.

Field B., Kerr, C. B. and Mathers, C. D., 1982, 'Incidence of Neural Tube Defects', *Developmental Medicine & Child Neurology*, 24: Issue Supplement s45, 861–2

Field B. and Kerr, C. B., 1988, 'Reproductive behaviour and consistent patterns of abnormality in offspring of Vietnam veterans', *Journal of Medical Genetics*, 25: 819–26 and subsequent correspondence (on line).

Fischer, F. E. L. von and Meyer, C. A. A. von, eds, 1854, *Index Seminum, quae hortus botanicus Imperialis Petropolitanus pro mutua commutatione offert . . .* St Petersburg, 1

Flora of Australia, 1981–, 59 volumes, Canberra, Australian Government Public Service, now on line as part of the Australian Biological Resources Study of the Department of Sustainability, Environment, Water, Population and Communities (*sic*)

Floyd, A. G., 1989, *Rainforest Trees of Mainland South-eastern Australia*, Melbourne, Inkata Press

— 2008, *Rainforest Trees of Mainland South-eastern Australia*, Lismore, Terania Rainforest Publishing

Forster, J. R. and G., 1776, *Characteres Generum Plantarum, quas in itinere ad insulas Maris Australis, . . .* London, B. White, T. Cadell & P. Elmsly

Fox, Marilyn D., 1999, 'Present environmental influences on the Australian Flora', *Flora of Australia*, 2nd edn, vol. 1

Frodin, D. G., 1976, 'Studies in Cryptocarya (Lauraceae) I', *Telopea*, 1: 3

Gammage, W. H., 2011, *The Biggest Estate on Earth: How Aborigines Made Australia*, Crow's Nest, New South Wales, Allen & Unwin

Geytenbeek, Brian B. and Geytenbeek, Helen, 1971, *Gidabal Grammar and Dictionary*, Australian Aboriginal Studies 17, Canberra, Australian Institute for Aboriginal Studies

Githabul People's Native Title Determination, North-eastern New South Wales, 29 November 2007, National Native Title Tribunal

Glauert, L., 1948, 'A Western Tiger Snake, *Notechis scutatus occidentalis*, subsp. nov.', *West Australian Naturalist* 1: 139–41

González, L., Souto, X. C. and Reigosa, M. J., 1995, 'Allelopathic effects of *Acacia melanoxylon* R. Br. phyllodes during their decomposition', *Forest Ecology and Management*, 77: 1-3, September, 53-63

Greathead, D. J., 1968, 'Biological control of *Lantana*. A review and discussion of recent developments in East Africa', London, Centre for Overseas Pest Research, Pest Articles and News Summaries, 14: 167–75

Greer, A. E., 1997, *The Biology and Evolution of Australian Snakes,* Chipping Norton New South Wales, Surrey, Beatty and Sons

Gresty, J. A., 1946–7, 'The Numinbah Valley: Its Geography, History and Aboriginal Associations', *Queensland Geographical Journal*, 51: 57–72

Groom, Arthur, (1949) 1992, *One Mountain after Another*, Sydney, Envirobook

Gross, C. L. and Weston, P. H., 1992, '*Macadamia jansenii* (Proteaceae), a new species from Central Queensland', *Australian Systematic Botany*, 5: 6

Groves, R. H., Biden, Robert and Lonsdale, W. M., 2005, *Jumping the Garden Fence: Invasive garden plants in Australia and their environmental and agricultural impacts*, CSIRO for WWF Australia

Guilfoyle, W. R., 1878, *Australian Botany: specially designed for the use of schools*, Melbourne, S. Mullen

— 1910, *Australian plants suitable for gardens, parks, timber reserves, etc.*, Melbourne, Whitcomb & Tombs

Guppy, Henry Brougham, 1887a, *The Solomon Islands and their Natives*, London, Swan Sonnenschein, Lowry and Co.

— 1887b, *The Solomon Islands: their geology, general features, and suitability for colonization*, London, Swan Sonnenschein, Lowry and Co.

Hall, J., 1986, 'Exploratory excavation at Bushrangers cave (Site LA: A11), a 6000-year-old campside in Southeast Queensland: Preliminary Results', *Australian Archaeology*, 22: 88–103

Hall, Pamela, Yaun, Donna and Gilmont, Noela, 1988, *Numinbah Valley: A Social and Natural History 1840s – 1988*, South Tweed Heads, Numinbah Valley Bicentennial Committee

Hall, P. and Selinger, B., 1981, 'Australian Herbicide usage and congenital abnormalities', *Chemistry in Australia*, 48

Hanlon, E. W., 1935, 'The Early History of the Logan and Albert Districts', *Journal of the Historical Society of Queensland*, 2: 5, 208–65

Harden, G. J., ed., 2000, *The Flora of New South Wales*, revised edition, 4 vols, Sydney, University of New South Wales Press

— and Williams, J. B., 2000, 'A revision of Davidsonia (Cunoniaceae)', *Telopea*, 8: 4

— McDonald, W. J. F. and Williams, John B., 2007, *Rainforest Climbing Plants*, Nambucca Heads, Gwen Harden Publishing

— McDonald, W. J. F. and Williams, John B., 2008, *Rainforest Trees and Shrubs: A field guide to their identification in Victoria, New South Wales and subtropical Queensland using vegetative features*, Nambucca Heads, Gwen Harden Publishing

Hardin, D. W., Harden, G., and Goddin, D., eds, 2000, *Proteaceae of New South Wales*, Sydney, University of New South Wales Press

Harms, H. A. T., Engler, H. G. A. and Prantl, K. A. E., 1896, *Die Natürlichen Pflanzenfamilien*, 3: 4

Hausfeldt, R., 1960, 'Aspects of Aboriginal Station Management', MA. Thesis, University of Sydney

Henderson, J., 1851, *Excursions and Adventures in NSW with pictures of squatting and of life in the bush: an account of the climate, productions, and with advice to emigrants etc.*, London, W. Shoberl

Hodgkinson, Clement, 1848, *Australia from Port Macquarie to Moreton Bay*, London, T. & W. Boone

Holden, Nick, 'Looking Back', 1981, *The Hinterlander*, 28 January, 4 February, 14

Holmer, Nils M., 1971, *Notes on the Bandjalang dialect, spoken at Coraki and Bungawalbin Creek, N. S. W.*, Canberra, Australian Institute of Aboriginal Studies

Home, R. W., Lucas, A. M., Maroske, Sara, Sinkora, D. M. and Voigt, J. H., 1998–2006, *Regardfully Yours: Selected Correspondence of Ferdinand von Mueller*, 3 vols, Bern, Berlin, Frankfurt-am-Main, New York, Paris, Vienna, Peter Lang

Hoser, R. T., 1998, 'Wells and Wellington: It's Time to Bury the Hatchet', *Monitor*, 9: 2, 20–41

Hrdina, Frances C., 1997, 'Marsupial Destruction in Queensland 1877–1930', *Australian Zoologist*, 30: 272–86

Huxley, Elspeth, 1967, *Their Shining Eldorado: A Journey through Australia*, London, Chatto & Windus

Johnson, L. A. S., 1954, '*Macadamia ternifolia* F. Muell. and a Related New Species', *Proceedings of the Linnean Society of New South Wales*, Series 2, 79: 1–2

— 1962, 'Taxonomic notes on Australian Plants', *Contributions from the New South Wales Herbarium*, 3, 3: 99

— and Briggs, B. G., 1975, 'On the Proteaceae: the evolution and classification of a southern family', *Journal of the Linnean Society, Botany*, 70: 176

Johnson, S., 2007, *Review of the Declaration of Lantana species in New South Wales*, Orange, New South Wales Department of Primary Industries

Keats, N. C., s. d., *Wollumbin: the creation and early habitation of the Tweed, Brunswick and Richmond Rivers of N.S.W*, Point Clare, New South Wales

Kidd, R., 1997, *The Way We Civilise: Aboriginal Affairs, the Untold Story*, St Lucia, University of Queensland Press

Kinsman, M., s. d., *Joshua Bray: A Tweed Valley Pioneer*, Chatswood, New South Wales, Bannerman Bros

Knight, J., 1809, *On the Cultivation of the Plants belonging to the natural order of Proteeae*, London, W. Savage

Kostermans, A. J. G. H., 1959, 'Monograph of the genus Heritiera Aiton (Stercul.)', *Reinwardtia*, 4: 528–31

— 1970, 'Materials for a revision of Lauraceae III', *Reinwardtia*, 8: 1

Kynaston, E., 1981, *A Man on Edge: The Life of Baron Sir Ferdinand von Mueller*, Ringwood, Victoria, Allen Lane

Langdon, R. F., 1981, 'The remarkable Mrs Clemens', in *People and Plants in Australia*, eds Carr, D. J. and S. G. M., Sydney, Academic Press

Lassak, E. and McCarthy, T., 2011, *Australian Medicinal Plants: A Complete Guide to their Identification and Usage*, Chatswood, New South Wales, Reed New Holland

Latham, J., 1781–1801, *General Synopsis of Birds*, London, Benjamin White

— 1790, *Index Ornithologicus: sive systema ornithologiae; complectens avium divisionem in classes, ordines, genera, species, ipsarumque varietates: adjectis synonymis, locis, descriptionibus, &c.*, London, Leigh & Sotheby

Lee, D. W., 1991, 'Ultrastructural basis and function of iridescent blue colour of fruits in *Elaeocarpus*', *Nature*, 349: 260–2

Leichhardt, Ludwig, 1847, *Journal of an Overland Expedition in Australia*, London, T. & W. Boone

Leighton, S., *Tamarisk – a Real Risk for New South Wales*, Alice Springs, Northern Territory Department of Natural Resources, Environment and The Arts

Leiper, G., Glazebrook, J., Cox, D. and Rathie, K., 2009, *Mangroves to Mountains*, revised edition, Browns Plains, Society for Growing Australian Plants (Queensland Region) Inc., Logan River Branch

Lentz, C. F. O., 1961, 'Memoirs and some History', unpublished typescript

L'Héritier de Brutelle, C., 1788, *Sertum Anglicum seu plantae Rariores qua in Hortes juxta Londinum, imprimis in Horto Regio Kewensi Excoluntur, ab Anno 1786 ad Annuum 1787, 18 Observatae*, Paris.

Linnaeus, C., 1753, *Species Plantarum exhibentes plantas rite cognitas, ad genera relatas, . . . secundum systema sexuale digestas*, 2 vols, Stockholm, Laurence Salvius

Lonsdale, W. M., 1994, 'Inviting Trouble: introduced pasture species in northern Australia', *Australian Journal of Ecology*, 19: 345–54

Lopez, M. Lisa, Bonzani, Norma E. and Zygdalo, Julio A., 2009, 'Allelopathic Potential of *Tagetes minuta* terpenes by a chemical, anotomical and phytotoxic approach', *Biochemical Systematics and Ecology*, 36: 8982–890

Lowman, M., 1999, *Life in the Treetops*, Newhaven, Yale University Press

Lumholtz, Carl, 1889, *Among Cannibals: An account of four years' travels in Australia and of camp life with the aborigines of Queensland*, New York, Charles Scribner's Sons

Mabberley, D. J., 1992, 'Robert Mudie (1777–1842) and Australian Botany, or the Saga of the Black Bean', *Australian Systematic Botany Newsletter*, 70

— 1998, 'Australian Citreae with notes on other Aurantioidae (Rutaceae)', *Telopea*, 7: 4.

— 2002, 'The *Agathis brownii* case (Araucariaceae)', *Telopea*, 9: 743–54

— 2004, 'European Discovery, Description and Naming', *Red Cedar in Australia*, Sydney, Historic Houses Trust, 23–41

— 2008, *Mabberley's Plant-Book: A portable dictionary of plants, their classification and uses*, third edition, Cambridge, Cambridge University Press

McGillivray, D. J., 1985, 'Proposal to Amend 2045 Grevillea R. Br. ex Knight, nom. cons. (Proteaceae)', *Taxon* 34: 536–7

— and R. O. Makinson, 1993, *Grevillea Proteaceae: a taxonomic revision*, Carlton, Victoria, Melbourne University Press at the Miegunyah Press

McMinn, W. G., 1970, *Allan Cunningham, Botanist and Explorer*, Melbourne, Melbourne University Press

Maiden, J. H., 1889, *The Useful Native Plants of Australia (including Tasmania)*, Sydney, Turner and Henderson

— 1891, 'Australian Economic Plants', *Sydney Mail*, 2 May, 15 August

— 1904–, *The Forest Flora of New South Wales* in 77 parts

— and Betche, E., 1897, 'On new species of Macadamia together with notes on two plants new to the colony', *Proceedings of the Linnean Society of New South Wales*, Series 2, 21: 624–7

— and Betche, E., 1899, 'Notes from the Botanic Gardens, Sydney No. 4', *Proceedings of the Linnean Society of New South Wales*, 24: 150

Marlow, B. J., 1961, 'Reproductive Behaviour of the Marsupial Mouse *Antechinus flavipes* (Waterhouse) (Marsupialia) and the development of the Pouch young', *Australian Journal of Zoology*, 9: 203–318

Mast, A. R., Willis, C. L., Jones, E. H., Downs, K. M. and Weston, P. H., 2008, 'A smaller Macadamia from a more vagile tribe: inference of phylogenetic relationships, divergence times, and diaspore evolution in Macadamia and relatives (tribe Macadamiae; Proteaceae)', *American Journal of Botany*, 95: 7

Mear, Craig, 2008, 'The origin of the smallpox outbreak in Sydney in 1789', *Journal of the Royal Australian Historical Society*, 94: 1

Meston, A., 'The Bunya Mountains', 1892, *The Queenslander*, 21 May, 987

Miquel, F. A. W., 1866, 'Prolusio Florae Iaponicae', *Annales Museum Botanicum Lugduno-Batavum*, 2: 200

Mudie, Robert, 1829a, *The Picture of Australia: exhibiting New Holland, Van Dioemenns Land, and all the settlements from the first at Sydney to the last at the Swan River*, London, Whitaker, Treacher

— 1829b, *A Description and History of Vegetable Substances, Used in the Arts and in Domestic Economy. Timber trees: fruits*. London, Charles Knight

Mueller, Ferdinand, 1857, 'Account of Some New Australian Plants', *Transactions of the Philosophical Institute of Victoria*, 2

— 1858–1881, *Fragmenta Phytographiæ Australiæ*, 11 vols, Melbourne, Government Printer

— 1872, *Lectures delivered . . . in the lecture room of the Museum during the second session of 1871*, Melbourne

Munir, A. A., 1984, 'A Taxonomic Revision of the Genus Gmelina L. (Verbenaceae) in Australia', *Journal of the Adelaide Botanic Gardens*, 7: 1, 109–14

Nadkarni, N., Parker, G. G., Rinker, H. Bruce and Jarzen, D. M., 2004, 'The Nature of Forest Canopies' in *Forest Canopies* (second edition), ed. M. Lowman and H. Bruce Rinker, Elsevier

Novotny, Vojtech, Clarke, Anthony R., Drew, Richard A. I., Balagwi, Solomon and Clifford, Barbara, 2005, 'Host specialization and species richness of fruit flies (Diptera: Tephritidae) in a New Guinea rain forest', *Journal of Tropical Ecology*, 21: 67–77

O'Connor, Rory, 1997, *The Kombumerri: Aboriginal People of the Gold Coast*, Bundall, Queensland, Rory O'Connor

O'Dowd, Dennis J., Brew, Christine R., Christophel David C. and Norton Roy A., 1991, 'Mite–Plant Associations from the Eocene of Southern Australia', *Science*, New Series, 252: 5002, 99–101

O'Reilly, Bernard, s. d., *Green Mountains*, Sydney, Envirobook

Pemberton, Robert W., 2000, 'Predictable risk to native plants in weed biological control', *Oecologia*, 125: 489–94

Peters, C. W. H., 1861, 'Eine Zweite Ubersicht der von Herrn Jagor auf Malacca, Java, Borneo, und den Philippinen gesammelten auf dem Kgl. zoologischen Museum übersandten Schlangen', *Monatsberichte der Königlichen Preussischen Akademie der Wissenschaften zu Berlin*

Petrie, C. C., 1904, *Tom Petrie's Reminiscences of Early Queensland (dating from 1837) recorded by his daughter*, Brisbane, Watson Feguson

Pinckard, George, 1806, *Notes on the West Indies: written during an expedition under the command of the late general Sir Ralph Abercromby: including observations on the isle of Barbadoes . . . in three volumes*, London, Longman, Hurst, Rees and Orme

Powell, Michael and Hesline, Rex, 'Making Tribes? Constructing Aboriginal tribal entities in Sydney and coastal NSW from the early colonial period to the present', *Journal of the Royal Australian Historical Society*, 96: 115–48

Praed, Rosa, 1902, *My Australian Girlhood: sketches and impressions of bush life*, London, T. Fisher Unwin

Preston, Diana and Michael, 2004, *A Pirate of Exquisite Mind: the life of William Dampier, explorer, naturalist and buccaneer*, London, Doubleday

Radlkofer, L. A. T., 1879a, *Actes du Congrès Internationale des Botanistes . . . Amsterdam for 1877*, 107

— 1879b, *Sitzungsberichte der Mathematisch-Physikalischen Classe (Klasse) der K. B. Akademie der Wissenschaften zu München* 9: 608

Recovery Plan for Davidsonia johnsonii *(Smooth Davidsonia)*, 2004, Hurstville, Department of Environment and Conservation (New South Wales), on line

Reichmann, K. G., Twist, J. O., Mackenzie, R. A. and Rowan, K. J., 1987, 'Inhibition of bovine alpha-glucosidase by *Castanospermum australe* and its effect on the biochemical identification of heterozygotes for generalised glycogenosis type II (Pompe's disease) in cattle', *Australian Veterinary Journal*, 64: 9, 274–6

Reynolds, S. T., 1984, 'Notes on the Sapindaceae', iii, *Austrobaileya*, 2: 38–9

Richards, Jonathan, 2008, *The Secret War: A True History of Queensland's Native Police,* St Lucia, University of Queensland Press

Roemer, J. J. in Roemer, M. J., 1846, *Familiarum Naturalium Regni Vegetabilis Synopses Monographicae,* 1

Roja, G. and Heble, M., 2006, 'Castanospermine, an HIV inhibitor from tissue cultures of Castanospermum australe', *Phytotherapy Research*, 9: 7, 540–2

Rotherham, E. R., Briggs, B. G., Blaxell, D. F. and Carolin, R. C., 1975, *Flowers and Plants of New South Wales and Southern Queensland,* Terry Hills, Reed

Rowley, C. D., 1970, *The Destruction of Aboriginal Society: Aboriginal policy and practice,* Canberra, Australian National University Press

Sanderson, C. A. and Rogers, L. A., 1981, '2,4,5-trichlorophenoxyacetic acid causes behavioral effects in chickens at environmentally relevant doses', *Science,* 211: 4482, 593–5

Savage, P., 1992, *Christie Palmerston, Explorer; with maps and an essay by Alan Boughton,* revised and enlarged by B. J. Dalton, Townsville, Department of History and Politics, James Cook University

Sharpe, Margaret, 1985, 'Bundjalung Settlement and Migration', *Aboriginal History,* 9: 101–24

— ed., *c.*1995, *Dictionary of Western Bundjalung, including, Gidhabal and Tabulam Bundjalung,* Armidale, M. Sharpe

— 1998, *Dictionary of Yugambeh (including neighbouring dialects),* Canberra, Pacific Linguistics

Shirley, J., 1910, 'A Bora Ring in the Albert Valley', *Journal of the Royal Australian Historical Society,* 23: 1

Shoobridge, Linda, 2000, *My Memories: Hopkins Creek and Chillingham Numinbah Valley NSW,* Linda Shoobridge

Simons, M., 2003, *The Meeting of the Waters: The Hindmarsh Island Affair,* Sydney, Hodder Headline

Skertchly, S. J. B., 1923, 'On Springbrook', *Brisbane Courier,* 7 April, 7

Smith, J. E., 1793–5, *A Specimen of the Botany of New Holland,* London, J. Sowerby

— 1811, *Transactions of the Linnaean Society,* 10

Spenneman, D. H. R. and Allen, L. R., 2000, 'Cultivar to Weed: The Spread of Olives in Australia', *Olivae,* 82: 44–6

Stanley, T. D. and Ross, E. M., 1995, *Flora of south-eastern Queensland,* 3 vols, Brisbane, Department of Primary Industries

Steele, J. G., 1984, *Aboriginal Pathways in Southeast Queensland and the Richmond River,* St Lucia, University of Queensland Press

Stevenson, R., 2005, 'Macadamia: domestication and commercialization', *Chronica Horticulturae,* 45: 2, 11–15

Stewart, K. and Percival, B., 1997, *Bush Foods of New South Wales: A Botanical Record and an Aboriginal Oral History,* Sydney, Royal Botanical Gardens

Storey, William, 1957, 'The Madacamia in California', *Proceedings of Florida State Horticultural Society,* 333–8

— and Saleeb, Wadie F., 1970, 'Interspecific Hybridization in Macadamia', from *Queensland Nut Trees,* California Macadamia Society Yearbook, 16, on line

Tindale, Norman, 1940, *Map showing Distribution of the Aboriginal Tribes of Australia,* Adelaide, Royal Society of South Australia

— 1974, *Aboriginal Tribes of Australia: their terrain, environmental controls, distribution, limits, and proper names*, Canberra, Australian National University Press

Tracey, Geoff and Webb, Len, 1984, 'A floristic framework of Australian rainforests', *Australian Journal of Ecology*, 9: 169–98

Turvey, Nigel, 2006, *Terania Creek: Rainforest Wars*, Brisbane, Glass House Books

Tweed Heads Master Plan Site Analysis Part 3, 3–5

Vader, John, 2002, *Red Gold: The Tree that Built a Nation*, Sydney, New Holland Publishers

Valance, T. G., Moore, D. T. and Groves, E. W., eds, 2001, *Nature's Investigator: the diary of Robert Brown in Australia 1801–1805*, Canberra, Australian Biological Resources Study

Webb, L. J., 1954, 'Aluminium Accumulation in Australian-New Guinean Flora', *Australian Journal of Botany*, 2: 176–96

— 1959, 'Physiognomic Classification of Australian Rainforest Vegetation', *Ecology*, 49: 551–570

Wells, C. H. and Lewty, M. J., 1984, 'A Team Approach to Forest Weed Control', *Proceedings of the Seventh Australian Weeds Conference*, 1: 215–19

White, C. T., 1922, 'An Australian Citrus Relative: Notes on the Russell River Lime', *Journal of Heredity*, 13: 119–21

— and Francis, W. D., 1920, *Botany Bulletin, Department of Agriculture, Queensland*, 22: 36

__ and Francis, W. D., 1924, *Proceedings of the Royal Society of Queensland*, 35: 75

Williams, David, Wüster, Wolfgang and Fry, David Grieg, 2006, 'The Good, the Bad and the Ugly: Australian Snake Taxonomists and a history of the taxonomy of Australia's venomous snakes', *Toxicon*, 48: 919–30

Williams, Geoff and Adam, Paul, 1994, 'A review of rainforest pollination and plant-pollinator interactions, with particular reference to Australian subtropical rainforests', *Australian Zoologist*, 29: 177–212

Williams, John B. and Harden, Gwen, 2000, 'A revision of Davidsonia (Cunoniaceae)', *Telopea*, 8: 4, 414

Willis, Margaret, 1949, *By their Fruits: A Life of Ferdinand von Mueller, Botanist and Explorer*, Sydney, Angus & Robertson

Woolley, Pat, Australian Academy of Science: Interviews with Australian Scientists, on line

ACKNOWLEDGEMENTS

The author has a great many people to thank for the help, support, encouragement and advice she has been given over the twelve years since she encountered the forest at Natural Bridge. Some of their names might not appear in the list that follows, but this doesn't mean that she has forgotten them, but rather that she has never known their surnames.

She thanks first of all, the redoubtable CCRRS workforce, especially Garry Mills, Will Miller, Simon Valadares, Luke and Rachael Morphett, Michelle and Barry Walsh, Ben Yaun and Mitchell Philp, also Bronwen Mark and Andrew Campbell; Ann Polis, and her daughter Mary Polis, for being so ready to give whatever help and support they could, Mary particularly for legal advice which Friends of Gondwana Rainforest could not have afforded otherwise; Professor Paul McHugh and Andrew Hardwick for coming on board as trustees at what turned out to be a very difficult time, and for weathering the storm of refashioning the charity; Nick Diss FCA of Reardon and Co. and Robert Meakin PhD of Stone King LLP for sorting out the muddle; Stephen Bligh and Andrew Swarbrick for listening to her anguished queries and steering her towards a solution; Eddie Stern of C. Hoare and Co. and Lucy Zheng of National Australia Bank for their prudent oversight; Brian Bayne and Tim Green for offering to act as directors of Djurebil Pty Ltd; Lynne and Duncan Turpie for helping her to find Brian and Tim; Lui Weber and Rob Price both for their astonishing depth of knowledge of the CCRRS rainforest and their willingness to share it; Christopher Spain BSc (Hons), now principal ecologist at Biodiversity Assessment and Management, for his work on the Cave Creek macadamias, and Dr Conrad Hoskin of James Cook University, for showing her some of the rarer fauna. Her debt to David Jinks should be obvious and she is very aware of the interest taken in the project by Dr Bill McDonald, and the friendliness of such rainforest heroes as Nan and Hugh Nicholson and Gwen Harden; for sharing expertise and supplying CCRRS with plants, Charlie and Cathy Booth at Bush Nuts Native Nursery, Tallebudgera Valley, Kris and Kim Kupsch of Ooray Orchards, Burringbar, and Lance, Sally and Matt Fitzgerald and Dave Woodlee at Burringbar Rainforest Nursery; for advice and assistance in selection of potting media, Tony Mullan and everyone at Green Fingers.

The author's thanks also go to the staff of the many libraries, archives and museums where she has foraged for information about the Numinbah Valley, its flora and fauna, and its human history. These include the National Library of Australia, the State Library of New South Wales, the Queensland State Archives, the Cambridge University Library, the Library of the University of Queensland, the National Archives (UK), the British Library, the Gold Coast City Library, the Tweed Heads Historical Society, the Richmond-Tweed Regional Library, Lismore, the Tweed River Historical Society, Murwillumbah, Murwillumbah Historical Society Inc., and in particular the Institute of Aboriginal and Torres Strait Islander Studies for expert help sensitively and discreetly given. Other archivists and scholars have given her help anonymously through websites and databases; her debt to them is obvious. Every day she has occasion to bless the International Plant Name Index, the Australian Plant Name Index, The Plant List, Tropicos and Botanicus. She also thanks Dr Mark Nesbitt of the Economic Botany Collection at the Royal Botanic Gardens, Kew, for help generously given on the occasion of her visit to the collection. Special thanks go to Brian and Margaret Palmer who introduced her to the conservation work going on in Northland NZ, and to John and Catherine Hawley of Maranui Conservation Ltd who took the time and trouble to familiarise her with the Gondwanan rainforest of the Brynderwyns–Bream Tail area.

Her sister Alida Jane Burke, and her husband Peter have let her drone on about the forest for hours without complaint; her brother Barry and his family have shown an abiding confidence in the value of the project even when she was wavering. Professor Jenny Morton has done her considerable best to turn the author into a scientist. The author's surrogate Fink family, especially Leon and Margaret, and Hannah Fink and her husband Andrew Shapiro, have helped her in

every imaginable way. Don and Janet Holt were charming and hospi-
table hosts at Delmore Downs. Erwin and Adrienne Weber have
served the cause of sustainability much longer than she has, and she
values their example and advice. Judy Diamond and Kerry Broome
have been good mates and have kept a watching brief at Cave Creek.

Above all, she thanks the denizens of the Cave Creek rainforest,
vegetable and animal; their lust for life is what has transformed her
uncertain efforts to rebuild the forest into a triumph over the forces
of depletion. This it is that makes her dare to hope that it is not too
late to save this most enchanting of small planets.

INDEX

A NOTE ON THE AUTHOR

Germaine Greer is an Australian academic and journalist, and a major feminist voice of the mid-twentieth century. She gained her Ph.D. from the University of Cambridge in 1967. She is Professor Emerita of English Literature and Comparative Studies at the University of Warwick. Greer's ideas have created controversy ever since *The Female Eunuch* became an international bestseller in 1970. She is the author of many other books including *Sex and Destiny: The Politics of Human Fertility* (1984); *The Change: Women, Ageing and the Menopause* (1991); *The Whole Woman* (1999) and *Shakespeare's Wife* (2007).

A NOTE ON THE TYPE

The text of this book is set in Bembo. This type was first used in 1495 by the Venetian printer Aldus Manutius for Cardinal Bembo's *De Aetna*, and was cut for Manutius by Francesco Griffo. It was one of the types used by Claude Garamond (1480–1561) as a model for his Romain de L'Université, and so it was the forerunner of what became standard European type for the following two centuries. Its modern form follows the original types and was designed for Monotype in 1929.